Historic Real Estate

EARLY AMERICAN STUDIES

Series editors:
Daniel K. Richter, Kathleen M. Brown, Max Cavitch, and David Waldstreicher

Exploring neglected aspects of our colonial, revolutionary, and early national history and culture, Early American Studies reinterprets familiar themes and events in fresh ways. Interdisciplinary in character, and with a special emphasis on the period from about 1600 to 1850, the series is published in partnership with the McNeil Center for Early American Studies.

A complete list of books in the series is available from the publisher.

Historic Real Estate

Market Morality and the Politics of
Preservation in the Early United States

Whitney Martinko

PENN

University of Pennsylvania Press

Philadelphia

Published by
University of Pennsylvania Press
Philadelphia, Pennsylvania 19104-4112
www.upenn.edu/pennpress

Printed in the United States of America on acid-free paper
10 9 8 7 6 5 4 3 2 1

A Cataloging-in-Publication record is available from the Library of Congress
ISBN 978-0-8122-5209-5

For my parents and my friends

Contents

Preface

One morning as I revised this book, I woke up to a headline announcing the demolition of the historic core of Philadelphia, just a few miles from my home. "Confident Philadelphia Officials Preemptively Raze Center City to Make Room for Amazon Headquarters" announced the *Onion*. The popular parody website lampooned Philadelphia's eagerness to attract a corporate headquarters with a picture of architectural destruction. "It was definitely bittersweet saying goodbye to the Liberty Bell before our controlled demolition of Independence Hall," says the satirical version of Mayor Jim Kenney, "but it's important we encourage businesses to invest in the city."[1] Displaced citizens, he assured, could travel to see relics of Philadelphia's past in a new museum thirty miles outside of its city limits.

The article's humor arises, in part, from treating some of the nation's most cherished historic sites as prime real estate for a new economy. Yet Philadelphians had faced this very situation two hundred years earlier when the commonwealth of Pennsylvania planned to subdivide the site of Independence Hall for private development. The resulting campaign to preserve the building and its surrounding green space featured the same critiques of urban development, capitalist greed, and corrupt public interest that appeared in the *Onion* two centuries later. Early nineteenth-century observers viewed Independence Hall as a bellwether of the values guiding economic development in Philadelphia and the nation at large. Their commentary shows us how U.S. residents long have shaped historic sites not simply to commemorate the past but also to define what should not be for sale during times of economic change.

Residents of the early United States regularly debated the fate of historic architecture during what some historians have called "the market revolution" and others have called "the transition to capitalism." In the following chapters, I trace the discursive and material definitions of what many early Americans called the "preservation" of the built environment. Proponents of these various methods all defined architectural permanence as a central, if contentious, strategy for defining civil society as a matter of moral economic behavior. In doing so, they produced a national historical consciousness designed to shape, not re-treat from, capitalism and its effects. U.S. residents formulated different modes of architectural preservation to influence the development of local markets, the social effects of capitalist economies, and their own places in these new orders. Their debates over the fate of historic architecture weighed in on some of the most pressing concerns of U.S. society and economy: whether corporations really served the public good, how a seemingly pervasive desire to be rich af-fected collective welfare, and what effects shifting modes of production and market instability had on American families.

In this book, I aim to understand my subjects on their own terms, not to pin-point the origins of particular preservation techniques used today or assess past projects by these standards.[2] As a result, I take a capacious view of *architecture*—a word I use to encompass all human-made modifications to the physical environ-ment. On the one hand, I recognize the inseparability of built and "natural" fea-tures, particularly when it comes to the landscape architecture of parks, domestic grounds, and cemeteries. I follow my subjects in framing earthworks, parks and plantings, battlegrounds defined by property lines, and even documentary im-ages as part of the built environment as much as churches, government build-ings, and houses. On the other hand, I do not attempt to trace efforts to preserve "natural" historic landmarks, such as trees identified as remnants of "original" North American forests or rocks characterized as witnesses of historic events.[3] In each chapter, I range over a number of architectural features that my subjects viewed as "historic"—not necessarily "old" but invested with the capacity to con-nect present and future viewers with the past—a moment in time that had termi-nated. I use the word *site* to refer to the geographic locality of these structures.

The projects and debates discussed in this book have shaped the built envi-ronment not only by determining the presence or absence of particular struc-tures but also by informing the ways that we value historic architecture today. Contemporary debates over cultural property ownership, real estate develop-ment, and the politics of demolition draw on designs, arguments, and legal structures created by the subjects of this book. A history of their projects of ar-chitectural preservation exposes a new view of the living legacies we must con-front today when we debate what to preserve, how to do it, and whom we should empower to decide.

Architecture, Society, and Economy in the Early United States

In April 1788, Rufus Putnam ascended an embankment of the Muskingum River determined to make history. Here, where the Muskingum poured into the Ohio River, he would lay out the first U.S. city to be built in the Northwest Territory. Putnam had spent three years preparing for this moment. He had worked with other veteran officers of the Continental Army to organize a New England land company whose shareholders wanted to make a future west of the Appalachians. The Ohio Company of Associates had negotiated the purchase of 1.5 million acres of Shawnee territory not from its Indigenous residents but from the U.S. Congress, which claimed the Ohio country as federal property. Putnam alighted on a corner of the massive tract poised to build a capital city not only for Ohio Company shareholders but also for a nation of settler colonists.

As Putnam traversed the site for the first time, he envisioned the future city by focusing on remnants of the site's past. On the high ground, above the confluence of the Muskingum and Ohio Rivers, Putnam marveled over a complex of earthen architecture (Figure 1). Mounded walls created a wide corridor from the banks of the Muskingum to a quadrangle above, where more walls enclosed three large forms. Their pyramidal bases lofted flat tops several feet above the heads of people below; gently sloped earthen ramps provided access to their elevations. Half a mile to the southeast, a conical mound stood thirty feet tall. A wide ditch encircled its base, limiting an approach to a narrow land bridge.

Indigenous Americans had built these monumental structures between 800 BCE and 500 CE as sites of astronomical ceremony, ritual deposition, and human burial.[1] The Muskingum complex was one of many along Ohio country waterways that drew Woodland era travelers from across the continent. Here, ancestors of the Shawnee, Miami, Ojibwe, and Kickapoo peoples and their kin forged connections across cultures, generations, and geographic distance.[2] In 1788,

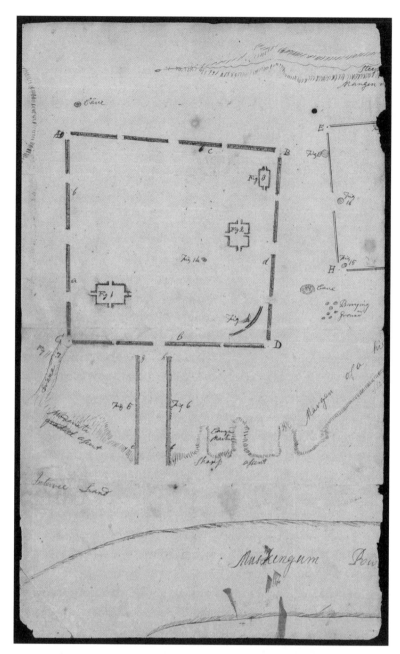

Figure 1. After arriving on the Muskingum River in 1788, Rufus Putnam delineated and described elements of the site's topography. He labeled his depictions of earthen architecture with numbers and letters that corresponded to his accompanying "References," which recorded his descriptions and measurements of the "artificial," or human-made, features. Putnam's survey would form the basis for U.S. conceptions of the site's "historic" features as well as plans for the development of the city of Marietta, Ohio, on the site. Rufus Putnam, "Plan of the Ancient Works," 1788, Rufus Putnam Papers. Marietta College Special Collections.

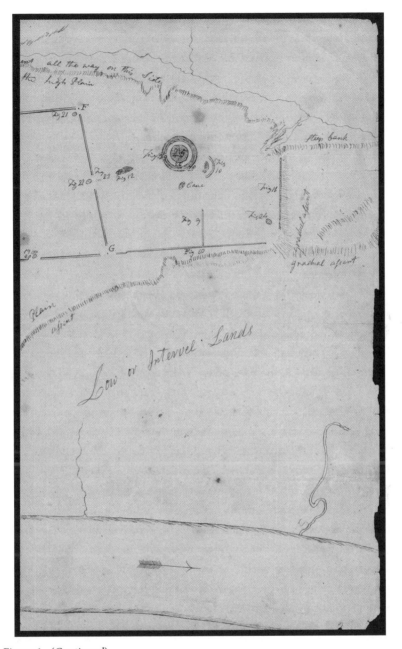

Figure 1. (*Continued*)

however, Rufus Putnam viewed these structures as evidence of an ancient history of the new nation: they formed the remnants of an American town comparable to classical Rome. As he translated an idealized urban grid to the particularities of the new site, he appropriated the earthworks as markers of this imagined past, making them centerpiece monuments of public squares. Ohio Company directors passed several rounds of directives affirming Putnam's plan. By their definition, construction of the new city would proceed as a project of preservation.

Rufus Putnam was not alone. In subsequent decades, residents of the early United States attempted to make architectural evidence of the past permanent, from mounds in the Ohio Valley to the old Pennsylvania statehouse in Philadelphia; from Benjamin Franklin's childhood home in Boston to St. Philip's Episcopal Church in Charleston, South Carolina; from the Van Rensselaer family manor near Albany, New York, to Henry Clay's Kentucky estate. Observers did not define these structures solely as vessels of historical memory or metaphors for the past. They also saw them as real estate. When individuals characterized these structures as historic and sought to secure their futures, they made preservation a way of defining what should not be for sale, how consumers should behave, and how certain types of labor should be valued. Preservation was, in other words, a strategy for making a moral economy.

Many residents of the early United States engaged in preservation to work out practical applications of a central concern in the new nation and, indeed, the early modern world: the relationship between public good and private profit.[3] Historic sites made compelling locales to test this correlation because they were places where the materiality of the past and the market economy met. Advocates of preservation defined architectural permanence as a statement of civic virtue—a willingness to balance communal and personal interests. In this light, it is not surprising that the earliest concerted project of architectural preservation in the United States started in its newest territory, where questions about the relationship of private profit to public good first bubbled up around the sale of federal lands. In the coming years, people as varied as Abraham Touro, a Jewish philanthropist; Stephen Gould, a Quaker artisan and antiquarian; Payton Stewart, an African American salesman of secondhand clothes; John Doyle, an Irish tavern keeper; and Ann Pamela Cunningham, the South Carolinian founder of the Mount Vernon Ladies' Association, defined different modes of preservation to demonstrate economic behavior as social virtue. Despite their disparate strategies, they all shared a common belief with the agenda that Rufus Putnam modeled in 1788: securing architectural evidence of the past for future generations displayed civility, or a self-cultivated fitness for participation in public life.

This definition of preservation framed it as a material practice that fomented the bonds of civil society and, in turn, determined who should be included in—and excluded from—"the public." Americans who championed this social model made claims of superiority over "uncivil" populations. One did not have to know or subscribe to the intricacies of stadial theory—the idea that human populations progressed through discrete, hierarchical stages of social development—to associate characteristics of the built environment with particular levels of social evolution. In this generalized worldview, savages and barbarians exhibited self-interest with temporary structures and architectural destruction; civilized people advanced the commonweal with permanent architecture. Early U.S. advocates of architectural preservation translated this materialist conception of civilization into racialized conceptions of savagery—often embodied by Indigenous Americans, Euro-American agrarians, and African Americans living according to "primitive" material standards.[4] Yet they also defined speculative capitalism as a form of barbarism. Individuals who sought maximal wealth in the market economy, they suggested, engaged in environmental destruction that degraded civil society as much as people who refused, or lacked the ability, to improve it. The impermanent architecture of both populations, in this view, demonstrated a self-interest that threatened early U.S. civil society—and the success of the new nation itself.

Of course, purveyors of preservation aimed to profit from their commitment to a so-called common good. They calibrated their designs for architectural permanence to portray themselves as agents of an incremental process of civilization. In turn, they advocated for the preservation of historic sites as a strategy for economic participation, not as a retraction from it. Rufus Putnam, for instance, appropriated the Muskingum earthworks as a way of making competitive appeals to investors as well as dispossessing Indigenous residents of the Ohio country. Other corporate trustees, land developers, household consumers, laborers, family heirs, and commercial entrepreneurs shaped designs for the historic built environment to paint themselves as moral economic actors who strengthened civil society. They applied their plans for architectural permanence to sites whose particularities seemed to fulfill a national promise of local self-determination, not necessarily sites whose past symbolized the nation whole cloth. As individuals proposed different physical, legal, and financial means of making structures and sites permanent, they shaped a national historical consciousness constructed in materiality as well as memory.

History and Materiality

Many scholars have studied architectural preservation as a process of making historical memory: the creation of a usable past for a contemporary purpose.[5] They have shown that residents of the early United States shared with European

counterparts a practice of historical place-making honed to define national identity in an age of revolution and imperialism.[6] After the War for Independence, many
residents of the United States looked to sites associated with the revolution and
its leaders to define the new nation and its citizenry. They attended anniversary
celebrations that enlivened battlegrounds with living memories of war and laid
monuments to military engagements and the birthplaces of their leaders. Tourists visited these sites to pay respect to men defined as national martyrs and to
experience the power of place to connect visitors to the past.[7] More broadly, travelers and antiquaries traversed the land looking for material evidence of local history. Indigenous Americans and settler colonists both created physical markers of
place invested with memories of past events, especially of colonial violence.[8]

Yet these Americans recognized a crucial difference between constructing new
monuments to the past and maintaining historic architectural features themselves.
As one writer put it in 1831, "If there is any good reason for our erecting mementos
of past occurrences, there is certainly stronger ones for preserving those which our
fathers have erected and are identified with themselves."[9] Historic structures could
serve as bearers of collective memory. Yet they also constituted physical remnants
of the past itself. I attend to this defining distinction of preservation in the early
United States by framing it as an environmental ethic: a set of moral principles articulated to guide how people treated the world around them. Residents of the new
nation did not see and shape their environments solely according to aesthetic
principles of beauty and contemporary style.[10] Proponents of preservation tried to
cultivate a built environment that engendered a moralizing historical consciousness that pivoted from a view of the past to a view of the future. They saw the forms,
fabrics, and situations of historic structures as evidence not only of the past but also
of the care that current denizens expressed for fellow citizens and future generations.[11] To reconstruct the broad environmental ethic of architectural permanence
that they promoted, I take a synthetic material cultural approach to analyzing the
built environment.[12] Written descriptions and visual depictions of architecture do
not simply convey evidence of environmental appearance or record environmental
features that their makers chose to memorialize or erase. Residents of the early
United States defined and contested the social meaning of architecture in the mate-
rialities of objects, images, and texts. They defined the built environment in genres
of prose as well as words, in the design of artifacts as well as their fabric, and in the
visual conventions of images as well as the features depicted.[13]

Each chapter of this book moves from an analysis of how some U.S. residents
used architectural materiality to embody evidence of the past to an argument
about how they deployed these forms of material culture to shape society and
economy to their own advantage. In doing so, it shows the necessity of interpret-
ing historical sources in their material contexts. We cannot understand how Ohio

Company leaders appropriated Indigenous earthworks if we do not understand the trappings of Masonic rituals. We cannot understand how business proprietors such as upholsterer John K. Simpson harnessed preservation to attract customers unless we analyze the precepts of antiquarian and commercial imagery. We cannot understand why writers such as Edmund Quincy began to call some sites sacred if we do not understand new methods of building construction and design. And we cannot understand why people such as John Fanning Watson and Anna Cora Ritchie organized associational efforts to buy historic houses if we do not understand the contours of domestic luxury goods.

This approach to the material world demands a broad view of the shared conventions of hemispheric and transatlantic material culture as well as a close look at the particularities of time and place. Residents of the early United States shaped the meaning of architecture, images, objects, and texts in conversation with early modern predecessors and transnational peers.[14] Rufus Putnam drew on preservation edicts of urban planning from Renaissance Rome. Congregants of St. Philip's Episcopal Church in Charleston followed the reconstruction model of British Gothic churches. Popular writers highlighted house museums in Germany and Switzerland as models for the former American residences of William Penn and George Washington. All developed vernacular theories of preservation decades before European architects John Ruskin and Eugène-Emmanuel Viollet-le-Duc published their treatises on the subject.[15] More broadly, these U.S. residents helped to define transatlantic strains of Eurocentric historicism that believed that architecture could inform rational studies of the past and, in turn, cultivate a shared love of country that would strengthen devotion to fellow citizens.

Yet U.S. residents made preservation a tool of nation building by designing architectural permanence in diverse environmental conditions and legal landscapes where architecture made visible local particularities and regional distinctiveness. Its practitioners sought to construct a national historical consciousness grounded in continuous change and progressive social development, not simply in the memory of Revolutionary founders or events. They defined nationalism not by the homogenization of Anglo-American architecture but by histories of Euro-American colonization of North America. In turn, they created a historic landscape that fashioned colonization as a process of civilization brought to fruition in U.S. civil society.

Permanence and Civil Society

Even before the War for Independence, elite Euro-Americans had shaped transatlantic currents of material culture to define civility in the context of specific

North American environments and peoples. Residents of the early United States adapted these practices to define new material markers of civility and cosmopolitanism in a postcolonial and colonizing nation.[16] Americans of various economic statuses strove to demonstrate civic virtue not only with conspicuous consumption and refined comportment but also with the collection of historic artifacts and the creation of historic archives.[17] The donation of excavated objects or family manuscripts to historical societies, for instance, defined civility in material meaning made outside the marketplace of goods.

Amid this interest in the materiality of the past, the preservation of historic structures activated a broader significance of architectural permanence. People indoctrinated in Enlightenment theories of civilization conceived of social and environmental development as a single process of improvement.[18] Individuals on both sides of the Atlantic made the preservation of historic architecture part of this campaign for so-called improvement when they framed it as a tool for creating environmental permanence. In the early United States, advocates of preservation made their plans a principal strategy for creating a new order of property and power promised by revolutionary principles.[19] By substantiating civil society in professedly historic architecture, they defined a national citizenry across time as well as space.[20] They framed the permanence of historic structures as a matter of public interest to this multigenerational populace. Yet unlike leaders of postrevolutionary regimes in France, U.S. citizens did not make historic sites the property of the national government.[21] Instead, they determined to let properties of public interest emerge from private holdings. Citizens would substantiate civil society in the United States, they believed, by working out local claims to the public or private nature of city squares, public buildings, domestic spaces, and commercial sites.[22] In this way, they made debates over the architectural permanence of historic sites as central to the formation of a U.S. "public" as state-funded infrastructure and the regulation of space.[23]

By the same token, many residents of the early United States made preservation a means of colonization by dispossession and spatial control. As an ethic of permanence, this conceptualization of preservation promoted the same campaign for "civilization" as did the praying towns in Nipmuc territory and the agricultural landscapes of Creek country.[24] In some instances, as with the earthworks in the Ohio and Mississippi Valleys, U.S. citizens appropriated Indigenous structures as markers of a settler colonial past. In others, they secured the architecture of European colonizers as evidence of the "founding" of America. Both propelled acts of possession by fencing, planting, and deeding Indigenous lands as private property. In rural as well as urban locales, advocates of preservation used claims to permanence to remove or surveil people who did not comply with material markers of civil society. Later generations of urban planners, highway engineers, and park superintendents would make this an enduring strategy for exerting power over residents of locales around the globe, from Lahore to the Blue Ridge Mountains.[25]

This ethic also enabled its practitioners to authorize demolition. By applying calls for permanence to some structures, U.S. residents cast others as expendable in the project of building the nation. In this way, they continued a long history of the demolition of sacred Indigenous sites begun by Spanish, French, and English colonists in previous centuries—what one scholar has called "settler iconoclasm."[26] More broadly, they abided, approved, or enacted the demolition of a number of buildings that certainly held collective historic meaning for many Americans and, in turn, excluded caretakers of "disposable" structures from civil society. At the same time, advocates of preservation shaped a politics of demolition that characterized the destruction of historic architecture as civic iconoclasm.[27] In this way, they created a new politics of preservation defined not only by backcountry savagery but also by market barbarity.

Market and Morality

In the early United States, observers defined the social value of architecture in the context of a market economy. Historic structures and sites were embedded in an environment thoroughly commodified by most Euro-Americans by the end of the eighteenth century. The federal government carved up its territorial lands for sale to private owners. Investors commissioned buildings as sources of rental and resale income. Financial booms and busts leveled new structures that had seemed grand and permanent just years earlier. Demolition crews sold salvaged materials from dismantled buildings. Even houses of worship and benevolent societies used their property to generate capital. These new conditions of U.S. real estate markets prompted observers to question the relationship between the financial and use value of buildings and sites invested with some degree of public interest.[28]

Advocates of preservation promoted a materialist conception of historical consciousness as a means of addressing this question. Like architects of new churches, penitentiaries, schools, and houses, they believed that architecture had the power to shape morality and behavior.[29] Yet proponents of preservation believed that architectural forms and fabrics of the past could advance social development, not block it. When individuals and institutions encouraged Americans to manage historic structures according to a use value rather than a solely financial one, they made preservation a key node of contention in defining morality in the early United States.[30] Their proposals show how debates over sacred space in the early United States arose not from the extensions of religiosity into secular spaces but from broader efforts to determine the limits of environmental commodification.[31]

Rather than disconnecting from capitalist economies, campaigns for architectural permanence aimed to shape them with a code of civic morality. Market participation alone did not cultivate civil society, they implied; in fact, the pursuit of capital according to strict rules of political economy could harm the public good. By framing the perceived problems of the economy as social, they confirmed the spread of capitalist markets by promising to make them moral.[32] Unlike the Indigenous Americans and Euro-American agrarians who tried to resist commodification of land by maintaining common property, advocates of preservation embraced the strictures of private property.[33] A variety of men and women offered up different and often conflicting expressions of historical permanence to fashion themselves simultaneously as moral economic actors, members of civil society, and deserving members of a national public.

Advocates of preservation addressed their growing trepidation about the social effects of capitalism by turning to sites that encapsulated their anxieties: corporate properties, commercial sites, and domestic spaces. I trace the development of preservation methods in pairs of chapters centered on these three types of sites and the economic and social concerns that they embodied. In the first two chapters, I examine efforts to secure "public" historic structures owned by collective entities: town squares, municipal cemeteries, landmark houses of worship, and governmental buildings. These sites attracted the attention of city residents in the first decades of U.S. nationhood because their fates were bound up in debates about the relationship between state authority and local self-determination embodied by corporate property. When residents of aspirational and established urban centers debated the material and legal perpetuity of historic sites, they engaged in larger efforts to define and enforce principles of corporate governance in the new nation.

In the next two chapters, I focus on commercial sites, or localities characterized by their positions in marketplaces of goods and real estate. Between the panic of 1819 and the depression recovery beginning in 1842, business proprietors and political partisans defined preservation as a means to create opportunities for and limits on commercial profit in speculative economies. Merchants, tavern proprietors, and imagemakers perpetuated historic architecture as a competitive market strategy, enticing customers with a historically conscious vision of respectable consumption. Some of their contemporaries, however, argued that historic sites should be set apart from commercial enterprise. Partisan political writers condemned the treatment of venerable public buildings, old houses, and Indigenous earthworks as commodities and encouraged readers to treat them as sacred spaces whose permanence should be secured outside the bounds of speculative markets. Both types of appeals operated in a broader constellation of economic schemes to define moral commerce for a new era of finance, labor, industrial production, and marketing.

The final two chapters examine domestic spaces, including house interiors and the seats of family properties. From the 1830s to the 1850s, men and women argued over the merits of old houses and ancestral estates to debate how capitalism affected family economies. As women exerted more authority over domestic economies—and sometimes their public-minded philanthropic extensions—some men moved to preserve domestic spaces as sites of public historic interest. Middling men created plans to make old houses the property of incorporated voluntary societies, where they developed an antiluxury mode of civic housekeeping that reclaimed a place for men as moral and material leaders of American home and society. By contrast, heirs of ancestral estates adopted new modes of rural improvement to position themselves as patriarchs for a new generation, maintaining familial homes while parceling off outlying tracts in suburban land markets. Men looking to maintain patriarchal authority in new modes of domestic living, both within family economies and urbanizing locales, shaped methods of preservation to maintain strains of "old-fashioned" economy and society as moral principles for a modern world.

This narrative progression, from corporate to commercial to domestic sites, tracks the expansion of efforts to define economic morality with architectural preservation in the early United States. In fact, observers often assessed the same structure in multiple ways. I end this book where many histories of preservation begin—with George Washington's former estate at Mount Vernon—to give a view of how advocates of preservation synthesized concerns about corporations, commerce, and domesticity by the mid-nineteenth century.[34] In light of the previous chapters, the epilogue offers a new telling of the efforts of the Mount Vernon Ladies' Association to purchase Washington's estate. It repositions their project not as the birth of preservation but as the consolidation of its popular practice as one that complemented market transactions and substantiated a supposedly moral form of capitalism for the "modern" era.[35]

This new history of preservation shows it to be a crucial component of the history of capitalism in the early United States. Architects of plans for preservation argued that social welfare demanded that citizens sacrifice not self-interest but the boundless pursuit of profits and luxuries afforded by capitalist marketplaces. They used architecture to define ways that citizens might demonstrate this commitment to the public good: forgoing maximal profits on real estate sales, contributing money to stewardship efforts, producing or purchasing documentary views, shopping in historic structures, or donating labor to the care of historic sites. Campaigns for preservation shaped not only particular sites but also the urbanizing society that stretched along roads, rivers, and railways into small towns and farms as well as growing cities.[36] Residents of the early nation fashioned the built environment to work out the contours of local markets, economic value, law, consumer culture, and conceptions of moral commerce and benevolent capital and labor.[37] U.S. residents, in others words, shaped the landscape of "modern" capitalism by cultivating dynamic forms of permanence as well as architectural innovation, new construction, and urbanization.[38]

This view of the early national built environment disrupts the clean narrative of the privatization of public space to which preservationists, environmentalists, and urbanists sometimes subscribe.[39] Early U.S. advocates of architectural preservation claimed to limit the influence of market mentality on the built environment. But their methods of securing environmental permanence have confounded distinctions between public and private since the eighteenth century. To confront the history of this entanglement is to see historical consciousness at the heart of defining commodity production, consumption, and the value of labor in the past and in the present.

PART I

Corporate Properties

CHAPTER 1

Capital Plans: Ancient Monuments in Public Squares

Late in the winter of 1791, Rufus Putnam and fellow Ohio Company leaders found themselves back where they had started: sheltered with area residents in the block-house that they had built on their arrival. Since 1788, they had worked to con-struct a capital city and fill it with U.S. citizens.[1] Rufus Putnam had led the effort to create a settler society marked not only by shared authority of company stock-holders and clear titles to land but also by refined urban society. This attention to the structural details of governance, land division, and architecture, he hoped, would distinguish company directors from the absentee land speculators who kept loose tabs on their trans-Appalachian tracts.[2] Three years later, however, Ohio Company members and Marietta residents faced conditions that threatened their development plans, investments, and lives.

For starters, many Indigenous residents of the Ohio country resisted coloni-zation. Late in 1790, Wyandot, Miami, and Shawnee peoples led by Michikinikwa, or Little Turtle, had defeated U.S. troops two hundred miles west of Marietta, near a new post at Cincinnati. Soon after, armed resistance spread eastward toward the Ohio Company tract. After Indigenous Americans killed Euro-American res-idents at Big Bottom, thirty miles up the Muskingum River from Marietta, area settlers streamed into the fortification at Marietta.[3] Pressed for monetary and military reinforcements they did not have, Ohio Company leaders lobbied the federal government for help reinforcing their blockhouse for "general war."[4]

At the same time, Ohio Company directors faced financial pressure from a second angle. Shareholders and outside observers alike mounted criticism that Rufus Putnam and fellow Ohio Company leaders Winthrop Sargent and Manasseh Cutler had engineered a fraudulent financial scheme to purchase their company's land in 1787. Accusers charged the men with entangling Ohio Com-pany business with the Scioto Company, a "private speculation" managed by notorious land speculator William Duer.[5] Amid a national financial downturn, Ohio Company directors in New England and the Northwest Territory scrambled to secure payments from their shareholders, attract new investors, and finalize their land claims with Congress. In turn, impatient shareholders pressed agents for outright deeds to their plots, hoping to resell their titles for a profit and end their dealings with the company.

Amid these crises, Ohio Company directors in Marietta set aside time to direct urban planning of a city built mostly on paper. Early in 1791, local leaders continued to make specific plans for "ornamenting and preserving" the earthworks in Marietta's public squares.[6] In February, prominent Marietta men Joseph Gilman, Daniel Story, and Jonathan Heart drafted a report that identified precisely where certain types of trees should be planted and which areas should be fenced and maintained in turf. They also charged individuals with stewardship of the squares. Leading shareholders reviewed and approved these plans the following month.[7]

At first glance, the company's attention to the earthworks seems like an escapist diversion from more pressing problems. Yet by characterizing themselves as agents of preservation, Ohio Company men angled for a competitive advantage in contests for financial capital and political capitals in the early nation. In the 1780s and 1790s, land speculators sought to turn a profit on land purchases not by cultivating the land itself but by pitching visions of what the land could be. Many speculators primed these visions by planning new construction of infrastructure, such as roads and public buildings. This is the strategy that George Washington and William Duer deployed in 1791 when they tried to encourage the development of Washington City as a prime location for the new federal capital.[8] Most of these plans, however, were more suggestive than constitutive of the commercial development and architectural refinement of urban life. Ohio Company leaders leveraged the materiality of the earthworks to invest their urban plans with material reality. In a moment of crisis, they framed the earthworks as monumental urban centerpieces to make a deliberately confident statement of U.S. sovereignty and urban growth. Marietta, they implied, was no ordinary venture in land speculation: ancient architecture proved the viability of urban development in this location. In turn, they suggested, it marked Marietta as a secure investment of financial and political capital in a landscape of high risk and reward.

An Ancient Town in a New City

When Ohio Company leaders determined to maintain Indigenous earthworks as remnants of American antiquity, they made preservation a tool of colonization. Massachusetts native Winthrop Sargent was one of the first Ohio Company members to entwine historical study and territorial expansion. Dissatisfied by the financial returns of seafaring out of his hometown of Gloucester, Massachusetts, Sargent joined the ranks of federal land surveyors hoping to profit from the colonization of trans-Appalachian lands. Great Britain nominally had ceded the lands northwest of the Ohio River to the United States in 1783. Yet it remained to be seen if U.S. citizens could establish national sovereignty over this territory.[9] Congress approached the task as a project of settler colonialism. They passed the Land Ordinance of 1785 to prepare the land for sale, hoping to fill national coffers while putting U.S. citizens on the ground to stake claims against European and Indigenous powers in the Great Lakes region and Mississippi River valley.[10] When the call went out for federal land surveyors, Sargent signed up to survey his own opportunities for economic and political gain in the region.

When Sargent arrived on the western banks of the Ohio in the summer of 1786, he saw the earthworks at the mouth of the Muskingum as a chance to claim notoriety for himself and his fledgling land company. A few months earlier, he had created the Ohio Company of Associates with other veteran officers of the Continental Army who saw limited prospects in post-Revolutionary New England. When he saw the geometric earthen architecture just across the Muskingum from the U.S. Army post at Fort Harmar, he judged it to be a prime spot for the men's endeavor.[11] Sargent set aside the logic of the grid that he projected across Indigenous lands and used the tools of survey to measure and draw the earthworks built by their ancestors.[12] His plan melded the conventions of land survey and antiquarian study to depict the site as one ripe for redevelopment. He recorded the site's elevation with linear shading, showing a complex of earthworks elevated above watercourses that bounded the site. A descriptive key explained the graphic delineations of earthen walls, raised earthworks, and "excavations" that formed the "Ruins of an Antient Town or Fortified Camp." Sargent used dashed lines to depict "graves" outside the ancient walls, a practice that linked this supposedly extinct American civilization to ancient Romans. He also included the footprint of Fort Harmar to indicate the presence of U.S. troops just across the Muskingum River and situate his plan in a present-day view that claimed the territory for the new nation.[13]

Like previous European colonizers, Winthrop Sargent engaged in environmental study to advance Enlightenment notions of science and imperial power. He had indulged his interest in natural history at Harvard College, and he used his studies of the Ohio earthworks to gain membership in the American Academy of Arts and Sciences and the American Philosophical Society in the late 1780s.[14] No longer a middleman in the British imperial production of knowledge, Sargent joined a variety of Americans in using rational inquiry to expand the intellectual respectability and the continental empire of the United States.[15] Like contemporary British antiquaries interested in Roman ruins and Druidical monuments, Euro-Americans turned to the study of "domestic antiquities" to create a national base of knowledge that contributed to transatlantic studies of world historical civilizations.[16] After requesting information from Ohio Company migrants in 1788, for instance, James Winthrop reminded Winthrop Sargent that his study of antiquities in the Ohio country would be a "great service in the history of mankind" because it was "by a comparison of these things with the familiar productions of other countries, and something with history, we may trace useful resemblances . . . and the degree of civilization may be tolerably ascertained."[17] When Sargent sent his observations of the earthworks and objects excavated from them to learned societies, he styled himself a public servant to the nation and "the literati in Europe."[18] For men newly resident in the Ohio country, these studies established cultural and intellectual inclusion with peers in the eastern states and Great Britain while shaking off colonial oversight from both.[19]

Sargent's survey contributed more directly to U.S. colonization of the Ohio Valley.[20] As Ohio Company leaders recruited shareholders and negotiated a purchase agreement for 1.5 million acres from Congress, land agents used Sargent's intel to entice New Englanders to purchase and migrate to Ohio Company lands. More broadly, company members circulated reports about the earthen architecture on the Muskingum to draw interest to their enterprise. Numerous investors in western lands published a serialized poem, "The Anarchiad," that celebrated the earthworks as a mysterious font of ancient knowledge. Jonathan Heart, a commanding officer at Fort Harmar and an Ohio Company investor, published a map and description of the earthworks in the *Columbian Magazine* in May 1787. Manasseh Cutler depicted the location of the "ancient ruins" on his map of the surveyed federal territory. And newspaper editors filled their pages with reports of the earthworks.[21] All offered an image of abandoned ancient architecture that mitigated a common "fear of savages," which Ohio Company leaders saw as a deterrent to migration.[22]

Many Ohio Company leaders used the tools of Enlightenment inquiry to translate the earthworks into a historical narrative of American civilization that projected the imperial authority of the United States. In 1787, the U.S. government still held very little control over the Ohio country.[23] In the Ohio Company tract, federal power came from Fort Harmar on the west side of the Muskingum River, built in 1785 for troops charged with removing residents who did not have clear title to land recognized by U.S. law.[24] Many Ohio Company members participated directly in this violent campaign to remove uncooperative residents from the area—often with limited success. Their simultaneous study of earthworks asserted a more confident authority over Ohio lands, sometimes in explicit ways. For instance, Ohio Company directors measured the Muskingum earthworks in the presence of the territorial governor and federal judges in 1788. The survey was a means of measurement characterized as scientific yet long used to establish colonial power.[25] The officers of the surveying party invested the event with federal authority. When Rufus Putnam certified Manasseh Cutler's records of site measurements as "Minutes taken in the presence of Governor St. Clair, the Judges, etc.," he explicitly linked the Ohio Company's private settlement to the federal project of national expansion and married the professedly disinterested practice of Enlightenment inquiry and historical study to the land development enacted by those projects.[26] The objective production of historical knowledge about the new nation, he implied, guided the colonial drive for empire.

Yet Ohio Company leaders also asserted their power over the Muskingum Valley by reading the earthworks as remnants of an urban plan, not simply ancient artifacts or curiosities. Most eighteenth-century Euro-Americans believed that architecture provided material evidence of the social values and intellectual development of its makers. In their minds, the construction of buildings and the living patterns engendered by town plans indicated where a community stood in the progressive course of human development from savagery to civilization. In the Ohio Valley, Sargent and his fellow land investors characterized the arrangement and scale of the Muskingum earthworks as remnants of a permanent, communal dwelling site—the hallmark of a civil society. This contrasted with dispersed and impermanent habitations, which Ohio Company leaders regularly characterized as signs of savagery among contemporary Indigenous Americans and Euro-American agrarians, often called squatters.

While many North American colonizers promoted town-building as a tool of civilization, Ohio Company leaders used urbanism to set up a socioenvironmental justification for the removal of territorial residents.[27] When Winthrop Sargent declared the earthworks the "ruins of an ancient town," he helped to create an early formulation of the "Moundbuilder myth"—a belief that the architects of Ohio and Mississippi Valley earthworks were Indigenous Americans who had mysteriously disappeared from the continent, either through death or mass migration to South America.[28] Company leaders contrasted the scale, permanence, and architectural complexity of these earthworks with contemporary Indigenous architecture to argue that present inhabitants of the region were less civilized than the moundbuilders and not descended from them.[29] Moreover, company members emphasized that Indigenous residents of the Ohio country expressed little knowledge of the origins and uses of the earthworks.[30]

Ohio Company members used the logic of urbanism to portray earthworks as abandoned towns that stood open for population by people who would revive civilization in the Ohio country. This belief in the civil character of urban architecture also spurred company members to define preservation as a guiding principle of urban planning. As company leaders mused on early plans for a city on the Muskingum in 1787, they settled on a grid created by a hierarchy of streets, filled with identically sized house lots and symmetrically distributed public squares.[31] Their adoption of orthogonal city planning, which echoed the grid that divided federal lands for sale, placed Ohio Company leaders at the forefront of U.S. city planners who used the urban grid to order a republican landscape and citizenry.[32] When Rufus Putnam adapted the proposed city grid to encompass the most prominent earthworks as landmark features of the new urban plan, he used a tool of systemic thinking to order the new city in relationship to the old and, in turn, signal environmental and social refinement (Figure 2).[33] On paper, this visual overlay implied that the Ohio Company had made the principal earthen structures more useful and convenient than the architects of the original earthen complex that surrounded them. This juxtaposition implied a straight line of progressive development between what company members viewed as an ancient *town* and their own *city*—a larger and more complex form of social organization.[34]

In this way, Putnam shaped the city of Marietta as a capital of empires past and future. Colonization of the Ohio country, he implied, restored civilization to the American equivalent of ancient Rome. Service in the Revolution and membership in the Society of the Cincinnati had primed him and his peers to formulate the project of nation building in classical terms.[35] Company leaders considered naming their new city Castrapolis to highlight how its urban infrastructure recalled the Roman castrum.[36] Instead, they invoked ancient Rome with their campaign for so-called preservation. Putnam appropriated Indigenous architecture through symbolic names and spatial metaphor.[37] He aligned one axis of streets with two parallel earthen walls that ran from the banks of the Muskingum to a plateau above its juncture with the Ohio. He named the wide swath of land it created Sacra Via—a transposition of ancient Rome's main thoroughfare known for triumphal imperial processions. Like its namesake, Marietta's Sacra Via led to the city's monumental landmarks, running past the company's blockhouse, named Campus Martius after the famous Roman plain, to two rectilinear platform mounds. Putnam dubbed them Quadranaou and Capitolium, in reference to the two Roman hills Quirinal, the political center of ancient Rome, and Capitoline, its highest point and citadel. To the southeast, Putnam denominated the tallest mound with a Latin descriptor, Conus, and disrupted the regularity of the street grid to create an open square around it.[38] By designating these sites as historic, public spaces, Putnam created a classicized urban metaphor that cast Marietta as a city simultaneously republican and imperial.

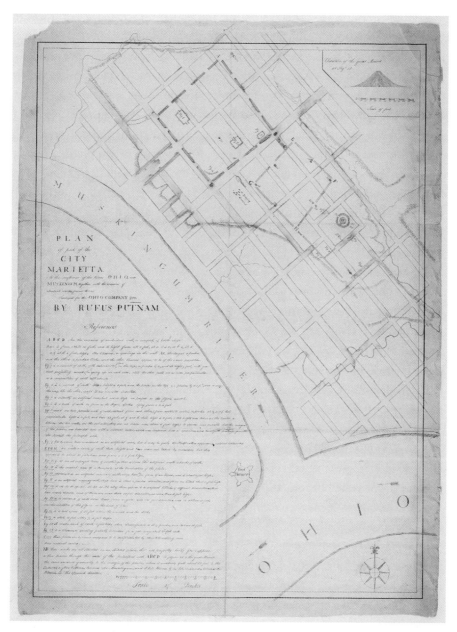

Figure 2. Soon after Rufus Putnam surveyed the earthworks and natural topography at the confluence of the Muskingum and Ohio Rivers, he projected an urban grid over the site. This plan shows how Putnam adapted the city grid to incorporate some earthworks as monumental architecture of the proposed city while planning the demolition of others, as well as the Indigenous "burying ground" on the site. Rufus Putnam, "Plan of Part of the City of Marietta, . . . together with the Remains of Antient Works Found There," 1788. Courtesy American Antiquarian Society.

Putnam drew on a long history of imperial leaders preserving structures built by previous societies to claim authority over newly acquired territory and its residents. No place demonstrated that better than the history of Rome itself. In sixth-century Rome, Ostrogothic ruler Theodoric characterized himself as heir to the ancient Roman empire by attending to the preservation of classical structures in the city. He proclaimed his care for the historic urban fabric to curry favor with Romans who had maintained these vestiges of the classical era under Visigothic rulers. In the next millennium, Renaissance urban planners made preservation a guiding principle for renovating the city as well. Particularly after Pope Martin V ordered heightened attention to the preservation of classical landmarks in 1420, papal administrators and city officials shaped preservation legislation and its enforcement to gain power in shaping the modern contours of the ancient city.[39]

In Marietta, Ohio Company leaders engaged in the same strategy of preservation to portray themselves as the heirs to an ancient American republic. They used the urban plan of Marietta to position U.S. sovereignty as a peaceful and constructive "revival" of civil society in the Ohio country. Yet urban planning was a tactic of imperial expansion that perpetuated violence and destruction used to dispossess Indigenous peoples and Euro-American agrarians.[40] Marietta founders demolished environmental features that did not suit their needs, leveling many earthworks and building over graves marked by pits rather than geometric earthworks. Many other landscape features that evinced the area's Indigenous and colonial pasts went entirely unrecorded. Preservation formed the obverse side of these erasures and demolitions while masking this violence in professedly disinterested historical study of the land.[41]

Ohio Company leaders chose to preserve earthworks that helped them specifically frame ongoing violence in their lands in classicized terms. At a time when observers sometimes described earthworks as fortifications, Marietta leaders read them as evidence of socialized warfare in ancient North America. By maintaining multiple earthworks, Marietta leaders encouraged viewers to see an ancient landscape of ritual and procession, where ancient American residents had conducted military activity as part of a coordinated social effort. Linking the Indigenous mounds to the ancient Roman landscape reinforced this view of defensive and temporary militarization. It worked with Marietta founders' membership in the Society of the Cincinnati to authorize contemporary violence with links to a distant past revered by Euro-Americans, implying that U.S. fortification of Marietta was necessary, defensive, and executed only for the social good.[42] In this way, Ohio Company members shaped the earthworks to cultivate a doubly historicized view of warfare conducted according to age-old military custom and set aside in favor of civilian life as soon as possible. This urban design cloaked the offensive project of U.S. expansion, as well as the piecemeal and disorganized nature of colonial violence, in the architectural language of civil society.

Ancient Monuments in Public Squares

Rufus Putnam and Winthrop Sargent used urban design to appropriate Indigenous architecture as declarations of national authority and imperial aspirations. They also shaped their appeals for preservation to assert themselves as arbiters of civility—the professed foundation of political power in the early nation.[43] In national borderlands feared to be uncivilized and to cause social regression, Ohio Company leaders faced a strong imperative to establish civil society not only in opposition to local "savages" but also for inclusion in a cosmopolitan American elite. Urbanism broadly connoted social development, but details of its design also signaled the taste of its founders and inhabitants. By applying principles of Renaissance urbanism and British antiquarianism to the Muskingum earthworks, Ohio Company leaders used preservation to create a monumental city both distinctively American and legibly refined. Marietta's historic monuments, they believed, would inculcate social values and cultural principles to serve all citizens of the new nation.[44]

Ohio Company directors pursued urbanism as a deliberate strategy for ordering society, not as a proclivity ingrained by their New England town origins. By the eighteenth century, Euro-Americans joined their European counterparts in adapting the principles of Renaissance urban planning to refine civic spaces. Ohio Company men laid out Marietta to cultivate a vision of urban grandeur marked by a regular street plan and public squares.[45] These features, they hoped, would attract desirable inhabitants and cultivate aesthetic enjoyment and refined behavior as well as commercial development.[46] In their vision, Marietta would grow into a major entrepôt on the Ohio-Mississippi corridor, more comparable to cities such as Philadelphia and New Orleans than to their New England hometowns, such as Rutland or Gloucester, Massachusetts.[47] On paper and on the ground, Marietta's urban features would signal that city founders engaged in the same principles of urban improvement that Europeans used to reshape medieval districts to improve the health of city residents.[48] But they also would convey what type of society the Ohio Company wished to build west of the Ohio River more broadly.[49]

Ohio Company leaders saw the Muskingum earthworks as a compelling element of urban design because they viewed the earthen architecture through a lens of Enlightenment inquiry ground with Masonic principles. A few Ohio Company men had been formally educated at Harvard College, but many more shared an intellectual foundation in freemasonry, which promoted rational learning and fraternity through a celebration of ancient architectural practices. For individuals who defined their social organization by the mysteries of ancient builders, divine geometry, and architectural symbolism, the forms and dimensions of the Muskingum earthworks seemed to offer evidence of a distinct North American culture of architecture and ritual. Like the British Masonic antiquaries who studied the monumental architecture of "ancient Britons," Ohio Company men believed that freemasonry might produce new national history in tandem with fraternal bounds.[50]

Freemasons in Marietta framed the earthworks simultaneously as subjects of study and sites of sociability. They saw the earthworks as a way to solve the problem of establishing a new Masonic lodge in federal territory. After the Revolution, freemasons in the United States could no longer look to Great Britain as a source of Masonic authority. Yet the Grand Lodges of the new American states held no authority over federal territory and could not charter a new lodge in the Ohio country.[51] As Ohio Company members considered how to incorporate a new lodge at Marietta, they framed the earthworks as sites that shared physical characteristics with Masonic meeting places. Rufus Putnam described the tops of two truncated pyramidal earthworks as being "as level on the top as a mosaic pavement." His excised description of the planar surfaces as "level as the Floor of the Scot[tish Rite] Lodge in Boston" reveals the depth of his association with ancient Masonic knowledge and contemporary fraternal practice.[52] Putnam invested so much significance in the forms of these structures that he emended depictions suggesting that the earthworks had pointed tops like Egyptian pyramids.[53] His representation of Marietta's public squares showed concern not only for outlining accurate footprints of the forms but also for depicting their platform tops and siting amid flat, open ground (see Figure 3 and Figure 4).[54] Ohio Company leaders placed these sites under individual Masonic stewardship. Freemasons Winthrop Sargent, Samuel Parsons, Rufus Putnam, Jonathan Heart, Griffin Greene, and Daniel Story all served on committees to direct their preservation or were invested with their care for the public good.[55]

Ohio Company freemasons sustained this attention to the material details of the earthworks because they believed that they substantiated the foundations of their fraternity and modern republican society. The floors of Masonic lodges, set atop stairs, represented the floor of King Solomon's temple (Plate 1). These perfectly level surfaces signified the full equality of all who stood on them.[56] To Putnam's mind, the flat tops of many of the earthworks formed an architectural parallel. He believed that they were "the foundation of some Spacious public buildings" for ancient Americans and served as evidence of the republican nature of their society.[57] These sites of ancient sociability offered a venerable legacy

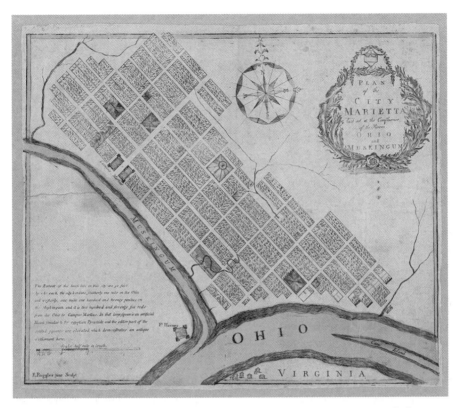

Figure 3. In 1789, the ambitious engraver Edward Ruggles Jr. hoped to profit from grand visions of the past and future of the Ohio Valley. He produced this print in Pomfret, Connecticut, for sale to local Ohio Company investors and regional residents who had made Marietta and its earthworks a topic of national popular interest. Ruggles carefully enumerated the city's house lots and hatched the public squares in triangular planes converging at a central point, likening the depicted features to Egyptian pyramids. Edward Ruggles Jr., "Plan of the City of Marietta, laid out at the Confluence of the Rivers, Ohio and Muskingum," hand-colored engraving, 1789. Courtesy American Antiquarian Society.

on which to build modern republican sociability as well—one that would transcend political and sectarian divisions.[58] Just as Masons ceremonially ascended steps to the mosaic pavement in private lodges, so too could ordinary individuals ascend the public earthworks and contemplate the lessons of ancient American architects, forming a civil bond among Americans by linking past, present, and future generations.

Masonic views of the earthworks infused plans to make them urban monuments and, in turn, create an image of a city that boasted refined public squares. Rufus Putnam's adaptation of the grid recalled monumental city plans such as the one that engineer Charles L'Enfant proposed for a federal capital on the Potomac River in 1791. Both Putnam and L'Enfant had honed their planning and

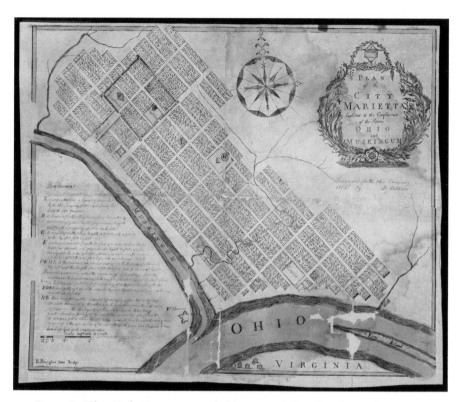

Figure 4. When Rufus Putnam emended his copy of the Edward Ruggles Jr. print, he took special care to revise the engraver's depiction of the earthworks on site. Putnam pasted tiny hand-drawn images of the earthworks and a more extensive description of them over the printed depictions and descriptions. He depicted the specific footprints of the earthworks as well as their flat tops and portrayed the earthworks amid flat, open ground. He also added sketches of earthen walls to show that he had aligned one axis of streets with a feature that he had named the Sacra Via. These detailed edits reveal how Putnam and his peers viewed the earthworks through a lens of Enlightenment inquiry ground on Masonic principles. Rufus Putnam emendations (c. 1789), "Plan of the City of Marietta . . . ," by Edward Ruggles Jr., Records of the Ohio Company of Associates. Marietta College Special Collections.

drafting skills in the military, and they incorporated monuments into city plans designed—in their minds—to civilize wilderness in the name of national power.[59] Putnam framed his monumental vision within the right angles of a grid manipulated to accommodate extant structures. His plan contrasted with L'Enfant's use of baroque urban design, with diagonal boulevards leading to circular places awaiting the construction of new monuments.[60] Both men sought to create urban centers of power marked by the visual grandeur and physical scale of public monuments. But Putnam's choice of urban and monumental forms characterized Marietta as a republican capital defined by shared use and local distinctiveness.

In Putnam's plan, the earthworks engendered a unique urban grid. Marietta's public squares visually linked the city to others with public green spaces, such as Philadelphia and London, and contrasted with new cities, such as Cincinnati, packed densely with private lots.[61] But preservation differentiated Marietta from these cities with an asymmetrical system of public squares. It married picturesque environmental features with orderly and rational ones and created an urban grid whose irregularities enhanced aesthetic variegation and guarded against criticisms of monotonous or disorienting uniformity.[62] Changes in elevation contributed to the picturesque features of the grid. For visitors disembarking from the Muskingum, the truncated pyramid that the Ohio Company named Capitolium slowly appeared above the crest line of the plateau as pedestrians ascended the Sacra Via. To the southeast, the largest mound stood as a monumental focal point for anyone approaching its surrounding public square.

Company leaders affirmed the monumental design of Putnam's survey by legislating the care of select earthworks as urban monuments in public squares. They voted to maintain four principal earthworks under collective company ownership and determined "to perpetuate the figure and appearance of so majestic a Monument of Antiquity."[63] They passed directives charging citizen stewards with keeping the features in their current forms, seeding them with grass, and ensuring that they were in "no other ways improved" and "hereafter occupied in no other way."[64] Their policies answered the appeals of nonresident antiquaries such as James Winthrop, who had implored Winthrop Sargent that "care should be taken to prevent people from building on, or plowing up such sacred ground."[65] Through environmental legislation, the land company leaders defined their city as a monumental one by designating the earthworks as seemingly unchanged—and unchanging—urban landmarks of an ancient past.

In the early days of city building, these written and visual plans for preservation invoked Marietta's intended public squares as refined urban spaces. The frequent label of "ruins" signified the earthworks as objects of contemplation and aesthetic appreciation while emphasizing their tangible links to ancient pasts. These features, along with views of the junction of the Ohio and Muskingum Rivers, were the elements of topographical and urban variety touted by Rufus Putnam when he wrote that "the situation of the City-plat is the most delightful of any I ever saw."[66] Migrant John May agreed. When he "spent the day in viewing and reconnoitering the spot where the City is to be built," he found "the situation delightfully agreeable, well calculated for an elegant City—the old ruins are a masterly piece of work of great extent." To May's mind, the ancient landscape made a refined contrast to the current state of Ohio Company infrastructure, which he judged to be "in a very backward state."[67]

A few months after Marietta settlers first praised the site's earthen architecture, company leaders cast the earthworks as monumental centerpieces of city greens to model the polite urban walks that elite Euro-Americans desired.[68] Beginning in 1788, company directors voted to cultivate the grounds surrounding the earthworks with ornamental plantings and public walks or public buildings. They invested a committee with management of these public squares, charging them "to point out the Mode of improvement for Ornament and in what manner the Ancient works shall be preserved."[69] It was this committee that in 1791, amid impending warfare with Indigenous peoples in the Ohio country and a declining national economy, set out detailed horticultural instructions, designating the precise places where particular species of trees should be planted. The square that surrounded the great mound, for instance, would be lined with mulberry trees, joined at each corner with an elm. Rows of honey locusts, weeping willows, evergreens, and more mulberries would frame the conical mound at the center. The committee wrote similar instructions for the care of Capitolium and Quadraniou.[70]

This vision of environmental refinement countered images of untamed Ohio Valley wilderness that engendered social regression in U.S. migrants.[71] In contrast to the seemingly wild vistas of the region, the regularity of the tree plantings, set between twenty and thirty feet apart and aligned with the streets and internal walkways, along with the patterned placement of species, created a public landscape cultivated for aesthetic appreciation of order and refinement. Yet company leaders tried to engender a more ambitious picture of urbanism along the Ohio by drawing direct comparisons to celebrated sites of urban leisure and sociability in the new United States. Trying to enliven a map of the earthworks and town plan for a Massachusetts correspondent, Rufus Putnam compared Marietta's green spaces to ones in Boston and New York. The Sacra Via was as "regular and uniform" as "the gravel walk of the Boston Mall," an arbored walk along the southeastern perimeter of the Common (Plate 2).[72] The ascents of Capitolium and Quadraniou were like the well-known flight of stairs leading from the edge of Boston Common to the front door of James Bowdoin, the former Massachusetts governor and Ohio Company investor.[73] The great mound, wrote Putnam, formed an ellipsis as "regular" as New York's bowling green.[74] When the environmental geometries of Marietta's public squares matched their most admired seaboard counterparts, he implied, they cultivated equally refined social life.

These invocations of the Boston Mall and the Bowling Green characterized the neighborhoods around Marietta's public squares as aspirational elite urban districts. Patriot citizens of New York had lodged the city's Bowling Green in the memory of fellow Americans as a site of Revolutionary iconoclasm when they toppled the statue of George III in 1776. Yet when Putnam referred to the site,

New York City merchants were consolidating their dwellings around the green space. Stepping into Manhattan's first public park, visitors got a view of the new four-story houses that ringed it. As these domiciles became the city's most expensive real estate, the Bowling Green attracted notoriety as the central feature of a well-to-do neighborhood. John May, for instance, noted the impressive fireworks and illuminated houses that he viewed from the green in the spring of 1789 on his way from Boston to Marietta.[75] Similarly, pedestrians on Boston's Mall could look across the Common to see elite Georgian mansions lofted above Beacon Street. Along with James Bowdoin's house, John Hancock's mansion formed a renowned point of public admiration.[76] By comparing Marietta's squares with these well-known urban recreational spaces, Putnam invoked the elegant domestic seats that he and his fellow Mariettans hoped to build around the city's public greens.

Altogether, Ohio Company leaders' professed preservation of earthworks as ancient monuments embodied their plans for an urban future. Their campaign to shape sites of sociability enabled early residents to stretch their imagination—and those of their interlocutors—to envision Marietta as a city, as Minerva Nye did when she wrote in September 1788, "We now live in the City of Marietta where we expect to end our days."[77] At a time when Ohio Company leaders devoted daily labor to building houses, fortifying the blockhouse, and planting gardens, they appropriated the earthworks as ready-made urban features. On the ground, their scale and relational expanse formed the most demonstrative features of the proposed scale of the nascent city. Earthworks oriented viewers in the city plan and aided the mental projection of house lots, rights-of-way, and municipal sites across the landscape. Making these historic features permanent made future generations of residents seem more present.

Public and Private in Territorial Lands

As company members appropriated the earthworks to bestow a sense of urban reality and historical gravity to a city built mostly on paper, they developed preservation as a competitive strategy for capital building—making Marietta an urban center of political power and private profit. From the beginning, company men had angled for their settlement to become the capital of the Northwest Territory. Shareholder John May noted these designs as he made his way to Marietta in May 1788. When he crossed paths with territorial governor Arthur St. Clair in Pittsburgh, May confessed that he wished to visit the governor in service of the "little selfish" desire of the Ohio Company, "as we wish him to make Muskingum the sea[t] of Government, and place of his residence." Success in this pursuit could be achieved, he believed, "if proper attention is paid to little matters as well as those of greater magnitude."[78]

Rufus Putnam and his compatriots used preservation to cultivate the sense of place needed to exert U.S. political power over federal territory and to make their city a capital of this domain.[79] Early descriptions of Marietta's distinctive plan created an image of a place that could serve as a seat of government. Local urban planning carried new import after company leaders succeeded in their campaign to make Marietta the territorial capital in July 1788. Ohio Company leaders invested their study and preservation of the earthworks with federal authority, as when they conducted a survey in the presence of Governor Arthur St. Clair and federal judges. But they also used descriptions of the urban plan to characterize Marietta as a place where individuals might angle for federal political power.[80] Marietta residents were not shy about pursuing political appointments. As Joseph Gilman wrote soon after his arrival in 1789, an Ohio Company proprietor "assured" him that "there was no impropriety in soliciting our friends in Government for such Offices as they may judge us capable of filling."[81] Indeed, many members of the Ohio Company translated their roles in building the city into territorial offices.

The company's interest in building a political capital, of course, was enmeshed with their goal of building financial capital. Land company investors had turned west in pursuit of personal profit. Rufus Putnam, Winthrop Sargent, and many of the Ohio Company directors had struggled to regain a financial foothold after military service in the War for Independence drained their personal resources. They used social connections fomented in the Continental Army to create opportunities for personal advancement through land development.[82] Investors did everything they could to profit from the favor that the federal government bestowed on their business venture. They worked with congressmen to obtain a low price for acreage, paid in depreciated land certificates, and then reaped the benefit of land values inflated by the passage of the Northwest Ordinance of 1787.[83] Company directors kept track of their labor for the association and submitted expenses for reimbursement and time for wages.[84] Other migrants, such as Dudley Woodbridge Jr., moved to Marietta with "a variety of *plans* to grow *rich*."[85]

The same men touted preservation of the earthworks as evidence that interest in the public welfare guided their land development. The resulting urban designs simultaneously advanced and denied their individual agendas for economic and political profit. Legislation guiding the survey, sale, and settlement of the federal territory northwest of the Ohio River had been born of a debate about the relationship of public good and private wealth in the United States. When Confederation legislators had debated the best way to divide this territory in 1784 and 1785, the proposal to prepare public lands for private sale sparked one of the earliest national attempts to encourage opportunities for individual profit in support of collective good. Architects of the Land Ordinance and Northwest Ordinance crafted policy that they thought would balance the interests of individuals who bought territorial lands with the welfare of a national citizenry.[86]

Ohio Company leaders strove to characterize themselves as model practitioners of this balance: private investors who acted in the interest of all U.S. citizens. They studiously sought to avoid characterization as land speculators, a practice as common as it was lamented by U.S. officials. Ohio Company shareholders pointed to the preservation of earthworks as one way of demonstrating that they were not driven by "aspirations . . . after money" but instead devoted to building a "permanent republick" of citizens joined by common manners and complementary interests.[87] Framed as ancient monuments in public greens, the Marietta earthworks bolstered the company's celebration of urban social organization as interest in common welfare. They also formed points of visual contrast to denigrate impermanent architecture, mobile lifeways, and dispersed settlement as evidence of the self-interest of Euro-Americans who did not recognize Marietta as a seat of authority. These settlers, as Samuel Parsons put it in 1785, shortly before he became a director of the Ohio Company, comprised "our own *white* Indians of no character who have their own Private Views without Regard to public Benefits to Serve."[88] In this view, Euro-Americans who looked out only for themselves formed as large a threat to U.S. state and society as did Indigenous Americans who resisted colonization and displacement. When the buildings of Marietta's first inhabitants looked unsettlingly similar to the dwellings of the backcountry residents they criticized, Ohio Company leaders saw earthworks as crucial elements of a planned urban order and environmental refinement demonstrated almost entirely by these structures.

As private purchasers of public lands, Ohio Company directors also used preservation to display a willingness to place limits on private holdings. When the U.S. government created the Northwest Territory, it defined these lands as public by virtue of ownership by the federal government. When the Ohio Company purchased their tract from Congress, they made the earthworks public by retaining them under collective ownership of company shareholders.[89] This rendered the city's public squares technically private land, as the company was neither a governmental nor a corporate entity. But Marietta leaders stressed their public nature by contrasting them with the private house lots deeded to individual shareholders. As Rufus Putnam wrote in 1788, "In laying out our Citty, we have preserved Some of these works from becoming privet [sic] property by including them within Lots or Squares appropriated to public uses."[90] The earthworks and their surrounding squares, in other words, would never be sold. Of course, if Ohio

Company goals came to pass, their permanence would drive up the market value of surrounding lands for sale.

A draft of Putnam's letter reveals how much care he took to explain the relationship of these public and private properties. Though he readily admitted that the company did not keep all of the earthworks intact, he self-consciously excised his explanation that some would disappear under private development. While the company secured the permanence of some of the largest earthen structures as monuments, "the rest of the works can ~~only~~ remain ~~on paper for they are covered with house lots~~ when the new Citty is built, on paper only."[91] By explaining the destruction of some mounds in a more passive voice, Putnam implied that the demolition served the collective good of building urban infrastructure rather than the private wealth created by individually held lots. He hoped to train sympathetic eyes to see the disruption of a perfectly regular grid as a sign of the town planners' attention to the public good. In this view, the linear perfection of the federal land grid, calculated only to facilitate the ease of sale for private profit, formed a crude contrast to the distinctive urban design that made public monuments of Marietta's ancient architecture.[92]

This environmental statement of public-mindedness served as a strategy for attracting attention and profit within a landscape of urban competition—a core element of the Ohio Company's speculative project. As Manasseh Cutler wrote of his early town plans, directors hoped that the urban form of Marietta would ensure that company members "shall be able to vie with our western competitors in city building."[93] By including the earthworks within the city, they made antiquarian correspondence about evidence of the past a vehicle for reports about their modern city building. In encouraging visitors to see the works for themselves, Marietta antiquaries ensured their reputations as informants in intellectual networks.[94] As one observer reported in 1791, he had not believed reports of the earthworks' complexity and size until viewing them firsthand.[95] Extant earthworks served as insurance for the accuracy of Ohio Company claims when observers could compare the structures to written descriptions. Company leaders thus dealt the earthworks into the confidence game of city boosterism, drawing interest with their notable features and buoying their own reputations in broader conversations about trans-Appalachian development.[96]

Rufus Putnam and his partners also used plans for preservation as an enticement for U.S. settlers with refined tastes—and hopefully heavy pocketbooks. The earthworks and their surrounding public spaces could not override economic disadvantages that potential settlers might perceive. But they might attract migrants eager to allay concerns that uncultivated environments might trigger social regression or signal uncivil residents. Showpiece urban monuments might also draw travelers into town before they continued down the Ohio River or even encourage investment in nearby lands in which many Ohio Company shareholders also had a stake.[97] City plans with public squares, cultivated through intellectual study as well as environmental refinement, also served as propaganda directed at increasingly skeptical eastern shareholders who sought to direct company business from Philadelphia or New York rather than Marietta.[98]

City boosterism voiced in the language of the public good countered accusations that a corrupting greed drove the business dealings of company directors. In 1787, Manasseh Cutler and Winthrop Sargent had blurred the already fuzzy lines between private speculation and the so-called public nature of the shareholding company by piggybacking the Ohio Company purchase on a larger land speculation scheme undertaken by the Scioto Company. Cutler freely admitted that Congress would not have approved such a low price for the Ohio Company's 1.5 million acres without the simultaneous sale of 3.5 million acres to the Scioto Company "for a private speculation."[99] Though signed in two separate contracts, the companies featured many overlapping investors, and Cutler described the purchase as a single one for nearly 6 million acres: "the greatest private contract ever made in America," by his account.[100]

Ohio Company leaders soon came under fire for their dealings with the Scioto Company. Manasseh Cutler and Winthrop Sargent's negotiation with Secretary of the Treasury William Duer had secured favorable rates for the Ohio Company purchase, but it also had entangled them with Duer's personal speculations in the Scioto Company. Ohio Company members who invested after 1787 raised concerns that Cutler and Sargent's investments in the Scioto Company formed a conflict of interest that would hurt the Ohio Company's success. Both men tried to quell the criticism of Ohio Company shareholders Rufus Putnam, Benjamin Tupper, and Samuel Parsons by giving them stock in the Scioto Company. A contingent of Ohio Company investors from Rhode Island met with no such appeasement in 1789, though, and protest grew when Cutler and Putnam engineered a reverse investment in 1790, selling 148 defaulted shares in the Ohio Company to three leading shareholders of the increasingly suspect Scioto Company.[101] Criticism of the Ohio Company directors' private dealings swelled as the economy declined, and solvent shareholders grew impatient for individual deeds to their holdings. By the summer of 1791, Cutler and Sargent found themselves defending against calls to investigate their land dealings in both companies.[102]

Demonstration of leading shareholders' interest in the public good was particularly important because the Ohio Company had never incorporated as planned. Ohio Company leaders first expressed interest in incorporation by Congress or a state in 1786; in 1788, they agreed to apply to Congress.[103] Lack of incorporation created legal and cultural liabilities for administrators of the association. Some congressmen had questioned the ability of Congress to sell public lands to a self-formed association that lacked a charter. Even after Cutler presented the Ohio Company's articles of association to Congress, some opponents "still objected that we were a self-created body, and not legally incorporated, and therefore Congress could not know us as such."[104] By Cutler's account, Congress was to blame: their refusal to incorporate the company or recognize it as a self-formed corporate association forced Cutler and Sargent into private dealings with the Scioto Company to negotiate the Ohio Company land sale.

As a result, Ohio Company directors lacked legal privileges and public authority invested in corporate trustees. Failure of the venture held greater personal consequences. Shareholders of the Ohio Company were keenly aware that its unincorporated status left leaders personally liable for company debts and so did their best to mitigate this risk.[105] Absence of a charter also denied them formal recognition of the public benefits supposedly derived from their business venture, which increasingly appeared to concentrate associational power in the hands of a few Marietta residents. By 1790, it became clear that nearly two-thirds of the initial shareholders had bought into the land deal not to emigrate to the Ohio country but to profit from the resale of the land.[106] Though company rules had capped buy-ins at five shares per individual, proxy votes and land claims quickly concentrated in the hands of a few residents. The founding of Marietta produced a balance of local power very different from a community of equal shareholders described by the association's founding documents.

Ohio Company leaders used their designs for preservation to consolidate their control over public land in Marietta. Stewards of the squares did not have free rein; they paid rent to the company and were charged with carrying out the committee's instructions for "the Mode of improvement for Ornament and in what manner the Ancient works shall be preserved."[107] In December 1788, a committee leased the three largest earthworks to Samuel H. Parsons, Rufus Putnam, and Griffin Greene, "so long a time as they are not wanted for the Uses for which they were reserved."[108] In the spring of 1791, another committee granted Rufus Putnam charge of the largest square for twelve years. Dudley Woodbridge leased Capitolium for eight years, and Benjamin Tupper took care of Quadraniou for a decade. Ohio Company shareholders also determined that the Sacra Via should not be leased, making it a right-of-way from the Muskingum River into Marietta. Still, they asked "that Judge Putnam be requested to attend particularly to its preservation in its present form & seed it to Grass."[109] As company members named individual men stewards of antiquity, the squares became monuments to their benevolence as well as prime pastureland singled out for their individual use.[110]

Lasting personal profit, however, rested on finalizing the Ohio Company's land purchase. No one could secure deeds in fee simple to individual parcels until investors made final payments to the association and the Ohio Company settled its debt with Congress. As violent contests over land and an increasingly frantic scramble for capital in the United States threw the Ohio country into greater flux, onlookers increasingly—and rightfully—doubted the solvency and dominion of the Ohio Company. Company leaders doubled down on preservation as a strategic overstatement of their authority. Early in 1792, they cited these urban plans in their pleas for partial debt forgiveness from Congress. They deserved financial favor once again, they argued, because "their object was not to raise the value of their lands at the expence, exertion, and risk of others, but to make an actual settlement."[111] Yet as Manasseh Cutler privately had confessed a few months earlier, many shareholders openly admitted their desire to sell their lands for profit rather than resettle in the Ohio Valley. In what Cutler called "the present rage for speculation," it was ultimately the promise of securing private property and elevating the price of real estate that committed Ohio Company shareholders to preserving the past in Marietta's public squares.[112]

Ohio Company Legacies

Despite the outstanding debts of individual shareholders and the association at large, Ohio Company agents finalized the purchase of half of their contracted land in 1792. Migration to the Ohio territory picked up after 1795, and as Ohio Company administrators conveyed deeds to shareholders, they dissolved regular meetings. Marietta did not explode into an Ohio River metropolis, but earthworks continued to attract travelers.[113] Marietta residents inscribed these sites not only with the moundbuilder myth but also with the company's founding narrative of the Northwest Territory. With the Ohio Company itself relegated to the past, travel writers rehearsed the history of the earthworks' preservation as often as they did theories about the architects of the earthworks. In his report of his travels to Ohio in 1803, Thaddeus Mason Harris reprinted an engraving of Rufus Putnam's map of Marietta that overlaid the planned city grid with the earthworks surveyed in 1788 (Figure 5). When other antiquaries pointed to Harris's description as authoritative in coming decades, they echoed the voices of his informants: Rufus Putnam, Dudley Woodbridge, and Joseph Gilman, all of whom either superintended town squares or sat on committees to direct their care.[114]

Travelers who continued down the Ohio and Mississippi Rivers often made the Marietta earthworks points of comparison or adopted urban perspectives of other earthen architecture. In the 1810s, Henry Brackenridge made direct reference to Marietta when he described mounds near St. Louis.[115] These earthworks, he believed, added interest to modern U.S. cities such as St. Louis, where

Figure 5. This engraving points to the lasting influence of Rufus Putnam's vision for Marietta's urban plan. Generations of readers viewed the city on the page, where earthen architecture and urban infrastructure coexisted in ways impossible on the ground. Thaddeus Mason Harris, "A Plan of part of Marietta with the remains of Antient Works found there," in *A Journal of a Tour into the Territory Northwest of the Alleghany Mountains, Made in the Spring of the Year 1803* (Boston, 1805), back matter. Albert and Shirley Small Special Collections Library, University of Virginia.

the "Indian mounds, and remains of antiquity; which, while they are ornamental to the town, prove, that in former times, those places had also been chosen as the site, perhaps, of a populous city."[116] At nearby Cahokia—a complex of earthworks built in a burst of large-scale construction around 1050 CE—Brackenridge explained the material traces of past habitation by imagining the ruin of modern Philadelphia, whose metropolitan population approached a hundred thousand residents.[117]

Ohio Company directors were not the only U.S. colonizers to appropriate earthworks with urban design. In the Scioto River valley, Daniel Dresbach built a new county seat for Pickaway County, Ohio, within a circular earthwork in 1810 (Figure 6).[118] Charged as town director of the aptly named Circleville, he set out two concentric bands of private lots separated by a circular road. The county courthouse, built in octagonal form, sat at the center of the plan amid a circular plot designated a "public area." Two principal streets transected the town and the earthwork at a right angle, while smaller radial streets provided rights-of-way in the town center. Dresbach also professed to set prices and stipulations of lot purchase, which mandated the construction of public curbs and walks as well as houses, to attract buyers "most likely to improve and prevent speculation."[119] Yet he also translated public amenities of this plan into financial valuation: lots ringing the public area at the center of town were appraised most highly.[120] Caleb Atwater, a Massachusetts native devoted to antiquarian study, was certainly not the only resident to take interest in this new town because of his Masonic beliefs. He peppered his efforts to found a Masonic lodge in Circleville in the 1810s with debates about what he and fellow freemasons should or should not reveal about Masonic interpretations of the earthworks.[121]

Circleville's urban form brought it notoriety when Ohio towns—and the competition between their founders—boomed.[122] Daniel Dresbach did not record as comprehensive a plan for preservation as did Marietta builders, but he drew attention to the earthen architecture to sell lots and settle town accounts. Newspaper notices deemed Circleville a "curiosity on account of its scite [sic] and form."[123] One writer reflected on the geometries of the circular earthwork at Circleville in comparison to a tangent square one to compare the advantages of round and rectilinear urban plans. To some, this distinctive engagement with evidence of the past made Circleville residents exemplars of "the enterprising spirit of our citizens" because they "profitted from the prior choice and works of the former owners of the soil."[124] These reports guided travelers in uniting their appraisal of the extant earthworks and the ongoing town-building efforts. In August 1816, for instance, Pennsylvania Quaker Leatitia Ware echoed a description in Philadelphia's *Weekly Aurora* when she described her firsthand view of Circleville as "a flourishing place" characterized by new as well as ancient architecture.[125]

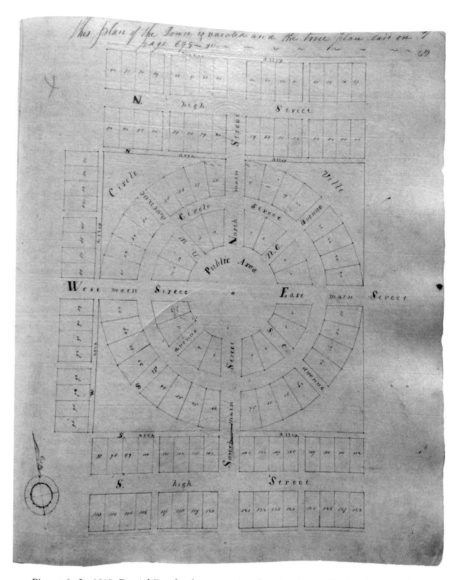

Figure 6. In 1810, Daniel Dresbach appropriated a circular earthwork in the Scioto River valley as an element of town planning for a new Ohio town named Circleville. He set an octagonal courthouse in the center of two concentric bands of lots. No municipal laws regulated the treatment of the extant earthworks, and Euro-American residents of the region removed them. Between 1837 and 1854, a private redevelopment company worked to replat this central part of the town in a grid. Town plat for Circleville, Ohio, Deed Book A, 67. Recorder's Office, Pickaway County, Ohio.

Yet the appropriation of earthworks as public monuments in Marietta did not just provide a prototype for U.S. migrants westward. It also drew town leaders into an increasingly fraught project of managing public buildings and grounds—an undertaking that they shared with their U.S. counterparts in colonial cities that had aging urban fabric. When Marietta residents successfully petitioned the territorial legislature for municipal incorporation in 1800, a city council replaced the Ohio Company board of directors as the primary body of local governance. The town's public lands, formerly held in trust by a handful of citizens, became city property governed by council members. When Marietta residents came into conflict over how the city should manage these sites, they joined residents in municipalities across the United States who argued over how historic public structures contributed to the public good. In doing so, they engaged preservation as a way to amplify disputes over local authority into broader statements about the powers of corporations in the early nation.

CHAPTER 2

Sacred Forms: Public Buildings and Urban Improvements

In 1811, Rufus Putnam spent another spring day sketching plans for one of Marietta's monumental squares. Twenty-three years after he had first delineated its boundaries, he joined two other city council members, Judson Gitteau and Paul Fearing, in redesigning what they now called Mound Square. The town council had charged the men with submitting a plan for how the public grounds might "be improved as a burying ground."[1] Again, they adapted a grid—this time within the public square—to showcase the parcel's central feature: the large conical mound at its center, now interpreted as an ancient burial monument. This time, the site plan divided land not into house lots and city streets but into family burial plots and access roads. Decorative plantings and fencing would bound the perimeter. This design made clear that its architects applied new principles of cemetery design circulating in the Atlantic world to fulfill the preservation mandate set out by Ohio Company leaders in previous decades.[2] Yet this new plan also made Mound Square itself—an urban feature created by the city's founders—a historic feature worthy of preservation as much as the earthwork at its center.

When Marietta councillors built a new cemetery in the name of preservation, they shaped a built environment that manifested municipal power with a statement of permanence. Their plan used environmental design and regulation to assert municipal authority over federal and state claims as well as recalcitrant town residents who countered municipal governance with resistance and noncompliance.[3] Many civic leaders in established cities across the early United States argued to preserve colonial "antiquities" for the same reasons. They pointed to many forms of public architecture—houses of worship, government buildings, burying grounds, and city greens—as historic evidence of the "founding" generations of Euro-American colonizers that had built them. This public architecture evinced the advent of civil society in North America, they argued, and the demolition of these sites exposed a creeping threat to that civil society: urban real estate speculators. As city improvers guided environmental change to facilitate the growth of commerce, advocates of preservation argued that city dwellers should not shape the built environment solely according to the market value of the land that it occupied. The permanence of some historic structures, they argued, formed a key element of environmental refinement and progressive social development in a market society, not evidence of economic stagnation or cultural backwardness.

Municipal leaders, corporate trustees, and city residents amplified these local contests over public architecture to speak to national debates about the relationship of corporate entities, the states that issued their charters, and the citizens that they were charged to serve. In disputes over governance and property rights, they argued about whether the permanence or destruction of historic sites served the public good. By homing in on sites created by colonizers, they defined a republic of citizens who looked to settler colonialism as a founding narrative. Yet by insisting that preservation and urban improvement could work together, they also defined an ethic of permanence that justified the removal of markers of the past that did not accord with ideals of urban order and public health.

Municipal Authority and Local Governance

Few U.S. residents saw the revolutionary break from Great Britain as a reason to ignore the histories embodied by colonial buildings. Like European antiquaries, they viewed the architecture of the early modern past with as much interest as "ancient" Indigenous structures. Antiquaries on both sides of the Atlantic Ocean saw the architecture of previous generations as a source of both local character and national identity. In the 1790s, British antiquary John Carter wrote one of the largest studies focused on documenting the historic built environment: a six-volume book series that recorded the "ancient buildings" standing in modern England.[4] But even writers of more modest local histories included descriptions of extant urban infrastructure, medieval buildings, and vernacular architectural styles as evidence of past generations to be studied and preserved, if not in place then on paper.[5]

In the new United States, many Euro-Americans highlighted the oldest extant features of Euro-American colonization to narrate the seeming transformation of the North American "wilderness" into a cultivated landscape. By observing the particularities of a site, they believed, Americans would build a distinctive national identity through historical associations. Articulated most completely by

Archibald Allison in his *Essays on the Nature and Principles of Taste* (1790), this associational theory held that individuals formed emotional connections with their countrymen through shared experiences of distinctive built and natural environments.[6] Subscribers to this view believed that residents of the United States could cultivate a strong national feeling by paying attention to the characteristics of structures that previous generations had put into place. The built environment marked the beginning of a national history that extended, as Philadelphia antiquary Deborah Norris Logan put it, "from the older olden time, to the Revolutionary War, down to modern improvement."[7] In historical perspective, locally distinctive evidence of Euro-American colonization in early U.S. communities seemed to reveal how previous generations had carved multiple paths that all led to the progressive development of a modern republic.

Appreciation of a site's historic value did not depend on an appraisal of picturesque beauty. Residents of the post-Revolutionary United States often joined their European counterparts in viewing architectural ruins with aesthetic as well as historic appreciation.[8] Yet antiquaries often reminded their audiences that valuable markers of the past might be ugly or visually unremarkable. In 1802, for instance, the Reverend Joseph Lathrop explained how the old meetinghouse in West Springfield, Massachusetts, informed observers' knowledge of the past and, in turn, their connections with each other. Some congregants, he acknowledged, might regret saying goodbye to the meetinghouse just as an old man hated to leave his "decayed and tottering house" that "assists his meditations, and recals [*sic*] to his mind past agreeable scenes."[9] Yet the antique features of the meetinghouse also evoked a deeper past that recalled the lives of the "founders of this ancient temple."[10] Lathrop explained, "The antiquity of this house carries our minds back to the time of its erection, which was an hundred years ago. . . . And, though, in this age of comparative opulence and refinement, it may appear as a wretched, unsightly pile, yet if we carry our thoughts back one hundred years, and contemplate the habits and manners, the poverty and paucity of the then existing inhabitants, it will assume a grandeur, which few modern temples can boast."[11] Lathrop urged his congregants to see the building in the context of its original construction, not in terms of modern standards of beauty, to vivify the historical development of American civil society.

Lathrop expounded on the historic qualities of the meetinghouse shortly before its demolition. Many stewards of public architecture across the early United States were leading similar campaigns of destruction in the name of urban improvement. As city corporations increasingly defined themselves as bodies of local governance that managed town affairs in the interest of all residents rather than regulating markets in the interest of merchants, municipal officials pursued environmental transformations to increase rational order,

health, and safety in the interest of the public good. Purveyors of these campaigns used local law to regulate the use of common spaces and enforce ordinances about noise, cleanliness, and other "nuisances"; fund and coordinate
the building, widening, and straightening of streets; and set building codes to
regulate private construction. Likewise, architects of new public buildings and
houses of worship employed architectural designs understood to invoke modern ideas of comfort and convenience.[12]

Yet some city dwellers argued for the preservation of historic public architecture to extend its salutary effects to future generations. They invested the fate of
local sites owned by corporate entities with national significance by linking their
fate to the broader definition of the rights of corporations and the states that
charted them. In some cases, city residents made arguments about the historic
character of public properties to shape a redefinition of city corporations sweep-
ing over the early United States. In the 1770s and 1780s, residents of many North
American towns enacted a wave of municipal incorporation to increase local political participation and autonomy during and after the War for Independence.[13]
In 1789, for instance, a number of white male citizens of Philadelphia drew up a
new charter to replace the original one, issued in 1701. Like ones in Boston, New
Amsterdam, and Albany, Philadelphia's first charter aimed primarily to hold
common property and regulate markets. It appointed a closed board of directors
to govern the corporation; lifetime members filled board vacancies by internal
appointment and legislated local rules of commerce in the interest of the mer-
cantile and artisan classes.[14] Philadelphia's new charter established an open corporation, run by a group of elected representatives living within the city's
geographic boundaries, as an entity of local governance. As one Philadelphia resident put it in 1804, this system replaced an older system that "was self elective,
and not accountable to the citizens, according to the arbitrary systems of the
mother country."[15]

Supporters of this "municipal revolution" broadly agreed on the usefulness
of the open corporation as a means of participatory self-determination in the new
nation. After 1800, residents of the United States incorporated new and growing
towns along this model as never before.[16] Freeholders in Marietta, for instance,
petitioned the territorial legislature that year to "be incorporated into a body politic, and corporate, vested with power to regulate the internal police . . . and provide for the incidental expenses arising within the sa[id Township] . . . , granting
them such privileges as are commonly enjoy'd by incorporate Towns in many of
the States, composing the United States of America."[17] Yet widespread efforts to
hammer out the details of municipal governance fed acrimonious political debates in the new nation. Disagreements about how to establish a local electorate,
enumerate powers of administrators, and articulate the terms of municipal

offices generated the same concerns over balance of powers and degrees of social and political democracy as did issues of state and national governance. Municipal corporations themselves became objects of scrutiny as they proliferated. Were they little republics that offered town residents a practical tool for tending to local welfare? Or did they enable elites to concentrate power spread more broadly by town meetings and state legislatures?[18]

Contests over the power to shape historic public architecture in early U.S. cities informed these larger questions about governance. Municipal leaders in places such as Philadelphia and Marietta turned to preservation to cast city corporations as stewards of the public welfare and assert the property rights of city corporations over the governmental entities that issued their charters. They invested their local proposals with national import by merging the language of historic memory with arguments about corporate property rights in the new nation. In 1811, Marietta councillors submitted their new plan for the preservation of Mound Square to wrest control over local land from federal and state authorities. The municipality did not technically own most of the land encompassed by Mound Square. After municipal incorporation in 1800, the newly formed town council claimed the public squares as city property, just as the Ohio Company had intended.[19] But the conical earthwork and lands around it fell in section 29 of the township laid out by the federal land survey (Figure 7). Congressional land ordinances from the 1780s designated this section for the support of local religion. Marietta leaders knew that house lots and public grounds in the city's plan overlapped these "ministerial" lands.[20] For years, they remained optimistic that they could swap the uniformly appointed section 29 with another township section and execute the promised land titles in the original locales. Yet the federal government refused to consent, and in 1800, the territorial legislature became the trustee of these public lands and appointed a county-level board of trustees to manage rents collected from them.[21]

Still, the municipal government did not give up its argument that it should control the public square that fell within section 29. In 1811, the town council used their plan for a new public burial ground to apply for a "permanent lease of Mound Square." Putnam, Gitteau, and Fearing rebranded the large conical earthwork as a burial site of founders of the ancient town by encircling it with deceased founders of the modern city. Just as Putnam had adapted the city plan itself, he and fellow committee members incorporated the "great mound" as a centerpiece feature of the cemetery, encircling it with a road and adapting surrounding plots to its conical footprint. The federally mandated, state-administered county board of trustees of the ministerial lands approved this request as the will of town inhabitants and issued a rent-free ninety-nine-year lease "renewable forever."[22]

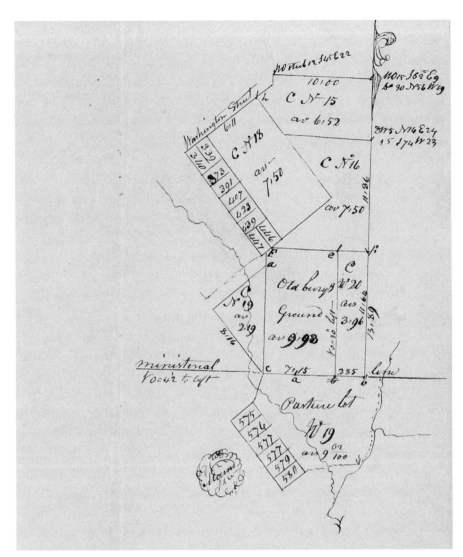

Figure 7. Federal land ordinances of the 1780s reserved section 29 of each township for the support of local religion. Early records of the Ohio Company depict the boundary line of the ministerial lot running through their city plan; company directors hoped that they could secure an exception to the policy and parcel out the land to private owners. When federal officials refused, Marietta town councillors closed the "old burying ground" of Euro-American residents depicted in this survey and plotted a new cemetery around the conical mound in the ministerial lot. Detail, plat map, c. 1789–1796, Records of the Ohio Company of Associates. Marietta College Special Collections.

Marietta town councillors translated municipal control of this public land into a broader statement about the corporate rights of city corporations. At the meeting in which they reviewed the initial cemetery plan in 1811, council members composed a formal protest against a state-incorporated county commission that had excised a piece of land comprising one-third of the municipality.[23] This manipulation of city boundaries served no particular need, town councillors argued, and left Marietta a "singularly awkward and inconvenient shape."[24] They insisted that they had nothing against a legal alteration of this type but the county commissioners could not infringe on the municipal rights and privileges endowed by the state's act of incorporation unless the town itself decided to forfeit those rights.[25] They looked to the past to explain the property rights of the city. The Revolutionary War, in their telling, had secured corporate charter rights first guaranteed by British law and now "sealed with American blood, and shrouded by American Constitutions." Corporate rights endured as "sacred" principles meant to be preserved in perpetuity: they formed "the basis of American Legislation that contracts should not be impaired and that property and vested rights should not wantonly be taken away."[26] The municipal right to maintain a permanent hold on its property, in this view, constituted no less than the national legacy of the Revolution.

Mariettans were not the only U.S. residents who invested historic squares and their centerpieces with such import at the turn of the nineteenth century.[27] In Philadelphia, civic leaders launched a heated campaign for the preservation of the old statehouse and its yard in 1813. The Pennsylvania Assembly had commissioned the building as the seat of the colonial legislature in 1729. The brick Georgian façade had made a grand statement of the assembly's authority over a growing city and the increasingly vast tracts of Pennsylvania land that colonists coerced from Indigenous American control. As craftsmen put the finishing touches on the building in 1735, legislators mandated that the open ground south of the structure never "be converted into or made use of for erecting any sort of building thereupon, but that the said ground shall be inclosed, and remain a publick open green and walk for ever."[28] During the eighteenth century, government officials and their constituents made the statehouse and its yard a seat of public authority. Political representatives, visitors, electors, and protestors all used the site to direct city affairs and colonial—and later national—politics.[29]

In 1813, Philadelphians became incensed when they learned that the Pennsylvania legislature proposed to divide and sell the statehouse tract as common real estate. The General Assembly planned to use the proceeds to build a statehouse in the new capital city of Harrisburg. When news of the plan reached Philadelphia, it reignited a dispute that had flared in the 1790s. Prominent city residents insisted that the law was clear: the statehouse grounds must remain open ground, reserved for public use in perpetuity. As trustees of the property, the Pennsylvania legislature had no legal standing to divide or sell the land. Any reforms imposed by the commonwealth, they argued, had to come from the state judiciary.[30]

City councillors did not stop with legal arguments. They also explained how the permanence of the square and building substantiated the public good. In an 1813 petition to the Pennsylvania legislature, members of the Common and Select Councils of the City of Philadelphia enumerated the value of the property in terms of civic health. The statehouse yard served as a critical source of air, light, and recreation necessary for the physical well-being of a growing urban populace, they argued. It also provided gathering space for the electioneering that ensured the political health of the city and the nation.[31] The historic character of the old statehouse contributed to public welfare as well. Councillors celebrated the building as the meeting place of the Second Continental Congress and the Constitutional Convention and the spot on which the Declaration "was first made known to the American people." In their words, "The spot which the Bill proposes to cover with private buildings, is hallowed to your memorialists, by many strong and impressive recollections. From it have issued some of the most important public acts, acts not confined to the limits of Pennsylvania, but which embrace the whole United States, and which have given birth, to the only free Republic the world has seen."[32] When they fought against a miscarriage of jurisprudence that would demolish the old statehouse, writers explained, they fought to maintain an irreplaceable monument to a watershed moment in the world history.

Philadelphia councillors insisted that their municipal fight against the Pennsylvania legislature arose not simply from local urban interests but also from a "sense of public duty" that encompassed a national citizenry at large—past, present, and future.[33] In their minds, historic features of municipal properties mattered not just as aides-memoires for the Revolutionary generation but also as real property whose fate linked the rights of U.S. citizens with the rights of the city corporation. Philadelphia city councillors framed this link between local governance and the national character of the statehouse property in opposition to governance by the state legislature. Since the 1790s, city councillors had engaged in legal disputes with the commonwealth over the ownership of Philadelphia's five original public squares. They cited the intent of seventeenth-century city founders William Penn and Thomas Holme as proof of municipal ownership. Throughout the early nineteenth century, civic leaders such as Thomas P. Cope used the language of preservation to promote a vision of urban improvement similar to the one promoted by Marietta town leaders. Philadelphians challenged state ownership of the squares by replacing their varied and

common uses with planted beds and geometric walks and building a municipal waterworks on Center Square.[34]

In 1816, William Duane engaged in this struggle for control over public lands
in Philadelphia when he cast the preservation of the old statehouse and its grounds
as a matter of the "rights of the city." In a diatribe published in his triweekly newspaper, *Aurora for the Country*, he charged the commonwealth with illegal and
immoral behavior in planning to carve up the public square without providing
a comparable environmental substitute.[35] But Duane also pointed to the irreplace-
ability of the historic character of the statehouse and its yard. As several of Duane's
allies detailed in newspapers, pamphlets, and appeals to state legislators, commonwealth law granted the property to a public defined as users of the site. This definition encompassed not only the city residents who gathered in the statehouse yard
but also the numerous people who visited the old statehouse because of its historic character.[36] In this view, old and new features of the site worked together to
bestow moral instruction and enjoyment to all who gazed at them.

Duane linked preservation with advances in moral governance by turning to
world history. According to him, "In Swisserland, the little cottage in which *William
Tell* and his associates declared the freedom of the Swiss, has been preserved
with a holy veneration for ages; the English erected a commemorative monument in Runnymede, where *magna charta* was obtained; in Greece and Rome,
whatever spot was consecrated by any great event propitious to liberty or public
virtue, it was customary to consecrate the spot by the erection of some noble and
useful public edifice." Pennsylvania leaders should add the old statehouse to this
group of historic landmarks. "In the spirit of ancient times," Duane wrote, "or of
that virtue which ought to govern all times, the *building* in which the *Declaration
of Independence* was deliberated and determined, would obtain veneration the
most sensible and endearing, as a monument of that splendid event."[37] A local
act of preservation, Duane suggested, would secure a place for the United States
among the enlightened nations of the world in a way that its founding documents
alone could not do.

While Duane and like-minded Philadelphians used the press to charge municipal bodies with this responsibility, other citizens used benevolent donations
to make city councils the trustees of historic sites. This is what Ohio Company
directors had done when they donated the public squares of Marietta to the city
corporation. The town council cited this duty to steward the trust of the donors
and of town residents when they engaged in a protracted battle with a citizen who
destroyed one of the earthworks designated for preservation. When Rev. Joseph
Willard began to plow the platform mound on the municipal land that he rented,
the town council insisted that he stop because the town founders had "ordered
[the earthworks] to be sacredly preserved in the form first discovered by our first

settlers."[38] When Willard demanded to "be furnished with evidence that the principal authority of this town had a claim, either in law or equity, paramount to his own," Marietta councillors showed him evidence of what they believed was "incontestably, the claim of the municipal authority of Marietta to control and regulate this public donation." In the councillors' telling, the "regulations of the donors and the feelings of the citizens" worked in concert. When councillors put Willard on legal notice, they reported, "many of our citizens resorted to the spot and restored, as well as might be, the ancient works to their original state."[39] In this account, municipal leaders and town residents worked together to secure the permanence not only of a historic site but also of the public legacy of a benevolent bequest.[40]

In Newport, Rhode Island, Abraham Touro sought to secure the town's synagogue as a historic property not with a land donation but with a charitable trust fund. Built in Palladian style in 1763, the brick building occupied a prominent place on a hill at the center of town.[41] Touro had attended worship there only as an infant, before his family left Newport during the Revolution. Like many of the city's Jewish merchant families, the Touro family never reestablished residence in Newport. After the war, town residents used the synagogue as a public meeting space. The Rhode Island state legislature and Supreme Court, as well as town meetings, convened there in the early 1780s. Former congregants of the synagogue cared for it from afar, returning for summer services and family burials and sending financial support for the property's care to the handful of Jewish residents of the city. By the time that Moses Lopez declared himself the final Jew in Newport in 1822, observers encouraged the preservation of the synagogue as "a handsome specimen of ancient architecture" and a marker of Rhode Island's long history of religious toleration, a principle confirmed by George Washington's celebrated letter to the congregation in 1790.[42]

When Abraham Touro found himself on his deathbed in Boston in the fall of 1822, he turned to government entities rather than private organizations to secure the permanence of the Newport synagogue. Touro drafted a will that gave the state of Rhode Island $10,000 to create a special trust fund to maintain the house of worship and its burying ground "in such manner as the said Legislature together with the municipal authority of the Town of Newport may from time [to time] direct and appoint."[43] He hoped that Jewish residents would return to Newport one day and take up regular worship in the building. Until then, however, Touro used the mechanism of a private charitable trust to make the preservation of the synagogue a municipal matter (Figure 8). By framing the synagogue as a property of local historic interest, not simply a religious one, Touro sought buy-in from antiquarian stewards. The benefactor could have left his bequest directly to Shearith Israel, a sister congregation in New York. When Moses

Lopez had moved from Newport to New York City a few months before Touro's death, he carried stewardship of the Newport synagogue with him to Shearith Israel. Abraham Touro made the first bequest in his will to this New York City congregation: $10,000 to settle its debts plus a waiver of the $1,000 it owed to him. This gift acknowledged the kinship between the historic Newport congregation and the modern New York congregation, of which Touro's sister Rebecca was also a member. Yet the significant debt of the New York congregation likely discouraged Touro from giving them funds earmarked for the care of the Newport synagogue. A trust held by the Rhode Island General Assembly secured Touro's bequest from debt collectors or misappropriation by the financially strapped New York congregation. It also reinforced the idea that the upkeep of the house of worship constituted a matter of public good defined by locality.[44]

While making the state his fiduciary agent, Touro looked to Newport's municipal government, incorporated in 1784, as the most likely architectural steward. His donation of $5,000 directly to the town council for the repair and maintenance of the street running from the burying ground to the city's main thoroughfare made clear that he understood the municipal corporation as an arm of local governance with growing authority over streets as a public space.[45] When he charged Newport's town council with caretaking duties of the synagogue and its grounds, he empowered the people geographically closest to the property to care for it as a matter of public interest to town residents. But he also made them reliant on state authorities for approval of and compensation for execution of their duties.

Touro's bequest drew Newport's town councillors into fraught relationships not only with the Rhode Island state legislature but also with local caretakers. When Touro had placed the purse in the hands of the state of Rhode Island, estate administrators realized that they needed to make Touro's trust itself "secure and permanent" before they could use it to ensure the same fate for the synagogue and grounds. Stephen Gould, a Quaker watchmaker and Newport resident with antiquarian interests, worked with Boston lawyer Titus Wells and Rhode Island General Assembly member William Hunter to define the legal architecture of Touro's trust "that it may be rightly managed in every respect."[46] The legislative act passed to administer the trust invested the Newport town council with the full responsibility of maintaining the repair of the building and its grounds. In the absence of Jewish town residents who could direct municipal maintenance, the assembly determined, the council should hire a qualified Newport resident to superintend the property's care.[47] This act confirmed that its stewards should treat the synagogue and burying ground as public buildings for the foreseeable future. It also forced municipal caretakers into larger debates about the nature of corporate property and authority in U.S. municipalities.

Figure 8. The gate at the synagogue in Newport, Rhode Island, commemorates the bequest made by Abraham Touro in 1822. Trustees used the maintenance fund to erect the granite gate and wrought-iron fence in 1842. The terms of this trust and ownership of the congregation's historic property, as defined by antiquarian caretakers and Rhode Island legislators in the 1820s, remain a source of legal dispute between Jeshuat Israel in Newport and Shearith Israel in New York City. Photograph by author, 2016.

Corporate Leaders and the Politics of Demolition

In the early nineteenth century, municipal leaders faced challenges not only to their powers of local governance but also to their authority as managers of corporate properties. Municipal incorporations flourished as part of a broader movement to incorporate religious and voluntary associations as well as business ventures, all intended to extend privileges of corporate legal structure and property ownership to organizations that professedly served the public good. State legislatures in the early United States granted corporate charters to banks, infrastructure projects, voluntary associations, charitable and religious organizations, and towns on the principle that the broad benefits of their functions justified their legal privileges. After the Revolutionary War, some states enabled general incorporation to bypass the need for legislature approval.[48] As corporate bodies proliferated, they filled the nation's landscape with properties understood by some measure to be public. Local culture, city directories, and town histories characterized churches, schools, cemeteries, benevolent institutions, town squares, and local government buildings as public structures. These sites joined wharves, bridges, turnpikes, waterworks, canals, and railroads to create a landscape of public architecture controlled by corporate officers.

As projects of corporate construction and demolition spread across the United States, U.S. citizens increasingly looked to the courts to resolve disputes over corporate properties and, in turn, refine definitions of corporations themselves. U.S. Supreme Court decisions, such as *Terrett v. Taylor* (1815) and *Dartmouth v. Woodward* (1819), sought to clarify the rights of corporations in relationship to the states that chartered them. Churches, *Terrett* decided, were private entities despite their public ends. States could claim their property only through a judicial ruling proving that the corporate body had misused or abandoned their property, not a legislative act. The *Dartmouth* decision linked churches with charities and business corporations as private entities whose contracts could not be infringed by the state.[49] Municipal incorporations stood apart as public corporations that could regulate private property for the public welfare. Though the state could limit municipal powers if the legislature reserved the power to amend the corporate charter, it could never take ownership of municipal property.[50]

These decisions established incorporation as a means of securing property interests not only of collective organizations but also of the private citizens who donated property or capital to public endeavors. In his 1815 *Terrett* opinion, Justice Joseph Story encouraged churches to use incorporation as a tool to secure their property against public interference.[51] In 1819, Justice John Marshall cited this protection of property as a benefit specifically for donors in two decisions—one for *Dartmouth* and another for *Philadelphia Baptist Association v. Hart*, which required associational heirs to have the legal certainty endowed by incorporation to accept bequests.[52] Incorporation, then, protected the property rights of "charitable or public-spirited individuals," in Marshall's words, to enact philanthropic projects beyond the grave.[53]

Jurists who decided these cases purported to clarify the relationship of different sorts of corporations to the market as well as the state: municipal corporations were public, acting as local government in the best interests of residents, and other corporations were private, endowed with special privileges as market actors that the state could not inhibit.[54] In practice, leaders of both types of corporations created more nuanced relationships with state and market powers. The classification of most corporations as private entities did not undercut the premise that they should broadly serve the public good.[55] U.S. residents continued to conceive of corporations as private-public partnerships until later in the nineteenth century. Yet the Supreme Court rulings of the 1810s that made it easier for corporate leaders to raise money for various moral reforms also made them more vulnerable to criticism that they used incorporation to advance personal interests that worked against the public good.[56]

To distance themselves from business corporations, the trustees of schools, churches, asylums, and other socially minded private corporations often turned to new architectural conventions to signal the public ends of their capital.[57] Conversely, municipal corporations sometimes claimed to harness market powers for the private development and growth of the city to benefit all residents. Campaigns of urban improvement and development frequently aimed not just to improve public health and safety but also to promote the operation of private markets. Cities, in other words, had public and private dimensions, and conflicts arose when constituents called on different sides of the city's character to preside over a particular tract of land.[58]

Observers often turned to the built environment to assess whether, and how, corporate trustees directed projects of "improvement" to serve the public welfare. In the early nation, the power of corporate leaders increased with the right to eminent domain, public coffers of taxpayer dollars, ever-larger pools of capital consolidated by shareholder contributions, and limited liability for corporate debt or failure. Many U.S. citizens worried about potential corruption of corporate leaders even as they maintained optimism that incorporation could serve the public good.[59] Could leading citizens put aside their private interests, they wondered, to direct city affairs in the interest of all residents? Did profits for shareholders of a waterworks company or a congregational windfall from the sale of a landmark church always constitute a public good? Observers assessed the built environment to answer these kinds of questions and make broader arguments about whose interests urban "improvements" really served.

In the first two decades of the nineteenth century, Americans who argued over the fate of historic sites participated in this nationwide project of defining the nature of corporate properties and the duties of their trustees. Some citizens called for the preservation of public buildings to criticize their sellers or demolishers as betrayers of the public trust with a selfish desire to maximize profit in urbanizing real estate markets. As urban improvers guided environmental transformations to facilitate the growth of commerce, advocates of preservation argued that city dwellers should not shape all elements of the built environment according to the market value of the land that they occupied. They held up the demolition of historic public buildings to condemn men who usurped public property for personal gain in urban real estate markets. These men, critics argued, did not profit as a by-product of environmental improvements that augmented a town's convenience, health, and beauty; they masqueraded in the name of public interest to garner profit for a few at the expense of many.

In this way, advocates of preservation created a politics of demolition that they deployed against partisan rivals. William Duane did this when he argued for the preservation of the old Pennsylvania statehouse under city proprietorship. He and fellow critics homed in on the state legislators' professed desire to maximize profit as evidence of a private agenda rather than a public one. When the Pennsylvania Senate laid out plans for the statehouse yard in 1813, they directed that the land be divided "in such manner as in their opinion will most conduce to the value of the property." Value, to them, was financial. State commissioners laid out two perpendicular streets and subdivided the quadrants into "lots suitable for building, so as that in their opinion they will accommodate purchasers and produce the best price."[60] The commonwealth would not accept less than $150,000 for the sale to private owners. They would, however, sell the property to the City of Philadelphia for $70,000, transferring title in fee simple if the city agreed to maintain the south lawn as public walks.[61]

Duane argued against the state's real estate plans by charging that places defined in law and in custom as "public," to be maintained in perpetuity, should not be divided to fill public coffers. When jurists William Rawle and Peter S. DuPonceau agreed a few years later, they cited Emer de Vattel's *Law of Nations* to argue that "property once appropriated to public use is to remain sacredly applied to that use."[62] Duane made this argument in terms of market morality. The commonwealth's plan to sell subdivided lots for real estate development constituted a "project for *robbing the city of Philadelphia* of its only open and ornamented square, and of making *a bargain and sale* between the *government* and the *city*, between the rulers and a part of the people, as if the city was no part of the *commonwealth*; or that the city had no right to those properties which belonged to it before the revolution; in fact, as if the city was part of another nation!"[63] While Duane cast local rights of governance as a matter of national significance, he formulated a broad principle about the duties of city officers. It was the duty of municipal leaders, he suggested, to prevent public officials from shaping the urban environment to maximize profit in the real estate market at the expense of city residents.

Writers in other cities echoed Duane's argument in the 1810s. In his 1817 historical geography of Boston, Charles Shaw criticized the Massachusetts legislature's management of the Province House, a seventeenth-century colonial governors' residence whose urban courtyard and old-fashioned architecture made it a distinctive marker of the city's past. In 1811, state legislators had given the property to the Massachusetts General Hospital in its founding charter.[64] In 1817, Shaw relayed the news that the state legislature recently had allowed the hospital to use the property to generate rental income rather than to house their operations. A hundred-year lease allowed renters to build a large commercial row of brick buildings, filling an open and airy green space with shops that blocked views of the landmark and renovations to enlarge it. Shaw lamented this development as a transformation of public property to private uses, not only in the arrival of commerce on site but also in the displacement of the governor's domicile to the private realm. "We cannot forbear to regret that the building was not enlarged and improved and used for the purpose for which it was designed," he wrote. "At present our governors who are not citizens of the town, are obliged to provide lodging for themselves, and must receive visitors of distinction in the style of private gentlemen."[65] Shaw, like Duane, was not satisfied with using market-generated capital to erect a new public building if it came at the loss of historic public use. In 1825, physician and historian Caleb Snow echoed this criticism in his *History of Boston.*[66]

City dwellers also campaigned for preservation to critique the corporate trustees of buildings considered to be public but not owned by municipal or state governments. In 1808, for instance, Benjamin Austin condemned the congregational leaders of Boston's First Church by launching a print campaign for the preservation of their meeting place as a local historic landmark. For years, Austin had watched what he saw as the intrusion of commercial interests and politics into the congregation's fold.[67] In 1799, wealthy congregational leaders—the so-called Brahmin class of Boston capitalists—enticed minister William Emerson to their pulpit with a generous salary and material comforts. After spending a miserable decade in a small-town post, Emerson reveled in the vibrancy of life among Boston's elites and experimented with ways to turn the accumulation of their private wealth into support for the moral agenda of First Church.[68]

When First Church leaders determined to sell the "Old Brick" to fund the construction of a new church elsewhere, Benjamin Austin pointed to its impending demolition as evidence of the moral corruption of congregational leaders who prized wealth and social ascendance. He regarded the First Church as stewards of one of Boston's historic public buildings. The Old Brick dated from 1713, and it stood where John Winthrop's generation had gathered for worship and town meetings beginning in 1639, when it was the town's sole congregation. Colonial New Englanders joined town and church as local governance, and the meetinghouse served as both a house of worship and a town hall. Though New Englanders had begun to separate the spaces of meetinghouse and townhouse by the second quarter of the eighteenth century, collective memory still saw old meetinghouses as sites of town history.[69]

The Old Brick remained a prominent marker of Boston's past even as denominational pluralism and municipal architecture disintegrated its monopoly on religious and political activity. Austin argued that the removal of the centenarian building left "scarcely a vestige of antiquity in the town" and showed the symptoms of misguided improvements threatening to rob Bostonians of their tangible heritage.[70] By 1808, the First Church congregation had evolved into a poll parish—a religious association supported by the contributions of members regardless of geographic boundaries.[71] Though Congregationalism remained the state religion, First Church members governed themselves and their property as a corporation.[72] In prose and poetry, Austin charged that their sale of the church property proved that congregants made decisions about public affairs in the interest of personal gain. Bostonians suffered the loss of a communally prized building, he argued, at the hands of individuals who pursued "the trifling profit anticipated by the sale . . . to gratify the rapacity of a few men who trouble society both in Church and State."[73] To some observers, the construction of commercial buildings on the site of the Old Brick confirmed Austin's indictment of the profit motive.[74]

By painting demolishers of historic public buildings as money-hungry capitalists, Duane, Shaw, and Austin spun calls for preservation into an illustration of social dangers that they saw emerging with the new market economy. When public leaders acted as real estate brokers rather than stewards of communal property, critics argued, they threatened civil society in the new nation. Demolition, under these circumstances, constituted an "outrage of civilization." As Duane put it, state legislators' proposals to demolish the old statehouse showed that "in Pennsylvania, under the *Gothic mist of ignorance and vice*, by which it is now governed—every thing is to be *pulled down*—virtue, personal and public, are trampled under foot—ignorance, vice, and crime, rules this once venerated state, founded by Penn, and exalted by the genius and sagacity of Franklin."[75] Much like the Ohio Company leaders who held up their preservation efforts to distinguish themselves as more enlightened than Indigenous populations and speculators in western territorial lands, Duane placed urban real estate speculators on par with "uncivilized" populations. "The argument of this barbarian," he explained of the state legislators, "may be presented in a few words—for, it is foolish to reproach *Cossacs* and *Cherokees* and *Pottawattomies*, with the epithet of barbarous, who know nothing of social duties nor moral obligations; and to say that men are *civilized*, who exhibit a total unacquaintance with the same obligations of morality and the same duties, which men owe each other in a community."[76] In Duane's analogy, the legislators at Harrisburg behaved like the "white Indians" of the Ohio country: their environmental actions constituted social regression, an act more damnable than a failure to progress.

In Philadelphia, Boston, Marietta, and Newport, advocates of preservation argued that greed-fueled demolition of historic sites—not the absence of them in a young nation—threatened the peer status of U.S. residents to Old World counterparts. "If a proposition had been made in London, Paris, or Amsterdam," Benjamin Austin wrote, "to the society owning the *First Church* of either of those respectable cities, to sell (on a principle of speculation) their ancient edifice, it would have been spurned at with indignation." Residents of those cities never would have abided the destruction of a house of worship both so old and in such good condition, he argued. Even the British troops who occupied Boston during the Revolutionary War, he continued, had not demolished the Old Brick or put it to profane uses, as they did by making the Old South meetinghouse into an indoor riding school.[77] Instead, architectural violence at First Church occurred at the hands of congregation members who sold the building as ordinary real estate and its bell and organ as secondhand goods.[78]

These American calls for preservation did indeed resonate with ones issued by European antiquaries. In the 1790s and 1800s, some residents of Great Britain and France sought to secure medieval churches as public, not religious, sites of architectural heritage and national history.[79] Some argued specifically against the encroachment of architectural "improvements" to buildings and urban fabric. In 1806, for instance, British antiquary John Carter criticized city leaders of York for encouraging the demolition of the city's medieval walls. During a visit in 1790, he had found the walls in good condition and lauded them as venerable memorials to previous generations. Sixteen years later, however, members of York's city corporation deemed these antiquities "nuisances" and demolished them in a wave of what Carter deemed "false improvement."[80] When the same leaders tried to remove the historic city gates, Carter disparaged them as "barbarian innovators, *alias* 'improvers.'" Preservation of the gate alone could not win Carter's approval. He also condemned the archbishop whose attempt to stop the demolition arose from financial rather than intellectual motives: the clergyman's chancery suit to maintain the historic gate as a means to control traffic and preserve his customary income from tolls collected on fair days. Carter found this argument as offensive as the destruction of the gate and lamented the inattention to local history shown by residents focused on urban improvement and finance.[81]

In the early United States, however, advocates of preservation spun their calls for permanence into a social commentary on what they saw as the distinct features of the nation's political structure and economy. As legal rulings steadily tied the value of land to its economic productivity, historic structures became imbricated in the speculative land economy.[82] Urban developers assessed the value of these sites by imagining the profit that future improvements might bring at that location. Men such as Duane and Austin saw a different vision of the future: one in which citizens who engaged in speculation—buying land and building on

credit to maximize personal financial gain—destroyed the intergenerational social ties fostered by historic buildings. Trustees who sold public properties to speculators were just as guilty as the real estate entrepreneurs themselves.

William Duane and Benjamin Austin turned their views into partisan barbs.
Both men were avowed Democratic-Republicans openly at odds with rival factions and Federalist opponents. Though Austin descended from an elite mercan-
tile family, he did not attend college and styled himself as an ally of the working
classes and an enemy of aristocracy.[83] He identified himself as a vehement Jeffersonian in a town full of Federalists and expressed his views from seats in the
Boston town council and Massachusetts state senate as well as from the pages of
the *Independent Chronicle*, which he coedited.[84] Austin published his views on
the Old Brick to weigh in on local debates over the morally correct relationship
between individual rights and the health of public welfare.[85] Bostonians read Austin's charges against speculative land dealings when the credit scheme of one of
Boston's biggest builders crumbled around them. Leveraged in the politics of the
ongoing U.S. embargo, which had slowed New England port traffic to a crawl,
Austin's depiction of the sale and demolition of the Old Brick indicted local
Federalists—not the Jeffersonian Republicans in national office—as culprits of
economic immorality.[86]

William Duane was an even more notorious Democratic-Republican fire-
brand. In 1816, his invective stoked a heated power struggle between Republicans in Philadelphia and Harrisburg. When Duane cast the state legislators as
enemies of the revolutionary principles set out in 1776, he invoked the impending demolition of the statehouse to inform long-standing efforts to work out state-
level Republican principles in a capitalist economy.[87] Their sale of the statehouse
and yard, he wrote, marked them as *"economic brawlers,"* working against common interests for the benefit of a few. It exemplified how "every thing in Pennsylvania (with its present rulers and their adherents) is for *barter and sale*—it is
proposed to deprive the ancient capital of Pennsylvania of its only improved and
ornamented square, and to *sell the ground* for *building lots!!*"[88] To Duane, plans
for the old statehouse confirmed the economic cupidity and self-interest of his
political enemies, proving that these "*fabricators* of *forty banks*," who levied taxes
inequitably on urban dwellers, were driven by corrupt financial principles.[89] Indeed, Duane published the letter of a state senator who dismissed public opposition to the sale with the reasoning that a monument "on the spot where American
Independence was declared in 1776" was "all nonsense, a solid dollar will do a
man more good than ten thousand such vagaries."[90] If politicians would sell the
nationally—even internationally—revered statehouse and public square to private developers, Duane reasoned, then surely they attuned their political influence to financial gain rather than the principles of the common good.

Nothing about the politics of demolition inherently aligned with partisan Republican ideology. When Austin and Duane condemned urban speculation, they contradicted the notion that individual enterprise and profit would usher in a public spirit among wealthy citizens and a golden age for cities.[91] In this way, they trafficked in the same ideas about the moral dimensions of land development as did Marietta Federalists from the 1780s throughout the 1810s. These partisans shared an engagement with urban improvements defined not by a particular size of local population but by municipal incorporation, which enabled them to leverage historic public architecture in partisan debates over governance and political economy. These public structures, they believed, were the places where U.S. citizens would work out the balance of powers between themselves and stewards of their collective interest.

Restoration as Public Good and Local Power

As some civic leaders engaged in the politics of demolition in print, many also turned to the material details of preservation to make an argument for the public good of permanence. In light of an increasing number of legal rulings that favored new land use, town dwellers from Newport to Charleston created new material iterations of the past to define preservation not simply as the maintenance of customary land use and ancient property rights but as a dynamic form of environmental management necessary for civil society. Town leaders drew new ideas about cemetery, church, and municipal architecture into the realm of local history to build "better" versions of the past that could not be mistaken for evidence of economic stagnation or cultural backwardness. In this way, they sought to create culturally defined forms of physical impassability that bolstered their power to shape the municipal landscape.[92] In turn, they opened the way for the demolition of historic landscape features that did not accord with modern standards of public health and urban order.

In the 1810s, Marietta councillors staked their claim for control of Mound Square with architectural design as much as written appeals. They conceived of a cemetery plan for the site that reversed the common practices of removing grave markers to resell old plots, burying corpses layers deep, and letting livestock graze on graves.[93] The Marietta men likely drew inspiration from the new burying ground of New Haven, Connecticut, surveyed by the brother of Ohio Company member Return Jonathan Meigs and widely publicized as a model for "improved" urban cemeteries. Like the new New Haven burying ground, the proposed cemetery grid in Marietta featured numbered burial lots assigned to families rather than individuals, streets that directed access through cultivated grounds, a sur-rounding fence, and corporate proprietorship.[94]

Yet municipal leaders in Marietta made the unusual decision to move their new cemetery closer to town when most municipalities aimed to remove bury-ing grounds from urban cores. Their placement of the cemetery around the con-ical mound used old as well as new mortuary architecture to secure a long-term lease and to diminish the chances that it would be revoked (Figure 9). This was not an idle fear. In 1816, for instance, Philadelphia's city councils refused to re-new a ninety-nine-year lease with a church congregation whose building stood on a public square.[95] Mariettans deployed new features of cemetery architecture as part of the site's preservation mandate to decrease the chances that the city's lease—and the bodies interred on site—would meet the same fate. As one local poet put it:

Then hallow the spot which incloses,
The ashes of warriors renown'd;
Tread light where the Hero reposes:
Disturb not the *Monument Mound*.[96]

Marietta councillors did not brand the mound an ancient burial site out of re-spect for Indigenous peoples; the same men who plotted the cemetery had built over graves when planning the city several years earlier. Rather, councillors shaped the mound's new identity as a historic burial monument to extend sanctity to the grounds around it before Euro-American graves consecrated the earth.[97]

Even when vernacular burial practice thwarted municipal planning, the ide-als that guided the burial ground's design and regulations entrenched a notion that the site was sacred: set apart from productive land development and kept permanently in place. As was common across the United States, cemetery devel-opment in Marietta did not proceed according to plan. Town residents buried their loved ones as they pleased, often refusing to apply to the town sexton for a lot assignment or pay him for his services.[98] It took years for the council to erect a fence. Private citizens, not municipal coffers, provided funds to ornament the square and "to protect the ancient works."[99] Yet by 1820, townspeople and trav-elers remarked on the new cemetery as a fitting tribute to the site's imagined an-cient residents. Caleb Atwater, for instance, characterized the Ohio Valley mounds as earthen tombs and temples that, like Greek and Roman examples, were made "to endure while the world itself shall continue, unless destroyed by the sacrilegious hand of man."[100] Mariettans deserved praise, he argued, for keep-ing the great mound "entire, standing in the burying ground of the present town."[101] Mariettans reinforced conceptions of Mound Square as sacred space by

Figure 9. In 1811, Marietta town councillors sketched a formal cemetery plan that made a large conical mound the centerpiece of a new municipal burial ground. Generations of Euro-American residents of Marietta have buried their dead in "Mound Cemetery" since then. Stone steps—placed before 1850—deface the Indigenous architecture but also testify to Euro-American attempts to shape the site as a space of rural-urban leisure as well as mourning. Photograph by author, 2015.

maintaining a separation of the burying ground from town business, noise, and traffic. The town council continued to rent an adjacent pasture to local citizens. But when the it proposed building a new courthouse on the west side of Mound Square in 1822, residents voted 116 to 75 to maintain the burying-ground tract in its established form, even though the original Ohio Company regulations allowed for the construction of public buildings near the earthworks.[102]

Unlike the town vote in Marietta, local and state courts increasingly adjudicated property disputes in favor of new development. The New York City street plan for the northern parts of Manhattan, begun in 1807 and filed in 1811, formed one of the most comprehensive projects of the era to override the claims of individual property owners with a development plan professedly designed to improve the collective welfare of city residents.[103] When U.S. citizens challenged the takings of public-use sites by eminent domain or the rights of land developers, jurists most frequently supported municipal regulation over customary use and land development over "ancient rights" of property.[104] In the 1820s, a cluster of suits in New York made these proclivities clear in rulings about the management of historic church graveyards. The city's Common Council cited public health concerns when it banned new burials in the city's densest neighborhoods. The council's arguments carried undertones of the belief that sites formed in the city's early years prohibited the growth and development of New York City.[105] Litigants challenged this view by arguing that the city's regulations infringed not only on private property rights given to churches by corporate charters but also on collective interest in keeping material markers of previous generations in place.[106] Jurists ruled in favor of the city. As Judge John T. Irving put it in 1824, though these burying grounds were a "hallowed species of property, . . . change was unavoidable and ought not to be hampered by antiquities and archaic practices."[107] Property owners who maintained long-standing uses of land in the most crowded part of Manhattan, in other words, made land stagnant when it could be put to better use.

Some men developed architectural designs for preservation that disputed the notion that environmental permanence equated to stagnation.[108] They built new forms of historic architecture to "restore" old structures and paint preservation as an active form of property management that served public as well as private interests. In turn, they translated antiquarian pursuits into statements of their own economic principles. In Newport, Stephen Gould treated the local synagogue as a vehicle of city improvement and evidence of his abilities as a public trustee. Gould had served Abraham Touro as a synagogue caretaker for many years before the benefactor's death.[109] When the Rhode Island General Assembly named the Newport town council as primary steward of the synagogue, Gould became the caretaker of a property claimed by two entities: the municipal government, legally mandated to manage its care, and the Newport synagogue's trustees, residents of New York City affiliated with a different congregation.[110] Throughout the 1820s, Gould shepherded communications not only between the city council and the New York stewards but also between both parties and the Rhode Island legislature.

Gould saw his mediation of the Touro trust as part of his long-standing antiquarian efforts to preserve tangible evidence of the region's past. At the same moment when he helped to found the Rhode Island Historical Society and became its first cabinet keeper, he adopted the role of synagogue steward, in his words, "not from selfish motives, other than the honor of our Town & state."[111] For years, he struggled to coordinate the interests of trustees in New York City, Newport, and Providence into a plan for repairing the rapidly deteriorating building. At first, Gould pushed the Newport town council to authorize work and the state legislature to disburse funds at the request of Moses Lopez, a mouthpiece of the steward congregation, Shearith Israel, and Rebecca Touro, the sister of Abraham Touro who also attended that congregation.[112] It took nearly two years for the town council to act. Council members who inspected the synagogue in the summer of

1825 found the structural masonry and interior plaster in bad condition. When they reported the immediate need for repairs to the New York congregation, they asked for the keys to the synagogue as well as directions for "the particular mode, or style in which they wished the said repairs to be made."[113] After months of no response, Newport councillors appealed to the state legislature for permission to fulfill their legal duty to preserve the failing building.[114] When the town council moved forward with building repairs on its own in the fall of 1826, Moses Lopez cautioned Gould against a backlash: "I am doubtful whether the Trustees of it will tamely submit to the forced agency of the Council to repair their own property without their consent," he wrote.[115] From Lopez's vantage, the town councillors overreached the limits of their public power into the affairs of private property.

Gould attempted to quell the power struggle between municipal administrators and distant trustees with a plan for restoration of the synagogue's historic features. After earning blanket approval for architectural decisions from Lopez, Gould executed a massive renovation of the synagogue between 1827 and 1829. Charged "to refit what may appear rotten & defective in the building," Gould introduced higher-quality craftsmanship in structure, finish, and ornament as historic features themselves. While keeping structural elements in place, Gould and his associates constructed interior details to fit their image of elite Anglo-colonial ideals. In the same way that he re-recorded a historic deed absent from the written record, Gould used restoration to create a vision of the past according to modern sensibility of what it should be.[116]

The renovations added a layer of finish that connoted a refined aesthetic and a communal prosperity in the cost of materials and maintenance labor. Outside, Gould ordered the red brick walls to be painted in brown and beige tones and finished the stone cap of the burying-ground walls with a coat of paint. Inside, Gould redesigned the ark according to architectural pattern books popular in the mid-eighteenth century. Rather than ordering a replica of the simple square wainscoted ark, Gould installed holy architecture embellished with carved draperies and a massive pedimented panel framed with curvilinear flourishes.[117] He also ordered a new painting of the Ten Commandments from fellow antiquarian Benjamin B. Howland, who had become the Newport town clerk in 1825.[118] Their "restoration" operated in the spirit of the building's architect, who had designed Newport's Redwood Library and Boston's King's Chapel from pattern books.[119] But it created for their town a more elaborate version of mid-eighteenth-century architecture than had stood on site.

Gould and Howland worked together to shape a project of so-called preservation that brought money out of state coffers and into the pockets of local civil servants, craftsmen, and laborers. They and other members of the Newport council leveraged the historic nature of the synagogue's architecture to justify the high costs of construction, which totaled nearly $3,500.[120] As one legislator summed up for the General Assembly, the donor and current synagogue trustees in New York wished that the building "be repaired in the most thorough and permanent manner possible." Fulfilling these wishes made it "necessary" not only to repair the poor condition of the building but also to work in the "style of the building required."[121] Moreover, it meant hiring experienced craftsmen whose high-quality work outweighed their reputations as slow workers.[122] In this case, preservation encouraged its practitioners to look to the future in more ways than one. When construction costs exceeded the interest accrued by 1828, town councillors secured permission from the General Assembly to finance a loan by borrowing against future interest of the trust fund's capital investment.[123]

Gould and Howland orchestrated a plan for preservation that created an "improved" vision of the past as a means of urban improvement. In a town frequently criticized for its shabby buildings and old-fashioned appearance in an inert real estate market, building new versions of historic features signaled well-being for the entire town.[124] In turn, it conveyed the prosperity and civility of synagogue stewards. Gould and Howland had personal reasons to make the synagogue a showpiece of the public benefit of permanence. Howland had become a clerk in the 1820s—not only for the town but also for the Marine Insurance Company, the Newport Savings Bank, and various historical societies—after financial failures in the previous decade.[125] His business in trade had landed him in debtors' prison, and efforts to recover solvency as an auctioneer had led to bankruptcy in 1815.[126] Gould sought to establish a reputation for responsible estate management after losing capital entrusted to him. A few years earlier, he had invested various estate funds in local financial institutions because money on hand was unprofitable to him. When the local bank failed in 1824 and the insurance company refused to pay dividends, Gould defended himself by insisting that his financial decisions were reasonable, not speculative, ones.[127] Gould did not have control of the Touro fund investments: he had heeded the state's treasurer and asked the estate's executor to weigh in on "what kind of Stock will be the most productive & safe" for the bequest's investment.[128] Yet his reputation as a capable trustee hung in the balance as litigation emerged to define what determined responsible management of trust funds in a boom and bust economy.[129] For men who had suffered financial losses, the preservation of a historic property under their care could convey financial stability and moral solvency that new structures could not.

Similar renovations played out around the United States in the 1820s and 1830s as civic leaders sought to create material arguments for the value of permanence in urbanizing locales. Their conversations extended the language of sacred architecture from houses of worship and burial grounds to the realm of public architecture. Here, advocates of preservation debated the best way to shape buildings that established permanence of architecture and property rights in historic but adaptive terms. In Philadelphia, city councillors became embroiled in an internal debate about how to preserve the historic character of the old statehouse. The city had purchased the building and its adjacent square from the Commonwealth of Pennsylvania for $70,000 in the summer of 1818.[130] A decade later, city councillors commissioned architect William Strickland to design a new tower that would form "in fact a restoration of the spire originally erected with the building, and standing there on 4th July, 1776."[131] Strickland's designs set the tower atop the building's square turret and endowed it with a bell and a new clock. Its crowning steeple, taller than the one that had graced the building in the eighteenth century, would give the old statehouse a commanding profile among the city's church spires.

When Philadelphia council members reviewed Strickland's plans, they disagreed whether its modern features fulfilled the promise of restoring the aspect of its Revolutionary predecessor. Benjamin Tilghman lauded the project as a reverent reinstallation of an old feature that "unhallowed hands" had desecrated by demolition. "If there were a spot on earth on which space might be identified with holiness," he enjoined, "it would be the spot on which the old state house stands. It is a sacred spot,—a sacred building." The councillor hoped it was the first step in a campaign for total restoration "to the state in which it stood in 1775." Francis Gurney Smith diplomatically corrected Tilghman. Only the cupola and spire "were exact copies of the original," and Strickland's plan called for a taller brick turret instead of a squat wooden one, a necessary accommodation for a bell and clock. The effect improved the building's public usefulness and ornament while making "as few changes as possible in the ancient appearance of the building." Critics chimed in to deny both appraisals. One judged that "the effect of the original is entirely destroyed," while another argued that the "deformity" of the new design would not conjure veneration for the statehouse of 1776 but would "efface the remembrance of it altogether."[132]

Both houses of Philadelphia's city council ultimately approved Strickland's design for the tower. So, too, did they approve John Haviland's designs for "restorative" renovations to the interior in 1831.[133] Neither Haviland nor Strickland unwittingly departed from the structure's colonial appearance. Philadelphia councillors ultimately approved their renovations to make the building permanent, not simply historic, in the modern city. Yet when civic leaders built new architectural features designed to constitute past conditions as well as material improvements, they opened themselves up to disagreements not only about what constituted the public good but also about what constituted the preservation of historic architecture itself.

Restoration as Improvement

Debates about the character of historic restorations added a new layer to contests about corporate property rights and municipal authority into the 1830s. In Charleston, plans to rebuild St. Philip's Episcopal Church prompted congregants, townspeople, and municipal and state officials to question what material qualities of a building preserved its historic character. As with the Newport synagogue and the Old Brick meetinghouse in Boston, Charlestonians characterized St. Philip's Church as a marker of local, colonial, state, and national history.[134] Completed in 1723, it stood as the oldest church in Charleston and one of the most impressively built eighteenth-century churches on the eastern American seaboard.[135] Even after South Carolina disestablished the Church of England as its state religion, the parish boundaries of St. Philip's remained a district of municipal governance in Charleston.[136] When the church building burned down in 1835, congregants issued a "lament, not for a private, but a public loss."[137] The editor of the *Charleston Mercury* agreed, writing that he had "never witnessed . . . such deep and general regret as prevails among our citizens" upon the destruction of the church. It "was dear to the affections and pride of every native of the city—and its antique walls and arches . . . carried the mind far back into our revolutionary and colonial history," he continued. "Every one felt in its fall, that a link was harshly sundered in the chain of cherished associations."[138] A writer for the rival *Charleston Courier* echoed these sentiments, writing that the church had displayed "all the solemnity and noble proportions of antique architecture—constituting a hallowed link between the *past* and present."[139]

Within days of the conflagration, the church's vestry and congregation decided to rebuild the new church "upon the same plan and on the same foundation as the old."[140] They cited a similar restoration at the medieval cathedral in York, England, as a model for fundraising as well as architectural reconstruction. After a fire in 1829, members of the York congregation had raised £50,000 in public donations because residents of England reportedly saw the fifteenth-century architecture as a marker of national import. "With the exception that the choir looks cleaner and fresher than formerly," noted one writer, "a person unacquainted with its destruction would be unable to perceive any change." The reconstruction, in his mind, succeeded in its aim "to preserve every detail of the building."[141] When Charlestonians nodded to the construction project at York Minster, they exuded a confidence that the restoration of the historic features of St. Philip's would serve the public good.

But debates arose over which features of St. Philip's must be restored to maintain a meaningful connection to the past. One set of contentions centered on the right of the congregation to rebuild on its former foundation. Some Charlestonians needled the municipal government to improve the city plan by insisting that St. Philip's rebuild on a different foundation. The portico of the incinerated building had jutted far into the street, disrupting a straight course of traffic by forcing travelers to arc around its front steps. Two months after the fire, some citizens began to lobby the city council to regulate rebuilding efforts to straighten the street. As "A Citizen" put it, claiming to speak "for the concurrent voice of the whole community (some of the Church members excepted)," city councillors should mandate this plan as a matter of "public welfare." He concluded, "Let the Church be remunerated for the loss of ground, and they could not have any reason to object to the improvement."[142] The congregants, however, found plenty of reasons to resist. They leveled rejoinders about property rights, sarcastic commentary about street safety, and defenses of their duties as congregational stewards.

In 1835, the Charleston city council ordered the church to move their new building forty-eight feet back from the street to create a straight right-of-way. Congregants responded by making the council answer to the state-appointed Commission for Opening and Widening Streets, Lanes, and Alleys. The colonial general assembly had founded the commission in 1764 to manage the urban infrastructure of Charleston in the absence of a municipal corporation. The commission endured after Charleston incorporated in 1783, with the state assembly affirming its authority over the municipal government in 1817.[143] When St. Philip's vestry members submitted their pleas against the city council's ruling to the state legislature, they cast the historic features of their church as material arguments for why they should not have to submit to a municipal directive about the management of church property.[144] In turn, state commissioners looked to the site itself for answers. After a site visit, they ruled that the congregation should move their structure only twenty-two feet from its original position (Plate 3). Their decision framed the reconstruction of the historic church as a contribution to the public good: improvements instituted by the city council's ruling "either in the way of use or of ornament" did not outweigh the costs it would impose. By citing the beauty of the church's portico and the maintenance of graves "consecrated by feelings the dearest to the human heart," state commissioners confirmed that the architectural elements that St. Philip's sought to maintain were worth more than the amount that the city would have paid for the land taken for a wider street.[145]

The commission's decision reflected the ongoing ways that U.S. citizens weighed the meaning of historic features to develop a working relationship among municipal corporations, so-called private corporations, and the states that chartered them.[146] At the end of their ruling, the state commissioners nodded to these larger questions of property rights:

> A question has been made whether the Public can legally or constitutionally, take away for a public purpose, Lands that have been consecrated, and set apart for pious uses; and that too, when they may have been derived either from Legislative Grants and appropriations, or the donation of Individuals—on this point your Committee have no doubt. All the Lands in the State are held under its Laws, and, with the necessary implication that private rights must always be subordinate to the public advantage, under the obligation, which is paramount to all Law, that full compensation be made for these rights. No individual can by dedicating a donation to any special object—charitable or religious— exempt it from the operation of this principle—a principle, however, to be ever exercised with the utmost circumspection, with the most sacred regard to justice, and with the deepest determination that the interests or rights of the few shall never without ample compensation be taken for the benefit of the many.[147]

When state officials affirmed the rights of the state to take away private property, including that of religious or charitable corporations empowered by legislative acts, for public welfare, they implied that they made their ruling about the church footprint in the interest of all Charlestonians. Keeping burial grounds intact and enabling a congregation to rebuild a church that still disrupted the urban grid could support the public good more than a perfectly straight street. Congregation members adopted this same language when they publicized their willingness to retract the footprint twenty-two feet. As one member put it, the congregation would "forego their own feelings and opinions, when conflicting with those of their fellow-citizens in general," and restore their historic church, as it was, on a revised site that benefited the local populace.[148]

Church members initially determined that the reconstruction would "be of the dimensions and order of architecture, and after the plan of the second, with the addition of a chancel."[149] This single change to the church's design, however, prompted some congregants to press for more alterations. They suggested that a raised floor, new pew styles, and lighter interior columns would improve the appearance and function of the old design.[150] Their proposals caused some Charlestonians to question what distinctive features needed to be rebuilt "for the sake of seeing again the interior of St. Philip's, as it was." In the words of one congregant, the church need not be an exact replica of the previous one, but it should "aid in awakening through the sense of sight, the thoughts and feeling appropriate to the sanctuary, or to make me feel in some degree at least, that I was again in the Church of my fathers."[151] Others argued for a simpler, cost-efficient interior that reflected modern sensibilities. Congregants fooled themselves into believing that they were erecting a replica, one argued, so they might as well build an entirely new design that embraced contemporary values.

The architect for the church's reconstruction sketched three options for interior details of the church: one that mimicked the former building, another that offered a modern classical design, and a third that replicated the English church St. Martin's in the Fields—supposedly the intended model of St. Philip's congregational leaders in the early eighteenth century.[152] Congregants ultimately chose the design that purported to make visible the intent rather than the product of the church's colonial builders. Labeled as preservation, this plan for rebuilding paradoxically claimed to make permanent a more authentic version of the past than the one that had burned down in 1835. It also constructed a historic St. Philip's design that conveniently shrunk the lamented interior columns of its predecessor.

The absent columns represent a more general principle of demolition engendered by debates over the preservation of historic public architecture. When preservation became a tool for urban and architectural improvement, it also became a justification for the demolition of tangible markers of the past meaningful to many Americans. Marietta leaders built over graves of Indigenous Americans. Planted beds and geometric walks intended to substantiate the colonial public squares laid out by Philadelphia founders erased the graves of indigent citizens and African Americans as well as evidence of the long-standing market activities on the sites.[153] New England residents who sought to preserve town commons as historic sites embarked on similar acts of demolition.[154] The insistence that preservation and improvement could operate in lockstep cleared the way for the removal of landscape features that conflicted with modern urban order even as it insisted that profit in the real estate market should not be the sole operating principle of its creation.

It would be easy to conclude that plans for the preservation of historic public structures succeeded when they created more convenient and useful versions of the architectural past. But this overlooks the coherent ethic that proponents of architectural preservation developed between 1785 and 1835. They characterized corporately held structures as tangible links to the previous generations who had built and used them and touted preservation as a means of establishing principles of property management that would promote the public good in a commercial economy. Good citizens, they argued, kept historic structures in place for public use rather than treating them as commodities. In the second quarter of the nineteenth century, many commercial proprietors adopted this principle and characterized themselves as purveyors of preservation to define themselves as public-minded businesspeople. When they offered consumers access to architectural evidence of the past, they framed their commercial ventures as a public service.

PART II

Commercial Sites

CHAPTER 3

The Business of Preservation: Antiquarian Views and Commercial Enterprise

In 1808, Benjamin Austin sought political gain by protesting the demolition of Boston's First Church. Five years later, J. T. Buckingham pursued financial profit from the building's preservation. The Boston publisher opened the July issue of his *Polyanthos* with the frontispiece "View of the Old Brick Meeting House in Boston 1808" (Figure 10). On the centennial of the building's construction, Buckingham hired James Kidder to engrave what he characterized as the last remaining view of the landmark building. John Rubens Smith had drawn the building just before its demolition, and the print conveyed to readers "an accurate representation" of the Old Brick's appearance at the end of its existence. It captured the meetinghouse's old-fashioned form, including its porch entrance on the long side of its rectilinear footprint and its cupola. William Emerson's recent history of First Church could give readers a much fuller account of the congregation, Buckingham wrote, but his magazine offered up a documentary view that preserved the building for future generations.[1]

Kidder's engraving of the Old Brick included a glimpse of the business landscape that replaced the religious one. Shops that framed the view of the meetinghouse on Cornhill Street in 1808 foretold the transformation of the site into Boston's Washington Street shopping district. The commercial block that supplanted the old meetinghouse typified new commercial architecture and urban transformation in the early nineteenth century. Land developers and shopkeepers across the North Atlantic world redesigned urban cores to transport, display, and sell a growing number and variety of goods produced by industrial growth and specialization. They did the same for the sale of niche services and refined leisure, including new forms of dining and lodging. Architectural projects to rebuild open-air markets, renovate shops and taverns, and construct shopping

Figure 10. In 1813, publisher J. T. Buckingham hired James Kidder to engrave a view of the "Old Brick" meetinghouse in Boston on the centennial of its construction. Kidder replicated a painting done by John Rubens Smith just before the building's demolition five years earlier. Both images typify attempts to profit from the creation of views of historic buildings made before their demolition. John Rubens Smith, del., James Kidder, engraver, "View of the Old Brick Meeting House in Boston, 1808," *Polyanthos*, July 1813, 169. Courtesy American Antiquarian Society.

arcades and hotels shaped new material conditions of commerce and social definitions of consumerism.[2]

In this environmental transformation, some businessmen framed the old-fashioned architectural features of their places of business as appealing points of historic interest rather than undesirable remnants of outmoded commercial spaces. Business proprietors worked in concert with imagemakers to profit from this attention to markers of the past. They depicted old buildings in ways that called attention to or even exaggerated the rapidity and inevitability of urban change to inflate their preservation of old architectural features as a rare and laudable action. These entrepreneurs married the antiquarian and economic principles of scarcity to entice customers with a social appeal to market exclusivity determined not by lavishness of commercial setting or high price of goods but by appreciation of views of historic buildings on the ground and on the page.

Businessmen who linked their sales appeals with preservation tied commercial enterprise and consumer discernment to the appreciation of historic features, not simply modern refinement. As U.S. residents worked out new material mark-

ers of respectability in a growing market economy, these entrepreneurs leveraged their places in the commercial landscape to define antiquarian viewing as
a way to pursue market profit by contributing to the public good. As social reformers and religious enthusiasts defined various ethics of moral consumption,
antiquarian businessmen defined a mode of moral commerce that purported to
endow its producers, vendors, and consumers with civic virtue.[3] Yet as imagemakers expanded the visual rhetoric of their documentary views to appeal to a
broader range of customers in the 1830s, they ultimately undercut the respectability of the people working in the sites that they depicted.

Preservation by Print

U.S. residents engaged antiquarian views in broader efforts to define citizenship
through consumption in the first half of the nineteenth century. Many imagemakers pursued architectural preservation as a supposedly enlightened business
strategy when they made and sold images intended to secure permanent like-
nesses of their subjects for future generations. When John Rubens Smith depicted Boston's Old Brick meetinghouse on the eve of its demolition, he worked
in a pictorial genre of antiquarian view making formulated during the Renaissance and carried out on both sides of the Atlantic Ocean.[4] By using what British antiquary John Carter called the "imitative hand," limners claimed to preserve
historic structures by fixing careful delineations of how they looked in the modern world. Their representational conventions conveyed attention to the Enlightenment principles of careful study rather than the aesthetics of picturesque
landscape painting. Carter, for instance, spent decades making a "minute series
of plans, elevations, sections, and detail of decorations" of ancient and medieval
buildings to record their appearance for posterity. He touted these pictorial labors
in 1806 by exclaiming, "What praise will not Futurity bestow on his name, as he
will leave behind him on paper representations of those works, which others of
contra-dispositions may have in a few years, transformed, or utterly destroyed!"
For those who could not secure buildings on the ground, view making offered
future generations evidence of the past embedded in the built environment.[5]

In the early United States, view makers deployed the conventions of this genre
to produce preservational views in a wide variety of media. A close look at the
life of one documentary view of the Dutch Protestant Church in Albany, New
York, shows how artisans aimed to profit from offering consumers a pictorial
mode of preservation in an era of urban improvement. In 1806, the same year
that John Carter praised views done by the "imitative hand," Philip Hooker
produced a view of the recently vacated church. Albany residents had erected the

distinctive square, stone edifice in 1715, building it around the smaller church erected by Dutch colonizers in the previous century. In 1797, the congregation hired Elisha Putnam and Philip Hooker to build a new house of worship in North Pearl Street.[6] The commission reflected the money that the congregation had earned from selling land parcels around the growing city, which had just been named the state capital.[7] After the congregation removed to the new church building, they also sold the site of their old church to the city of Albany and parceled out its movable features. Hooker would go on to make a name for himself as a celebrated architect of public buildings in the state capital.[8] However, he also preserved one of its most notable colonial buildings when he drew a view of the Dutch Protestant church building just before its demolition.[9]

Hooker may have sketched the building as part of his own antiquarian pursuits. As an architect, he likely took great interest in the building's distinctive construction and antiquated materials and style. He may have wished to contribute to associational efforts to document the history of the city in visual as well as textual records. Members of Albany's Society for the Promotion of Useful Arts, which included Hooker, and of the recently formed New-York Historical Society in Manhattan collected just these sorts of views. Or perhaps the members of the congregation asked the architect to ply his drafting hand to render the old church as well as the new one. This is what members of St. John's Lutheran Church in Charleston, South Carolina, did a decade later. While congregants of the historically German congregation built a new church to stake out their place in Charleston's Anglophile mainstream, they used views of their old church to carve out a place for the congregation in the city's history. Two exterior views preserved the gambrel roof, tower cap, wooden clapboards, lean-to additions, asymmetry, and other architectural features that the congregation replaced with the monumental, classicized architecture of their new house of worship.[10] As builders created a more homogenous, classicized public architecture in the United States, views of the old Dutch church and St. John's preserved ethnic vernaculars in archivable form that made way for modern architecture.

Philip Hooker's view also offered a business opportunity to engraver Henry W. Snyder as well. In 1806, Snyder translated Hooker's picture to the copperplate (Figure 11). He rendered the building's materials, surfaces, and architectural features in exceptionally fine detail to convey his documentary attention to its distinctive and recognizable characteristics.[11] This included delineating its façade from a thirty-degree angle to capture the building's pyramidal roof and vestibular entryway. Snyder's representation of surface details drew viewers' eyes to the decorative ironwork, asymmetrical façade, crowning bell tower, and rooftop finials. His abstraction of the building from its environment kept viewers' attention there; by setting the structure in a starkly blank field, he rendered the building

A VIEW OF THE LATE PROTESTANT DUTCH CHURCH in the CITY of ALBANY.

This Venerable Edifice was situated at the junction of State Market & Court streets. It was erected A.D 1715 & demolished A.D 1806. It included within its walls the site of a Church the corner stone whereof was laid by Rutger Jacobsen A.D 1656.

Figure 11. In 1806, Henry Snyder engraved two views of a Dutch American church in Albany, New York, at the time of its demolition. Snyder made this first print of the structure an object lesson or an artifactual depiction of the building as a discrete structure absent its surroundings. Philip Hooker, del., Henry Snyder, engraver, "A View of the Late Protestant Dutch Church in the City of Albany," 1806. Photo credit: Yale University Art Gallery.

an object lesson. Snyder also composed a caption to place the building in geographic and chronological context. "This venerable edifice," it stated, "was situated at the junction of State, Market, & Court-streets. It was erected AD. 1715, & demolished AD. 1806. It included w[ithin] its walls the site of a Church the corner stone whereof was laid by Rutger Jacobsen, AD. 1656."[12] This caption conveyed that Snyder worked from an original image taken on the spot, and its credit to both Hooker and Snyder simultaneously drew on their reputations as skilled craftsmen and advertised their fuller body of work to viewers.[13]

After handing the copperplate over to a printer, who likely struck off a few hundred prints in Albany, Snyder returned to the plate to engrave a fuller scene and a second appeal to consumers (Plate 4). This new image also constituted a preservational view of the demolished church building. However, it transformed it from an object lesson of Albany's past into an environmental view of the city's historical development. In this elaborated view, Snyder leveled the ground of the first image to depict partial façades of two State Street buildings peeking out from the left side.[14] On the right, he showed the western side of Market Street running down to the headhouse in the center of the street. In a stretch of perspective, Snyder depicted the distinctive double towers of the congregation's new church in the distance. He devoted exacting attention to the caption text, rubbing out "demolished" and replacing it with "pulled down." The change of tone from material destruction to disassembly matched the revised tenor of the image. This view appealed to observers with a narrative of progressive change: the congregation had moved from the old church and to the new one as part of a broader wave of urban improvement depicted in the frame. Demolition of the depicted building opened room for traffic at a major intersection in the commercial core of the growing city. The print invited viewers to muse on the environmental and social changes that had removed the subject of the print while studying the architectural features that made it interesting and instructive evidence of Albany's past.

Snyder's production of two views points to the way that imagemakers regarded demolition as a business opportunity. The destruction of buildings whose architectural particularities or historic associations attracted attention, they anticipated, would create a market for views of them. Imagemakers began to produce a growing number of views of historic buildings on speculation—to hawk to customers in the general public—rather than by commission or subscription before publication. Snyder took his plate to New York City, where bookseller and publisher John Low added his name below the caption and then pulled a run of prints for sale to store patrons. These fine prints, some of them hand colored, sold for a higher price than the previous object-lesson engravings that Snyder had printed in Albany. They also brought attention to the high quality of images that Low published and offered for sale. From the walls of public spaces and domestic settings and the leaves of bound portfolios, this second view of the demolished Albany church brought attention both to the Dutch heritage and early national growth of the state capital and to the skills of the three men who advertised their roles in making the image. In Albany in 1815, *American Magazine* editor Horatio Gates Spofford commissioned a copy of the same view from engraver John Scoles.[15] He used the view of the demolished building as a frontispiece, just like J. T. Buckingham did with a view of the Old Brick Meeting House in 1813. Both men hoped to entice consumers with a desire for preservational prints, either as volume illustrations or as prints to be cut away for individual display or for extra-illustration.

Other artisans looked to these prints to profit from antiquarian view making as well. When they translated the abstracted view of the Albany church onto domestic goods, they invested the social uses of the objects with the virtues of preservation.[16] The maker of a lavish looking glass carefully reverse-painted a copy of Snyder's view on glass panels set into a pillar frame for the mirror plates. This delicate rendering of the building, made for members of the Gansevoort family, singled it out as the only representational image of the six landscape views depicted in decorative panels.[17] The painter used the print to earn a handsome fee for investing a luxury good with a recognizable view of a local family landmark, reflected back to generations of Albany elites who gazed into the Gansevoorts' looking glass. Pattern makers for Albany's school of printwork embroidery also profited from the work of Hooker and Snyder. One artist drew the church view on silk, setting it amid a memorial scene dedicated to young Julia Gourlay in 1813. The building's pyramidal roof and gabled vestibule visually echoed the stout obelisk of Gourlay's burial monument in the scene. Neither the deceased nor her elder sisters, who likely worked the picture, had worshiped in the old building; their needlework formed a lesson in local history and geography as well as in fiber art and mourning.[18] Across the Atlantic, British potter Andrew Stevenson cashed in on the environmental view of the church by placing it on pitchers of his Staffordshire "Stone China," running the dates of the building's erection and demolition along its roofline. Whether he encountered the print in Britain or during one of his sojourns in Manhattan in the 1820s, Stevenson added it to his line of popular blue-and-white transferware.[19]

The proliferation of views of Albany's demolished Dutch church exemplifies the transatlantic popularity of antiquarian views in print and material culture. Yet these images also participated in a distinctively national visual project of colonization whereby Euro-American artists professed to "preserve" the peoples and environments they believed to be disappearing under the growth of U.S. sovereignty and society. Beginning in 1816, Thomas L. McKenney used his position as superintendent of the Indian Trade Bureau to assemble "archives" of Indigenous peoples that included representational portraits along with objects and written records of cultural knowledge.[20] In 1821, he commissioned Charles Bird King and James Otto Lewis to paint portraits of Indigenous American leaders of peoples he saw doomed to extinction.[21] In the late 1820s and 1830s, itinerant portraitist George Catlin took up a similar project. He declared himself a "historian" of Indigenous peoples, animals, and environments of the United States and made images that purportedly "preserved" these subjects "by literal and graphic delineation."[22] John James Audubon did the same for North American birds. He aimed to counteract the death of his avian subjects by committing life-size copies of their bodies to the page, preserving individual specimens and waning species for future generations.[23]

Documentary images of historic buildings contributed to this distinctive strain of U.S. visual culture by purporting to replicate evidence of the past that seemed to be vanishing at great speed.[24] Makers of these views leveraged preservation as a strategy for commercial profit by translating antiquarian principles into marketing strategies. They emphasized the rapidity of environmental change and exaggerated the scarcity of historic buildings to define the value of the views that they offered to customers. Consumers who availed themselves of their products, they implied, would distinguish themselves by demonstrating attentiveness to accurate views of an instructive past as they navigated the modern world.

Preservation as Commercial Strategy: City Guides

Imagemakers made preservation a strategy for promoting an ethic of moral consumption in the second quarter of the nineteenth century. Americans long had used consumerism to define good citizenship, first in the British Empire and later in the new nation. By the 1820s, many residents of the United States defined consumer choice as both a right and a decision that shaped civil society as well as the national economy.[25] Some reformers, such as organizers of the free produce movement and craftsmen who founded cooperative salesrooms, promoted the consumption of particular goods to support ethical labor practices. They sought financial profit in support of economic and political change, such as the end of slavery or the attenuation of bourgeois capital.[26] In other strains of moral commerce, producers of religious texts sold goods purporting to promote morality, and women headed fundraisers that sold goods to support charitable causes.[27] All of these pursuits encouraged consumer morality as a business tactic: a dollar well spent, they implied, fulfilled a consumer's desire while improving the lives of others.

In this commercial landscape of moral appeals, some imagemakers made preservation a marketing strategy by presenting their visual goods as a critique of the marketplace in which they operated. Audubon's ornithological record, for instance, tried to counteract the instability of the speculative economy in which he operated and continually suffered financial losses.[28] Catlin moralized about American consumerism more explicitly, condemning the demand for buffalo robes as one of "the fashionable world's luxuries" that destroyed the peoples and environments that he depicted.[29] In his mind, the trade, manufacture, and consumption of buffalo products exemplified the commercial hypocrisy of U.S. civil society. Catlin conveyed little confidence that readers would institute his vision of a moral economy, where legislators disincentivized the manufacture of buffalo robes, traders stopped dealing in whiskey, and wealthy consumers chose woolens over hides. In fact, the American Fur Company funded his travel.[30] Yet by encouraging an alternate model of production and consumption, he defined the project of preserving historic and environmental features as an act of civility as well as a moral economic enterprise.

Makers of antiquarian views appealed to customers with a critique of the transformative effects of market capitalism on the built environment and civil society.[31] Preservational views of recent demolitions or rare survivals offered visual evidence of the past that encouraged viewers to see and assess urban change itself. In the 1820s, publishers of geographically informed history books adopted antiquarian view making to create comprehensive guides to viewing cities at the intersection of the page and the environment. Authors used the rhetoric of "on the spot" description and depiction of historic sites to define the value of their work as preservation and make it a central part of navigating the modern city.[32] On the one hand, guidebook views sought to direct readers to precise sites of historical import on the ground. On the other hand, publishers made clear that printed views themselves preserved architectural evidence of the past that readers could see nowhere else.

Authors of city guidebooks sold books by advertising updated historical content as well as the latest information about urban improvements and expansion. In 1828, for example, A. T. Goodrich characterized the value of his new edition of *Picture of New-York, and Stranger's Guide to the Commercial Metropolis* with a historicized mind-set.[33] In his previous preface, printed in 1818 and 1825 editions, Goodrich described the book as a guide to the present city, useful primarily to visitors as a handy reference.[34] In the third edition, however, Goodrich touted the enlarged "commercial, statistical, and historical facts" of the new edition along with its new map, made expressly to show the "ancient" core of New York City as well as the recently laid urban plan, filled land, and new wharves. Details that might appear trivial to readers in 1828, he remarked, would prove useful in the future as "valuable materials, in tracing the history and progress of this city." These features made the new edition beneficial to "the curious antiquary, the inquiring stranger, or the fellow-citizen" of Manhattan.[35]

Likewise, history writers took geographic turns that prompted them to modify the organization and physical formats of their books to enable antiquarian viewing as urban exploration. As local history writing flourished, authors more frequently organized their histories geographically rather than chronologically.[36] When Charles Shaw published *A Topographical and Historical Description of Boston* in 1817, for instance, he noted that the volume's history would be familiar to anyone who had studied the records of colonial Massachusetts. What was new, he explained, was the work he had done to locate these events in Boston's contemporary landscape.[37] Several years later, Abel Bowen commissioned Caleb Snow to expand the geographic as well as the historical scope of Shaw's history, to which he owned the rights. In the *History of Boston*, published in 1825 and 1828, Bowen added maps of Boston in 1722 and 1824, as well as a directory of street locations in the modern city, to help readers locate historic sites in the modern city. He also commissioned new illustrations of historic buildings.[38] A few years later, Snow and Bowen modified the format of their city history to appeal to new markets of readers. Bowen published a "convenient pocket volume" of Snow's work in his *Picture of Boston*, and Snow issued an abridged city history for schoolchildren, tailored even more strictly to municipal geography in its organization by ward.[39]

The differences in architectural views in these volumes exemplify how guidebook authors claimed to improve readers' vision of a changing city with preservational views. In 1817, Shaw depicted six historic buildings standing in Boston, ranging from "ancient" buildings that Shaw believed "should be carefully ascertained and preserved" to the relatively new Massachusetts statehouse.[40] In 1825, Bowen and Snow printed new engravings of some of the same buildings specifically because they did not still stand. By noting recent demolition dates, they framed their views as the last visible remnants of particular buildings.[41] They took pains to indicate that their views of demolished buildings had been taken from images done from firsthand observation. Bowen's woodcut of the triangular warehouse, built around 1700 and demolished in 1824, looked similar to the view that Nathaniel Dearborn had engraved for Shaw's 1817 history. Both views depicted an expansive building whose triangular footprint, finial-topped turrets, and asymmetrical fenestration spoke to its construction in a distant era. Dearborn and Bowen portrayed the building from the same perspective and abstracted it from the built environment, contextualizing it only with ground and sky. Readers engaged in close comparative looking might have attributed minor variations in fenestration, surrounding ground cover, and building fabric to differences in the engravers' hands. But small differences implied that Bowen must have portrayed the building as it looked on the ground just before demolition—whether or not he did.

Shaw and Bowen used geographic as well as visual devices to bolster these insinuations. Unlike Shaw, who noted locations simply by street name, Snow and Bowen contextualized their views with cardinal, relational, and cartographic directions. Whereas Shaw had labeled his view simply "Triangular Warehouse, Town Dock," Snow and Bowen noted that their image was a "view from the S. E. corner of Faneuil-Hall."[42] They also created a geographic location system to help their readers place historic views of demolished buildings on a map of the modern city. For instance, Snow located the former place of the Triangular Warehouse by pointing readers to the triangle in square *H e* of the map's grid.[43] At the demolished birthplace of Benjamin Franklin, Snow indicated that the artist had taken the firsthand view from the south side of the celebrated Old South Meetinghouse, a landmark whose location was well marked in local knowledge and the book's directory. Snow's notation that a furniture warehouse stood on the building's former site could help readers pinpoint the location on the ground and visually compare the current building with its predecessor.[44]

The authors helped readers discern former appearances of extant buildings as well. Most notably, Bowen revised his woodcut of Faneuil Hall that he had made for Shaw's 1817 topographical history. Boston residents would have recognized the site of this perspective view as the new market building being constructed by Boston mayor Josiah Quincy. For readers who were not familiar with the new market, the authors published a more distant perspective of Faneuil Hall's façade to show its new situation behind the massive, pillared façade and domed profile of the new market.[45] Yet Bowen and Snow also made the old view of Faneuil Hall a vision of progressive development for their readers. Bowen edited the old woodcut to include a ghost architectural profile on Faneuil Hall's opposite façade (Figure 12). As Snow explained, Boston town leaders had overseen a significant expansion of the colonial building in 1805, and "the white line in our view of the Hall exhibits the line of demarcation between the original building and the addition."[46] In this way, Snow and Bowen brought Faneuil Hall into view as it had existed during Revolutionary resistance to imperial policies, making the old print a new guide to seeing evidence of progressive change in the building itself, not just in contrast to its surroundings.

As Bowen and Snow guided their readers in seeing urban transformation in views of historic buildings, they transformed antiquarian views into commercial statements of fashion. They were only two of many guidebook, directory, and periodical authors who emphasized the rapidity and scale of environmental change to make the case that customers needed newer, up-to-date versions of their texts. These men touted their publications as *au courant* because of their depictions of what these changes had removed from the landscape as well as what new features replaced them. By their reasoning, the latest architectural and urban fashions of new construction and economic development demanded that customers buy updated antiquarian views of the structures that they made history.

Antiquarian Views and Moral Commerce

Business proprietors operating out of historic buildings were not passive bystanders to these depictions. They, too, merged antiquarian view making with

NORTH EAST VIEW OF FANUEIL HALL.

Figure 12.   Abel Bowen made this view of Faneuil Hall to depict its development, not just its contemporary appearance: he outlined the shape of the original building with a white line on the left half of the façade. Abel Bowen, engraver, "North East View of Faneuil Hall," in Caleb Snow, *A History of Boston, the Metropolis of Massachusetts* (Boston: Abel Bowen, 1825). Courtesy American Antiquarian Society.

modern commercial practices to define their business pursuits as moral commerce undertaken by historically conscious participants. Their appeals tried to convince consumers that the new commercial architecture arising in U.S. cities did not always demarcate the most respectable consumer choices. As tourism increased in the 1820s, commercial men might profit not only from proximity to a popular landmark but also from making a historic destination of commercial sites themselves.[47] They encouraged the idea that taking a meal in an old-fashioned tavern or shopping in a dry-goods store in an antiquated building could show admirable appreciation for historic sites being lost to capitalist transformations of the built environment. These actions, they implied, marked a civil consumer society more than dining at new hotels and restaurants or shopping in the most fashionable districts.

Many business proprietors used commercial imagery and architectural renovation to advertise their stores and taverns as places where consumers might view interesting and rare evidence of the past amid a modernizing commercial landscape. Real estate developers transformed previously mixed-used buildings and neighborhoods into devoted commercial buildings and districts. Business owners installed bulk windows that thrust displayed goods into the sidewalk and story-high fenestration whose large windowpanes made whole façades transparent. Storekeepers, who frequently rented commercial spaces, created interiors that catered to specialized display and organization of niche goods. They also clustered into districts organized by wares and price points that conveyed different levels of social status. Businessmen shaped the meaning of these architectural designs and commercial displays through urban texts and commercial imagery, hanging ever-larger signs and posters around the city and funding an explosion of print advertising in the second quarter of the nineteenth century.[48]

Together with consumers, commercial proprietors redefined the edification that visitors might receive from visiting these spaces. Storekeepers competed for customers by shaping their places of business as semipublic. They extended retail space into the street, drawing potential customers into their orbit with windows, sidewalk displays, and awnings that encouraged pedestrians to linger. Early experiments with exclusive interior shopping spaces, such as urban arcades, failed when they did not attract enough support from merchants and customers. To be sure, proprietors used architecture to create physical as well as social barriers to delimit who could enter and patronize their stores or taverns. Stores formed more private settings than the informal economies of the street or the regulated but porous public marketplaces.[49] But in the first half of the nineteenth century, urban proprietors opened retail stores to people sent on errands for employers, recreational browsers, and anyone who could appear to be a potential customer. Indeed, a wide variety of early U.S. residents defined themselves and their places in society not only through the purchase of goods but also through the performance of consumption in these semipublic venues.[50]

In this new commercial landscape, some men advertised the historic features of their places of business to draw attention to their commercial pursuits. Sometimes retailers sought to draw foot traffic to businesses outside new, fashionable commercial corridors. This is what John K. Simpson did for his upholstery business when Boston's Washington Avenue shopping district developed several blocks away. Around 1824, Simpson exploited the visual distinctiveness of the seventeenth-century building in which he operated by hiring William Hoogland to engrave a copperplate view of the structure on a trade card (Figure 13).[51] Etched after a drawing by James Kidder, the image harnessed the conventions of preservational view making to commercial imagery. It took an elevated perspective, setting the building at a forty-five-degree angle to capture two elevations that showed distinctive features of its age: irregular fenestration, an upper-story jetty, peaked gables, central chimney, and inscription of 1680 in the roughcast stucco.[52] Hoogland depicted commercial activity with goods on the sidewalk and a horse cart parked out front. He arced Simpson's name over the scene and identified him as an "Importer of Upholstery Goods," located at

Figure 13. John K. Simpson harnessed the visual conventions of preservational views to profit from antiquarian interest in his place of business. Simpson sent an image of the distinctive seventeenth-century building—likely a copy of this trade card—to Caleb Snow for inclusion in his *History of Boston* in 1824. James Kidder, del., William Hoogland, engraver, 1820–1829 (likely 1824?), American Antiquarian Society. Courtesy American Antiquarian Society.

No. 1 Ann Street. The final product, a remarkably fine image on a three-by-five-inch card of heavy stock, identified Simpson as a man of prosperity and taste informed not only by business principles but also by an appreciation for visual arts and historical subjects.

Simpson channeled Bowen and Snow's *History of Boston* as advertising space as well. On learning that Abel Bowen was preparing a geographically oriented history of Boston, he wrote to him with an image and description of the old building. Simpson characterized the building as a rare historic specimen, "probably the oldest wooden building in the city which retains its original appearance." Its gables, he insisted, stood "precisely as they were first erected, the frame and external appearance never having been altered." Its original roughcast remained intact, as did its timber skeleton, "perfectly sound, and intensely hard."[53] In his detailed attention to the material condition of the old building and its history of occupation, Simpson presented himself as a model steward of a commercial place where visitors could partake in a rare view of the past. His plan worked. Bowen engraved a woodblock view of the building, likely from Simpson's trade card, and Snow printed Simpson's description almost verbatim.

The *History of Boston* and its subsequent editions, in this case, emerged from the commercial designs not only of its author and publisher but also of an enterprising retailer.[54] Though Simpson remained anonymous in the first edition, he effectively inserted a description, location, and image of his business in a widely circulated text and garnered a superlative label—the oldest building in Boston—that might attract readers to his door. This is not to say that Simpson's interest in the historic building was purely mercenary. He also supported the commemorative aims of the Bunker Hill Association and, later, the Bunker Hill Monument Association.[55] But Simpson could not have ignored the advantages of generating appreciation for the old features of his building to attract attention to his business, which sat adjacent to the new Faneuil Hall Market.[56] He gained additional attention from Bowen's newspaper advertising, which touted the view of his building as one of the prime selling points of Snow's *History*.[57] In 1838, when Abel Bowen revised his *Picture of Boston*, he named Simpson as the proprietor of the building and gave it a lasting moniker that denoted his upholstery business: the old feather store.[58]

Business proprietors also encouraged antiquarian appreciation of their buildings to elevate the respectability of their commercial ventures and, in turn, their consumers. Around the corner from Simpson, Payton Stewart tried to leverage the historic associations of his store to carve out a place for himself in the secondhand clothing market. In the 1830s, he faced growing competition from the increasing number of salespeople catering to consumers of limited financial means. As a person of color, Stewart also confronted racist and classist suspicions of secondhand clothing dealers as merchandizers of stolen goods—and the mounting municipal regulations that resulted from these fears.[59] While many salespeople pedaled used goods on foot or from temporary quarters in cellars, Stewart distinguished himself by renting a ground-level storefront on Union Street, and a notable one at that. More than a century before, Benjamin Franklin had grown up under its roof. Stewart deployed his knowledge of this association to earn social capital that could translate to financial and political security. Stewart used his attention to the historic features of his creaky, subdivided wooden storefront to demonstrate an interest in civil society that other marketers of secondhand goods struggled to convey. His interest in preservation conveyed a residential permanence that countered the itinerancy common among secondhand vendors and, in turn, the attendant fears of their ability to defraud customers and disappear. Stewart also parlayed his place of business into a powerful social connection: Edmund Quincy, a wealthy friend of abolition and a devoted antiquary, who made a visit to Stewart's store to study its interior.[60] Stewart's concern for a historic site valued by elite white Bostonians would have eased the scrutiny of police and store visitors inclined to question whether he sold goods obtained by illicit means. At the same time, the modest appearance of the century-old, sub-divided store did not affront racist anxieties about the social ascendance of free black Americans.[61]

In Philadelphia, the Irish tavernkeeper John Doyle rebranded his business after he realized that historical associations might attract additional financial earnings and respectability. On November 4, 1824, he received a surprising group of customers: eighteen of the city's most prominent men arrived at his tavern to order a celebratory meal. The men styled themselves the Society for the Com-memoration of the Landing of William Penn and sought to celebrate in what they believed to be Penn's prior residence—now Doyle's tavern.[62] These visitors, by their own accounts, did not fit the profile of Doyle's usual customers, character-ized by Peter DuPonceau as uncouth patrons of a "common caravansary, whose daily inmates think little of the sacredness of the ground on which they are tread-ing."[63] Doyle, they reported, was surprised to see such esteemed men enter his establishment. His surprise, of course, may have stemmed from the fact that they had the wrong building: William Penn never had lived there.

Nevertheless, Doyle immediately recognized antiquarian interest as an op-portunity for his business. He appealed to the Penn revelers by claiming to forgo his own profits in support of their commemorative interests. As one diarist re-ported, "The honest Hibernian who keeps the Public House could scarcely be-lieve the Gentlemen intended to dine at his Old Dwelling, but when he found it was a reallity [*sic*] and not Quiz, he exerted himself to the utmost to procure them a good dinner without paying the strictest regard to his own remuneration."[64] Doyle's savvy earned the men's approbation, certainly in a manner more calcu-lated than they credited. By DuPonceau's account, the building had been "prov-identially preserved from the fate of contemporary buildings." Yet Doyle's generous service enabled them to restore the "former dignity" of the place by ven-erating antique architecture that revived scenes of Penn's life before their eyes. In lengthy reports of the dinner, they lauded Doyle as a generous host whose "sumptuous and well-served repast" enabled a civic transcendence of worldly con-cerns where "the animosities and Party Bickerings of the present day found no place."[65] The success of the meal prompted the men to propose an annual return to Doyle's tavern that would fill the small dining room to capacity.

Members of the society did some of the advertising work for Doyle. They prominently published the name and location of his inn in local newspapers. They also inscribed his name and establishment into the presentation copy of their as-sociation's constitution and register, which members saw as they signed their annual pledges of support and registered their attendance at celebratory dinners. In these lists, Doyle enjoyed the rare confraternity of an Irish American worker with Philadelphia's elite men for posterity. The Penn Society continued to publicize

Doyle's establishment in printed accounts of their celebrations and the house even after the association's dinner outsized Doyle's dining hall in 1825. Many members likely visited the tavern on their own.

Doyle, however, immediately leveraged his tavern's purported historic forms and associations into a new advertising campaign. He hired the city's leading sign painter, John Woodside, to craft a new tavern sign featuring a portrait of William Penn. Doyle used this commercial imagery to signal that a building that some might consider shabby or old-fashioned merited preservation. The sign's appeal also projected Doyle's notoriety beyond the street, earning him praise for his architectural stewardship from newspapers as far away as Trenton, New Jersey.[66] Doyle's sign also aimed to quell any doubts that William Penn had resided there. Despite popular emphasis on the rarity of early colonial buildings on the modern urban landscape, another visibly old house stood nearby. As Deborah Norris Logan pointed out when she walked by Doyle's tavern, "There is an ancient house in the Court fronting the East with a Pediment over the Door considerably carved, that being opposite to the lott on 2d street, described by William Penn as opposite 'to my Cousin Markhams' which will divide the attention of conniseurs [sic] in such affairs, with John Doyles mansion."[67] Some members of the Penn Society even questioned the attribution of Doyle's tavern to Penn's era. As John Fanning Watson cautioned Roberts Vaux after the first association dinner, "The Committee should be careful, as I have, to avoid making Doyles Inn, as peculiarity, Penns house."[68] An old man who lived around the corner from Doyle's place had attested to the erection of Doyle's building in the mid-eighteenth century. Its architectural features also evinced this late date, Watson continued, and historic maps showed that the tavern stood just outside the tract owned by Penn. Doyle used his tavern sign to assert a Penn provenance in the face of these doubts.

Doyle advertised the historic features of his establishment to extend his appeal for visitation to a broader public of potential customers. In many ways, the license required to operate an inn and the regulations that governed tavern operations made Doyle's establishment a public building. But his place of business stood in stark visual contrast to the "palaces of the public" springing up in Philadelphia and across the United States.[69] New hotels and restaurants featured plush lobbies, lighter interiors, more spacious accommodations, and private rooms that offered visitors more refined dining and lodging than old-fashioned taverns and inns. In this new commercial landscape, Doyle recast the old features of his building as architectural signs of the respectability of his business practice. By rendering Penn's portrait as a business sign, he framed his establishment's small rooms, creaky floorboards, low ceilings, and dim interiors as alternate appeals to the respectability of historic tourism, not undesirable contrasts to modern hotels and dining rooms.[70] His tavern, he implied, offered patrons access to more than just liquor and lodging: it offered them a view of the past that brought them into a fraternity that extended beyond the domestic and gustatory to the civic and historic.[71]

Historic associations could not entirely remove the social barriers that prevented passersby from entering Doyle's establishment and partaking of a meal or a night's stay. Deborah Norris Logan, for instance, took a great interest in Doyle's tavern. As the keeper of many Penn-era documents and artifacts that had descended through the family of her late husband, the elderly Quaker widow was an integral part of a Philadelphia network of antiquaries that included John Fanning Watson and John Jay Smith. On their regular visits to her home at Stenton, she provided them access to colonial records and historic artifacts as well as oral histories and personal memories of past places and people. Her role in the Penn Society celebration even earned her recognition in newspaper accounts of the event: she had lent a chair formerly belonging to William Penn to the men for their dinner. Reports of that celebration drew her to Doyle's tavern to appraise the building for herself. Yet Logan carefully noted that she and her young female companions remained outside when they "walked up Letitia Court to take a view, (an outside one only) of the Beef Steak and Oyster house reputed to have been once the mansion of William Penn."[72] For Logan, her sense of propriety barred her from an interior view. Wealthy men could partake of a meal at Doyle's tavern alongside lower-status men and women without fearing a loss of respectability. Yet she judged that a view of the building's historic interior might threaten a different standard of respectability set by her gender, her religious beliefs, and the youth of her companions.

Doyle sought to diminish these barriers and entice more customers into his historic establishment by renovating it with modern hotel and dining accommodations. In 1825, the Penn Society had passed him over for the celebration of the second annual dinner in favor of a larger venue. Doyle had lost out on a hefty income because of the spatial constraints of the old tavern: the society paid nearly four hundred dollars to Daniel Rubicam, one of the city's leading cooks, to cater dinner and champagne for sixty celebrants in the Grand Saloon of the Masonic Hall, which they had rented for seventy-five dollars.[73] Hoping to lure back the society, as well as other potential celebrations, Doyle renovated the tavern to include a three-story brick addition that could serve large dinner parties in more modern accommodations. In 1826, Doyle advertised the completion of these renovations under the new moniker of the "William Penn Tavern," announcing that the "additions and improvements . . . in and about his *Old Establishment*, will, for the future, enable him to entertain either *large or small* parties in the most comfortable manner." Penn Hall, the large new dining room on the second floor of the addition, boasted room for 150 diners in an "airy, well ventilated" room with a high ceiling. With additional "attention to business, the qualities of his liquors, and the contents of his larder," Doyle aimed to use the architecture of modern hotels and dining halls to make the historic features of his place of business more accessible and profitable.[74] When Doyle sold his share in the building the following year—perhaps because of the debt accrued by these renovations—proprietor Joseph Donath continued to advertise the tavern's history and the Penn Society's interest in the building as selling points for prospective renters.[75]

Doyle's tavern renovation points to the ways that business proprietors walked a fine line between incorporating fashionable changes to their places of business and preserving architectural evidence of the past. Philadelphia clothier William Brown promoted himself as an agent of preservation to benefit from a critique of the pursuit of fashion in retail goods and settings. Brown appealed to consumer morality with an advertising poster that depicted his historic storefront and its abundant display of menswear (Figure 14). Floor-to-ceiling display windows, a modern sidewalk, and a centerpiece display case spoke to Brown's modern commercial sensibilities. Yet as a purveyor of ready-made attire, Brown sold clothing that was cheaper than bespoke items from tailors and luxury stores. His location on Market Street also stood a block from the more fashionable retail stores on Chestnut Street. Brown's poster, however, contended that he offered customers a more exclusive and respectable shopping venue than did his upscale competitors. A large sign above the door announced that this building was no ordinary clothing store: it was the "Birth-Place of Liberty," where Thomas Jefferson had drafted the Declaration of Independence.[76]

Brown's advertisement merged the act of shopping for ready-made clothing with veneration of a historic site to increase the respectability of his business. In doing so, he modeled his ideal of a moral consumer: one who eschewed luxury for frugal quality. On the left of the poster, two men studied the ready-made garments hanging on forms in front of large shop windows and an open door. "Life, Liberty, & genteel Garments at the birth-place of Liberty, S. W. Cor. 7th & Market Sts.," one announced to his companion. On the right, two interlocutors remarked on the building. "How often I have read of this Establishment," one marveled. "The Clothing is as well made as in Chestnut st. I'll buy mine here in future & save my money." The copy below adapted the opening lines of the Declaration of Independence to a call for patronage of Brown's store: "a decent respect for the Memory of our Revolutionary Patriots demands that they should all call and purchase their external covering at the Birth-Place of Liberty, which is the identical and time-honored edifice in which the immortal patriot, Thomas Jefferson, penned the Glorious Declaration of our Inalienable Rights."[77] Clothes

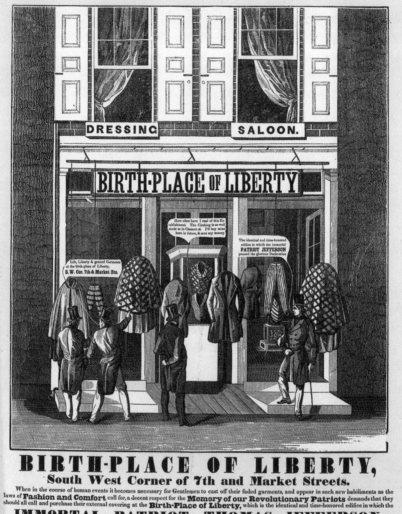

Figure 14. Philadelphia clothier William Brown appealed to consumer morality with a view of a Revolutionary landmark: the building in which Thomas Jefferson lodged while he wrote the Declaration of Independence. Brown's strategy for marketplace competition defined interest in historic architecture as an element of respectable consumerism. "Birth-Place of Liberty Dressing Saloon, South West Corner of 7th and Market Streets," undated, wood engraving. PR 031, Bella C. Landauer Collection of Business and Advertising Ephemera, New-York Historical Society, image number 44565.

alone did not make the man, Brown implied; the place where he shopped enriched his character too. By offering quality goods at economical prices in a historic setting, Brown offered men the chance to fulfill the patriotic duties of citizenship with the pursuit of their individual desires as fashionable *and* frugal consumers.[78]

Retailers who engaged preservation as a market strategy shaped modern commercial practices even as they critiqued them. Men who merged antiquarian views into commercial imagery formed the leading cusp of a widescale transition in advertising imagery. Their attention to the architectural details of particular storefronts in the 1820s and 1830s helped to usher in the turn of commercial visual culture toward architectural views of stores as sites of consumption in the 1840s. These engravers and retailers also became some of the earliest business proprietors to promote the idea that the shopping environment defined consumer respectability as much as the goods purchased. When business proprietors renovated historic buildings, modern features of commercial architecture, such as large windows and open doors, beckoned viewers to take a closer look at the old building itself as well as the goods it housed. It was not just new commercial architecture that made shopping and the act of individual consumption a means of self-improvement and moral expression, they implied.[79] Rather, good citizens who patronized a historic storefront partook in moral commerce that supported a civil society defined by a shared past as well as personal economy. Yet as these proprietors situated historic buildings in urban marketplaces of goods, they risked presenting themselves as men who corrupted historic buildings with the pursuit of profit.

The Demolition Market

In 1830, George Pope Morris treated subscribers of his weekly *New-York Mirror* to a new series of architectural views. In preceding years, he had commissioned Alexander Jackson Davis to engrave front-page images and descriptions of the "Public Buildings in the City of New York," which included institutions of higher learning, the Bowery Theatre, the bowling green, and over a dozen local churches whose histories the editors deemed "interesting to the historian and antiquary."[80] On the front page of his eighth edition, however, Morris opened with a picture of an old Dutch house standing on Manhattan's Broad Street (Figure 15). It was the first in a series of views and descriptions that the authors published "to secure correct views of the few that are yet left standing, . . . and consign them to the safe keeping of the New-York Mirror; which will, if our wishes be verified, reflect their venerable images down the long vista of distant futurity to the latest posterity."[81] Even if ironwork had not dated its construction to 1698, the form of

THE NEW-YOR

A REPOSITORY OF POLITE LITERA

VOLUME VIII.   NEW-YORK, SATURDAY, JU

DUTCH ARCHITECTURE.

Davis, del.   Mason, sculp.

THE OLD HOUSE IN BROAD-STREET.

WITHOUT advancing any claims to the honourable profession of an antiquary, either local or general, we still feel it a

In those days, however, whatever migh materials or dimensions of the edifice, its faced on the street, and generally terminate which resembled two opposing flights of stai eves on each side of the front, ascending wit roof, and meeting at a little brick turret, w its apex, and was commonly ornamented wi or vane to indicate the course of the wind.

The acute angle of the tiled roof was hap avert the danger to which buildings of a diffe have been exposed from the heavy falls of prevalent at that early period. On the gal mentioned, were displayed four large iron fig the year in which the building was erected, time serving the purpose of what modern bui irons which secure the walls to the floor-tim

As regards the interior of these buildings, low, and the apartments seldom ceiled over oak beams, either whitewashed with lime, o by frequent applications of the scrubbing-br indications of strength and durability. Th composed of three distinct sashes; two of hinges, and opening on the inside, like lit while the third, of more narrow dimension: zontally across the top, where it remained glass, which was cut into small panes of a by four, was set in lead. Few specimens, style of glazing can now be found in the city, a the ancient Dutch houses have all been mode a principal feature in the real Knickerbocker ture has become extinct. The windows wer by outside shutters, which were hung by hing and every morning let down to a horizont forming a convenient platform for the displa as were offered for sale by the occupant.

Figure 15. In the 1830s, editors of the *New-York Mirror* published a series of views of historic Dutch American architecture. Many of the images—like this view of H. N. Ferris & Co. Grocers—depicted the commercial trappings of resident businessmen as well as the antiquated architectural features of the buildings. As demolition of these structures increased, these images suggested that commercial tenants posed a threat to the preservation of historic structures. "Dutch Architecture: The Old House in Broad-Street," *New-York Mirror* 8:1 (July 10, 1830), 1. The Library Company of Philadelphia.

the building showed its age. The gable end street façade, with its steeply stepped roof line, formed a recognizable profile of buildings erected by Dutch colonizers who remained in New York after it became an English colony in 1674. The author of the accompanying article filled in the material details of this building type, made famous by Washington Irving's contemporary tales: distinctive yellow and black bricks, tile roofs, and small diamond-paned lead casement windows that intervening generations had removed. Though the writers knew nothing of the specific builders or inhabitants of this old house, they celebrated its age.

The view of the house also depicted its place in the modern commercial landscape of the booming nineteenth-century city. A sign above the door announced the shop as the home of H. N. Ferris & Co. Grocers, one of the growing number of retailers who honed their businesses to specialized trades. They displayed bottled goods in a twenty-five-pane show window—an enticing visual grid of goods that opened half of the ground-floor façade. This large window, along with a smaller show window and an open front door, created the porous exterior that merchants of the era sought. An abundance of crated goods out front extended Ferris's operation into the public sidewalk, forcing pedestrians into commercial space as they passed the building at 41 Broad Street, as it was designated in the new street address system. These commercial trappings marked Ferris, as the *Mirror* editors put it, "a good citizen, who 'keeps constantly on hand a general assortment of first-rate groceries, cheap for cash.'"[82] Yet it was his presence in an old building that singled out his business for a visual and verbal portrait circulated to thousands of readers in New York City and beyond.

As view makers portrayed commercial residents of the buildings they sought to document, they implicated commercial men in the urban change that they guided their viewers to see. The two men who created the views of old Dutch architecture for the *New-York Mirror* produced their work for a visual marketplace driven by demolition. Alexander Jackson Davis, the sketcher, and Abraham J. Mason, the engraver, trafficked in the currency of visual preservation to earn acclaim and remuneration for their work. At first glance, the *Mirror* commissions constituted a small job for men who had earned attention in Manhattan design circles.[83] Yet impending demolition of their subjects invested their work with a significance that the modest size and skill of the image did not convey. Signed and circulated to the *Mirror* readership, the images served as an advertisement for the artisans as citizens who preserved historic buildings that otherwise would disappear from sight.

In fact, Morris marketed the *Mirror* as a medium of preservation for the city's disappearing architectural past. In 1833, for instance, the *Mirror* ended its series of Dutch colonial buildings of Manhattan with "a correct and striking view of the last of the Dutch houses, which has survived the progress of improvement in this changeable city, and is now, as we are informed, about to be pulled down."[84] The loss was striking, in the minds of the editors, because few "improvements" had marred the façade. *Mirror* editors used image quality as a competitive strategy to distinguish their publication from similar periodicals with antiquarian goals, such as Abel Bowen's *City Record, and Boston News-Letter,* founded "to observe and preserve" items of historic note.[85] *Mirror* editors paid particularly close attention to the visual composition of their views and the high quality of their printing to establish their preservational quality.[86] As detailed woodcuts offered armchair readers a chance to view historic sites from afar, they also offered future readers an opportunity to see demolished buildings as they had stood in the past. Indeed, the *Mirror* became a source for other publishers looking to capitalize on views of demolished architecture: many views of extant historic buildings printed in the *Mirror* in the early 1830s reappeared in William Dunlop's *A History of New York, for Schools* in 1837 as examples of demolished buildings.[87]

As weekly editions offered up-to-date commentary on transformations of New York City's urban environment, they also formed an archive of the buildings removed by the rise of modern commercial districts. In one instance, the *Mirror* ended a profile of Manhattan's long-standing German Lutheran congregation by noting that they recently had vacated their old church building for an improved one, suggesting it would be "giving place to a block of modern stores." When the demolition ensued, publishers applauded their own foresight. "Aware of this probability [of destruction]," they wrote, "we took the precaution to secure its portrait, for the gratification of such as may have never seen the original."[88] *Mirror* views also documented commercial enterprises that had converted mixed-use domestic buildings to sole purpose businesses. In their first view of an old Dutch house and its accompanying article, they depicted Ferris's store as a laudable, modern enterprise in a historically interesting abode. Yet two views that followed in 1831 offered less adulatory commercial portraits. Editors limited the explanatory text of the "Old Dutch House in William-Street" to a short caption, "*Built* 1648. *Modernized* 1828."[89] With the stepped gable, small shuttered upper windows, and off-center door placement still in place, the single modern feature appeared clear: a large, bowed shop window. A few months later, a view of the "Old Dutch House in Pearl-Street" depicted a building "*Built* 1626.—*Rebuilt* 1697.—*Demolished* 1828."[90] A commercial sign over the door announced the residence of a purveyor of drugs, paints, and dyes. In this series, signs of commerce marked the last stage in a historic building's existence and then themselves became architectural relics; proprietors of these stores became final tenants who did not or could not stop demolition.

By the 1830s, imagemakers regularly capitalized on views that undercut commercial proprietors in historic buildings by presenting them as tenants of structures

soon to disappear. As they intensified their production of views meant to preserve buildings facing demolition, they suggested that the intrusion of commerce into old buildings spelled the end for these structures. Imagemakers
strengthened this effect by pairing a preservational view with a depiction of the
structure's demolition. In the final issue of the *New-York Mirror* for 1831, for instance, editors printed a lengthy history of "the Old Stuyvesant Mansion." The
article's author, Samuel Woodworth, framed the history of the house as a critique
of popular views of improvement.[91] The seventeenth-century abode had housed
the final governor of New Amsterdam, Peter Stuyvesant, and several generations
of his descendants. Now the house would disappear under the roads and building lots that extended the city northward. Woodworth cast a sarcastic aspersion
on the "sapient editors" of the *Mirror* for calling this urban development "public
improvements," and he condemned fellow city residents who embodied the same
ethos, which "stalked through this city with giant strides, and laid waste almost
every thing that bore the features of antiquity."[92] Much like the treasure hunters
who had pockmarked Stuyvesant's fields in search of buried gold, modern developers created a landscape marred by their desire to get rich from the land.[93]

Abraham Mason accentuated Woodworth's argument with an engraving of
the Stuyvesant house that implied its impending demolition. Alexander J. Davis
had made two watercolors of the house. One depicted the flat, five-bay western
façade of the house with the East River as a backdrop. Excavations formed sloping ascents in an undulating landscape; short runs of stairs enabled pedestrians
to reach the house. Land removal seemed occur at a slow pace at the hands of a
single man with a horse cart.[94] The second view offered a closer rendering of the
house's opposite façade (Figure 16). This perspective brought into view the house's
jettied upper story and asymmetrical gambrel roof gable profile, both features
that marked the house's age in obsolescent forms.[95] When Mason engraved this
view, he portrayed the building atop a land mass both taller and steeper than the
one that Davis depicted (Figure 17). He also erased indications of a two-tiered
land platform in favor of a sheer bluff, perching the house on an earthen pedes-
tal above starkly cleared and leveled land. Two cattle tucked themselves next to
the earthen wall. Drawn to the last tiny remnant of Stuyvesant's fields, they stood
as artifacts of a decimated pastoral environment. A crag created by land excava-
tion held two pedestrians at bay as they regarded the precarious edifice. They had
done what Woodworth encouraged readers to do: visit this old building before
its "final demolition" took place.[96] Mason's view made clear that readers would
have to hurry if they hoped to see the old building for themselves; soon his image would provide the only available view of it.

In printing Woodworth's article and Mason's engraving in a feature position,
the *Mirror* appealed to readers who held dissenting views on the value of old

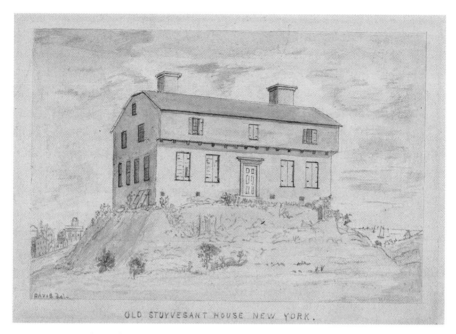

OLD STUYVESANT HOUSE NEW YORK.

Figure 16. Alexander Jackson Davis, then a young architect beginning to explore an interest in Gothic Revival architecture, drew two views of the seventeenth-century Stuyvesant House as its impending demolition approached. He sketched a partial floor plan of the house on the back of this image. His other view documented the opposite side of the house as land excavations approached its doorstep. Alexander Jackson Davis, Stuyvesant House ("Petersfield"), New York City, 1831. Brown ink and wash over graphite on paper, 6 1/2 × 9 in. Gift of Samuel V. Hoffman, New-York Historical Society, 1912.32.

buildings in the modern world. This critique of urban development bolstered editorial claims to impartiality and sought to appease readers who thought that commercial development should have limits as well as those who cheered its seemingly limitless expansion. Throughout the 1830s, imagemakers began to cater to customers with a similar approach: offering views that aimed to critique the demolition of buildings as well as preserve their subjects. William Breton did this by making pendant views of the old courthouse in Philadelphia. By the time he drew the structure in 1837, he had spent a decade making a living by depicting the city's historic structures in a variety of media. After arriving from England, Breton started out by selling small watercolors of area landmarks for twenty-five cents. He later set up a gallery in Philadelphia's Arcade, a new building at the corner of Sixth and Chestnut Streets. Here, shoppers could browse Breton's images under the same roof as retail stores, other galleries, and Peale's Museum. Views of historic buildings attracted particular attention and earned him a number of commissions. In 1827, members of the Historical Society of Pennsylvania

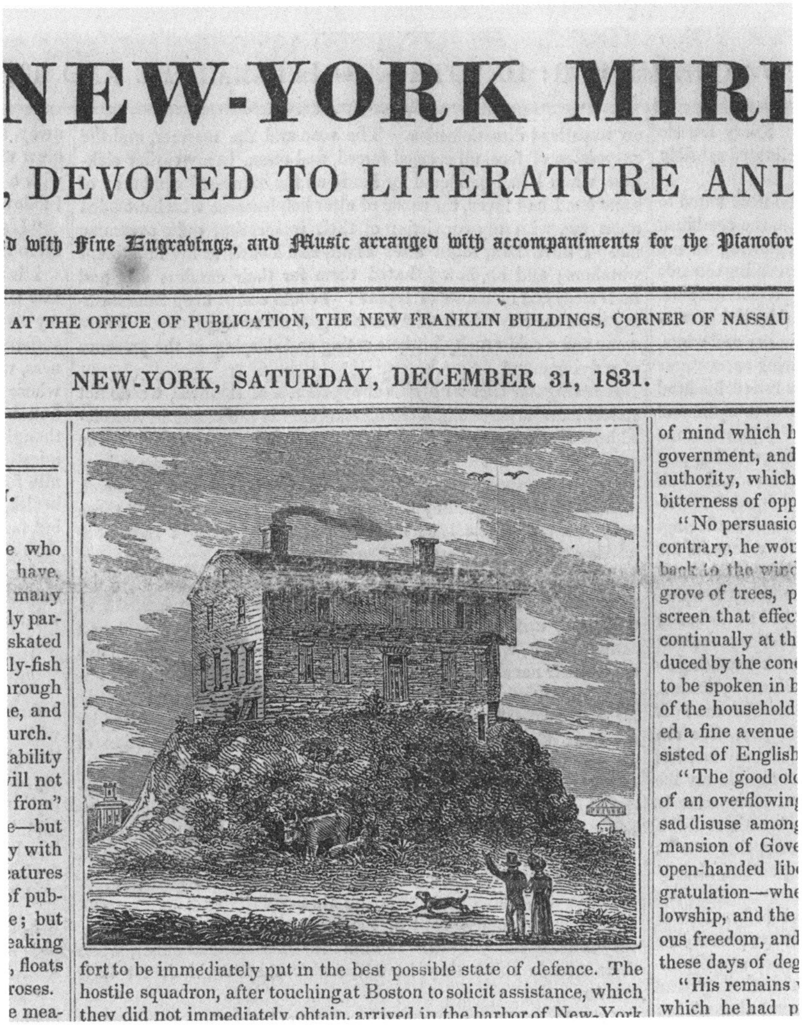
NEW-YORK MIRR

, DEVOTED TO LITERATURE AND

d with Fine Engravings, and Music arranged with accompaniments for the Pianofor

AT THE OFFICE OF PUBLICATION, THE NEW FRANKLIN BUILDINGS, CORNER OF NASSAU

NEW-YORK, SATURDAY, DECEMBER 31, 1831.

fort to be immediately put in the best possible state of defence. The hostile squadron, after touching at Boston to solicit assistance, which

Figure 17. When Abraham Mason engraved Alexander Jackson Davis's view, he exaggerated the height and slope of the land mass on which the Stuyvesant House stood. The resulting print depicted the structure in a more precarious situation than Davis's view had conveyed. Abraham Mason, engraver, for Samuel Woodworth, "New-York Antiquities: History of the Old Stuyvesant Mansion," *New-York Mirror* 10:26 (Dec. 31, 1831), 201. The Library Company of Philadelphia.

contacted him about his drawings of "Ancient Buildings," and antiquary John Fanning Watson ordered twenty-six of these views to be lithographed for his *Annals of Philadelphia* in 1830.[97] Breton also engraved a number of these views for the *Casket*.[98]

Commercial enterprise drew Breton to the old courthouse in April 1837. Though Breton had drawn views of the building before, he wanted to make more detailed images before impending demolition removed it from the landscape. As the artist sketched the eastern façade of the building, erected in the early eighteenth century, he captured one of Philadelphia's vibrant market scenes. The building, once the seat of municipal government, had come to serve as the head house for market stalls that formed the spine of Market Street (Figure 18). His "N. E. View of the Old Court House in Market St, Philada." fit the established conventions of preservational views.[99] It depicted the pedimented gable end, showing its shingled dormer windows and bell tower as well as the line of shambles that extended westward. Female vendors clustered on both sides of the arched central passage. A dozen posters papered the brick walls up to the second story, where a door to the balcony sat ajar. On the left side of the view, Breton depicted a glimpse of the brick storefronts on the south side of Market Street.

He did not stop with this single image. Like Davis had done with the Stuyvesant house, Breton went to the opposite side of the building to capture another view. In doing so, he depicted a different stage of demolition (Figure 19). Eight workmen stood amid skeletal roofing trusses, opening the building to the spring sky as they throw shingles and bricks to the street below.[100] The scar of an awning, visible above the building's western arch, marked where workers had decapitated the head house from its backbone of commercial stalls. Three respectably dressed women bent down to inspect the rubble. Perhaps they salvaged building material or looked for antiquities, such as the old spoons, engraved cornerstones, and colonial coins that so many newspapers reported were uncovered by demolition. A shadowy figure peered out a second-floor window. Perhaps he came to inspect the remnants of early eighteenth-century construction techniques revealed when workers gutted the interior. He might leave the site with wood from the floorboards, suitable for framing lithographs of the building or fashioning into relic boxes like the ones made by John Fanning Watson. A portly man stood in the foreground amid crates and barrels. His breeches, Quaker hat, and cane marked him as an old-fashioned resident. Rooted to a fine vantage point, he likely recalls scenes that he witnessed there over the previous decades. On the north side of the street, fashionable young men gathered to watch the demolition as well. Perhaps they had read the history of the building in Watson's *Annals* or in Carey and Hart's guide to the city.[101] They might remark on past events that took place within the crumbling walls even as they discussed business prospects for the cleared parcel.

Breton offered two views of the old courthouse to appeal to two strains of preservation contending for popular support by 1837. The fate of the old courthouse had come under debate when the *Public Ledger* announced the building's impending demolition. At least one citizen had written to the newspaper to argue for keeping the old building standing. The newspaper's editors had published a

N.E. View of the OLD COURT HOUSE in Market St, Philad.ª

Figure 18. After more than a decade making views of historic buildings in Philadelphia, William L. Breton composed a lithograph of "the old court house" just before its demolition in the spring of 1837. His view showed the building as the head house of the market shambles stretching several blocks west. William L. Breton, "N. E. View of the Old Court House in Market St, Philada." (Philadelphia: Lehman and Duval Lithographers, 1837). The Library Company of Philadelphia.

S.W. View of the OLD COURT HOUSE in Market St. Philad a

at the time of its being taken down (7 th April 1837)

Figure 19. William L. Breton rendered a demolition scene when he made a view of the opposite façade of "the old court house." Workers were taking down the masonry walls after removing the market shambles, gutting the building, and taking off the roof. Figures 18 and 19 speak to the market that Breton and his publishers identified among a local population who had made the demolition of the historic structure a matter of public debate. William L. Breton, "S. W. View of the Old Court House in Market St. Philada. at the time of its being taken down (7th April 1837)" (Philadelphia: Lehman and Duval Lithographers, 1837). The Library Company of Philadelphia.

scathing condemnation of his position. At a moment of widespread economic collapse, such demolitions offered signs of financial optimism and employment opportunities for laborers, they said. Imagemakers and publishers generated the most commercial success when they made views that appealed to people who saw their products as preservation *and* to consumers who challenged their ability to make historic architecture permanent. Their success fed the growing marketplace of images and, in turn, promoted the mounting belief that men who undertook commercial enterprise at historic sites were anything but moral.

CHAPTER 4

Moral Real Estate: Sacred Historic Space and the Politics of Speculation

Charles G. DeWitt was on his way to Washington when he stopped in Philadelphia in December 1829. One week before he would take up his seat in the Twenty-First Congress of the United States, the new representative from Kingston, New York, strode down Chestnut Street to inspect the meeting spot of the First Continental Congress. As he turned south into an alleyway between Third and Fourth Streets, Carpenters' Hall came into view. DeWitt beheld its three-story brick exterior and modest steeple, tucked away in an urban courtyard. The Carpenters' Company of Philadelphia had built the hall in 1770 to house trade meetings. Soon after, they had begun to rent its rooms to raise funds for their association.

When DeWitt stepped inside, he met an auctioneer who worked where colonial representatives had tested arguments for national independence (Figure 20). Charles J. Wolbert had set up his modest business in the building just a year earlier. He may well have seen the building's historic associations as a way to elevate his social status and sales at a time when auctioneers came under fire as suspect businessmen.[1] Wolbert proved sympathetic to DeWitt when he ceded his desk to the traveler so that he could record his impressions of the place. Yet DeWitt could abide only limited, anonymous praise for the auctioneer because the very nature of his business clashed with the veneration that the traveler wished to bestow on the building. "His voice stuns my ear," DeWitt wrote, "and distracts my brain, crying 'how much for these rush bottomed chairs? I am offered $5—nobody more? going! going!! gone!!!' In fact, the Hall is lumbered up with beds, looking-glasses, chairs, tables, pictures, ready-made clothes, and all the trash and trumpery which usually grace the premises of a knight of the hammer."[2] The setting did not elevate Wolbert's business, in DeWitt's mind; auctioneering diminished the visitor's ability to meditate on the past enlivened by historic interiors.

Figure 20. The ground floor of Carpenters' Hall—the meeting place of the First Continental Congress in 1774—served as an auction hall in the first half of the nineteenth century. The building's stewards faced mounting criticism of allowing the incursion of commerce into "sacred" historic space. Today, the ground floor of Carpenters' Hall reflects the "restoration" that the Carpenters' Company undertook in 1856 when they removed their business tenants and refurbished their building's interior in eighteenth-century Georgian style. Ground floor interior, Carpenters' Hall, Philadelphia. Photograph by author, 2019.

In his account of his visit, published in a number of periodicals, DeWitt characterized historic structures in seemingly original condition as sacred. Carpenters' Hall stood as a "consecrated apartment" and "Hallowed hall" because its purportedly unchanged architecture gave visitors a spatial experience that created a threshold between present and past. "O that walls could speak!" DeWitt exclaimed, as he described how the building's rooms revived an echo of the speeches given under its roof.[3] In a city transformed by demolitions and so-called restorations, DeWitt praised the Carpenters' Company for maintaining the structure as it had always looked. Resident tenants, however, attracted his reproach for cacophonous endeavors that attenuated the power of architecture to evoke the past.

DeWitt's account of Carpenters' Hall marked a watershed in accounts of historic sites. During the economic swings of the late 1820s and 1830s, writers such as DeWitt touted the perpetual care of supposedly rare and untouched historic structures as a way to quell the "rage to be rich" pervading the market economy.[4] They described the built environment to characterize and condemn a new generation of capitalists as worshippers of Mammon—people who threatened civil society with their desire to exploit speculative economies for their own gain and the ruin of others. DeWitt leveraged his valuation of the historic architecture of Carpenters' Hall on the popular notion that auction houses hosted speculative schemes for outsized profits, often made on the misfortunes of debtors or the defrauding of buyers.[5] Other writers used calls for preservation to speak against the speculative building economy, where flimsy rentals and opulent mansions crowded out sturdy, if modest, structures and open green spaces of previous generations. The preservation of sacred historic sites, these writers implied, encouraged the pursuit of financial competence—a level of prosperity that secured independent support of a family and comfortable retirement and created social stability in a marketplace where risk of collective ruin ran high.

The sacred language of these appeals for preservation operated in conversation with an emergent gospel of wealth, whose ministers preached that it was godly to aspire to and achieve personal riches.[6] But when writers promoted this view of sacred historic sites in the partisan presses, they sought to align their various political agendas with a civically defined principle of moral market behavior that evaded the divisiveness of sectarian moral reforms. Whereas men such as Benjamin Austin and William Duane had called for preservation to shame corporate stewards of public buildings, DeWitt's contemporaries trained their criticism on individual owners of private properties. They portrayed the failure to keep these historic sites sacred, or set apart from the speculative market, as a mark of speculators' intent on building money power in a political system swayed by it. Men aligned with the Jacksonian Democrats, the Young America movement, Garrisonian abolition, and nascent Whigs all promoted this brand of sacred preservation as an ethical doctrine that framed perpetual but voluntary property ownership as a moral check on the pursuit of capital. Aristocracy, they suggested, was not synonymous with money power. By printing their calls for sacred preservation in the partisan presses, they painted their political agendas as ones informed by financial sacrifice for the collective good. In turn, they disengaged from more radical calls for democratized landownership that sought to redistribute private property across class or generation.

Sensing the Past at "Original" Sites

By his own account, Charles DeWitt's walk through Carpenters' Hall in 1829 bordered on sensory overload. The clatter of a live auction downstairs, the commotion of schoolchildren upstairs, and the speeches of Patrick Henry all ran through his mind as he looked around the rooms and vestibules. Despite the clamor, the fabric of the eighteenth-century building drew him into the proximate presence of Patrick Henry. "In this consecrated apartment, in which I am now seated—this unrivalled effort of human intellect was made!—I mark it as an epoch in my life. I look upon it as a distinguished favour that I am permitted to tread the very floor which Henry trod, and to survey the scene which, bating the changes of time and circumstance, must have been surveyed by him."[7] By sitting in the same room, walking over the same floor, and seeing the same walls as Patrick Henry had decades earlier, DeWitt believed that he gained insight into the life of his fore-bear. Yet DeWitt was careful to describe this encounter in a rational way. He did not feel teleported to the past. Rather, DeWitt believed that he was able to access Patrick Henry's life through a shared point of architectural contact, even though new occupants put the spaces to new uses. He had caught a glimpse of 1775 while remaining rooted firmly in 1829.

DeWitt was one of many U.S. residents who reported that moving through a seemingly unchanged building or environment made him feel as if he were par-taking in a doubled spatial experience with previous inhabitants who had moved through the space in the very same way.[8] Five years earlier, Peter DuPonceau had used similar language to describe a visit to John Doyle's tavern, writing that "we feel [William Penn's] spirit in the atmosphere that we breathe, we seek in every nook and corner of it for some traces of the illustrious man, we see in imagination the spot where he used to sit while dictating laws to a virtuous and happy people, we have a right to fancy that we are sitting in the same place where he used to take his frugal repast."[9] For writers such as DuPonceau and DeWitt, a visit to a historic environment in the present day had a comprehen-sive effect on the senses, reviving the sights, sounds, feel, and sometimes even the tastes and smells of the past. Modern visitors to immersive environments could access evidence of what the past felt like at a particular time and then contemplate historical developments by contrasting this experience to the con-ditions of the modern day.

Visitors to old spaces often described the effects of this experience as creat-ing visions of the past before the mind's eye. Several years after he managed the renovation of the Newport synagogue, Stephen Gould described this phenome-non while exploring a seventeenth-century house before its demolition. In 1835, when he "went into it and examined every part," he reported that his "immagi-nation [*sic*] was on the alert, far more than common for me." When Gould at-tuned his senses to the surrounding environment, the features of the old Coddington house transported his thoughts to the past. "As I walked thro' the rooms I could go back, and mentaly [*sic*] behold the yearly meeting there gath-ered under a solid reverend frame of spirit." He imagined the debates between George Fox and William Coddington, funeral sermons made by his ancestor

Daniel Gould, and Coddington's accounts of his passage on the *Arabella*. The walls evoked the meetings that had taken place within the house; the massive fireplaces called to mind the meals that Coddington shared with his associates; the house's siting on the landscape conjured visions of the funeral processions that wended their way from the front door to the nearby orchard. For Gould, "it was reasonable to fancy [past occupants] seated very solidly in those rooms."[10] Writers who described such vivid views of the past likely had especially high neurological capacities for forming mental images.[11] But they believed that these sorts of sites could evoke the same experience for any person willing to hone his analytical eye and historical knowledge.

Gould's letter exemplifies how writers carefully emphasized that envisioning the past was a roundly rational response to empirical study of the built environment, not a fantastical flight of imagination. Gould's linguistic mixing of the words *imagination* and *fancy* does not reveal an inconsistency in his thinking.[12] Though Gould's vernacular did not reflect the linguistic differentiation recently begun in European intellectual circles, he emphasized the empiricism of his exploration of the Coddington house. The men who promoted the instructional value of historic sites in supposedly original condition believed that individuals had to cultivate their imaginations to reap the instructive benefits of a doubled experience. They regarded imagination as the intermediary function of mind, which translated sensory perception of objective physical realities to reasonable conclusions.[13] A historical imagination was an empirical tool for analyzing material evidence of past lives, events, and eras. When well cultivated, it could create a complete and accurate vision of the past before the mind's eye.

These observers demanded rational analysis of historic spaces to elicit a morally instructive emotional response, not to quell it. Writers recounted the effects of looking in language of the auditory to characterize the rational emotion produced by doubled spatial experiences. Charles DeWitt's description of Carpenters' Hall as a sonic environment in 1829 was typical. "Yes!" he exclaimed, "These walls have echoed the inspiring eloquence of Patrick Henry," the great orator of the Revolution. "O that these walls could speak!" DeWitt wished, "that the echo which penetrates my soul as I pronounce the name of Patrick Henry in the corner I occupy, might again reverberate the thunders of his eloquence!"[14] DeWitt highlighted the famed rhetoric of his subject, whose notoriety had grown with the publication of William Wirt's multivolume biography beginning in 1817.[15] But DeWitt also used auditory language more broadly to characterize historic spaces as ones that elicited emotional effects as well as intellectual ones.

As DeWitt said, the act of pronouncing Henry's name on the spot where the orator had spoken echoed in his *soul*—the seat of emotion and feeling. Hearing had been linked to emotional responses since the Enlightenment, when thinkers had invested the eye with intellectual authority and warned against letting auditory perceptions cloud visual ones. As more Americans valued individual feeling as a source of religious authority and moral improvement, however, they invested hearing with a new importance. As John Fanning Watson reflected in 1830 after a visit to one of William Penn's former abodes, it was necessary "to think and feel" to appreciate the value of historic spaces.[16] Good citizens honed their perceptual skills, training both eye and ear, to ensure that rational thought and emotional response worked in tandem, not opposition.[17] DeWitt's labeling of the upstairs rooms of Carpenters' Hall as "sublime" emphasized their emotional effects. In 1818, Wirt had labeled Henry's voice itself sublime, his "wild and grand effusions" a stark contrast with the "chaste—classical—beautiful" rhetoric of fellow Revolutionary orator Richard Henry Lee.[18] Henry delivered his addresses "in accents which spoke to the soul, and to which every other bosom deeply responded," in Wirt's description.[19] Indeed, Henry's contemporaries later confessed that they remembered how they *felt* when they heard Henry speak, not the content of his orations.[20] In Wirt's view, modern generations could best know Henry's speeches through reminiscences of these feelings; after all, the famed orator never wrote down any of his addresses. DeWitt's view revised Wirt's: Carpenters' Hall could evoke these same feelings by enabling modern visitors to walk in Henry's footsteps. This doubled spatial experience produced an equivalent emotional response to hearing Henry himself speak—a possibility lost upon his death. In this view, Carpenters' Hall formed a sounding board whose emanations resonated in visitors' hearts rather than their ears.

DeWitt and his contemporaries used a particular phrase to invoke the emotional effects of historic spaces as rational responses: "O, that these walls could speak!"[21] Variants of this phrase were not entirely new in the 1830s. The expression "if walls had eyes and ears" appeared in English-language print culture around 1800, when writers wished that interior architecture could bear witness to recent events, particularly crimes.[22] In an era when new devices held the potential for aural and visual surveillance, the phrase carried an unseemly connotation of voyeurism when applied to private spaces.[23] Even legitimate observation of interior spaces, to solve a crime or maintain prison discipline, could seem shocking or improperly titillating. Early nineteenth-century writers generally used the expression in service of Gothic tropes, implying that even under the best circumstances, the possibility of knowing what occurred within interior spaces threatened to offend or shock the sensibilities as much as it promised to inform.

But in the early 1830s, writers began to use this phrase in a different way. They linked the established phrase "if walls had tongues" to the rational exploration of historic places. Edmund Quincy, the young antiquary and antislavery activist who visited Payton Stewart's store, exemplified this trend in private and printed prose when he repeatedly interjected, "If walls had tongues, what histories might they unfold!"[24] As the precursor to the modern parlance "if walls could talk," the phrase connoted that old spaces imparted a special kind of sensory experience that could teach onlookers valuable lessons about the past. When deployed in a historic environment, surveillance of domestic spaces offered an edifying view of the private realm.[25] The conditional tense of the phrase was particularly important. While its auditory vocabulary registered the emotional effect of historic spaces, its conditional construction insisted that interlocutors derived that emotion from rational perception. "If walls could speak" was a claim to authority in an early national culture that wanted to join a rational intellect with a feeling soul in civic as well as religious life. Intact historic spaces were special, this parlance suggested: their physical conditions could revive a simulacrum of the past and fill gaps in the written record. But writers simultaneously used this idiom as a shorthand way to distance themselves from superstitious beliefs in haunted houses, deceptions by ventriloquists, and crude phantasmagorias that promised to bring to life the spirits of historical figures.[26]

These writers retooled this turn of phrase to mark a new mode of engagement with the built environment. Historic sites in seemingly original condition were sacred, in their eyes: they formed thresholds to the past. Like other sacred spaces, they enabled visitors to have a morally instructive encounter with another realm. Church architecture enabled worshippers to encounter the divine.[27] Cemeteries brought living generations into communion with deceased ancestors.[28] Sublime sites of natural wonder, such as Niagara Falls, prompted tourists to contemplate transcendental truth.[29] Historic sites in original condition, these accounts explained, gave present-day visitors a view of past lives that had shaped the conditions of the present day.

Writers who labeled a historic structure sacred not only characterized its features but also issued a directive about how to treat it. Their insistence on the rational effects of historic spaces on minds and hearts echoed religious revivalists who emphasized the predominance of reason and order during emotional displays of conversion and devotion.[30] Yet to characterize a historic site as sacred was not to define its nature in the context of religion. Charles DeWitt's description of Carpenters' Hall made this clear: it was "a structure that will ever be deemed sacred while rational liberty is cherished on earth."[31] Writers such as DeWitt invoked the sacred to indicate that stewards should maintain historic architecture in perpetuity. In the second quarter of the nineteenth century, this ethic charged the owners and inhabitants of sacred structures to extract them from the speculative real estate market driven by unbacked paper money, cheap construction, and transactions between parties looking to get rich quick.

Sacred Sites in an Age of Speculation

Writers developed commentary on the sacred character of historic sites to condemn two popular concerns about the economy: the rage to be rich and the business transactions that it inspired. In the early nineteenth century, travel writers steadily began to charge U.S. citizens with a peculiar brand of market-based self-interest that revealed itself in the built environment. They pointed to Americans' seeming irreverence for historic sites as evidence that they cared for nothing except the financial profits that real estate might accrue. European and American travelers steadily remarked on the demolition of Indigenous earthworks in the Ohio and Mississippi Valleys to illustrate the character of land developers in the western United States. In Circleville, Leatitia Ware and Caleb Atwater both noted that early town residents were reducing the earthworks. By 1826, a writer who printed a diagram of the earthen architecture noted that they had "been much injured and thrown down, and barbarous as it may seem, the walls have been much destroyed by carting away the earth for the purposes of brick making."[32] Farther west, in the Mississippi Valley, many travelers expressed surprise that "individual taste and municipal authority . . . failed to avail themselves of the moral interest of these mounds" and ensure that they "were preserved for future generations." Instead, as Edmund Flagg observed in St. Louis, the farmhouses and city reservoirs that intruded on these sites marked a singular devotion to "practical utility" that drove land use in the western United States as a solely economic endeavor.[33]

In Philadelphia, British traveler Basil Hall pointed to the old Pennsylvania statehouse as an example of the same phenomenon. The adoption of the Declaration of Independence at the site, he wrote, "should have hallowed the spot in the estimation of every native of that country." Yet he found "all the rich paneling, cornices, and ornamental work of this room, have been pulled down, and in their place, tame plastering and raw carpentry have been stuck up, on the occasion of some recent festival."[34] To underline his point about Americans' immoral relationship with profit, the traveler pointedly noted that he arrived at Independence Hall directly after a tour of the Second Bank of the United States just down the street. The contrast of its prominence with the neglect of the old statehouse indicated that U.S. residents profited from commercial enterprise without paying due honor to the preceding generations that had enabled it.

This critique was not just a trope that travelers used to paint passing judgments in broad strokes. U.S. residents used similar language to express growing worries that their fellow citizens pursued personal wealth at the expense of the greater good. In 1822, Bostonians became uneasy about the sale of land where the battle of Bunker Hill took place. Announcements of the impending auction did not sidestep the history of the subdivided lots.[35] Some readers certainly lamented the publication of historic associations as a sales pitch. The auctioneer of the land seemed to defend himself against such charges a few days after the initial sales announcement. Construction was booming in this neighborhood, he explained, and the land must be sold to settle an estate. However, a man of means, he suggested, might buy the battleground to preserve it and its defensive earthworks as open space, as it had stood in 1775.[36] Editors at the *Independent Chronicle and Boston Patriot* made a more direct appeal. "As a site so memorable should not be covered with buildings," they pled, a "gentleman of wealth" should make it a place "to be held sacred" for future generations.[37] Perhaps some readers reflected on the demolition that they had witnessed years before, when real estate developers in Boston had leveled Beacon Hill and its Revolutionary monument. "The spirit of speculation has in an evil hour laid it low," Caleb Snow bemoaned in his *History of Boston*, "and posterity must satisfy themselves with a dull description instead of enjoying the reality."[38]

Bostonians were not the only ones to reappraise real estate development after the panic of 1819. In Philadelphia, economic changes of the 1820s had given Deborah Norris Logan a new perspective on the sale of her family estate. In 1818, her brother had sold their childhood home on Chestnut Street to the director of the Bank of the United States for $102,000. Logan recorded several visits "to take leave of the dear Old House" before and during its demolition. It was for her "a melancholy consideration," as her time in it inspired a feeling of closeness with her deceased mother and memories of how the city looked fifty years earlier. Initially, however, she repeatedly insisted that she could not blame her brother for the demolition, "as he gets an extraordinary sum for it, and his large Family claims consideration."[39] The sale price seemed reasonable rather than greedy given his financial responsibilities.

In hindsight, however, Isaac Norris profited from an entity that had tipped off the greatest financial crisis that the young nation had faced. The bank recalled its loans as it prepared to build a new edifice. Land speculators were left holding properties suddenly devalued by half or more. Credit disappeared, and unemployment rose across the nation. Many blamed the "hard times" on citizens who had wanted to get rich quick by exchanging unbacked paper bills for inflated real estate deals rather than earning a living through labor.[40] Deborah Norris Logan never openly condemned her brother's decision. But in 1829, when Jacksonian banking policies prompted another economic dip, she characterized the bank building as a beautiful but deceptive edifice. Reflecting on the family hearth that it had replaced, she recalibrated her urban compass, remarking that she recognized the spot only by its proximity to the old statehouse. Her shift of view removed her primary reference point from the new structure that marked the site of her former family home to a century-old landmark whose stewards professed to maintain—and even restore—its historic form.[41]

Charles DeWitt encouraged a similar reorientation with his description of Carpenters' Hall: it also stood in the shadow of the Second Bank of the United States. DeWitt's description of the humble brick walls of Carpenters' Hall drew an implicit contrast with the soaring blue marble façade on the neighboring block. After its completion in 1824, the bank became a popular destination for Philadelphia visitors and one of the most celebrated buildings in the country.[42] Its eight Doric columns, perched atop a flight of stairs, propped up a massive pediment looming high above pedestrians on Chestnut Street. The bank's architect, William Strickland, delimited a paved court for the bank with a decorative cast-iron fence. By setting the freestanding building back from the street, he swelled its monumentality in an urban fabric full of conjoined row buildings set close to the street. In engraved views of the building, artists reinforced Strickland's use of classical markers of the sacred to provoke awe from viewers and convince them that they entered a special space when they stepped through the gate (Figure 21).[43]

By 1829, many observers saw the bank as a symbol of the U.S. economy. Some argued that this building attested to the modesty of private fortunes in the United States in comparison to collective wealth. In the words of one Philadelphian, it showed that "all our great works are the common property of the nation—at once the evidences and the fruits of public prosperity."[44] Observers might balk at the use of sacred forms of ancient architecture for commercial purposes, the writer continued, but history bore out the modern idiom because ancient Greeks themselves had used temples as banks. Yet critics were not swayed by this explanation, and they pointed to the contrast between the classicized forms of modern banks and the pecuniary nature of their business to characterize them as sites of moral corruption.[45] Deborah Norris Logan, for instance, registered her disapproval of the Second Bank by wistfully remarking that the building's templar form belied the profane character of its inner workings.[46] Like-minded commentators saw architecture as yet another feature of the speculative economy that could deceive as ably as confidence men and counterfeit bills.[47]

Charles DeWitt offered a different appraisal of how architecture could index morality. As newspapers reported Andrew Jackson's initial assaults on the bank and began to splinter confidence in paper money issued from its doors, DeWitt turned readers' gazes to Carpenters' Hall and invited them to enter a humbler temple of republican virtue. He described the contemporary scene to offer up thoughts on how the stewardship of particular buildings, not their

Figure 21. The Second Bank of the United States, designed by William Strickland and completed in 1824, became one of the most celebrated U.S. buildings of its era. Travel accounts rarely failed to comment on its appearance, and they frequently remarked on the implications of housing a financial institution in a temple-like building. Commentary on the bank was part of a broader conversation about the architecture of the market—a subject that encompassed historic buildings as well as new ones. George Strickland, "United States Bank," engraved by William E. Tucker, frontispiece, *Souvenir* (Philadelphia, 1827). Courtesy American Antiquarian Society.

symbolic design, spoke to concerns about the speculative economy. In an age when many property owners sold historic properties to the highest bidder or leveled old structures to maximize revenue, DeWitt praised the artisan owners for keeping the building in its original state. Noisy occupants made clear the drawbacks of renting out the edifice for quotidian business. Indeed, the Carpenters' Company let rooms for the "best rent" that they could procure.[48] But their tenants also demonstrated their landlord's decision to maintain the historic building rather than sell the property or renovate it for a bigger windfall. In DeWitt's account, the resident auctioneer provided more of a foil for the carpenters' stewardship than a sign of their failure. While the salesman trafficked in second-rate goods for the highest profits he could bring, the carpenters used their professional skills and their rental income to keep the building in original condition, as they would "by no means part with it, or consent to any alteration." When DeWitt called for the continued preservation of the building "for ages," he held up the carpenters as models of moral real estate management in the modern commercial economy.[49]

Views that shifted from the Second Bank to historic buildings nearby heralded the growth of commentary on the sacred character of historic structures after the economic dip of 1829. To some observers, the commercial use of sacred buildings as commodities or settings for speculative transactions formed a cardinal sin of republican morality: the worship of Mammon. Writers who advocated for the preservation of historic sites in this language joined a broader conversation about the nature of capitalism and society in the late 1820s and 1830s. Many Christian reformers in Britain and the United States evangelized by condemning a seemingly new materialism as a form of Mammon worship. They pointed to people who pursued the accumulation of worldly riches as sinners who ignored the lessons of the gospels. Secular writers also adopted this vocabulary as social commentary on the evils of industrializing society. Too many capitalists, they wrote, aspired to live in the lap of luxury by eschewing labor in favor of speculation. Many contrasted the material conditions of laborers and countryfolk with industrialists and the new urban bourgeoisie to expose unjust inequalities of wealth created by men who got rich at the expense of others.[50] Political cartoonists joined the conversation as well, condemning elected officials, economic leaders, and voters with depictions of wealth and luxury. They often characterized the Second Bank of the United States as the object of their devotion, portraying it as the Temple of Mammon in popular prints that filled taverns, streets, and parlors (Figure 22).[51]

Commentary on the materialism of Mammon worship gained traction in the partisan press during the economic instability of the 1830s. When Andrew Jackson removed federal deposits from the Second Bank of the United States in late 1833 and redistributed the funds in various state banks, paper notes flooded the market. After a brief panic, this paper money propped up a boom in speculation well under way by early 1834.[52] Credit, inflation of paper bills, and speculation in real estate expanded steadily for three years. Speculators targeted western lands not yet populated by U.S. citizens and population centers ripe for urban development, clearing forests and town lots to put up new buildings. Jackson's Specie Circular, demanding hard money in exchange for federal lands, had little effect on the broader speculative real estate market in buying and building. A broad array of individuals bought into the fiction of land owning by putting down a small amount of paper money, often seeking to perpetuate a loop of selling higher and faster the next time.

As market bubbles burst, many commentators turned to historic structures to condemn real estate speculators as a source of collective economic woes. When the panic of 1837 unmasked the illusory state of property value and ownership across the United States, a number of writers contrasted the enduring presence of historic architecture with the evanescence of land titles and prices in the

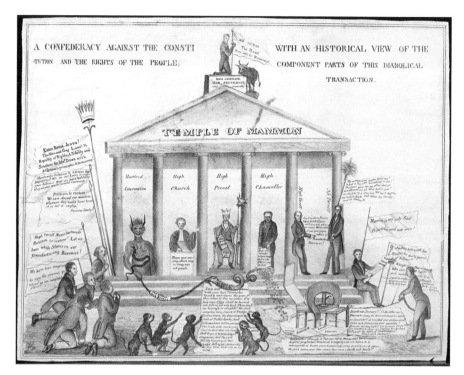

Figure 22. Political cartoonists joined social reformers in expressing concerns about speculative economies in the terms of Mammon worship. Here, a lithographer labels the Second Bank of the United States as the Temple of Mammon to portray men such as Henry Clay, Nicholas Biddle, and John C. Calhoun as supplicants to false wealth created by the institution. The notoriety of the bank building informed appraisals of historic structures whose architecture formed a stark contrast to its classical, templar form. [Seth Luther?], "A Confederacy Against the Constitution and the Rights of the People; with an Historical View of the Component Parts of the Diabolical Transaction" ([1833?]). The Library Company of Philadelphia.

speculative market.[53] If speculation was, according to one critic, "justly considered gambling—giving fictitious property a value, and affixing to actual property a fictitious and exaggerated worth," then preservation accounted for the worth of property in stable terms of material viability and social use.[54] Unlike previous generations, these advocates of preservation turned their sights to properties owned by individual citizens rather than corporate entities. Under their lens, the demolition of historic architecture exposed the falsehoods of speculative dealings in the solidity of old structures.

Take, for instance, a newspaper report of the demolition of the oldest house in Springfield, Massachusetts, in 1831. Anglo-American colonizer John Pyncheon had built the structure in Pocumtuc and Nipmuc territory around 1660. Generations later, the antiquated features of the house, like its jetty, peaked gables, composite chimneys, and porch tower, drew the attention of onlookers. In 1831, one writer pointed to the solidity of the fabric to double the weight of arguments for its preservation. The "immense chimneys," brick walls "of considerable thickness," "ponderous oaken door," and "timbers of massy oak" that had withstood nearly two centuries of battering "would probably have stood firm another hundred years." It was a shame, he continued, "that something had not been done to spare the old fabric—to continue it along to generations that would look upon it with more interest than we possibly can,—or at least suffer it to go to natural decay." The townspeople of Springfield "could have endured that the hand of time should remove brick by brick from the edifice till all should be levelled by stern Ruin's ploughshare," he continued. "But that the only remaining structure reared by the first settlers should be demolished at once—that the last visible link in the chain that bound us to those venerable men should be broken at a blow, seems like sacrilege."[55] The writer summoned sacred language to criticize the property owner for ignoring the architectural significance of the house to cash in on the value of land in the real estate market.

Other writers developed this critique by drawing attention to the shoddiness of new construction that replaced sturdy predecessors. In the 1830s, speculative builders used new methods of construction and finance to build structures qualitatively different from previous ones. On both sides of the Atlantic, investors with no connection to the building trades began to use mortgage finance to commission construction projects solely for the generation of capital. The terms of credit encouraged laborers to build quickly and cheaply, producing rental properties not intended to survive multiple generations. New construction technologies and materials that enabled builders to raise structures with unprecedented speed and scale formed a visual contrast with older buildings. Lighter frames of uniform dimension lumber, often nailed together, replaced the hierarchical construction of mortise-and-tenon beams uncovered by the era's demolitions. Standardized façades and exterior finishes of new buildings often aligned with the same regularity as their interior framing members. Inside, speculative builders often skimped on finishes out of public view.[56]

In the United States, observers associated these architectural characteristics with a new type of distinctively American real estate speculation. As the economy vacillated and then plunged into a five-year depression in 1837, writers expounded on this contrast to critique a market culture that threatened economic and social collapse when shaky morals met flimsy materials. In the months after the 1837 panic, twenty-nine-year-old Edmund Quincy issued an extended commentary on the subject in his essay "Old Houses." In the persona of an elderly man, identified by the pseudonymous initials Y. D., the young son of Boston's recent mayor narrated a walk through the streets of modern Boston.[57] As he recounted the appearances of old houses and their historic associations, Quincy

adopted the sensory language of the sacred to express the value of these structures. From the mansions of exiled loyalists to the humble wooden abode of
Benjamin Franklin's childhood, his narrator explained, old houses "speak to me
of the Past" as they evoked the sights and sounds of previous generations. "If
walls had tongues as well as ears," exclaimed the narrator, "what histories might
not these unfold!" When they were demolished, he felt the loss deeply: "The pick-
axe," he wrote, "enters my soul."[58]

Quincy's narrator warned that all old houses risked becoming figments of his
imagination in the hands of the city's real estate developers. Like Caleb Snow had
done thirteen years earlier, Quincy pointed to the former courtyard of the
seventeenth-century Province House to exemplify his fear. There stood "a star-
ing row of vulgar modern brick houses; presuming, like some upstarts newly rich,
to turn their backs to their betters." Another tract once occupied by a Georgian
pile had "given place also to a crowd of upstart heirs, who perk their common-
place, vulgar visages in your face as if they were of better worth than the noble
ancestral stock from which they sprung." These new types of buildings, such as
the line of brick rowhouses that the author described, were "all stark alike, as if
they had been run in the same stark mould—meaningless, soul-less masses of
matter."[59] They represented the "style of house, carriages, dress and table" that
another writer had described in Boston that same year: they marked a fortune
newly enriched—and often suddenly deflated—by speculation.[60]

In Quincy's view, many new buildings personified the thinness of character
and instability of their investors, whom Quincy characterized as Mammon worshippers. This "round-hatted, frock-coated, breeches-less generation" kowtowed
at templar banks and their fonts of paper money. Looking to get rich quick, these
speculators assessed the value of real estate solely in terms of dollars and cents.
"Too few, alas! of these abodes, consecrated by the memory of departed worth,"
exclaimed Quincy, "have escaped the ruthless hands of the money lovers of our
age; who regard one of my dear old houses as only so much improveable real estate; and who think of nothing when they gaze on its time-honored walls but
how much the old materials will bring." When it came to real estate transactions,
no property was off limits for development by this "stereotyped edition of
humanity—all bound alike, and not differing much in the nature and value of
their contents," much like the monolithic new rowhouses that they built. They
enacted their damage most often in the form of business corporations, which mul-
tiplied thanks to recent acts of general incorporation. "It is well that corporations have no souls," Quincy bemoaned, "or I fear that the one that delivered up
this last stronghold of the Past into the hands of the Philistines would stand in
fearful peril of utter perdition."[61] By enabling the proliferation of economic actors with no intellectual, spiritual, or emotional constitution, Quincy implied,

Plate 1. This Masonic apron, created and used in Rhode Island during the 1780s, depicts the architectural imagery of freemasonry in the early United States. Ohio Company members from this tristate region of New England would have envisioned the stairs and floor of King Solomon's temple in a similar way. This imagery informed their conceptions of Indigenous earthworks and their appropriation of these sites for urban sociability and Masonic ritual. Davis W. Hoppin, Masonic apron, leather and fiber with pencil drawing, 1783, RHi X17 1265. Courtesy Rhode Island Historical Society.

Plate 2. This view of Boston Common depicts the type of urban improvement of public greens that Ohio Company leaders hoped to inculcate in Marietta. Well-attired couples of men and women stroll along the mall, represented by an alley of trees in the foreground of the image. John Hancock's mansion sits on the opposite side of the grassy expanse behind a uniform line of planted trees and a neat fence. Rufus Putnam invoked these features of the site when he articulated his plans for Marietta's urban squares. Christian Remick, "A Prospective View of Part of the Commons," watercolor, 1768. Courtesy Concord Museum, www.concordmuseum.org.

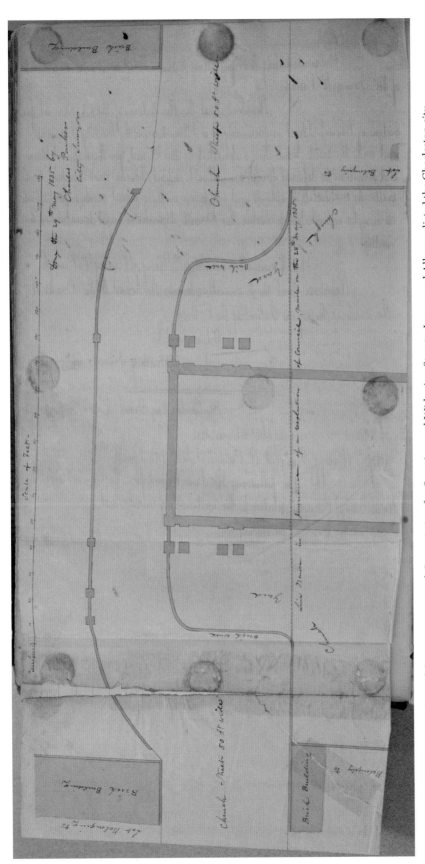

Plate 3. Members of the state-appointed Commission for Opening and Widening Streets, Lanes, and Alleys enlisted the Charleston city surveyor to make this plan of the St. Philip's site on May 29, 1835. Pink figures represent masonry features, including the foundation, column piers, and churchyard wall of the burned building. The yellow line marks the street width planned by the city council—a proposition that required the vestry to set back its church building forty-eight feet. The state commissioners overruled the city council and widened the street by only twenty-two feet in part because of the historic features of the church and its burial ground. Journal of the Board of Commissioners for Opening and Widening of Streets, Lanes and Alleys, June 6, 1835, p. 61, Charleston Archive. Courtesy Charleston County Public Library.

A VIEW OF THE LATE PROTESTANT DUTCH CHURCH in the CITY of ALBANY.

This Venerable Edifice was situated at the junction of State Market & Court streets. It was erected A.D. 1715 & Pulled down A.D. 1806. It included within its walls the site of a Church the corner stone whereof was laid by Rutger Jacobsen A.D. 1656.

Plate 4. In 1806, Henry Snyder produced a second print of a recently demolished church building in Albany. He returned to the plate after an initial run of architectural prints and set the church building in its urban context. This environmental view preserved an image of the demolished building in a narrative of city development. Philip Hooker, del., Henry Snyder, engraver, John Low, printer, "A View of the Late Protestant Dutch Church in the City of Albany," 1806. Courtesy American Antiquarian Society.

Plate 5. Benjamin Henry Latrobe was only one of the most notable travelers who sketched historic houses to record the appearance of antiquated architectural features and the historical associations embedded in them. Here, Latrobe depicted the seventeenth-century mansion of colonial Virginia governor William Berkeley, when the architect was invited to assess the structure's potential for renovation. Latrobe enumerated the interesting historical features of the house's interior and exterior and lamented that the house would not suit the new proprietor's desire for a modern domicile. Benjamin Henry Latrobe, "Greenspring, home of William Ludwell Lee," c. 1796, in Latrobe Sketchbooks, Museum Department. Courtesy Maryland Historical Society, item # 1960.108.1.2.33.

Plate 6. In 1831, domestic writer Eliza Leslie published *Cards of Boston*, a game that would teach players about historic sites in the city. She denominated categories of sites that included domestic spaces, such as the "Clarke House" and "Old Houses," as well as public places such as "Cemeteries" and "Churches." As players drew cards to match their category suits, they gleaned interior views of historic houses through Leslie's prose. Eliza Leslie, *Cards of Boston: Comprizing a Variety of Facts and Descriptions Relative to That City, in Past and Present Times* (Boston: Munroe and Fennels, 1831). Courtesy American Antiquarian Society.

Plate 7.   The brick house built by James B. Clay and Thomas Lewinski still stands at 120 Sycamore Road in Lexington, Kentucky. Clay's widow, Susan Jacob Clay, sold Ashland to Kentucky University in 1866, but Henry Clay's granddaughter purchased the estate for a family residence in 1882. It is administered by the Henry Clay Memorial Foundation, founded by Henry Clay's descendants in 1926, and is open for public tours ten months of each year. Courtesy Ashland, the Henry Clay Estate, Lexington, Kentucky.

Plate 8.   At nearly two-by-three feet, John Sartain's 1853 engraving of Ashland was reportedly the largest landscape view to be produced in the United States at the time. Sartain rendered his engraving from a triptych of daguerreotypes taken by Kentucky's prominent photographer John M. Hewitt; Henry Clay's son Thomas declared it to be so accurate that it preserved the old home from decay. One owner of this print, however, merged this image of the old Ashland with a vision of the new one by coloring the walls of the house red, invoking the brick façade of the new house on the form of the demolished one. John Sartain, engraver, "Ashland, the Homestead of Henry Clay" (Louisville: F. Hegan, 1853). Kentucky Historical Society, 1985.6.

BOSTONIANS!

SAVE THE

OLD JOHN HANCOCK MANSION

THERE IS TIME YET, ALTHOUGH THE WORK OF

DEMOLITION HAS COMMENCED

It is a question of some perplexity to decide how far it is wise or proper for the city government or for individuals to interfere to prevent the act of modern vandalism which demands the destruction of this precious relic; for that it is destroyed, in effect, if removed, we conceive admits of no question. Will it, or will it not, be a mitigation of the public disgrace to establish the house itself elsewhere as a perpetual monument of the proceeding.

Without wishing in the least degree to discourage the public spirit and the patriotism of those gentlemen in the City Council who are seeking at this moment to do the best thing they can for the preservation of the house, we still think it right that one preliminary appeal should be made to the present owners. They are gentlemen of wealth, they have made an honest purchase, and of course may plead that they have a right to do what they will with their own. It is with full recognition of their rights in this respect, and withal in the utmost kindness to them, that we would admonish them how dearly is purchased any good thing which costs the sacrifice of public associations so dear and so noble as those that cluster around the Hancock House.

These purchasers must at any rate be prepared to hear, during the whole of their lives and that of their remotest posterity, so long as any of them may live in the elegant modern palaces which shall supplant the ancient structure, the frequent expression of public discontent. Argument may show them blameless, but sentiment will ever condemn the proceeding in which theirs will be perhaps the most innocent, but nevertheless the most permanent part. It is not often that an opportunity is given to men of wealth to earn a title to public gratitude by an act of simple self-denial. Such an opportunity falls to the lot of the purchasers of this estate.

Published by T. O. H. P. Burnham, Boston, June 6, 1863.

Published by Burnham

Plate 9.   T. O. H. P. Burnham's broadsides urged Bostonians to save the Hancock House from an "act of modern vandalism." Though historians have pointed to this call for preservation as one of the earliest public campaigns, Burnham's posters drew on appeals to market morality and civil society that U.S. residents had used to encourage architectural permanence for many decades. T. O. H. P. Burnham, "Bostonians! Save the Old John Hancock Mansion," Boston, Mass., dated June 6, 1863, broadside. Courtesy Historic New England.

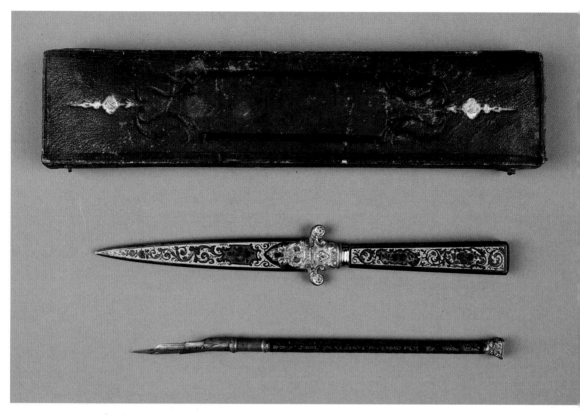

Plate 10. Ann Pamela Cunningham, founder of the Mount Vernon Ladies' Association, bequeathed to the organization this pen, which she used to sign the contract to purchase Mount Vernon from John A. Washington III. Its importance to Cunningham in shaping her legacy—and that of the MVLA more broadly—speaks to the culmination of early national debates over preservation in a definition that complemented rather than challenged the operations of a free real estate market. Pen, letter opener, and case, object M-661/A-C. Courtesy Mount Vernon Ladies Association.

U.S. corporation law minimized personal responsibility for market behavior and threatened the health of society.[62]

Quincy's essay consolidated a popular view of architecture as a bellwether of the motives of market actors. To many, buildings encapsulated the ways that immoral market behavior could wreck not only individual fortunes but also the health of U.S. economy and society.[63] Such commentaries swelled in 1837. In the wake of a transatlantic financial constriction, legal rulings in the United States seemed to propel a particularly nationalist rage to be rich that drove excessive speculation. In settling disputes over corporate property, U.S. courts regularly equated the public good with change in the built environment. The U.S. Supreme Court seemed to consolidate and confirm this trend in February 1837, when justices handed down the *Charles River Bridge v. Warren Bridge* decision that introduced the philosophy of "creative destruction" to the business landscape and built environment. This principle held that governments should not be bound to enforce legal terms, such as charters, deemed to be detrimental to the public. As it diminished the exclusivity of corporate privilege in the name of removing monopolistic holds on local economies, it encouraged the proliferation of new corporations. This translated to increased support for environmental change in conflicts over land use, as U.S. courts equated the public good with business development that engendered environmental impermanence.[64]

Critics turned to the past to define the values that they wished to guide modern economy and society. In an 1837 pamphlet, a writer calling himself "Old-Fashioned Man" identified the youth of the United States as its blessing and its curse: "We do not regret that we have no time honored abuses to cling to—but we do regret that there is not something to check the spirit of innovation."[65] With individualism unrestrained by national institutions, "overweening confidence in self, overrated ideas of capacity or ability,—excessive *self-esteem*" was "a main cause of the crazy speculations, and false pride, which have done their share" toward producing economic downturn.[66] U.S. residents, as a result, spent every dollar and false compliment possible "to appear in the eyes of the world, rich and liberal."[67] This desire to create appearances engendered rivalries at every level of social organization in the United States: nations, states, towns, families, and individuals.[68] All Americans, the writer charged, not just political leaders or bankers or speculators, bore the blame of promoting an economic culture that valued self-interest and acquisitiveness over honest industry.

Writers who described historic sites in sacred language believed that architectural preservation could provide the check to self-love that drove acquisitiveness and threatened to destroy civil society. They characterized historic structures as sacred not because they were timeless but because their historically specific forms created a temporal threshold that brought observers closer to a particular moment in the past. Demolition of these sites, in this view, constituted a deliberate act of individual and generational self-centeredness. A person who destroyed a site such as the old Pyncheon house or Carpenters' Hall severed a connection to the past for himself, his contemporary peers, *and* succeeding generations. As Edmund Quincy put it in 1838,

> It is hard to summon to our mind's eye, by the necromancy of the imagination, the venerable forms in which our fathers dwelt upon the earth, and to place ourselves, as it were, in the bodily presence in their midst. . . . It is hard to reconstruct by fancy's aid, the abodes in which our fathers dwelt on earth, after the hand of the destroyer had passed over them, but it is harder still to recall into a realized existence the chambers of the soul, the labyrinthal mazes of the human heart, and people them with the emotions which struggled for the mastery within their secret recesses.[69]

The demolition of sites in seemingly original historic condition, in other words, perpetrated an uncivil act whose damage to intergenerational ties and civic feelings was irreversible.

When writers such as Charles DeWitt and Edmund Quincy encouraged citizens to think of future generations as they shaped the built environment, they defined their vision of preservation as an act of empathy—a quality that religious and humanitarian reformers increasingly prized as the prime expression of moral character.[70] This historicized form of empathy pivoted to look to the future as well as to the past and constituted a multigenerational citizenry in secular civil society. Participants demonstrated care for fellow citizens—past, present, and future—by making individual sacrifices of maximum financial wealth to achieve environmental permanence. This definition of preservation delineated the physical bounds of the real estate market to minimize the social impact of personal financial risk. Property owners, it argued, should practice market restraint and keep these properties out of speculative deals. This meant that property owners needed to secure a clear title, not burdened by unbacked debt or mortgage, and resist selling the tract for the highest price. If they had to sell, they should seek a long-term steward as grantee to prevent the real estate from becoming "fast property," exchanged in transactions that occurred in quick succession and without residual obligations.[71] In so doing, property owners minimized the risk that historic spaces would be shaped by the whims of the market, falling into the hands of a financially powerless debtor or a speculator or creditor with interest only in maximizing profit. Secured by these principles of real estate management, historic structures promised to reinforce moral limits on the pursuit of profit in ways that muted growing sectarian divides, expanded the exclusive bounds of familial ancestor worship, and constituted evidence of so-called national progress.

Preservation and Jacksonian Politics

Many U.S. residents responded to the intensification of economic booms and busts by developing fuller-throated calls for the in situ preservation of historic sites in original condition. Purveyors of this discourse of sacred preservation plied it to give moral heft to their political stances in a shifting landscape of partisanship and factions. Supporters of Andrew Jackson had thrashed together a national coalition just long enough to put the Democratic candidate in office under the name of political reform. But urban workers, yeomen farmers, elite planters, and some scions of northern families all continued to hash out what sort of changes the new regime would bring. They did so against lingering nationalists, much more willing to legislate support for manufacturing and transportation improvements as well as codify religiously inspired moral reforms.[72] A number of young and middle-aged partisans developed calls for sacred preservation to advocate for agendas that many mainstream political partisans considered progressive or even radical.[73] They hoped their appeals would constitute a type of moral reform that strict political economy could not inculcate. The ethic of architectural preservation, they hoped, might appeal to men who shunned the paternalistic and restrictive moralizing of reform societies and the growing economic power of their subscribers but who wanted to engage with an issue of common concern: economic morality.

Charles DeWitt's description of Carpenters' Hall exemplifies the way that Jacksonians used preservation to define market morality in a partisan coalition reluctant to join evangelical social reforms. On his way to Congress, DeWitt united the interests of New York and Virginia Democrats with an appreciation for the enduring strength of a Pennsylvania workingmen's association and its property ownership.[74] DeWitt supported Martin Van Buren's alliance of Jacksonians who championed expanded rights for common men, including public education and universal white male suffrage. It is no surprise that he looked to Carpenters' Hall as well as the Virginia statehouse as sites that exuded the spirit of Patrick Henry and Thomas Jefferson, historic champions of democratic rights.[75] As late editor of the *Ulster Sentinel*, DeWitt used the partisan press to foster an interregional partisan consciousness with a celebration of these sites and their previous inhabitants: he directed his letter to the influential Virginian Thomas Ritchie, who reprinted it in his well-read Richmond *Enquirer*.[76]

Like many of his peers, DeWitt drew on the contemporary politics of Revolutionary memory impelled by the fiftieth anniversary of the War for Independence. At a moment of great partisan transition, DeWitt invoked the Revolutionary generation to cohere a new national party under the banner of the Old Republicans, united in their desire to attenuate the powers of the federal government. DeWitt linked Henry's ascendance from humble origins and his antiaristocratic politics to Philadelphia carpenters in the present day to channel new goodwill between northern and southern Democrats. Yet DeWitt spoke primarily about the treatment of Carpenters' Hall in the modern city to praise the virtues of artisans in contrast to commercial men. He characterized the building's owners and occupants not according to their knowledge of the building's revolutionary occupants but in light of their care for the structure. DeWitt's account of the sensory effects of the building's architecture acclaimed the artisans for maintaining it. It also reproached the tenants who sullied these spaces with commercial activities.[77]

Whereas DeWitt sought to inspire interregional solidarity against commercial men, a number of elite white writers turned to fiction to promote market morality in partisan arts and culture. Evert A. Duyckinck and Nathaniel Hawthorne both described the edifying effects of historic architecture in periodical organs of the Young America movement. Their prose modeled an ethic of voluntary market restraint in a literary form that also fulfilled the platform's cultural ambitions for the modern United States. Their tales operated as instructive counterparts to Gothic stories about superstitious beliefs and hauntings of old houses. The stories of Edgar Allan Poe, for instance, sketched architectural characteristics and historical associations so sensuously compelling that they threatened to swell the imagination to predominate over reason. When his protagonists let this happen, personal ruin ensued. Poe's "Fall of the House of Usher," for instance, turned an ancestral estate into an infectious environment that threatened physical illness and mental unrest.[78]

The prose of Duyckinck and Hawthorne, however, modeled the maintenance of a rational, embodied view of the past over a superstitious one. Hawthorne frequently played on the spooky entertainment value afforded by old houses. As he put it in one of his tales of the Province House in 1838, "In the course of generations, when many people have lived and died in an ancient house, the whistling of the wind through its crannies, and the creaking of its beams and rafters, become strangely like the tones of the human voice, or thundering laughter, or heavy footsteps treading the deserted chambers. It is as if the echoes of half a century were revived."[79] Yet readers and visitors to historic sites, he suggested, could revel in a sensorial simile—"It is *as if* the echoes of half a century were revived"—only if they first pinpointed the logical cause of eerie sounds.[80]

When Nathaniel Hawthorne published his "Legends of the Province House" in four installments in the *U.S. Magazine and Democratic Review* in 1838 and 1839, he encouraged readers to make this rational view of historic sites and their preservation a part of their political campaign for modernization.[81] Under the editorship of John Louis O'Sullivan, the magazine served as the most popular mouthpiece for a Democratic faction that promoted the expansion of locally funded transportation, national borders, and market capitalism as engines of popular prosperity.[82] Hawthorne's stories offered readers a narrative frame that followed a protagonist into the seventeenth-century Province House as it stood in contemporary Boston as a tavern kept by Thomas Waite.[83] By viewing the building through the eyes of a modern visitor, Hawthorne gave himself a platform not only for telling the history of the Province House but also for teaching his readers how to see architecture as laudable evidence of past lives that should be maintained apart from commercial development.

Hawthorne described a building that contemporary passersby would recognize. Waite advertised its history on his tavern sign, much as John Doyle did in Philadelphia.[84] The building's features attested to its past as well: its Dutch bricks, red freestone steps, Indian weathervane, wide front door, wrought-iron balustrade, and anchor plates in the "letters and figures—16 P.S. 79" all marked its age. Inside, however, commercial society obscured extant evidence of the past. The new stores on Washington Street cloaked the rooms in shadows, and a "bar in the modern style," stagecoach schedules, and partitions for boarding rooms filled the colonial interior. Yet for those willing to look hard enough, original elements of the house provided a portal to another era. The building's façade, wainscoting, Dutch fireplace tiles, staircase, and "ponderous whiteoak framework, so much more massive than the frames of modern houses," all helped to enliven the historic tales that Hawthorne recounted for his readers.[85] "In truth," sighed Hawthorne's narrator, "it is desperately hard work, when we attempt to throw the spell of hoar antiquity over localities with which the living world, and the day that is passing over us, have aught to do."[86] Yet as Hawthorne told a story about his protagonist bringing attention to the house's history, the author himself brought Waite's "forgotten mansion almost as effectually into public view as if we had thrown down the vulgar range of shoe-shops and dry-good stores, which hides its aristocratic front from Washington street."[87] In this way, Hawthorne made his fiction a civic counterweight to the market development that he and the *Democratic Review* championed.

Park Benjamin published stories of the same ilk in the *American Monthly Magazine*, including the essays of Evert A. Duyckinck writing under the pseudonym "Felix Merry."[88] Duyckinck, who carried the name of his colonizing forefather, espoused the expansionist, improvement-oriented, and internationalist ethos of budding Young America. In one installment for the magazine in 1838, Duyckinck propounded the virtues of city dwellers. To his mind, urban density cultivated benevolence and intellectualism, not the vice and deception more typically attributed to it. City environments spoke to this superiority, remarkable not only for the security of communal living but also for the local historic record it created. Churches, tombs, and old houses provided supremely evocative sources for history and literature. "If walls had but human voices," Duyckinck wrote, "they could tell more interesting tales than the most inventive novelist ever contrived; they are strange confidants to all the goodness and evil of life." For passersby willing to take a look, the buildings' carved wainscoting, floral wallpaper, and turned balusters made old houses ancient interlocutors. Duyckinck heard them "utter . . . homilies" in their distinctive visual language, and he "listened to many a discourse from the frequent ruins of some old family mansion" in the developing city.[89]

That these "treatises" arose from the work of wrecking crews spoke to a shortcoming of city life, in Duyckinck's account: the love of wealth that shaped urban society. Across Manhattan, the rubble of family homes, old churches, and even ancestral tombs marked the remnants of sites "removed before the march of Mammon." This "premature destruction" contrasted with one admirable feature of country life, that rural residents let "the slow hand of time" work at a steady pace without the "rude violence" of demolition. Country churches decayed, whereas Manhattan laborers lit upon houses of worship "like a band of evil spirits in an Arabian tale sent to destroy the favorite work of a good deity."[90] Duyckinck's use of this sensory and sacred language insisted that readers see architecture as more than commercial real estate. In turn, he imagined a new way of urban life that insisted that U.S. improvement must attend to the intellectual value of the material world, not only its financial potential.

Hawthorne's and Duyckinck's prose echoed the exclamations of the "Old Houses" essay that Edmund Quincy had published in the *American Monthly Magazine* in 1837.[91] Yet while Quincy's moralizing prose rang true for Young Americans in the late 1830s, he rehearsed critiques of capitalism for a different cause: Garrisonian antislavery. Quincy subscribed to the *Liberator* the same month that he published "Old Houses," and he began meeting regularly with Maria Chapman, Wendell Phillips, and antislavery activists who traveled to Boston.[92] Quincy's family wealth arose in part from slaveholding, and returns on real estate enabled him to forgo a paying job in legal practice after he graduated from Harvard College in 1829. He used this seat of privilege, perhaps uncritically, to write historical and abolitionist prose condemning the market economy with harmonized critiques of the exploitation of land and human capital.[93] In the 1840s, when Quincy edited and wrote for the *National Anti-Slavery Standard*, he used his observations of historic sites in the 1830s to diagnose commercial corruption for a new audience.[94] In 1847, he invoked his visit to Benjamin Franklin's childhood home in 1838 to advance his political agenda. By contrasting the building's seemingly original appearance under the care of Payton Stewart with later renovations that demolished its façade with "two monstrously disproportionated show-windows," Quincy equated the African American man's loss of the building with a loss for U.S. civil society. Commercial interests would demolish the building soon, Quincy predicted, "when the rise in real estate in that neighbourhood shall seal its doom."[95] Quincy's preservation appeal was already a decade old when he printed it in the *Standard*, yet it presaged the critique of capitalists that free labor ideology would make in the following years.

Newspaper editors expanded their commentaries on the character of historic structures not only to support preservation efforts but also to oppose them. Many inflected the partisan stances of their periodicals by arguing that old buildings made worthy sacrifices for communal prosperity. Some lauded the ways that architecture connected onlookers to the past only to elevate the structures that replaced them as worthy substitutes. In the spring of 1839, a writer for the Salem, Massachusetts, *Observer* chronicled the material history of the so-called Henfield house. It stood as one of the oldest buildings in town, "a complete specimen of the dwelling-house architecture of olden time—huge oak beams, sharp roof and low stud,—the lower room being only about five feet, eight inches in the clear." The writer gave a view of the house and the artifacts revealed by its disassembly as workers demolished it to make way for a railroad. "What a story of events and changes, this old house could have told, had it the power of remembrance, and a tongue!" the writer exclaimed. Yet he used his praise to demonstrate the superior value of the financial prosperity enabled by its demolition. In his mind, it was a "wonder that such an old shell has been suffered so long to stand in the very heart of the city—upon some of the most valuable land in the centre of business." Its demolition, he continued, would "add much to the value of several estates upon each of these streets,—Those in the rear of the old house in question, will be brought out upon a spacious street,—while the opposite block, will be, as it were, thrown into Essex street,—as eligible for business as those directly upon our thoroughfare."[96] This imagery reversed common complaints of new commercial buildings occluding ancient edifices to praise the demolition of old buildings as a lamentable but necessary cost of economic growth.

After the panic of 1837, editors of the Philadelphia *Public Ledger* appealed to underemployed workers with the outright condemnation of characterizing historic buildings as sacred. This reversed the position that they had taken the previous fall, when they lamented the poor condition of the old statehouse as a disgrace to city residents. Its shabby condition and sign-plastered walls stood as a source of local shame, they argued, under the gaze of visitors to the birthplace of the Declaration. The presence of commercial enterprise under the roof of Independence Hall particularly rankled the editors: "We perceive that councils have at length passed a resolution forbidding its devotion to purposes for which money is taken, without their special consent. It ought not to be devoted to such a purpose, even with their consent; but should be set apart as a sacred spot, and never be profaned by being converted into a booth for the exhibition of shows and its walls disfigured with lying placards and scurrilous lampoons."[97] When credit dried up the following spring, however, and laborers struggled to make a living, *Ledger* editors changed their tune.[98]

In the absence of a committed partisan readership and funds from long-term advertisers, *Ledger* publishers appealed to the city residents who needed jobs to draw in daily readers.[99] When one reader sent them a condemnation of the demolition of the old courthouse, *Ledger* editors reported it only to refute it. The writer venerated the old courthouse as a cherished remnant of the city's past. For him, it evoked the voice of the famed evangelist George Whitefield, who had "hallowed" it with sermons preached from its balcony in the mid-eighteenth century. A grander, modern headhouse planned in its place constituted a "modern misnamed improvement," he argued; it did not ease traffic jams and made an opulent genuflection to market culture.[100] *Ledger* editors pushed back. The writer exemplified the local attitude that they had bemoaned the previous month: Philadelphia remained inert, "sitting with folded arms," while other cities, such as New York, sped ahead, "advancing with rapid strides on the road to improvement and wealth."[101] Preservation formed "a check to all advancement, to all exertion for improving the physical and moral condition of mankind." Whitefield, they argued, "imparted no sanctity to the brick and mortar of the Court House." It, and even the old statehouse, should come down to make way for improved architecture that would inculcate a "salutary moral effect" among city residents. Contemporary generations could honor the memory of Whitefield and architects of U.S. independence, they argued, by continuing the legacy of their deeds and hanging their portraits in public buildings. In the *Ledger*'s editorial opinion, "To say that an awkward, inconvenient, rat devoured, worm eaten edifice is to be preserved, because this great man once inhabited it, or dined in it, or slept in it, or paced its mouldering floors, is to make a draft upon ignorant superstition, and not upon enlightened veneration."[102] Advocates of preservation, in other words, succumbed to the very irrationalities that they tried to deny.

The newspaper editors did not stop there. They launched a preemptive defense against charges of Mammon worship. "We are not among those who would prostrate every thing, even to the tombs of our fathers, in vile worship of the 'almighty dollar,' for we thoroughly detest and despise all the feelings of such worshippers," they wrote. "We have no respect for wealth in the abstract," they continued, "and no other sentiment than contempt for those gilded blockheads, those specimens of wealthy *animalism*, before which a majority of mankind crook the knee with profound obeisance."[103] The lengths to which the *Ledger* editors went to disengage their arguments from the archetypal speculator marked the success of preservation proponents in twinning the condemnation of the destruction of historic sites with the greed of their demolishers.

In slaveholding states, writers harnessed sacred appeals for preservation to vindicate political stances defined by sectional discord. In the fall of 1837, for instance, recently retired Senator John Tyler gave an anniversary address at the Yorktown battlefield that argued for its preservation as a stand against economic and political corruption. Tyler had returned to Virginia the previous year after resigning his Senate seat and his Jacksonian loyalties. Disheartened and broke even before the panic, he composed his Yorktown address as he sought to build new financial and political standing.[104] Tyler saw the battleground as an enduring landmark, unchanged amid a field of decay. The "ennobling objects around him, picture to his mind deeds there enacted in days long gone by," he explained, each "a proud memento of a glorious past: they speak to us of other times, and of other men."[105] True to genre, Tyler used auditory language to describe the emotional as well as intellectual effects of the doubled spatial experience enabled by the field. The site's "speaking relics" gave onlookers a direct view of the past and moved Tyler to narrate the battle as if it unfolded before the celebrants. Though he began to tell the history of the spot in the past tense—"*that* redoubt was stormed by Lafayette"—he quickly fell into the present tense. "Silence at length succeeds the thunders of artillery. A white flag is seen waving from those ramparts. . . . It pleads for mercy," he narrated. Yorktown was not a hub of commerce or a particularly beautiful place in 1837, Tyler admitted, but it deserved reverent study by visitors because it was a place where "the memory of the past comes over us like a living reality."[106]

In describing Yorktown as sacred, Tyler articulated a moral critique of the U.S. economy in principle rather than policy—a strategy that would help forge a new partnership with southern Whigs, who worked to bring him and other disaffected conservative Democrats into the fold. The committee of Virginians who requested John Tyler's speech at Yorktown—the "Williamsburg Guards"—felt that his speech would work "to stop the onward course of corruption, ere we rush into the maelstrom where nought is heard but the continual death-song of nations."[107] Tyler leveled his own entreaty for preservation as a diatribe against Mammon worship. "Corruption now spreads over the land; the spirit of cupidity stalks abroad, and Mammon comes to be worshipped as the only true God. The day of doom then rapidly approaches, and the end is not far. A republic can only be sustained by virtue—stern—unbending—uncalculating virtue."[108] For Tyler, the Yorktown battlefield was not simply a stage for lauding the sacrifices of the men who had dealt the deciding blows of the War of Independence. It also formed a proving ground for historic republican virtue in modern-day markets.

Southerners, in fact, turned the market critiques of northern writers back on their regional peers to support domestic slavery in the late 1830s. After John Tyler's Yorktown address appeared in the *Southern Literary Messenger*, so, too, did Edmund Quincy's "Old Houses." Two years after its original publication, southern editors recalibrated its message by removing Quincy's pseudonymous initials and attributing its authorship solely to its place of origin: Boston. Quincy had critiqued the city's capitalists from an invented generational remove. Southern editors framed his critique as evidence of commercial Yankee greed.[109] From a regional remove, they used Quincy's prose to portray northern industrial urbanism as a socioeconomic system that cultivated a rage to be rich and destroyed care for the common good. In this context, the abolitionist's invective rang true with proslavery advocates. Just two issues earlier, the *Messenger* had published Abel Upshur's justification of domestic slavery as one of the South's "peculiar institutions." In a speech to the Historical and Philosophical Society of Virginia, Upshur argued that slavery created long-term social stability, in part, by fostering agrarian civilization dotted with moderately sized commercial centers. This labor regime, he argued, prevented the growth of "swollen capitals" that defined northern urbanism. These cities spawned a desire for luxury, "seductive pleasures," and class strife that dissolved all facts of "public spirit" and civil society.[110] To Upshur and Tyler, calls for the preservation of sacred historic sites provided ready-made critiques of market culture that could help them consolidate proslavery political power in both a regional idiom and a new national regime.

Benevolent Preservation

In 1840, Tyler and Upshur both ascended to national executive office thanks in part to a Whig convention at a Revolutionary War battleground in the midst of a preservation debacle. Tens of thousands of citizens had gathered at Bunker Hill near Boston to support the new party platform outlined by Daniel Webster in advance of the coming presidential election. Before them, an unfinished granite obelisk attested to a commemorative design supported by many people in the partisan throng. For nearly twenty years, the Bunker Hill Monument Association had raised money to preserve the spot as open land. Dr. John Collins Warren, one of the Whig revelers, had answered the first call to "public spirited and patriotic capitalists" to stop the encroachment of real estate development in 1822.[111] After he purchased the subdivided tract in Charlestown, the place where his uncle famously had died for the patriot cause, a number of his Boston peers incorporated the Bunker Hill Monument Association to purchase surrounding acreage from private owners, including Warren. Association members combined monetary pledges with credit extended to them by the Suffolk Bank and exercised the state-given right of eminent domain to stitch together a new parcel that they characterized as the original battleground.[112]

Yet the monumental stump divulged the association's failure. By 1840, its members had lost over two-thirds of their land holdings to creditors. In 1829, a fundraising campaign for "the monument" was really an effort to save the association's title to a fifteen-acre parcel. Unless the association paid off its $25,000 debt, the expanse of land that was "open to the eye" from the monument's base would "be sold, and the opportunity lost for ever of reserving it from being covered with buildings which would disfigure it."[113] The impending loss of this land and view may well have inspired donors. After all, many people believed that the "open battle field, undisturbed and unaltered through all time, would be for many far preferable to any monument."[114] In 1834, however, the directors were forced to sell nine acres. A newspaper reporting this arrangement in 1836 assured, "The gentlemen who took the land did it more as security for the money advanced by them, than for any purposes of speculation, and there can be no doubt that they will readily yield their claim to the interests of this great public work."[115] It was an easy view to take when the economy boomed.

Yet after the financial downturn in 1837, the land fell into default. In 1838, newspapers called to "stay the sacrilege" by buying back the land: "Mortgagees have come in possession of the old battle ground, and unless money is speedily raised to purchase it, the ruthless hand of speculation will remove the remains of the old breast work, and erect buildings on the spot which ought to be kept sacred to the memory of those who fought on 'Bunker's height.'"[116] These words may well have been John Collins Warren's, conveyed to directors of the monument association just days before when they determined "to see what sacrifices the land holders were willing to make."[117] The answer, as Warren suspected, was very little. Newspapers as far away as New Orleans reported when laborers began to grade the sloping acreage for new construction.[118] Real estate developers netted over $48,000 from lot sales within a year, but they donated a mere $1,500 to the construction of the monument.[119] When partisans invoked Bunker Hill during the years of party reformulation, they conjured this fraught project of preservation along with the memory of Revolutionary forefathers it was meant to honor.[120]

These politicized appeals for the preservation of "sacred" historic properties ushered in a new type of philanthropy. Fundraisers transformed political appeals for market restraint into benevolent requests for money. If property owners would not reserve historic sites from the market, they argued, virtuous citizens should buy them. In the 1820s, wealthy individuals began to expend personal fortunes for that purpose. Abraham Touro did this with his bequest to the Newport synagogue. Others, such as John Collins Warren at Bunker Hill and Uriah Levy at Thomas Jefferson's Monticello, made private real estate transactions for public benefit. Newspapers from Maine to Georgia reprinted news of these men's purchases as points of national interest. Such benevolent outlays of capital seemed to ensure the moral worth of these men's fortunes as the accumulations of "safe and laudable enterprise" rather than the rage to be rich.[121]

Yet Americans also organized fundraising campaigns that solicited modest contributions to benevolent real estate deals. Leaders of these initiatives channeled donations through voluntary societies to leverage corporate privilege for architectural preservation much as corporate businesses did to build improvements. When preservation-minded societies funneled numerous financial contributions into a single corporate entity, they could remove property from market exchange with a title that promised perpetual ownership. They also made all donors shareholders in the moral proceeds generated by financial investments in a sacred historic property. Wealthy benefactors contributed large sums to these voluntary campaigns. At Bunker Hill, for instance, merchant and textile industrialist Amos Lawrence donated tens of thousands of dollars to the battleground campaign. Yet associational leaders also solicited modest donations from workingmen and children.[122] In 1830, they sanctioned Sarah Hale, editor of the *Ladies' Magazine*, to solicit donations of no more than one dollar from New England women as well. At the same time, the monument's architect, Solomon Willard, excluded contributions of labor from men who had been incarcerated or born abroad. He insisted that it ensured an economical and peaceful workplace, but it also prevented particular types of men from claiming honor by contributing to the site's preservation.[123] For Willard, Hale, and many associational leaders, donors had to have moral capital to invest in their financial donations.

Calls for the preservation of sacred space did not subside with economic recovery in the 1840s. As concerns about the moral dimensions of the market economy grew, more individuals sought to make historic sites permanent. As Hale's fundraising efforts for the Bunker Hill project exemplify, women began to extend their work in benevolent societies into the realm of preservation. Many businessmen and workingmen also withdrew evidence of commerce from historic sites that they wanted to portray as sacred. In the 1840s, for instance, historian Benson J. Lossing sharpened his criticism of commercial activities at Carpenters' Hall. He condemned auctioneer Charles Wolbert by name in his popular *Pictorial Field-book of the Revolution*, describing his presence as "a desecration!

Covering the façade of the very Temple of Freedom with the cards of groveling mammon!"[124] The growing intensity and circulation of these denunciations likely motivated the Carpenters' Company to evict the hall's tenants in 1856 and to refurbish the interior and reoccupy it the following year.[125]

Concerns about economic morality not only enlivened associational life but also shaped new ideas about the family home. As U.S. residents characterized the domestic realm as a moral one in the second quarter of the nineteenth century, public interest in old houses followed. Payton Stewart and Edmund Quincy's attention to Benjamin Franklin's childhood home marked a rising interest in the former homes of famous figures. Yet broader participation in preservation campaigns fed anxieties about the social effects of the market economy as much as it quelled them. As advocates of preservation turned their attention to domestic spaces, they confronted new conflicts about who could participate in making these sites public as well as permanent.

PART III

Domestic Spaces

CHAPTER 5

Civic Housekeeping: Voluntary Associations and Domestic Economy

In his "Old Houses" story in 1837, Edmund Quincy lauded domestic architecture as a particularly compelling type of historical evidence. Grand mansions revived images of colonial elites recorded by portrait painter John Singleton Copley. Other dwellings recalled inhabitants of more modest circumstances, "of whose existence not a single trace remains in any mind on earth." One small brick building enlivened the humble origins of Benjamin Franklin. "Reader," Quincy entreated, "if you are worthy to look upon this hallowed scene, make haste—delay not your pilgrimage till tomorrow, nor even after dinner—for even while I write its fate may be sealed and its destruction begun. In other countries," he continued, "the roofs which have sheltered less eminent men than Benjamin Franklin are preserved with filial reverence, and visited with pilgrim devotion. It should be so here."[1] Bostonians, he implored, should treat the building as a sacred structure.

A year later, Quincy got his first chance to go inside the former Franklin house when Payton Stewart invited him to inspect the building and advise him on its purchase. Though Quincy saw only a portion of the subdivided original, he reported that he "went over the rooms with no small emotion, knowing that Franklin had lived and played in those very rooms, had stood upon those very windowseats in his childhood and had always throughout his long and eventful life recurred to that humble roof as the scene of his earliest recollections." His experience seeing the interior spaces that Franklin had described in his autobiography prompted Quincy to repeat his entreaty for preservation of the old abode in Boston's cramped and aging core. It is impossible to know if Quincy discouraged Stewart from the purchase, but the clothier was not Quincy's ideal buyer. In his journal, the young patrician declared that the building "should be preserved at public expense as a memorial of one of Bostons greatest sons."[2]

Quincy's response to his tour of Franklin's childhood home exemplified a new strain of preservation in the 1830s and 1840s that called for house interiors to be preserved by public entities. Interest in historic houses was not new; Quincy himself pointed to European precedents. But as shifting architectural and cultural ideals of home redefined houses as private space, many U.S. residents projected these standards into the past. Their new perspectives on domesticity made house interiors evidence of the private lives of illustrious former residents—and in turn, windows on their true characters. As popular biographers cast historic abodes in this light, they and their readers explored domestic interiors for themselves and called for their preservation.

As interest in historic houses grew, so did the unpopularity of living in them. By the 1830s, few Americans wanted to inhabit old houses in their original condition: the material standard of living that they offered stood in stark contrast even to modest homes of middling Americans. Growing numbers of visitors who demanded to see house interiors further discouraged people from living in them when standards of civility demanded domestic privacy. In turn, storekeepers faced intensified scrutiny for introducing commercial architecture and activity into former domestic space. Inhabitants of rundown abodes or subdivided tenements who might earn praise for showing their residence to interested visitors opened their domestic lives to critique as well.

In the 1830s, a number of men who shared Quincy's interest in old houses began to propose specific plans for making them public. Members of state historical societies and voluntary associations organized to purchase historic houses, maintain their domestic interiors as they looked in the past, and open these spaces to visitors. In this way, they developed a masculine mode of civic housekeeping that made historic houses public statements of the private virtues not only of their former inhabitants but also of their modern stewards. These men engaged in historically minded organizations to model moral market behavior.[3] Yet they also made claims to authority over modern family homes. When they informed their discussions of how to purchase, furnish, maintain, and hire caretakers for these properties with new tenets of domestic economy, they resisted the ideological bifurcation of home and market that cast women as the moral compass of the domestic realm. In this way, they pushed back against the authority claimed by female authors of housekeeping manuals and their disciples by aiming to articulate a model of "old-fashioned" economy for the modern world—one that posited men as moral managers of public *and* private spaces, past and present.

House History

In the early United States, houses helped to establish social order. Like Edmund Quincy, many residents of the nation turned an eye to domestic architecture to assess how economic changes affected that order. Euro-Americans long had linked patriarchal family governance with the operation of the state, and colonial men constituted household, social, and political power in domestic architecture.[4] In the late eighteenth century, residents of the United States began to see the houses of national "founders" as evidence of a civil society created in private family life as well as state and society. Domestic façades attested to the personal tastes of their patrons. Renaissance classicism evinced cosmopolitanism while local vernaculars spoke to distinctive conventions of particular times and places. Domestic interiors formed lived spaces that registered the character of inhabitants in the private realm.[5] As biographer Caroline Kirkland explained, "The most commonplace man has an inner and an outer life, which, if displayed separately, might never be expected to belong to the same individual. . . . So with regard to public and domestic life."[6] Interior spaces gave insight into the familial relationships, emotional contours, moral development, and intellectual life of public leaders.[7]

To look to houses as evidence of the American past was to portray the colonization of North America as one of domestication. By poking into the former abodes of previous generations, U.S. residents might learn "not how men learned to conquer, but how they endeavored to live," as British biographer Oliver Goldsmith put it.[8] In this view, the presence of European vernaculars marked the first phase of the "civilization" of the continent. In 1796, this view informed Benjamin Henry Latrobe's appraisal of the sprawling seventeenth-century Green Spring mansion of Virginia colonial governor William Berkeley. Latrobe characterized the provincial political leader in his portrayal of the house's Jacobean architecture (Plate 5). The clustered chimneys, dormer windows, asymmetrical façade, fenced courtyard, and porch tower with "some clumsy ornamental brickwork about it of the stile [*sic*] of James the 1st" all formed approximations of cosmopolitan modes.[9] Inside, Latrobe's view of the governor's quarters infused a naturalized conception of colonial violence: "Many of the first Virginian assemblies were held in the very room in which I was plotting the death of Muskitoes, and many of their deliberations were directed to the same end in respect of the Indians, and for the same reason—they were weak and troublesome."[10] To Latrobe, the house enabled him to round out colonial histories of Virginia written by Berkeley and William Stith with his own assessment of the local past.

Early U.S. citizens informed their historical perspectives with houses of less wealthy colonizers as well. In 1796, serial diarist and Massachusetts clergyman William Bentley recorded his view of a seventeenth-century house near Salem that seemed to provide a glimpse of early colonizers of Naumkeag territory. From the outside, the house's unshaped stone step, hinged windows with diamond-paned glass, and wooden latches marked the old age of the frame house. Inside, aged bachelor John Symonds had kept a domestic time capsule: large fireplaces, old-fashioned furniture, pewter tableware, hanging textiles, and a wardrobe filled with outmoded habiliments seemed to preserve a view of the seventeenth century. "Everything," Bentley wrote, was "in its own likeness, and away, far away from present fashion." To Bentley, the interior revealed the "primitive manners . . . when we see society only in its first stages."[11] His appraisal of this particular domestic scene proffered a view of American "civilization" as a process of social development common not only to continent but also to the world.

By the 1820s, U.S. residents started to identify early eighteenth-century expressions of Renaissance classicism as a move toward American refinement. Bostonians pointed to a pair of mansions on Garden Court Street as examples. One was an imposing three-story mansion known for its intricate inlaid floors and elaborate wall panel paintings, commissioned by William Clarke. It acquired an air of intrigue under the later proprietorship of Charles Henry Frankland, a wealthy Boston merchant who married his impoverished mistress after she saved him from the rubble of the Lisbon earthquake in 1755.[12] The other house, built by John and Abigail Foster in 1692, featured a three-story brick façade notable for its symmetric design, full-length pilasters, second-floor balcony, and ornate decorative carvings.[13] In 1765, it became notorious under the proprietorship of Lieutenant Governor Thomas Hutchinson, when a mob attacked the house to protest his support of the Stamp Act. By the second quarter of the nineteenth century, however, local residents appreciated both houses as "specimens of the arts as they existed in Boston a century ago."[14] They saw these structures as early examples of the Anglicization of architectural style that elite and middling colonists made pervasive markers of cosmopolitan manners.[15]

Popular print culture prompted a growing number of writers and readers to seek out historic houses for themselves. In the late eighteenth century, Europeans had translated biographical interest into curiosity about the former homes of Petrarch, Milton, Luther, and Shakespeare. Elite American tourists trekked to these sites as well. In 1812, for instance, Thomas H. Perkins reported a repeat visit to the birthplace of William Shakespeare. The Boston merchant already had seen the room in which the writer had been born, but this time he wanted to show the site to Joseph Curwen, a British transplant to Philadelphia. Visitors had filled the house walls with their signatures, so Perkins brought the resident butcher and his wife a guestbook for future tourists that they welcomed.[16]

Residents of the early United States extended this biographical interest to the homes of Euro-American political leaders. No house attracted more visitors than Mount Vernon, the home of the late George Washington. Here, visitors believed that they could catch an unmediated glimpse of Washington's true character.[17] As one traveler put it in 1822, visitors treated Washington's house and grounds as "public property as to entitle them to run through them and round them without regard to the convenience of the present proprietor." Far from condemning the behavior, the observer deemed it "reasonable that the possessor of the estate of so illustrious a man should permit any of his Countrymen to examine whatever may awaken recollections of his greatness or afford a glimpse of his private life."[18] A decade later, a set of visitors took this belief to a shocking extreme. They rebuked enslaved workers who tried to bar them from the house when its proprietor was ill. The party, which included a U.S. congressman, pushed its way in and created such a commotion that they distressed John A. Washington Jr., as he expired on his deathbed upstairs.[19]

Washington's fame made Mount Vernon an exceptionally popular tourist destination. But it exemplified the conundrum of historic houses: perceptions that domestic interiors revealed the taste and private virtue of their previous residents simultaneously diminished opportunities to view them in the modern day. As with Mount Vernon, many historic houses in the early United States remained private residences. As such, they manifested the civility of modern-day residents as well as past ones. New standards of refinement and polite sociability worked against the preservation of old house interiors in the nineteenth century. A broad span of wealthy and striving citizens prized finished surfaces, fashionable design and ornament, larger windows for interior light, and higher ceilings and larger rooms for the circulation of air. In urban and rural settings, they also created more architectural and social boundaries to increase domestic privacy, making the front door a starker division between private and public worlds and using interior divisions to sharpen distinctions between sociable and intimate domestic space.[20]

Houses of elite Euro-American colonizers invited fashionable renovations well into the nineteenth century. U.S. residents were most willing to maintain eighteenth-century Georgian houses as single-family dwellings because their central halls and four-room plans allowed for specialized spaces and controlled access to private quarters. Edmund Quincy, for instance, judged his old family house in Massachusetts to be "an excellent one for any period and extraordinary for the times it was built. . . . The rooms in the newer part of the house are exceeding good size and the abode looks like a great gentlemans seat."[21] Yet pervasive remodeling and construction created a converse canon of "old-fashioned" architectural features: gabled roofs, casement windows, irregular fenestration, rough surfaces, visible framing members, low ceilings, large hearths, dirt floors, and undivided interiors. Many U.S. residents saw these elements as valuable markers of past lives. But they also believed that an unadulterated constellation of them could mark its inhabitants as uncivil. In the eyes of Americans who subscribed to material notions of modern living, domestic situations that did not substantiate modern aesthetics of beauty, taste, and domestic sociability risked detracting from early national civic life. They did not uphold modern architectural notions of public health, and they often marked the dwelling places of people who did not engage in productive labor. In fact, they were often inhabited by elderly residents who had remained unmarried and failed to reproduce.

As a result, U.S. residents who saw historic houses as valuable evidence of private histories had a hard time envisioning a future for their "original" forms. William Ludwell Lee, for instance, had invited Benjamin Latrobe to Green Spring to assess the house's potential for renovation. Latrobe appraised the house according to its historical as well as its structural condition, but the conventions of modern living meant that he did not see how the new heir could maintain it. "The antiquity of the old house, if in any case, ought to plead in the project," he wrote, "but its inconvenience and deformity are more powerful advocates for its destruction." Lee soon pulled down the manor house "to erect a modest Gentleman's house near the spot," and Green Spring remained standing only on the pages of Latrobe's sketchbook.[22]

Folks who lived a form of domestic anachronism preserved a comprehensive view of the past temporarily but also ensured its demise. In 1796, William Bentley recognized that no one would keep the antique estate of John Symonds intact. It was an unsustainable mode of living, in his mind. Its domestic furnishings would make "proper materials for a Cabinet," but unfortunately, Salem had no such repository. "With the loss of this man," Bentley surmised, the estate would disperse, the house would come down, and "the appearance of the last and the beginning of this Century is lost."[23] The death knell of elderly residents tolled for their domiciles too.

In the coming decades, some Americans preserved architectural fragments as object lessons in domestic civility. These relics did not rely on fabric alone to evoke connections to the past.[24] Rather, viewers believed that their design elements encapsulated the taste displayed by the entire structure from which they were taken. Bostonians created these types of artifacts when developers demolished the Garden Court Street mansions "to make room for . . . dwelling-houses of more fashionable and economical construction" in 1833.[25] City residents purchased or salvaged painted panels, decorative tiles, built-in cabinetry, and sections of parquet floors to decorate their own homes with architectural keepsakes and historic art.[26] The developers of the site, however, donated a capital from the Hutchinson house to the Massachusetts Historical Society immediately after demolition.[27] While generations could gaze at the façade of the house in an engraving first published in the *American Magazine of Useful and Entertaining Knowledge* in 1836, the exquisite craftsmanship and baroque design of the architectural artifacts embodied the lavish character of the mansion in more refined detail than a woodcut or a written description could.[28] Site developers certainly wanted to demonstrate their interest in the history of the houses that they had demolished to prevent attacks on their character as commercial men interested only in maximizing profit.

Yet artifacts alone did not satisfy the swelling popular interest in historic domestic interiors. Visitors long had approached the homes of prominent individuals, hoping to gain entry, and residents of these spaces had struggled to restrict access of guests to various rooms. George Washington, for instance, had felt bound by the conventions of hospitality even as he complained that visitors imposed upon his private space. The Washington family responded to these intrusions by constructing a gate at the base of the house's central staircase to discourage guests from ascending to family quarters. But by the 1820s, growing conventions of domestic privacy eclipsed the older notions of hospitality toward guests outside immediate social circles.[29] Gaining admission to historic house interiors was often a contentious or impossible process, even with the most willing proprietors. In 1831, Worcester antiquary Christopher Columbus Baldwin knocked on the door of the Boston house where he supposed Increase, Cotton, and Samuel Mather had lived. Perhaps he had learned about the house from Abel Bowen's *Picture of Boston*, which mentioned that it was still owned by descendants.[30] When a woman opened the door, he told her that he "came out of respect to the memory of the ancient occupants and wished to visit her garret to see the famous study and to search for old papers." Its occupant refused. Baldwin "insisted upon going into the garret, but she refused outright, and persisted in it to the last."[31] He left without seeing the Mathers' study, garret, or personal papers.

Ellen Randolph Coolidge expressed deep animosity toward such people as Baldwin, who professed to visit houses to honor former occupants while disrespecting the privacy of current ones. At Monticello, Coolidge and her family confronted visitors who flocked to her grandfather's former mountain home, several miles outside of Charlottesville, Virginia. She expressed outrage that they treated her private family home as public property. As she wrote to her mother in 1831,

> No feeling of delicacy ever restrained crowds of idle and curious visitors from intruding themselves upon you when you lived at Monticello before, and now I fear your time, your health, your quiet would be sacrificed without

scruple and without remorse to the gratification of the vulgar impulses which have turned the dwelling of Thomas Jefferson into a shew-place, a puppet-dance or a caravan of wild animals; for let not Virginia or Virginians dare to ascribe any better motive to their lawless curiosity. let them not presume to talk of national feelings of gratitude, or patriotism. they have [tram]pled on the memory of their [. . . bene]factor, driven his children [into] sorrowful exile, and let them not add effrontery to ingratitude and meanness, by pretending to venerate ought that remains of him. individuals have formed honorable and generous exceptions to the general rule, but a few individuals do not constitute the State.[32]

These affronts to family home life, she believed, saddled Jefferson's descendants with an uninhabitable property. They could not live there in peace, nor could they sell it to a respectable inhabitant. Ellen's sister, Cornelia Randolph, saw a return to nature a more acceptable outcome than conveying the estate to someone who would open the house to "the prophane [*sic*] eyes of those who respect no more the house of Thomas Jefferson than that of one of themselves and who would turn it into a boarding house probably if it was sold to them; to me this seems like prophaning [*sic*] a temple and I had rather the weeds and wild animals which are fast taking possession of the grounds . . . grow and live in the house itself." Destruction by neglect would be a more suitable fate: "I would see the house itself in ruins before I would see it turned into a tavern," she declared.[33] Her indignation stemmed not only from the idea of a commercial proprietor profiting from interest in her grandfather's legacy but also from the thought of opening his private domain to such common forms of lodging and entertainment.

In the end, Jefferson's daughter, Martha Randolph, justified a modest price for the estate in 1831 because the "evil of visitors has increased to such a degree as to be a tremendous drawback on it as a residence."[34] Indeed, individuals flocked to the estate to get a look at Jefferson's private quarters and grounds even after Charlottesville physician James Barclay bought the mountaintop estate and began to transform its domestic grounds into a farm. When John H. B. Latrobe visited Monticello in 1832 and found Barclay away, he reported looking into the house "by the peeps I made into peepable places."[35] By envisioning Latrobe pressing his face against house windows, it is easy to see how popular interest in domestic interiors could make historic houses undesirable places to live.

Some visitors comported themselves according to contemporary notions of social respectability. In 1833, for instance, Christopher Columbus Baldwin restrained himself from asking for admission to the Hoyt home near Deerfield, Massachusetts. The resident family had been caretakers of the late seventeenth-century house since moving there in 1742. Though they had operated it as a tavern during much of the eighteenth century, they made it solely a private residence after the Revolutionary War. Its deceased proprietor, Elihu Hoyt, had celebrated the historical associations of the old-fashioned wooden abode, which still bore the scars of violence between Pocumtuc residents and British colonizers in 1704.[36] In 1833, Baldwin was not shy about examining the exterior of the house, describing the door knocker as "the bigness of one's middle finger" and the largest hatchet hole as "large enough to run the arm through" it. But, he noted, "I did not go into the inside of the house except into the entry. I did not wish to disturb the family, especially at this time, as the late occupant, Col. Hoyt, brother of the Author of the Researches, had deceased only two weeks before."[37] The Hoyts were well known for indulging the curiosity of visitors, and the decedent himself had sold his pamphlet about the site's history to interested parties who approached the house.[38] Baldwin felt comfortable going into the house's public vestibule, but he believed that contemporary conventions of mourning and privacy barred his access to the historic interior.

Yet historical print culture such as Hoyt's pamphlet encouraged a growing belief that historic houses formed a sort of public property guided by conventions of civil behavior that differed from ordinary domestic spaces. The booming popularity and distribution of local histories, travel guidebooks, and historical fiction all generated conflicts of increasing number and note between visitors to historic houses and their residents. In particular, the rise of U.S. historical biography in the second quarter of the nineteenth century expanded and intensified this interest. In 1830, one article about the ensuing "biographical mania" argued that the desire to peer into the homes of notable citizens was a sign of an enlightened democratic society that held its leaders—past and present—up to the scrutiny of the "universal gaze."[39] As ever-larger numbers of literate Americans saw reading as a method of self-improvement, they reached for biographies as a didactic genre that would enrich their characters and intellects.[40]

As beliefs in the importance of childhood to shaping morality also grew, biographical texts expanded the gaze of readers to houses inhabited by their subjects in youth as well as adulthood. Samuel Goodrich's children's edition of *The Life of Benjamin Franklin* (1836), for instance, included illustrations of Franklin in particular settings, including the young subject reading a book in his childhood home. When Jared Sparks compiled the papers of Franklin and reprinted his autobiography between 1836 and 1840, he departed from previous editions by identifying the specific locations of Franklin's birthplace and childhood home in contemporary Boston.[41] Charles Frederick Briggs expanded his view of Franklin's family homes even further. After reading the *Life of Franklin*, he sought out the Nantucket house of Franklin's mother and grandfather Folger, rambling around the house and "wondering in which of its little rooms the grandfather of the philosopher sat."[42] Washington Irving spoke to the ways that biographies impelled these ventures. "If our love of country is excited when we read the biography of our revolutionary heroes, . . ." he wrote, "how much more will the flame of patriotism burn in our bosoms . . . when we move among the scenes where were conceived and consummated their noblest achievements."[43] The double entendre of Irving's words conveyed the growing belief that no spaces in the former homes of American worthies were off-limits to the public eye.

Edmund Quincy's proposal to preserve Benjamin Franklin's childhood home as a public site attempted to reconcile the conflicting demands in this historicized view of domestic civility. On the one hand, Quincy hoped to provide access to the interior spaces of Franklin's childhood highlighted by contemporary texts about his life. On the other hand, he hoped to remove commercial activity that was doubly dismissed as an intrusion in sacred historic space *and* the ideal home—even though the building had housed the artisan productions of Franklin's father alongside the family's domestic quarters. Quincy shaped his vision for the historic house to accord with his idea of the modern American home: a center of family development made moral by separation from market activity. This ideal defined the home as the realm of women who managed their households with a form of domestic morality calculated to counteract the self-interest that could impel men's actions in the outside world. Yet men who shared Quincy's vision believed that they might open the private rooms of historic houses to public view by becoming housekeepers themselves. Some turned to the moral authority of voluntary associations to resolve the tensions of domestic privacy in a civil manner.

Historic Homes

In the late 1820s, the imperative to keep historic houses intact doubled under new conceptions of the modern home as a sacred space. U.S. residents consolidated the ideal of the family home as a bastion of sentimental attachment, affection, and morality in a world of market competition and political strife. Architectural and cultural appeals sought to define these realms as separate spheres of gendered authority. In this archetype, women shaped the moral and material dimensions of domestic interiors while men earned money outside of the household. Home, then, characterized houses as a site of social stability, where citizens would build a civil society with familial affection and seek refuge when oscillations of the market threatened it.[44]

It was this new conception of home that prompted many U.S. residents to plan the preservation of historic houses as public domestic spaces. Some individuals

deliberately tried to preserve historic houses as modern homes that accommo-
dated family life and public access. When they opened their halls to curious
strangers, they reframed personal privacy as a sacrifice that they made for the
public good. When Uriah Levy purchased Monticello in 1834, for instance, he
tried to bridge the gap between public demand to see the house and his desire to
make it his seasonal residence.[45] James Barclay lasted only two years under public
scrutiny as the proprietor of Jefferson's former estate. Levy purchased the property
from him specifically for its "historical associations" advertised by the seller.[46] As
the first Jewish commodore of the U.S. Navy, Levy admired Jefferson as a propo-
nent of religious liberty and bought the estate as a tribute to him. Newspapers
across the nation reported that Levy would "commence immediately such improvements and repairs as will fully restore the buildings, &c. to their original
condition: afterwards it will be accessible to visitors once a week."[47] The Richmond
Enquirer added an addendum: "For the present, however, the proprietor does not
wish the public to visit the premises. Due notice will be given of the completion of
repairs."[48] Levy attempted to set up a comfortable seasonal home for himself away
from New York City, and he made his mother a full-time resident of the mountaintop at the end of her life. Yet visitors in the 1830s and 1840s paid little heed to
entreaties to visit only when the Levy family issued invitations.[49]

The Washington family continued to struggle with public incursions at Mount
Vernon. Jane C. Blackburn Washington tried to balance her desire for a private
home life with allowing the public to see George Washington's house. By 1837, she
complained that the burden of visitors had worn her down and that she would not
stay at the house any longer than necessary. She refused to let steamboats unload
passengers at the Mount Vernon wharf and admitted only persons who could
show a proper letter of introduction.[50] Still, she constantly weighed the benefit of
opening the house to the public with the cost to her privacy, writing in 1840, "I
never would have submitted to the endless intrusions, and sacrifice of every thing
like a private right and domestic privacy to which we are liable here, but that I believe it arises frequently from a sincere (though thoughtlessly indulged) desire of
honouring the memory of Genl. Washington."[51] Even as she recognized the "social
advantages the place confers," she counseled her son that "a situation more retired
from public interest and intrusion, is more fitting for rearing and providing for a
family and ensuring domestic privacy and comfort."[52] No matter how much the
Washingtons opened their home, the public complained about limited access.

The efforts of Uriah Levy and Jane Washington contrasted with the elite residents of other celebrated houses who designed domestic furnishings to discourage such public desire to see the interiors. Henry Wadsworth Longfellow adopted
this strategy at his home in Cambridge, Massachusetts. He and his intended wife,
Fanny Appleton, had determined to buy the "grand old mansion" in 1843 partly

because of its interesting history. The Georgian mansion, built nearly a century earlier by a wealthy member of the Vassall family, attracted the most public attention for its association with George Washington, who had used the house as his headquarters.[53] During the first year of the newlyweds' residence, George Washington Greene had "excited an historical association, or rather reminded us how noble an inheritance this is—where Washington dwelt in every room." Washington biographer Jared Sparks also led Longfellows around Cambridge to show them "Revolutionary landmarks" that related to the history of their home.[54] The couple themselves wrote a manuscript history of their abode that included accounts of its loyalist builders and post-Revolutionary occupants as well.[55]

The young couple wanted to keep architectural evidence of this multilayered past in place. As Henry Longfellow put it in the spring of 1844, the house was "decidedly conservative; and will remain as much in its old state as comfort permits."[56] Yet his nod to domestic comfort pointed to the new inhabitants' primary goal. They had chosen the residence not only for its historical associations but also for its potential to accommodate modern standards of living. Fanny Appleton Longfellow had convinced her father—one of the richest men in Boston—not to build the couple a new house only by insisting that the house was "large enough to introduce every modern comfort we should desire, and there is no position in Cambridge that can compare with it for the views and air."[57] Indeed, the Longfellows began refurbishing the house right away with fashionable furniture, window seats, kitchen updates, and structural repairs.[58] Over the next fifteen years, the couple retained the mid-eighteenth-century character of the estate while introducing enough modern features for visitors to declare that the couple had "refitted it."[59]

The Longfellows refrained from fashioning the house in the image of former occupants to discourage incursions on their domestic comfort. When Philadelphian John Jay Smith offered them a bookcase owned by George Washington, Henry Longfellow declined. He explained, "On many accounts, I should like to have a room furnished with articles, which had grown familiar with the august eyes of the great patriot: but I have never had any intention of attempting it; because on many, and more accounts, it would be very inconvenient; chiefly by rendering the house a kind of *show house*, which would be excessively disagreeable."[60] Indeed, questions about the house's interior abounded. A number of "inquisitive ladies" wrote to Jared Sparks, demanding to know exactly which rooms Washington had inhabited in his Cambridge headquarters in 1775 and 1776.[61] Longfellow wished to hold these prying eyes at bay by cultivating the best view of the house's Revolutionary appearance from the new sidewalks of Brattle Street, not his family quarters.

A number of men sought to resolve these tensions by replacing domestic matriarchs with associational stewards. In the 1820s, a number of middling and elite men added historical societies to the growing number of voluntary associations directing civil life in the United States. These organizations raised money to support mechanisms of social welfare most frequently fulfilled by the state in Europe and Asia. Beginning in the 1790s, women and men alike formed benevolent organizations to support impoverished populations and educate children of limited means. They also founded mutual benefit societies to support financial security and education of members as well as institutions to inculcate religion and social reform among the masses. Organizational leaders generally sought incorporation to manage charitable property. For most, this meant collecting and disbursing money and constructing buildings devoted to their aims.[62] But when it came to historical societies, leaders incorporated not only to manage funds and build repositories but also to possess property in trust for future generations. They characterized their goal of collecting historical records and artifacts as one calculated to secure the public interest in the permanence of property kept out of the market.

In the 1830s and 1840s, numerous men drew on the moral and legal weight of voluntary associations to articulate plans for "preserving" the domestic spaces of famous men while opening them to public view. Their proposals offered a calculated alternative to state ownership. In the late 1820s, for instance, the Randolph family had pressed Congress to buy Jefferson's estate from them to preserve as state-owned public property.[63] Beginning in the late 1830s, Jane Washington followed suit by seeking a congressional buyer for Mount Vernon.[64] Associational men offered a different solution for making historic houses public—one that used the private-public character of corporations to maintain the private character of home for public viewing. This voluntary means of preservation substantiated national claims to self-determination with organizations that many observed to be a distinctive feature of civil society in the United States.[65] In this way, associational men sought to secure the homes of American leaders in a way that called attention to the distinctiveness of the civil society that these historical figures had helped to build.

Take, for instance, John Fanning Watson's proposals to preserve a former home of William Penn. Watson, a bank clerk from Germantown, a few miles outside of Philadelphia, had spent years researching the former residences of the colonial proprietor by visiting extant buildings, speaking with elderly residents, and delving into property records.[66] He had warned members of the Penn Association in 1824 that John Doyle's tavern might not be a former dwelling of William Penn. In 1828, he tried to redirect their attention to a different building nearby: a small brick structure, known as the Letitia House and the old Rising Sun Tavern. He and Roberts Vaux were convinced that Penn and his daughter, Letitia Penn Aubrey, had called the building home.[67] The following year, Watson expressed lofty hopes that the Penn Association would raise funds to buy it, have it "consecrated to future renown" by furnishing it with his collection of Penn family relics, and "retain for public exhibition the primitive house of Penn."[68]

Watson cited several European examples of historic houses that provided worthy models of preservation. Travelers to German and Italian states would find the houses of Martin Luther, Philip Melancthon, and Petrarch maintained in their antiquated forms, filled with the belongings of these luminaries and furnished with guest books. Yet Philadelphians need not rely on the benevolence of monarchs and aristocrats to establish these houses, Watson suggested. Whereas the king of Prussia had bought Luther's birthplace at Eisleben and an aristocratic family in Padua had turned Petrarch's house into a museum, Philadelphians might celebrate democracy by preserving Penn's house with voluntary charitable giving and associational stewardship.[69]

Watson's efforts to purchase the house intensified in the Philadelphia real estate market of the 1830s. The old buildings attributed to Penn's era all stood in the city's oldest district. Despite the dilapidated condition of these structures, their landlords charged high rents because of their proximity to the Delaware River docks and the urban core. Deborah Norris Logan noted this in 1830 when she recorded a false report that another supposed abode of William Penn—"the Old Slate House in Second Street"—had burned down. It stood in a neighborhood where "the Buildings are very old and scarsely tenable, yet commanding a good rent from their situation, otherwise not a loss, but I am sorry for the Slate house on account of its antiquity and associations."[70]

Antiquaries confronted these inflated prices when a market dip in 1833 and uptick in 1834 prompted many property owners to liquidate real estate. What spurred developers to buy impelled others to preserve. Yet when Watson rushed to acquire the Letitia House, his plan revealed the practical shortcomings of associational purchases. In 1834, he dashed off a letter to fellow antiquary John Jay Smith sounding the alarm that the owner of the Letitia House, merchant Henry Heberton, planned "to pull it down!" In Watson's mind, this was the last opportunity to make a building of this vintage a permanent feature of the cityscape. "All of our other memorable buildings—of private ownership are gone or going," he wrote, "or are in situations too high priced to be bought and preserved—This one alone is so placed, as to not be capable of a high price." Though he still hoped that it could serve as a meeting space for the Penn Association, he knew he could not count on a speedy assembly of members who attended to a broad set of voluntary and professional responsibilities. Instead, he sought a benefactor to make an immediate purchase for the society's use. Hence his letter to Smith: he proposed that the two men enter into joint ownership of the building. Smith certainly had more expendable capital than Watson, and he also could keep a closer eye on the Philadelphia property. Forgoing associational ownership, however, meant that Watson and Smith needed to cobble together a workable plan for permanence that corporate ownership would have provided. Watson suggested that they would need to establish a safe chain of inheritance and apply to the city for potential tax exemption "for the sake of its public object."[71]

In this case, Watson tried to act as a moral real estate broker on behalf of a historical association. He believed that he had convinced Heberton to make a deal in the interest of the public good. The grantor needed to turn his property into cash, but he supposedly agreed to make the antiquaries preferred buyers and give them a good deal—though he had not quoted Watson a price. Watson recognized that even as a benevolent owner, he and his joint tenants would have to manage the property with an eye to its market value, as he considered it the most viable way to sustain the building's care. He assured Smith that he would evaluate the asking price of the property in proportion to the rent paid by current occupants and could "foresee means by which we could enhance its value in our own hands." Attempts to maximize real estate profits could be moral, in this view, when calculated to secure historic features rather than demolish them. This means of financial management would support the "perpetual preservation" of the house as "a memorable City Relic, . . . as the actual contrast at all times, between the beginning and the Progress of our City."[72] Of course, the new landlords would have to find tenants with the same sensibilities of stewardship.

Watson was not the only antiquary to think this way. Members of the Rhode Island Historical Society tried to make the association a moral real estate agent as well. In the summer of 1835, they directed their secretary, Thomas H. Webb, "to ascertain the condition of the old Gov. Coddington house at Newport, and to see if the same can be preserved from destruction."[73] Built by Rowland Robinson in the late 1660s, the house was "well-known" as the domicile of colonial governor William Coddington.[74] In 1835, Webb found the house "in a very dilapidated state, and from its exposed situation it is daily liable to farther injury from depredations that may so easily be committed upon it." The building had an absentee owner, a woman who "not being much interested in its preservation, from a regard to the historical associations connected with it," planned "for the purpose of improving the lot and increasing the income therefrom, to pull it down." After touring the house and consulting with local antiquarian Robert Johnston, an old-house aficionado, Webb recommended that the society "make some effort to preserve this relic of other times" because "it was the residence of one of the founders of the State, [and] is the oldest tenement now standing in Newport."[75] Webb reported that the former Coddington property might be purchased for $800, but "as there is sufficient land attached, for two or three house lots, the disposal of these, would enable one to obtain the house at a moderate price."[76] Like Watson, the Rhode Islanders calculated the property's market value to form a sustainable plan for its care. In this case, they collapsed the historical value of the parcel into the house and sacrificed the open land around it to generate maintenance fees for the building.

In 1839, a number of Hudson Valley men chartered a new association to purchase the Newburgh headquarters of George Washington. As petitioners put it to the New York legislature that year, "It remains as yet in nearly the same condition as that in which Washington left it; but circumstances are such, that it must soon fall before the march of village improvement, unless efficient measures are taken to preserve it."[77] They incorporated the Washington's Head-Quarters Association on the model of a business corporation "for the purpose of preserving and perpetuating in such manner as they deem proper," aiming to hold $60,000 stock in shares valued at $25 each.[78] Commissioners would earn 5 percent of the contributions that they collected. They aimed to buy the property that proprietor Jonathan Hasbrouck III had been trying to sell since 1834. For years, his family had asked for financial help to keep up the house for the many Hudson Valley tourists who visited. By 1839, Hasbrouck struggled to repay the mortgage that he had placed on the property. The association hoped to relieve him of his financial troubles with the public privileges of incorporation.[79] In their minds, corporate ownership would insulate the property's fate from the fiscal tribulations of private owners while collectively bearing the burdens of a public site.

All three associational efforts aimed to preserve historic houses specifically for the instructive value of their interiors. Commentators on the Hasbrouck house valued it as a private place where Washington had made decisions of great consequence. In the 1830s, printed descriptions of the house began to emphasize the importance of seeing its inner chambers. In a *New-York Mirror* issue that included a full-plate engraving of the old house, Gulian Verplanck assured readers, "The interior remains very nearly as Washington left it." He went on to describe the various rooms, with their low ceilings and large hearths, and how Washington had used each one to dine, sleep, ruminate, and host guests in his "liberal, though plain hospitality." The oft-described central room with seven doors served as Washington's parlor and dining room while offering sleeping quarters to his officers at night. A small adjacent room attracted veneration as the place where Washington wrote imperative letters that quelled discontent from an overextended and underpaid army and seemingly secured the fate of the nation.[80] Petitioners to the New York state legislature pointed to this room specifically when they applied for incorporation to preserve the building. Here, they wrote, "the imagination can almost conceive him, on that occasion, as personating the genius of American liberty, dictating his orders . . . and preparing an address" to his soldiers. Though Washington's residence was fleeting, his private quarters in the house evoked his presence and deeds.[81] Several Hudson Valley men hoped to harness the power of association to preserve that architectural experience for future generations.

John Fanning Watson planned to recall the domestic past of the Letitia House with furnishings as well as architectural preservation. In 1830, he had suggested that an associational buyer might maintain the exterior appearance of the building while removing some interior walls to create meeting space.[82] In 1834, however, Watson committed to keeping the interior entirely "in its original character and appearance." If functional needs necessitated the opening of some partitions, Watson explained, alterations should be reversible to maintain the original spatial design. "Its rooms should all stand as now," he continued, with the interior "in all respects old-fashioned," including sanded floors, pewter table settings, and seventeenth-century furnishings donated by Philadelphia area families. By lining the walls with his views of old houses, framed in relic wood, Watson believed that he would make the Letitia House into the "perfect museum," designed to meet ends both "patriotic and pious."[83]

Watson envisioned daily operations that would generate moral returns rather than financial ones. He continued in the vein of a moral real estate manager by subverting the most likely use for the building: instead of a tavern, like John Doyle's establishment, he would make the former Penn abode a temperance house. He thought that a widow would make an ideal proprietor for this antiquarian establishment, though he would settle for "a small Family of good character." The hostess might "secure good company" by serving light fare—"something alluring for ladies"—as well as providing a place of respite for marketgoers from the countryside. But the hospitality should not outshine the historical enterprise. As Watson put it, "To proper minds, the going into the alley and narrow court to find the hallowed spot, should constitute its chiefest interest." Temperance and matronly hospitality was a means of supporting the preservation of a historic structure. Watson saw depravity in demolition as well as drinking: "It will be sinful apathy to let the house go down!!!" in his words.[84]

Watson was not the only man to busy himself with the details of housekeeping as an antiquarian enterprise. Members of the Rhode Island Historical Society monitored the housekeeping of a tenant family at Whitehall, the former residence of Bishop George Berkeley. From 1729 to 1731, the British intellectual had lived outside of Newport and renovated the seventeenth-century clapboard house to include five bays and a double front door surrounded by a stately pediment. After his departure, he bequeathed it to Yale College for the support of scholars. In May 1835, the *Newport Mercury* had reported that Yale intended to tear it down.[85] Robert Johnston and Andrew A. Harwood went to sketch the house in case its landlords did not listen to their pleas to keep it standing.[86] But the society also sent their secretary Thomas Webb to meet with Johnston and inspect the house and its residents: the large family of Abraham Brown, who had rented the house and farmed the surrounding land for a decade.[87] Johnston and Webb blamed the Browns for inattention to the house's care and left "fully satisfied, that the expense, of repairing the present tenement, would be far less, than that of erecting a new one, and that its present condition must be attributed more to neglect upon the part of tenants, than to the ravages of time."[88] When they conveyed this report to Yale president Jeremiah Day, he assured them that he would not demolish Whitehall and would be more vigilant in ensuring that tenants kept the residence in good repair.[89] For leaders of both institutions, an agreement to cast an agrarian family as uncivil smoothed over a potentially acrimonious exchange.

In these plans for historic houses, middling Euro-American men combined the structures of associational and domestic life to experiment with making historic homes permanent and public. They appealed to the corporate nature of historical associations to act as moral real estate agents, buying homes from families who would not or could not make these houses sites of civic morality on their own. But they also used the voluntary status of male members to make old-fashioned interiors exemplars of modern civility—and their associational stewards moral exemplars for future generations. In this way, they shaped emerging ideas about the sanctity of homes with ideas about history.[90] In turn, they articulated a masculine form of domesticity as a brand of civic housekeeping that challenged the growing economic authority of women.[91]

Old-Fashioned Domestic Economy

In 1847, Henry King Hoyt announced his plan to tear down the house that his family had stewarded for over a century. He had inherited the Deerfield house on the death of his father, Elihu Hoyt, in 1833. After fourteen years of proprietorship, he was ready to build a new one in its place. Residents of western Massachusetts immediately established an association to raise money to purchase the old house. John Wilson initiated the negotiations with Hoyt. As one newspaper reported, "He proposes to preserve the ancient structure *as it is*—the old door that bears the marks of the savage tomahawk, *as it was*," along with the rooms that bullets had perforated in 1704. The purchasers would maintain it "for the inspection of the inquiring traveller," indulging its notoriety as "a relic of public interest, which few travelers omit to visit on their passage through the village."[92] The house, as association spokesmen put it, evoked a shared past and "is, in a sense, common property; interesting to the antiquary, wherever he may dwell." To let the house be demolished would "be a subject of regret and self-reproach, more perhaps to the people of Deerfield than to those of other places; but not peculiar to them."[93] It should be preserved as is, they argued, for all interested parties to explore.

As usual, the market value of the land far eclipsed the market value of the building. One newspaper writer judged the old house to have "no intrinsic value" and suggested it might be purchased for a small sum and removed to another site for preservation. Hoyt was willing to sell the house for $150. But the association members decided that the 150-year-old structure would not survive the move, and a loss of its locality would diminish its ability to connect visitors to the past. With his designs set on a new house, Henry Hoyt demanded $2,300 for the six-acre property. In a broadside to the public, the committee judged the price to be extortionate. However, they avoided labeling the proprietor greedy—likely because signatories included his uncle Epaphras Hoyt. Instead, they framed the asking price as a reflection of the seller's familial attachment to the land. Paying a premium for the tract, they argued, would repay him for his family's stewardship over the years: "We, the public in general," they wrote, "are indebted to them for the cheerful and courteous reception, which for successive generations, the family have given to visitors at all hours of the day, although it has been often attended with personal and domestic inconvenience."[94] Like associational plans in Philadelphia and Newport, the Massachusetts men planned to fund the perpetual preservation of the house with returns from the real estate market. The committee might lease or sell five acres of land for $600 to $800 dollars, and after putting some of that money into house repairs, they could rent the house and remaining land to a "decent family" of caretakers who would admit visitors to the house.

After the historical association failed to raise the money quickly enough, Henry Hoyt demolished the house in 1848. Explanations of his motives expose the ways that associational efforts to preserve historic house interiors formed pointed critiques of domestic luxury. One newspaper reported that Hoyt demolished the old house when it became "so inconvenient for a residence" that modern comfort necessitated a new one.[95] Accounts recorded in private histories and local conversations placed the onus of demolition on someone else: Hoyt's intended wife, Catherine Wells. Locals explained that she had accepted Hoyt's marriage proposal on the condition that she would not live in the old house. Hoyt's decision to move forward with the demolition was a decision not to delay his marriage—a late one for a couple who were already thirty-seven and forty-two years old. The couple moved into a new white clapboard house, near the spot of the old one, on their marriage in 1849.[96]

The Hoyts' domestic upgrade was one of many that fed a strain of popular commentary on the social effects of domestic consumption. For twenty years, U.S.

industries had been turning out a growing number of specialty goods. Clocks, chairs, carpets, and stoves were only a few types of home furnishings that craftsmen produced in ever larger quantities. Manufacturers encouraged consumption of these goods by speaking about the social leveling that they engendered. As refined goods came within the reach of modest earners in rural and urban areas, they insisted, U.S. residents eliminated the social distinctions defined by the material culture of previous decades. Consumption of new products, makers and merchants continued, supported the development of U.S. economy *and* society. They directed these appeals to the people charged with the responsibility of household management: women.[97]

Yet, in an age when market instability frequently turned personal fortune into ruin, many commentators warned against the siren song of frivolous purchases and consumer luxuries. As popular culture empowered women as the household's lead consumer, it also socked them with the blame of a poor household economy.[98] After years of managing a household through an economic depression, Martha Coffin Wright fumed when she reflected on the proclivity to blame a feminine love of luxury for a family's financial strain. "Women are very apt to look on with apprehension and endeavor to avert by such arguments as they can use, the mania of speculation, the reckless endorsing for others and the thousand unprofitable schemes that are hurrying [men] to ruin, but those arguments are not spoken through a trumpet, nor on the house top," she wrote in 1841. Instead, women worked with little fanfare to cushion household economies from financial blows of variable markets. "The innumerable acts of self denial that [women] practice with the hope of keeping back the crisis are untold," she concluded.[99] Like many, she managed consumer expenditure alongside the labor of sewing, cooking, cleaning, and childrearing as duties of domestic economy performed by women.

Many women adopted a historical view of the home to articulate principles of domestic economy that promoted thrifty practices of labor and consumption. Deborah Norris Logan made her extensive diaries a record of how she informed her modern methods of housekeeping with an appreciation for old-fashioned markers of home. Like many women of her generation and the previous one, Logan maintained sentimental connections to deceased family members in domestic architecture and collections of texts, objects, and images. She also made her home a node of antiquarian sociability and proffered her personal collections for historical studies. Like her contemporary Hannah Mather Crocker in Boston, Logan wrote local histories, lent items to male antiquaries, and earned an honorary membership in a historical society for her contributions.[100]

Though Logan professed a "strange predelection [*sic*] for old things," she appraised the world around her with an eye for modern housekeeping.[101] When she visited Jane Haines at her seventeenth-century stone house, Wyck, she noted that "the house [was] old fashioned, neat, comfortable and convenient, beyond in my estimation, all shew an elegance of modern living." As Logan explained a year later, "An old mansion looks very comfortable when well kep't and in good order, and even a degree of decay does not offend when all is clean, but reverse the matter—and all is dismal and disgusting." Logan found pleasing domestic renovations at Belfield, where her young cousin Sarah Wister had set up housekeeping in the former Peale family house—"an old one it is true and an odly [sic] contrived one enough, but made neat and convenient and furnished suitably, by her kind and good father." Three years later, Logan made another visit and reflected, "In the *Present*, I was pleased with the moderation and economy of my niece—and in the *Past* the memory of my kind old friend and neighbour Charles W. Peale and his estimable wife, is everywhere preserved at that place where the distribution of the ground and many of his seats and inscriptions are still to be seen. And as to the future, what has been may be again. One generation succeeds another, and alterations take place every where."[102] For Logan, a home renovated to balance old and new features formed a pivot point for viewing the progress of history, from past to future.

At her own home outside of Philadelphia, Stenton, Logan took great pains to make clear that she curated a selective set of domestic artifacts. As she ruminated on the past invoked by her home and family archives, she also documented her constant attention to keeping up the house and grounds. She made modern renovations to her century-old house at the same time that she celebrated its antique features. In 1833, when she decided, "I should like a picture of my morning and evening hours to be preserved," she limned a picture of how a housekeeper might integrate old-fashioned features into a modern home. The "repairs and new covers" of her old-fashioned armchair, which she had found in the house fifty years before, made it "respectable" for modern use. Her daily routine included time "spent in the old dining room with the great improvement of my Coal stove and Lehigh Coal." Stenton was no time capsule of eighteenth-century living.

Logan offered this historically informed model of modern housekeeping as one that eschewed the pursuit of rapidly changing fashion. The impulse to institute the latest practices and styles disrupted households with false notions of domestic improvement. In 1832, she bemoaned the destruction of the historic interior of the Dickinson family house, which had stood on Maryland's Eastern Shore since 1681. Logan reported that the owner of the "Old Mansion . . . has given the place up to his son who has lately married a gay and fashionable girl—with a manageing [sic] Mother! and so the Old inmates have to clear out and take care of themselves—and I fear the old furniture and the Antique Cupboard are doomed to removal and destruction also."[103] This situation illustrated what many critics characterized as the self-interest of the young generation. The new bride shrugged off her domestic responsibilities to her mother with instructions to set up her husband's family house according to the latest fashions. From Logan's perspective, the woman's immediate dismissal of long-standing domestic arrangements carried out a regrettable change in house architecture and household structure.

Logan foregrounded her antiquarian interests in private musings on home life. But authors of the era's popular domestic economy manuals infused their advice for modern housekeeping with historical views of home too. Lydia Maria Francis Child, for instance, began her writing career with antiquarian study that took her into the old houses of Boston. She opened *The Rebels* (1825) with a description of the Foster-Hutchinson domestic interior and used a footnote to pinpoint its location in the modern city. Her view of pre-Revolutionary Boston reflected her visits to the former abode of Mather Byles, kept as a domestic time capsule by his spinster daughters.[104] Child's housekeeping manual, *The American Frugal Housewife*, reflected her historical interests in less obvious ways. First published in 1829, the remarkably popular guide set out principles of thrifty housework that mirrored principles of antiquarian labor. "The true economy of housekeeping is simply the art of gathering up all the fragments, so that nothing be lost," Child began. Housewives as well as antiquaries practiced their art by piecing together collected scraps. This "patchwork" sustained what otherwise would be wasted; it was a form of preservation that served the commonweal. The neglect of such "good economy," Child wrote, was "morally wrong, so far as the individual is concerned; and injurious beyond calculation to the interests of our country." As such, mothers should teach children "to save everything . . . not for their *own* use, for that would make them selfish—but for *some* use."[105] In this model, domestic economy and modern antiquarianism both encouraged preservation as a selfless practice that bolstered the stability and prosperity of U.S. economy and society.[106]

Child distinguished her *American Frugal Housewife* from other domestic manuals as one for women of truly meager means. Yet authors of contemporaneous guidebooks also framed "old-fashioned" forms of domesticity as laudable features of modern homes. Eliza Leslie, the author of the decidedly unfrugal *Seventy-Five Receipts for Pastry, Cakes and Sweetmeats*, first published in 1828, also saw old houses as instructive views of the past for the modern era.[107] Her historical geography game, *Cards of Boston* (1831), gave descriptive views of several of the city's historic domestic interiors (Plate 6). She, too, had visited the Byles house and frequently reflected on the ways that modern women could appreciate the benefits of old-fashioned homes while avoiding the uncivil stance of the Byles sisters, whose loyalist proclivities and self-love matched their material backwardness.[108] In her *Treatise on Domestic Economy*, first published in 1841, Catherine Beecher promoted old-fashioned domestic practices as a matter of efficiency. Households, she wrote, were "bound by the same rules as relate to the use of property" and should be governed by a business-like sense of "systematic and habitual industry."[109] Newer was not always better. As late as 1869, Beecher maintained that old brick bake ovens served women better than new stoves. She also modeled her ideal house plans after seventeenth-century New England structures because her vision of domestic economy promoted small rooms used for multiple purposes rather than large rooms devoted to occasional activities. This spatial organization conserved the energy of the housekeeper and the domestic environment.[110]

All of these manuals emphasized that thrift promoted generosity, not acquisitiveness. Many women extended these domestic values into campaigns for benevolence that articulated principles of moral money management. U.S. women had organized benevolent associations since the 1790s, first to care for and educate citizens in need and later to inculcate popular moral reform. In the 1830s, organizers of charitable causes began to frame fundraising campaigns as moral market transactions in which women might sell products or spend money for a good cause.[111] When directed to historical sites, contributors linked the sustaining ethos of domestic economy with environmental permanence. In 1830, for instance, Sarah Hale published a lengthy column entitled "The Worth of Money" to raise funds for the Bunker Hill Monument and the preservation of its surrounding acreage. She launched this campaign in her *Ladies' Magazine* with an argument that the edicts of strict saving fed the desire of Americans to be rich. "This is the age of economy," she opened, and U.S. citizens could not operate according to classical or European principles and expect to escape the corruption of materialism. Saving money was the selfish acquisition of individual wealth that fed the pursuit of luxury. Benevolent spending, however, would make citizens of the United States "the first to endeavor to shake off the dominion of selfishness, and make the object of their ambition, moral and mental excellence, rather than wealth."[112] The proportional sacrifice of funds to individual means and the donor's intention substantiated money's worth, not the financial value of the contribution, she argued. Women had a particular responsibility to cultivate this lesson by guiding the management of money, she continued, not just domestic labor.

Hale encouraged donations to the Bunker Hill campaign by highlighting the vice that it would stop as well as the historic site that it would preserve. Local men recently had proposed running a state lottery to fund the monument with "an appeal . . . to the avarice and the gambling propensities of the people." Benevolent women could prevent the exploitation of men's tendency toward risk and avarice, she hoped, and marry "the love of country, of liberty, or social order and the refined enjoyment of doing good." Her goal was to raise $50,000 from the women and children of New England who earned their contributions through "industry, economy or self-denial," not by asking their husbands and fathers for a donation. This would demonstrate that "the true value of money is to use it for purposes that purify the affections, improve the intellect, and strengthen and exalt the best feelings of our nature."[113] Hale's fundraising campaign articulated a vision of domestic economy that shaped the home *and* the public sphere with moral financial principles of earning and spending.

The consternation that Hale received for her efforts illuminates how men's associational plans for historic homes rebuffed the moral authority of women. In the subsequent issue of the *Ladies' Magazine*, Hale made extensive efforts to allay concerns that her fundraising campaign disrupted the gendered order of household and society. She had not intended to draw attention away from the associational men who had initiated efforts to preserve Bunker Hill and raise a monument, she insisted; her campaign aimed to encourage female "*helpers*," not competitors, who participated only with the "consent of her immediate protector." Hale pointed to "the present depression of business, and insolvences," as the circumstance that necessitated the contributions of women and children: their efforts acted to cushion the effects of a fickle marketplace not only in the home but also in public fundraising endeavors. She also backtracked on her directive that women must earn their contributions.[114] By affirming men's control of the household purse, Hale reinforced the notion that only men's labor had market value and erased the authority that many women—including herself—exercised over income that they earned from work or investments. Calls for donations the next month limited contributions to a dollar per person—an amount that would not tempt women to work for pay or draw capital away from men in their household.[115]

Hale's campaign and associational efforts to raise funds for the preservation of Bunker Hill exemplify how U.S. residents merged public and private mechanisms to support their conception of the public good. Yet efforts to enact ideals that separated the purportedly private sphere of the home from the public sphere of the market intensified conflicts over their inherent entanglement. The environmental conditions of preservation exposed this friction. Sarah Hale pointed to the source of this conflict when she acknowledged the nature of the Bunker Hill project as one "usually considered as belonging exclusively to the province of men, namely, building." Fundraisers operated "in a public manner, and for a public work" when they sought to contribute to these projects.[116] Women, many contemporaries insisted, had no place in these endeavors. In 1833, Hale admitted the "failure" of the women's committee and announced that the women "sacredly reserved" the $3,000 that they had raised to the Massachusetts Charitable Mechanics Association, another voluntary organization that was assuming construction management from the Bunker Hill Monument Association. Hale hoped that the money would be used to care for the remaining grounds preserved apart from development.[117]

Historic houses came to embody this tension like no other sites in the nineteenth-century United States. When observers valued them as evidence of both the domestic architecture and the lived space of past residents, their façades and interiors became inseparable markers of a modern morality that insisted on their separation. Men and women meditated on these sites to develop an ethic of old-fashioned domestic economy that condemned the pursuit of luxury and offered a model of moral consumption in the modern marketplace. But when men fashioned a form of masculine domesticity in associational life, they sought to demonstrate a moral authority that secured their financial control of the private household. They resolutely framed historic houses as men's space—only in later decades would they participate in reconstructions of colonial kitchens that foregrounded women's labor in historic homes.[118] As women more frequently earned money, made consumer purchases with cash instead of credit, and hired household help, associational men devised plans for preservation that demonstrated their ability to do these same tasks with the public good in mind. When they aimed to preserve historic house interiors under the construct of a voluntary association, they framed civic housekeeping as an activity in which any self-improving man could partake—with or without a family home to call his own.

Deals Unsealed

Support for associational plans for preservation rose and fell according to domestic ideals of morality and economy, not love or disdain of the past. In 1834, Ellen Randolph Coolidge, still bitter at her family's loss of Monticello, condemned associational efforts to buy the property. She gasped at the uncouth behavior of a man trying to solicit donations to purchase Monticello from James Barclay. "I am glad Monticello is no longer in the market to be hawked about by that crazy creature Mr. Hart, who has been lately in Boston tormenting the natives to subscribe for the purchase," she wrote to her sister. "He called to see me and his mind was so evidently wandering that I was glad to have him out of the house and dissuaded him all I could from going round among persons who, besides having no friendly feelings for the name of Jefferson, were about that time almost crazed by their own pecuniary troubles."[119] To Coolidge, Hart pursued supposedly benevolent designs in a manner no better than a speculative auctioneer: he encouraged unwise spending by playing on people's emotions.

Other proposals for the associational preservation of historic houses met similar criticism and insufficient financial support. But members of voluntary organizations continued to solicit allies. In Philadelphia, John Fanning Watson failed to purchase the Letitia House in 1834. Still, it remained standing and would later be removed from the urban crush along the Delaware River to the verdant banks of the Schuylkill, west of the city's nucleus.[120] The Historical Society of Pennsylvania periodically expressed interest in buying other historic buildings in Philadelphia. In 1846, one committee decided to "confer with the present owner of the Norris House and ascertain if she would consent to sell the same if the Society could provide a purchaser pledged to its perpetual preservation."[121] Five years later, another committee tried to find a third-party buyer for Penn's Slate Roof house. When they failed, they lobbied fellow society members to authorize an associational purchase.[122] At Newburgh, the Washington's Head-Quarters Association failed to raise the money they needed to buy real estate—$40,000 subscribed with a quarter of the amount collected.[123] The property landed in the hands of New York State when Jonathan Hasbrouck defaulted on his mortgage in 1848. In 1850, the celebrated purchase of Newburgh's headquarters occurred when the state legislature paid the $2,000 owed to the U.S. Deposit Fund for the foreclosed property.[124]

Yet the limited success of plans for collective ownership did not indicate a popular apathy toward old houses in the second quarter of the nineteenth century. By the 1830s, a preponderance of U.S. residents agreed that architecture could form permanent links to the past in ways that written documents could not. The desire to see domestic interiors of historic figures continued to grow. By mid-century, readers could buy volumes that offered geographical biographies of famous men, such as George P. Putnam's *Homes of American Authors* (1853) and *Homes of American Statesmen* (1854). These books promoted the idea that each house "had a certain individual character and expression of its own," and it evoked the "individual and private memories" of the men who lived in it.[125] The art of discerning the character of men from these houses, wrote Edward W. Johnston, was like studying handwriting or physiognomy; just as the form of a hand or the shape of a skull gave insight into the inner workings of the brain, houses "might connect the structural efforts of individuals with the cast of their minds and feelings."[126] Birthplaces, family homes, and adult residences could offer deeper insight into an individual's character than could his public actions and writings. Even as these volumes warned against prying eyes that disturbed the sanctity of leaders' domestic spheres, they fed an interest in viewing these spaces after their famed inhabitants had departed. In some places, viewers found descendants of U.S. "founders" still in residence. These heirs of family estates faced growing demands to manage public interest in their homes as inheritance patterns, regional economies, and real estate markets of suburbanization all put new pressures on stewards of multigenerational estates. Many turned to the architecture of rural improvement to monumentalize their family's prominence in a statement of permanence for a new age.

CHAPTER 6

Ancestral Estates: Patrimonial Property and Rural Improvement

In 1835, Rebecca Warren Brown turned to the life of her great-uncle Joseph Warren to capitalize on her family history. She appealed to popular interest in the domestic lives of "great men" by opening her children's biography of the Revolutionary War general with a description of his birthplace. Writing pseudonymously as "A Lady of Boston," she described her ancestors' estate from the perspective of a mother teaching her children. When General Warren was the age of her young listeners, she explained, he lived with his family in a farmhouse near Roxbury. Modern travelers regularly passed this house on the way to Boston; it stood in full view of a busy road. "It is now almost fallen to pieces," she noted, "but it was once a beautiful place, and had a great many fine fruits around it."

Brown's view of the estate reflected a different vision of the family home from the one that Eliza Leslie or Edmund Quincy characterized. Rather than peering into the private quarters of the old farmhouse, which was presently filled with tenants, Brown took a step back to survey the domestic landscape. In doing so, she gave her readers a view of the Warren estate through the lens of the environmental reforms promoted by New England's agrarians and country gentlemen. These principles of rural improvement cast the house as a poor monument to the past. Its decayed condition and old-fashioned features spelled its obsolescence. A different feature of the homestead, however, preserved the Warren family legacy: the "Warren russetting," a popular green and blush apple supposedly first cultivated by the general's father. Young Joseph's father had died picking one of these prized apples, Brown's narrator explained, but the fruits still filled New England orchards, cider bottles, and baked goods (Figure 23).[1]

As popular interest in the houses of illustrious men grew, Rebecca Brown's depiction of the Warren estate drew attention to a particular type of historic home: an ancestral estate owned by descendants of the same family. Her brother, John

Figure 23. Nathaniel Currier hoped to profit from popular interest in the homes of famous men when he published this lithograph of the birthplace of Joseph Warren in 1840. His view presents a different image from the dilapidated one that Rebecca Warren Ball described in her 1835 biography of Warren: Currier shows a neatly kept, if old-fashioned, clapboard farmhouse and picket fence. The contrast of Currier's and Ball's characterizations exemplifies competing visions of the value of old houses for modern U.S. society. Nathaniel Currier, "The House in Roxbury, Mass. (As It Now Stands, August, 1840) in which General Joseph Warren was born in the year 1741." Collection of the Massachusetts Historical Society.

Collins Warren, had inherited the property from their bachelor uncle, Samuel Warren, in 1805.[2] Brown's description of the dilapidated farmhouse strategically avoided mentioning her brother's proprietorship and the tenants who rented his patrimony. At the time, John Collins Warren preferred to memorialize his famous uncle at the Bunker Hill battleground rather than his Roxbury birthplace. Ten years later, however, he determined to preserve the Roxbury property as a memorial to Warren family history. Warren adopted the doctrines of rural improvement that his sister had invoked: he demolished the old house and built a new one according to the principles of Andrew Jackson Downing, an architect who published popular house and horticulture designs intended to cultivate residential permanence at country estates. John Collins Warren celebrated the renovated property as "Warren Manor," the historic seat of his American ancestors.

Rebecca Brown and John Collins Warren defined an evolutionary mode of preservation with rural improvement to participate in broader conversations about the social effects of inheritance. At a moment when most U.S. residents saw landed inheritance in terms of monetary rather than productive value, observers questioned whether permanent family holdings constituted laudable social stability or the consolidation of aristocratic wealth. Interlocutors on both sides of the argument supported their claims with family genealogies and progressive narratives of historical change defined by the process of civilization. Some argued that perpetual family estates preserved colonial forms of property ownership that inhibited the free circulation of property. In their minds, the division of inherited real estate enabled the economic independence necessary for democratic citizenship. Others forged an argument for estate preservation at the intersection of sentimental domesticity and environmental sustainability. Heirs who maintained ancestral estates with rural improvement, they argued, cultivated a modern form of domestic permanence that promoted civic health by nurturing an intergenerational attachment not only to family homes but also to historic places.

Men who shaped their ancestral estates with this evolutionary form of preservation sought to capitalize on the transformation of agrarian lands into suburban developments. They used the architecture of rural improvement to fix environmental remnants of the past not in "original" forms but in transformations of distinctive features. In this way, they promoted modern standards of domestic privacy by redirecting public interest from domestic interiors to landscape views. But they also constructed a logic of preservation that sanctioned the subdivision of inherited property for new land and labor markets. They used Downing's revivalist forms to inscribe agricultural pasts of extensive land holding into domestic gardens, renovated houses, and newly grafted trees. If heirs could preserve ancestral estates as living memorials, they could make their historic properties permanent while selling unproductive lands—or even unprofitable people.[3] This mode of preservation encouraged men to imagine themselves as ancestral patriarchs of the future while affirming the moral leadership of historic estate proprietors at the top of racial, gender, and social hierarchies. But as more proprietors reshaped ancestral estates with rural improvement, critics deployed the politics of demolition to challenge the ability of familial heirs to preserve historic estates as sites of public interest.

Ancestral Estates

When Rebecca Brown published her description of the Warren homestead, many Americans saw an estate preserved by multiple generations of familial descendants as a rare thing. The Revolutionary generation had defined wide-spread land ownership as a necessary feature of a modern republic, and political leaders shaped estate law to encourage dispersion of land to freeholders rather than consolidation of family property in aristocratic land holdings. Lawmakers cleared the way for the sale of real estate to settle debts of a decedent. They also directed the equal division of intestate estates among a decedent's heirs, regardless of sex or birth order. Testators tended to follow suit. Estate divisions, paired with economic change, prompted many heirs to convert landed inheritance into cash rather than place it in a family trust or take possession of subdivided parcels. A descendant who wanted to preserve an ancestral estate intact would have to purchase it at a sheriff's sale or buy out fellow heirs—prospects that generally demanded an outlay of disposable capital.[4]

As a result, most Americans saw the dissipation of ancestral estates as a way of life in the United States. Louisa Catherine Adams took this perspective when she reflected on the fate of the Hamilton family estate outside of Philadelphia in 1822. The most recent owner had been the fourth generation of his family to own it. When he died intestate and childless in 1817, the Schuylkill River estate descended to his nieces and nephews. Adams saw the impending fate of the property as a typical one. "The Woodlands is really a beautiful spot," she reflected, "but like most of the property in our Country, it is to be sold and can no longer remain in the hands of the old proprietors; as it must be divided between the family."[5] Some Hamilton heirs tried to secure ownership of the Woodlands by purchasing it from their uncle's estate. But standing debts and high expenses landed the property at sheriff's sale in 1827. One of the Hamilton heirs bought the estate only to sell it to a different buyer a week later so that the family could reap some financial benefit.[6]

In the 1830s, an increasing number of U.S. residents saw landed inheritance as an opportunity to generate the cash and mobility needed to navigate new conditions of industrializing economies, not as a means to continue their family's land use for another generation. This was particularly true for families embedded in agrarian economies. Freeholders and landlords managed real estate in response to swings in agricultural markets, transformative effects of new transportation, environmental degradation, and the rise of cash and contract transactions. Many turned to land sales to generate the cash needed to pursue new modes of capital generation or move to locations with more promising markets.[7] When heirs confronted complications to securing clear title to their landed inheritance, they often invoked the right to property as a foundational principle of the nation. However, they adapted it to new economic conditions by characterizing land as the foundation of independence, not as a means of subsistence production but as a way to generate financial capital. In this line of thinking, U.S. citizens cultivated civic health by sustaining a robust real estate market. The right to claim landed inheritance was the right to sell it.

The stakes of these transactions were highest for Americans of limited capital. When they confronted hurdles to profiting from the sale of ancestral lands, many crafted histories of family and nation to make reinforcing claims to personal property rights and a place in U.S. civil society. Strictures that perpetuated colonial forms of property holdings, they argued, stunted economic and social improvement. Either they locked Americans in old economic and social relationships or they empowered landholders to exploit old privileges without fulfilling the responsibilities once linked to those advantages. The preservation of family estates as permanent features of the modern United States, critics argued, were uncivil. Landholders demonstrated their support for a modern democratic citizenry, in this view, by supporting the division and sale of family lands as a mechanism of improvement.

Thomas Commuck used this strategy to navigate an exploitative trusteeship of Narragansett lands and secure a title to his family farm near Charlestown, Rhode Island. In 1823, Commuck had left his natal community to join a new Indigenous nation in upstate New York: the Brothertown Indians.[8] Members of several Indigenous communities in New England had established the Brothertown nation in the mid-eighteenth century and taken up residence on donated Oneida land soon thereafter. While many Brothertowns maintained some identification with their distinctive communities of origin, they embraced forms of property ownership, economic production, and participation in U.S. politics that departed from ancestral lifeways continued by many of their kin. Young Thomas Commuck likely saw membership in the Brothertown nation as an opportunity to leave the economic hardship, state guardianship, racial discrimination, and dispossession endured by residents of Narragansett lands.[9]

Fifteen years later, Commuck sought to turn his landed inheritance in Narragansett country into capital that would support a new family home among Brothertowns, who themselves sought a new home on the western side of the Great Lakes. Beginning in the 1830s, Commuck worked with Rhode Island legislator Wilkins Updike and Narragansett clergyman Moses Stanton to petition the General Assembly of Rhode Island to issue to him a deed in fee simple for his grandfather's farm. The acreage fell within the swath of Narragansett land that the state had designated as tribal property, preserved in a trust managed by the state of Rhode Island. In petitions to the state legislature, Commuck narrated two accounts of his personal past to position himself as the rightful owner of his ancestral farm. One was a genealogy of his Narragansett ancestry.[10] Commuck drafted numerous declarations of his exclusive "right of Inheritants [sic] in the Narragansett Reservation" as the "just and legal heir to certain

Landed Estates through kinship which Estates Descended to him in a Direct Line."[11] He recounted a chain of property descent from his direct ancestors to himself and noted that the most recent resident of the family house was distant kin with no claim to ownership. Commuck played to his audience when he translated this genealogy to a statement of racial purity. When he asserted himself to be "one of the very few full blooded Remnants of that Once numerous and Powerful Tribe known by the name of the Narragansett Tribe of Indians," he boosted his own claim to title by diminishing competing appeals that might arise from Narragansetts with African ancestors as well as Indigenous ones.[12] This argument leveraged the "vanishing Indian" trope for personal power, implying that legislators should release lands intended for perpetual preservation because no future need for it would exist.[13]

Commuck paired his genealogical account with a moralizing narrative of personal improvement. He deployed colonizing conceptions of civilization to tell his family history as one of Indigenous "progress" away from traditional Narragansett living toward the "modern" life of the Brothertowns. Commuck made this argument by separating his claims of Narragansett biological racial identity from his membership in the Brothertown nation. For instance, he reported that his grandmother had taught him the only six Narragansett words that she had learned from her mother. "You may judge from this," he wrote to Wisconsin historian Lyman C. Draper, "how long it must be since the Brothertowns used their native tongue."[14] Similarly, Commuck emphasized that the tunes in his songbook *Indian Melodies* did not originate from Indigenous musical traditions. He had learned to sing "scientifically," he told readers, and had written these songs only after years of musical study.[15] Commuck characterized individual property holdings deeded in fee simple as the final step of this "rise and progress" of Indigenous people who adopted Euro-American modes of dress, language, architecture, and Christianity.[16] In this view, the Brothertown Indians achieved the pinnacle of this ascent in 1839, when the U.S. government awarded them U.S. citizenship and fee simple deeds to land in Wisconsin territory. To Commuck, this new locale was "Home, Sweet Home."[17] With this popular expression of sentimental domesticity, Commuck calibrated his moral center of gravity to modern material standards of Christian family life rather than established ways of living on ancestral lands.[18] Yet he also claimed his right to possess—and sell—the lands that had descended to him through familial inheritance backed by U.S. law.

Commuck believed that Indigenous Americans should secure a permanent place in the United States by possessing land as individual holdings of private property, not as collective tracts of tribal nations. His arguments against the preservation strictures of his ancestral estate responded to the particular forms of

Indigenous dispossession and oppression that he had witnessed in three separate regions. In the 1820s, the General Assembly of Rhode Island began to cleave off land parcels to settle the debts that they ascribed to Narragansett residents—an act in blatant disregard of the U.S. Non-Intercourse Acts that outlawed this practice. The Brothertowns had engaged in years of disputes to secure and sell property in their New York parcel. Their attempts to purchase land west of the Great Lakes generated conflicts as well, not only with the U.S. government but also with the Menominee and Ho-Chunk nations.[19] To Commuck, these cases confirmed that collective tribal land claims posed two threats to Indigenous Americans' wellbeing: the risk of land confiscation and, paradoxically, the capital immobility of perpetual land ownership. Holding lands in fee simple, in his view, empowered Indigenous Americans to possess, bequeath, and sell family lands as individual managers of real estate rather than usufruct stewards—a position too frequently usurped from tribal leaders by state entities.

Though Commuck confronted particular exigencies as a Narragansett and Brothertown man, his concern over access to land ownership resonated with the arguments of a growing number of white laborers. Commuck sought to reverse old patterns of property holding that denied him the rights promised by the American Revolution. In the 1830s and 1840s, white workingmen and agrarian reformers launched similar arguments about anachronistic strictures of property holding as oppressive to laborers.[20] Agrarians in New York's Hudson Valley generated one of the largest and most sustained campaigns to this effect. These "anti-rent" activities challenged the region's heritable system of leaseholding. For two centuries, proprietary land rights had directed area residents to pay yearly rents of cash, labor, and agricultural products to their landlords. The sale of heritable leases also incurred fees.[21] Like Commuck, Hudson Valley agrarians saw enduring proprietorships as a vestige of the past that attenuated economic and social improvement in the United States.

When Stephen Van Rensselaer IV expressed a particularly tenacious resistance to land reform, a coalition of "anti-renters" characterized the preservation of his family's landholdings as an antimodern maintenance of feudalism. Van Rensselaer inherited the western half of his ancestral estate, Rensselaerwyck, on the death of his father in 1839. His colonizing progenitor had received the land as part of a patent of Mohawk and Mahican lands issued by the Dutch government in 1629. The parcel encompassed the growing post of Beverwyck and extended for twenty-five miles along the Hudson River and just as far from both sides of its banks. As Beverwyck developed into the capital city of Albany, generations of Van Rensselaers maintained their proprietary holdings through transitions to British colonial administration and then U.S. governance. In 1785, Stephen Van Rensselaer III took up proprietorship of the estate with a manorial celebration that "revived" feudal practices that had never existed on the manor.[22] He developed his land holdings by attracting more renters to clear the land and profited not only from increased agricultural output but also from consumerism directed toward Van Rensselaer businesses. The panic of 1819 and subsequent depression of the region's markets shook the prosperity of Rensselaerwyck into decline. Van Rensselaer converted unpaid rents due in bushels of wheat into cash debts and pressed his tenants for repayment. As agricultural production on exhausted lands slowed and transport provided by the Erie Canal diminished market prices for these attenuated harvests, farmers had to generate much higher yields to settle cash debts accrued according to old market prices. Some renters settled their accounts, but others resisted Van Rensselaer by ignoring his demands or challenging the terms of his leases.[23]

When the proprietor died in 1839, many renters hoped for a new era of land tenure that would erase back rents and issue deeds in fee simple—or at least offer revised leases. They were sorely disappointed. Stephen Van Rensselaer's will divided his proprietary holdings in half to convey landed inheritance to the oldest son of each of his two wives. He favored his eldest son and namesake with the historical authority of family proprietorship: Stephen Van Rensselaer IV received lands west of the Hudson River that contained the family's two manor houses. Yet he also inherited his father's debts. The will of Stephen Van Rensselaer III instructed executors to collect the massive sum of back rents to settle his accounts. His sons would have to pick up the remaining balance if they were not successful in collecting the $400,000 due.[24] While Stephen Van Rensselaer IV's half-brother William expressed more patience with insolvent renters on his tract east of the Hudson, Van Rensselaer IV initiated an aggressive campaign to shake down tenants who did not immediately remit payment.

Like Thomas Commuck, tenants fought these unfavorable terms with historical narratives of property ownership. They challenged their landlords by characterizing them as corrupt aristocrats who perpetuated unjust features of colonial life invalidated by the Revolution. Some tenants tried to prove that the Van Rensselaers did not possess a clear title to their inherited tracts. They dove into family histories and imperial records seeking evidence of problematic chains of descent or legal authority that would invalidate subsequent inheritance transfers.[25] Others framed historical arguments for the abolition of the rent system. They invoked their own family lineage to claim rights to their leaseholds with permanent improvements created by ancestral labor and cultivated grounds marked by the graves of their forefathers. Leaseholds that denied families a clear title to these properties, they argued, constituted a form of labor theft that kept renters in a "feudal slavery" characteristic of the European past.[26] When tenants donned "Indian" costumes to perpetrate violence against proprietary interests, they invoked histories of revolutionary resistance to monarchical power to cast their landlords as holdovers of exploitative colonial interests.[27]

New York legislators took up the anti-rent cause to formulate broader arguments about the role that inheritance and labor should play in defining property rights. They confronted especially precarious work when they tried to weaken vested proprietary interests without endangering an ordinary citizens' right to inheritance. "Great landed property and the descent of enormous and unbroken fortunes are, on any large scale, wholly incompatible with our institutions," wrote state legislator Theodore Sedgwick Jr. But "the right of property, the right to enjoy undisturbed the fruits of legitimate acquisition, whether of one's own or of ancestral labor, is the first badge of a civilized society, and to it every other principle gives way."[28] In attempts to work out this conundrum, reformers used the language of feudalism to characterize particular property regimes as regressive forces. As one legislator put it, "In England, all is stable; here all is changing. There a man reveres as sacred the ancient stone walls of the family mansion occupied by his ancestors a thousand years ago, however uncouth or inconvenient; here we would demolish them and build better."[29] Any U.S. citizen who did not subscribe to this ethic, he implied, let ancestor worship impede improvement. Another politician agreed when he framed manorial rents as "relics of barbarism, incompatible with the institutions of a free people and the spirit of the age."[30] Writers pointed to Russia and China as places where feudalism stunted the development of "pre-modern" nations in the contemporary world.[31] Some made the racial limits of their arguments explicit when they worried that exploitative land practices would make "white slaves" of workers rather than citizens.[32] Only at the end of the 1840s did some anti-rent supporters join Free-Soilers and antislavery advocates in extending the metaphor of feudalism to condemn African American slavery as an anachronistic form of labor.[33]

Anti-renters leveraged this vision of living history in the politics of capitalism. They portrayed the anti-rent struggle as a contest between old ways and new ones. Manorial land tenures, they argued, kept the past in place instead of driving historical development. Yet critics decried the pecuniary motives of manor proprietors as thoroughly modern ones: they were money-hungry elites who kept tenants in a form of "voluntary slavery" to maximize their profits in the new economy.[34] In their view, proprietary heirs who preserved their ancestral estates exploited economic privileges inherited from the colonial era by ignoring the terms of U.S. civil society. Men such as Stephen Van Rensselaer IV managed their property only with an eye to financial profits, neglecting the social responsibilities of both an old-fashioned manorial landlord and a modern republican citizen. They acted, in the words of one commentator, in "the interest of a capitalist."[35]

As proprietors of ancestral lands faced these attacks, they shaped the built environment to make the case for the perpetuity of family property in modern civil society. In Rhode Island, legislators regularly permitted Narragansett petitioners to sell their family estates in fee simple deeds with no restrictions on future land use or sale. Yet many Narragansetts who remained built distinctive and durable masonry structures that maintained ancestral lands. These buildings, fences, and memorials formed an architectural means of resisting dispossession and detribalization by staying in place.[36] Other Indigenous residents of New England did the same to preserve tribal lands in parcels legally defined as privately held family farms. The stone boundary walls and 1801 homestead built by descendants of Moses Printer, for instance, mark the Nipmuc land now preserved as the Hassanamisco Reservation.[37]

In the Hudson Valley, Stephen Van Rensselaer IV argued against the charges of anti-renters through architecture as well as court cases. When he inherited the western half of Rensselaerwyck in 1839, he embarked on a building campaign to fashion himself a progressive landlord. He immediately demolished the oldest manor house on the property—Watervliet, a one-story stone structure built by the family's first American proprietor, Jeremias Van Rensselaer, in 1668.[38] He then hired architect Richard Upjohn to renovate the newer manor house, a Georgian mansion built in 1765 by the heir's grandfather. Upjohn was making a name for himself as a leading designer of revivalist architecture—iterations of medieval designs created to secure architectural permanence for a modern era.[39] Van Rensselaer made these renovations a material rejoinder to anti-rent arguments. But he also modeled a type of evolutionary preservation that other heirs of landed patrimony would adopt in the coming years.

Rural Improvement and Evolutionary Preservation

Van Rensselaer used the revivalist architecture of rural improvement to frame his proprietorship of Rensselaerwyck as a laudable means of historic preservation, not an anachronistic relic of the colonial past. Upjohn's renovations and Van Rensselaer's gardens invoked environmental reforms designed expressly to cultivate residential permanence. The Hudson Valley hummed with men who defined these tenets for a national audience. In Albany, Jesse Buel published the *Cultivator*, a popular clearinghouse for lessons in agricultural improvement. Its readers sought to cultivate social and economic stability by combating soil exhaustion, designing more efficient implements, and developing new cultivars for higher yields.[40] Improvers of rural abodes aimed to cultivate stability with the architectural design of buildings and landscapes. Andrew Jackson

Downing and Alexander Jackson Davis—the architect who had drawn views of Dutch colonial buildings in Manhattan years earlier—elaborated architectural and horticultural principles of rural refinement. Their designs worked in concert with agricultural reforms to encourage intergenerational proprietorship of country estates.[41]

These rural improvers cultivated historical consciousness as a principle of wealth accumulation that strengthened civil society.[42] In their view, residential stability produced steady financial profits by counterbalancing a U.S. proclivity for fast profit derived from environmental waste and frequent migration. Buel, Davis, and Downing promulgated new modes of agrarian production, landscape architecture, and house design to encourage families to invest in long-term occupancy of a single locale. They and their disciples encouraged proprietors to shape a coherent domestic setting that drew out a site's distinctive features— Downing characterized it in the words of eighteenth-century poet Alexander Pope as "the genius of the place."[43] Architecture would shape family properties into "sacred patrimony" that heirs would cherish for perpetual use rather than market value. This eye toward environmental perpetuity, they believed, would inculcate economic and environmental self-restraint that would build social ties across time.[44]

Stephen Van Rensselaer IV saw rural improvement as a way to define his colonial inheritance as a boon rather than a hindrance to U.S. economy and civil society. He defined his family's past as one of the particularities of place that he sought to perpetuate. His estate renovations won the approval of Andrew Downing himself. In his first edition of *A Treatise on the Theory and Practice of Landscape Gardening*, published in 1841, Downing highlighted the "geometric" gardens of the manor house as a model of the landscape architecture that his treatise wished to inculcate in North America.[45] Three years later, Downing's revised edition singled out Van Rensselaer's architectural renovations for praise. The manor house, "lately remodeled and improved by that skilful [*sic*] architect, Mr. Upjohn, of New-York," he explained, formed the finest domestic example of Roman revival, or Italianate, architecture in the United States. To Downing, the renovated house embodied a family past much older than the structure itself: he labeled the abode the "Patroon's House," making no mention of the recently demolished Watervliet when he described it as "the ancient seat of the Van Rensselaer family."[46] In yet another edition in 1849, Downing inflated the profile of the estate by adding a second description to the "Historical Sketches" that opened his book.[47]

Van Rensselaer and Downing exemplified rural improvers who believed that they secured rather than erased the work of previous generations at family estates. As interest in old houses continued to rise, they defined the historic home not as the domestic interior of a nuclear family household but as the landscape of an intergenerational family seat. They used rural improvement to fashion an evolutionary mode of preservation that conceived of historic permanence of place akin to biological inheritance. Like-minded proprietors reshaped ancestral estates with architectural styles, building materials, landscape architecture, and plants designed to preserve the character of their ancestors' estate just as sexual reproduction perpetuated their heritable traits. In this way, rural improvers inscribed inherited properties with a genealogical view of land that framed their estates as living legacies of colonizing progenitors.[48] Observers pointed to "revived" buildings, trees, and planting schemes as evidence of the health of the property's architectural, horticultural, and human "stock."[49] Preservation of these remnants of the past could serve the public good, they implied, when estate proprietors carried out the work of previous generations. Yet in defining generations by transitions of property title, rural improvers articulated patrilineal chains of descent that overrode the complexities of biological family history with a naturalized claim to ancestral wealth and family authority.

Proponents of evolutionary preservation used revivalist architecture not to rebuild features exactly as they looked in the past but to create a landscape aesthetic that provoked interest in and care for the architectural remnants of the past that did remain. Beauty was irrelevant to individuals trying to keep old houses in place as they stood in the past; buildings described as ugly or humble could evoke intellectual and emotional connections to past residents. Rural improvers, however, valued beauty as a landscape feature that could generate a connection to the history of a specific place. Guides to rural improvement offered landed heirs a grammar of permanence that they used to tie remnants of the past into a historic whole defined by place and property lines.

In 1841, for instance, John Pickering (1777–1846) ordered a Gothic renovation of his seventeenth-century family property to restore the house's "original" character—something that both he and his father had studied.[50] His great-great-grandfather of the same name had built the core of the house near Salem, Massachusetts, around 1664 and enlarged it twenty years later.[51] Pickering had known the house only after a Georgian overhaul created a more spacious upper story and straight roofline in 1751.[52] John Pickering had grown up in this house under the mentorship of his bachelor uncle—another John—and inherited the property from him in 1811. Yet Pickering spent his adult life moving between Boston, Philadelphia, Washington, and Cambridge, building a career in law and linguistics. In the meantime, the house served as the final abode for a number of elderly relatives and later as a boardinghouse for local workers.[53]

Figure 24. Many of the estate renovations made by John Pickering and Jonathan F. Carlton in 1841 still stand today at 40 Broad Street in Salem, Massachusetts. The Pickering Foundation—a nonprofit organization founded in 1952 and still run by members of the Pickering family—manages the property and opens it to public tours on Sundays for five months of the year. Photograph by author, 2013.

When Pickering determined to make the house his summer retirement home, he hired master carpenter Jonathan F. Carlton to overhaul it with the design elements of rural improvement.[54] In 1841, these renovations replaced the straight roofline with a nearly symmetrical pair of gables (Figure 24). Repetitive quatrefoil cutouts on the balcony and the property's new board fence appropriated the decorative element from local Gothic churches built in the preceding years.[55] A round window in the center of each front gable, modillions on the roof eaves, large window surrounds under heavy cornices, and prominent obelisk finials on the roof rail and fence posts all appeared as distinctive markers of rural English Gothic cottages in Downing's *Treatise* that year.[56] Shrubbery supposedly imported from England a few years later also evoked a modern taste for British history in the United States.[57]

When viewers recognized these British Gothic designs as a contemporary architectural style, they saw the renovation campaign as an effort to maintain evidence of the property's colonial past. In June 1841, one newspaper writer reported it as a notable example of "Salem Improvements": "The old Pickering house," he wrote, "has been lately refitted in an antique and peculiar style, much resembling some of the picturesque old mansions of England."[58] By recognizing the renovations as elements of a coherent style, the writer invoked the associational qualities of architecture that Downing and his peers defined for it. In their view, revivalist architecture called to mind the historical era from which its forms derived.[59] At the Pickering house, however, approximations of

Figure 25. Joseph B. Felt published several views of seventeenth-century houses in Salem that—in his mind—exemplified the ways that the town's colonial architecture embodied revivalist design principles encouraged by Andrew Jackson Downing. The Curwin Mansion, depicted here, shared with the Pickering house a three-bay design with peaked gables, rooftop finials, and a central chimney. Joseph B. Felt, "Curwin Mansion," *Annals of Salem*, 2nd ed., vol. 1 (Salem, 1845), p. 410. Courtesy American Antiquarian Society.

medieval English architecture channeled the first generations of Massachusetts Bay colonizers.

Observers believed that the renovations reestablished architectural markers of the house's first era. In 1845, for instance, local historian Joseph B. Felt explained that recent renovations had "restored two of the three peaks, which formerly belonged to its front."[60] Viewers did not naively believe that the renovations re-created the look of the old house exactly. The gables and decorative details evoked the "class" of "ancient houses" built by early Anglo-American colonizers (Figure 25). Felt imagined that these houses connected modern-day viewers with forefathers in the same way that the original houses had tied their builders to English peers. "When we catch a glance of the remnants, which belonged to edifices, thus portrayed," Felt wrote, "we are carried back to the scene, when they began to peer above the cottages around them, attract the gaze of the untutored Indian, and renew, more impressively, the emigrant's association of domestic art in the land of his fathers."[61] In this telling, the

Pickering house had been an agent of American civilization, and its current owner—who shared a name with the house's builder—reactivated this power for the modern era.

Features that evoked the character of the original Pickering house also created a specific kind of memorial landscape, one that used rural improvement to secure permanent markers of individual lives in a familial domain. In the 1830s, Mount Auburn Cemetery outside of Cambridge, Massachusetts, and Salem's Harmony Grove became some of the first rural cemeteries to use Gothic revival architecture, picturesque conventions of landscape architecture, and fee simple deeds to family plots to secure the permanence of ancestral burials.[62] The architects of these sites built fences, chapels, and gatehouses in the Gothic revival style because they believed that its materiality encouraged permanence. Once reserved primarily for church architecture, architects carried it into rural cemeteries and houses as a way of expressing the newly sacred nature of those spaces.[63] Some elite men founded private cemetery companies that merged these new conventions of rural architecture with old ones to preserve former family estates as historic sites and green spaces. This is what happened to the Woodlands several years after Louisa Catherine Adams reflected on its impending sale: the Woodlands Cemetery Company preserved "the country seat of the Hamilton family" from industrial development by fixing many features of the eighteenth-century estate in the winding paths, horticultural landscape, and family plots of a nineteenth-century cemetery.[64]

In the mind of Henry Dearborn, a founder of Mount Auburn Cemetery, rural cemetery plots withstood the test of time in a way that family homes could not: "The moss-grown stone outlasts the most durable habitations of our fathers," he wrote.[65] Yet others believed that the same architecture of rural improvement could in fact secure historic homes as monuments that perpetuated memory of their previous residents in permanent dwellings and evocative grounds. In 1841, for instance, one writer—after reporting on a visit to Monticello—likened the renovation of the Pickering house to the tending of a parental grave plot. He described the house as "the picturesque birthplace of Col. Pickering, which the pious hands of his children have recently repaired and beautified in a style correspondent to the dignified simplicity of character of that inflexibly honest statesman."[66] This act of filial devotion preserved the home of a national luminary: Timothy Pickering, a former Revolutionary War general and U.S. statesman. The English style of the house and grounds highlighted his Anglophilic political and personal tastes while new plants, garden paths, and a modern stable evinced his devotion to agricultural improvement.[67] Future generations of Pickerings would keep the memory of their predecessor alive by caring for the estate according to his personal principles.[68]

In other words, preservation by rural improvement defined the character of past residents by the character of changes to their property, not the unchanged relics of their lives. John Collins Warren exemplified this principle with a domestic monument on his ancestral estate. In 1846, he replaced the clapboard farmhouse described by his sister with a stone house (Figure 26). On its façade, between the first and second stories, he inset a pair of engraved marble slabs. "On this spot stood the house erected by Joseph Warren, of Boston," the left one explained, "remarkable for being the birthplace of Gen. Joseph Warren, his grandson, who was killed at Bunker Hill, June 17, 1775." The right slab extended the family's history at the site: "John Warren, a distinguished anatomist, was also born here. The original house being in ruins, this house was built by John C. Warren, M.D., in 1846, son of the last named, as a permanent memorial of the spot."[69] These plaques made the new house a tombstone for the old one, marking stages in its life and death by residential epochs. A new stone wall bounded the front yard as memorial grounds. Nearly a decade later, Warren would transpose many of these elements into Roxbury's rural cemetery, Forest Hills, where he reinterred the remains of relatives exhumed from the old Roxbury burying ground and the family vault in St. Paul's Church in Boston.[70]

Yet the house design engaged the marble slabs in a campaign for preservation of the family estate, not just memorialization of the demolished house. Warren placed the engraved markers in a house that approximated the ornamental farmhouse design in Downing's *Cottage Residences*, which Warren purchased in 1846.[71] A symmetric, rectangular three-bay façade, finished with corner quoins and topped by two decorative chimneys, greeted visitors in place of a four-bay saltbox house with an off-center front door and central chimney. A diamond-shaped, diamond-paned window set into a steeply pointed central dormer, heavy stone window lintels, and a front portico crowned with a balustraded balcony all appeared in sharp contrast to the unadorned windows and plain entry cornice on the old house. A new dressed stone wall, replete with corner finials, took the place of wooden pickets and rough rocks. A new gardener's cottage sat at the back of the lot.[72]

The new house did not resemble its predecessor. But its design and materiality signaled its attempt to draw out the particularities of the site to perpetuate evidence of the past described on the plaques. John Collins Warren materialized family history as local history when he ordered new house walls built from conglomerate rock known as Roxbury puddingstone.[73] This distinctive geological feature, recognizable by its color and texture, naturalized the family's connection to place and likely had been quarried from a large outcropping on the Warren property. It also suggested that the men listed on the commemorative tablet had been instrumental in shaping the natural environment into a domes-

Figure 26. The stone house commissioned by John Collins Warren remains standing at 130 Warren Street in Roxbury, Massachusetts. The distinctive color and texture of the puddingstone walls express the popular domestic designs of Andrew
Jackson Downing in a recognizably local idiom. Inscribed plaques, visible between
first- and second-story windows, convey the history of the house that Warren set in
stone in 1846. The structure was rented as apartments and office space throughout
the twentieth century and remains in private hands, inaccessible to public visitors.
Photograph by author, 2014.

tic, civil one. The revivalist details of the new house invoked the early modern
progenitors of the Massachusetts Warrens. John Collins Warren traced this genealogy in family homes as well as people, imagining a domestic lineage that
matched Andrew Downing's statement that "the Anglo-Saxon love of home is
gradually developing itself out of the Anglo-American love of change."[74] In 1854,
Warren published a genealogy that traced a pedigree from the "ancient seat" of
the family in Devon, England, to the "Warren House, in Warren St., Roxbury.
Built in 1720 by Joseph Warren," to the "Warren House, in Warren St., Roxbury.
Rebuilt in 1846, by Dr. John C. Warren."[75] Observers followed the renovator's
lead in imprinting the stone cottage with its clapboard predecessor and the
Warren family's heraldic crest.[76]

When evolutionary preservation campaigns expressed the genealogical
view of land implicit in rural improvement, they framed the perpetuation of
ancestral estates as a manifestation of familial love that served the public good.
Heirs who continued family projects of so-called civilization cultivated historical anchors of civil society that fed a collective desire for "the old house at home."

Homecoming celebrations of the era attempted to gather far-flung migrants back to hometowns for public celebrations of civic progress. But they often elicited a nostalgia for the past rather than a celebration of its remnants.[77] As a writer opined in one Ohio newspaper, "Few are the instances where a family have resided for more than one generation; and should we have recollections, and attempt to re-visit our early homes, we find all changed."[78] In 1851, Henry Clay wrote to John Cleves Short that he recently had visited the old home place of his correspondent. "Every thing is totally changed," Clay reported. "Not a vestige remains of the old buildings. I should hardly have been able unassisted to recognize the spot. But, to do the present proprietor justice, he has built an excellent dwelling house and made a capital grazing farm out of it."[79] No less an advocate of agricultural improvement than Henry Clay regretted the disappearance of family homes while admitting the financial and moral value of environmental reforms that erased them.

Ancestral estates cultivated by consecutive generations seemed to model domestic economy that arose from devotion to family and home. As one writer noted of the New Hampshire family estate of U.S. historian William Prescott, "To possess an estate like that at Pepperell, which has come down by lineal descent through several successions of owners, all of whom were useful and honorable men in their day and generation, is a privilege not common any where, and very rare in a country like ours, young in years and not fruitful in local attachments." The writer did not deny that landed inheritance was a privilege. Yet he praised the Prescott heirs as honest workers who maintained the estate as an act of emotional care rather than economic calculation. "Family pride may be a weakness," the writer continued, "but family reverence is a just and generous sentiment."[80] In this view, the estate stood as evidence of the Prescott family's consistent devotion to the moral hearth of domestic life over market opportunities that would have dispersed it.

These accounts called up the language of sentimental domesticity to distract from the exploitative economic calculations made by Americans who forcibly removed African Americans and Indigenous Americans from their homes. These explanations also strengthened the language of development used to colonize Hispanic America in the 1840s and 1850s. Many observers praised mission churches, houses, and towns in former Spanish American colonies as material access points to "Old Spain." Through this lens, the architecture of California, Mexico, Texas, and Florida appeared as a new colonial past for the imperial United States. Many U.S. observers condemned the decay of these structures as evidence of the moral degeneracy of residents who practiced poor economy.[81] As one U.S. booster of St. Augustine, Florida, explained in 1848, "The blighted stocks of desolate orange groves—the tokens of decay—the obvious lack of industry and taste, and the consequent want of thrift—on a close inspection are relieved by a constant succession of images of the past, illustrative of the character of Castilian mind in a heroic and barbarous age." The "ancient city," however, "is being transformed into American features, both in the external appearance, and in the habits and customs of the people." These changes made the city more, not less, "interest[ing] to the antiquary and to the historian. If not old Spain in miniature, it is a chip of the block of the old in the new world, a relic of past interwoven with the texture of the present age."[82] These architectural assessments echoed the racial theories of historian William Prescott to characterize the so-called Americanization of the landscape as the preservation of venerable colonial legacies with environmental improvement.[83] Scions of early North American colonizers provided a model for how U.S. real estate developers might do this to best personal advantage.

Family Real Estate

Stephen Van Rensselaer IV, John Pickering, and John Collins Warren all used the architecture of rural improvement to transform their landed inheritance into suburban real estate. They designed their renovations broadly to curtail what they and other environmental reformers saw as the decay of the countryside during changes to agrarian economies. But they developed their mode of evolutionary preservation as a logic of suburban development. When they consolidated family lineage and local history in domestic renovations, they made outlying lands extraneous to the character of place. These heirs shaped the residential cores of their ancestral estates to portray the subdivision and sale of land parcels as a continuation of the improvement set in motion by their ancestors—not the decay of their legacy. From this perspective, they managed their landed inheritance in the interest of public good by civilizing the process of urbanization with suburbs that embodied local pasts and futures as well as country and city.

Van Rensselaer, Pickering, and Warren all sought financial profit when residents of nearby cities eyed the open lands of their ancestral estates as prime locations for homes removed from hubs of urban commerce and industry. Stephen Van Rensselaer IV came into conflict with his renters over how to determine a financial value for his lands in this changing land economy. When Van Rensselaer first tried to collect back rents in 1839, tenants pressed him to revise the terms of their leases to accord with new realities of agricultural production, including soil exhaustion and diminished market prices for wheat.[84] Tenants wanted their landlord to forgive debts, reassess land value to reflect the soil quality, and then offer farms for sale to current tenants. Van Rensselaer was willing to sell parcels

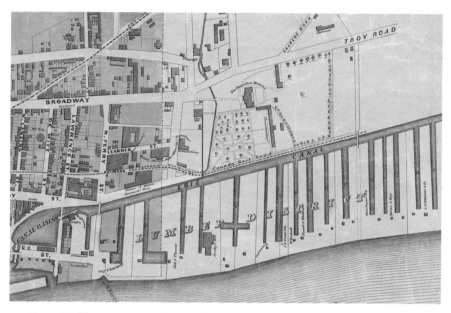

Figure 27. The geometric gardens at the center of this map detail, along with the adjacent mansion and conservatory, mark Stephen Van Rensselaer IV's estate, as it stood adjacent to the growing city of Albany in 1857. The estate sits just outside the city limits and municipal Ward 7. A railroad, canal, and strip of lumber wharves on the Hudson River form the property's eastern boundary; foundries and factories sit just to the south. Eight years earlier, Andrew Jackson Downing had described this once-rural situation as suburban. E. Jacob and Reuben H. Bingham, detail of "Map of the City of Albany" (Albany: Sprague and Co., 1857). Photo credit: New York Public Library.

to their tenants after the collection of back rents. But he calculated prices according to situation for commercial development. Rather than the price of two-and-a-half dollars per acre of productive land proposed by tenants, he offered to sell parcels at a baseline of five dollars—and later four dollars—per acre. He demanded higher prices for land closer to towns. By Van Rensselaer's calculations, proximity to urban markets and transportation made these tracts more valuable real estate not only for farmers taking products to market but also for urban developers.[85] Van Rensselaer got a close-up view of their work from his own manor house: by 1849, A. J. Downing described its location "in the northern suburbs of the city of Albany" (Figure 27).[86] In 1853, Van Rensselaer found a developer who would pay his asking price for manor land. He sold his hereditary leaseholds to Walter S. Church, who collected back rents—or evicted tenants—before selling off the lands in fee simple deeds. Van Rensselaer retained the former seat of the vast estate as a suburban family home and died there in 1868.[87]

John Pickering used the architecture of rural improvement to integrate his house into an urbanizing neighborhood that he himself had enabled. In the first quarter of the century, he and his cousin Pickering Dodge took the lead in the residential development of Chestnut Street just north of the family estate. They encouraged town administrators to double the width of the new street and built a number of fashionable Federal-style residences along the famed avenue. By the 1840s, John Pickering also had sold off house lots to the south of the old house. His land deals continued the work of the estate's previous proprietor, who had sold land for the development of the Broad Street neighborhood.[88] John Pickering's renovations collapsed the history of his family estate into a single house lot while integrating it into a suburban landscape. Historian Joseph Felt described how images of Salem's oldest houses could call to mind new houses recently built in a similar style—"'cottages ornate,' which are making their appearance in the vicinity of our metropolis and thus reviving a style of architecture, which has been long disused in our communities."[89] The Pickering house managed to maintain evidence of early Anglo-American architecture while resembling the new houses that characterized suburban districts.

Pickering and Warren used the double valence of revivalist architecture to frame their estates as ones that resisted decay. New houses that went up around their old ones created a visual contrast that threatened to cast their landed inheritance as an obsolescent piece of the past. Rural improvers were primed to see old-fashioned clapboard houses, unsculpted service yards, and coarse fences as evidence of rural decay.[90] Nearby houses with modern styles and refined landscape architecture appeared to make better use of land that had fallen fallow. Urban and rural observers saw environmental decay as moral decay. Physical dilapidation that once had constituted venerable age and sometimes even picturesque charm now signaled undesirable residents.[91] Subdivisions of decaying ancestral seats could signal that proprietors wished to maximize financial profit from real estate sales. Pickering and Warren were particularly susceptible to this criticism since they rented out their aging ancestral homes to persons in modest circumstances. In fact, John Collins Warren's own son explained that his father had let the eighteenth-century Warren farmhouse slip into disrepair when his career and party politics consumed him.[92] The renovation of the Warren and Pickering estates with revivalist styles suggested that their proprietors had rehabilitated themselves by setting aside time from business and politics to attend to the sacred subjects of family, home, and past.[93]

Yet, just like associational stewards, private estate owners assessed the moral valences of domestic architecture in financial terms. Old-fashioned houses in good repair could attract commendation as instructive evidence of past lives. But their physical attributes and the interest that they attracted continued to make them unappealing domiciles. As builders developed suburbs to create homogenous enclaves of wealth, old buildings—even those in good repair—would not attract the buyers and renters that developers desired. Lucius Manlius Sargent spoke to this concern in 1845, when he asked a correspondent to scout the former abode of a matrilineal ancestor. He was interested in purchasing "the old Turner house" to claim a piece of domestic genealogy. But he first wanted to know "whether it is capable of being sufficiently repaired for the occupancy of some poor, tidy family."[94] Sargent faced the realities of the rental market and modern standards of housekeeping when he assessed the purchase of an ancestral property.[95] What he stood to gain from possessing an ancestral estate he stood to lose if a rental became a tenement of ill repute.

John Collins Warren shaped his Roxbury estate according to the same calculations. Unlike Van Rensselaer and Pickering, Warren had no intention of living at the home place of his forefathers. He sent his real estate agent, Amos Cotting, to inspect the house's structural condition in the summer of 1845 and to make a recommendation for its rental prospects. Cotting reported the structure's dimensions and concluded, "The House can easily be repaired in its present shape, but it will cost quite as much as it would to build a new House. I know no reason why the House will not command a good and respectable tenant when finished."[96] Warren, it seemed, faced a decision about the house's fate in which the cost of renovations played no decisive role.[97] He made several trips "to examine the old Warren house" for himself as he debated what to do. In the end, Warren took relics from the old house and replaced it with a Downingesque cottage.[98] For the rest of his life, he earned a healthy rental income from George Blackburn, a Boston merchant.[99]

Warren made the new house part of a strategy for turning financial profits from residential development of his landed inheritance. The physician kicked off a suburban real estate boom in Roxbury when he first sold a parcel from the property in 1833. The group of investors, which included his brother-in-law John Ball Brown, laid out two roads and sold the property to a house builder a year later.[100] In 1845, Warren renovated his ancestor's home place to profit from the development of his initial sale.[101] He allowed a new road to be cut through his remaining property and sold off lots immediately north of the old house. Two years later, he earned $2,000 by allowing the city of Roxbury to place a drain through his property. Warren ceded a small section of this "front land" to street widening in exchange for permission to build a retaining wall on his property line and assurance that he could preserve the old elm tree that subsequently fell just outside these bounds.[102] A decade later, this wall would divide the estate from the new horse-drawn streetcar that carried passengers down Warren Street.

Warren retained his ancestral home to cast his real estate management as civil urban development. Many Americans characterized suburban development as a project of domestic morality achieved by setting single-family homes apart from

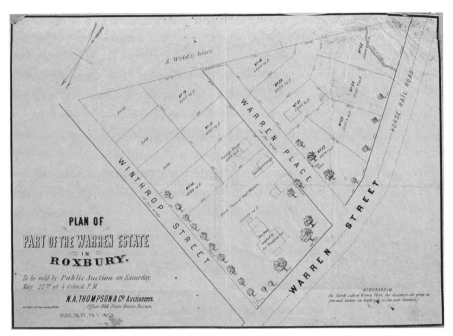

Figure 28. Developers of suburban Roxbury imprinted new house lots and streets with the history of the Warren family estate. This real estate map, for instance, identifies the truncated lot surrounding the stone house built by John Collins Warren as the "Birth Place of Genl. Warren." It also marks the "Old Elms" of the historic estate that stand on subdivided lots ready for sale. "Plan of Part of the Warren Estate in Roxbury" (Boston: Meisel Brothers Lithography, n.d. [1858?]), box 1 oversize, John Collins Warren Papers. Collection of the Massachusetts Historical Society.

urban districts. In 1855, *Ballou's Pictorial Drawing-Room Companion* recognized John Collins Warren as a participant in this endeavor by celebrating "the General Warren House" as one of the exemplary "suburban residences" in Roxbury. An editor placed an engraved view of the house at the center of four other house portraits printed to "show the variety of tastes and styles exhibited in domestic architecture . . . to those about to erect dwellings for themselves."[103] While admirers characterized the qualities of these properties in contrast to the urban character of Boston, they saw this residential landscape as an integral part of an urbanizing one: suburban homes fostered moral development of residents who worked, shopped, and socialized in the nearby city. Yet they also believed that the Warren house cultivated civil society as a suburban historical flagship for properties cut from its original plot (Figure 28). Labeled as the birthplace of General Warren, even by those who recognized that the stone house was "substituted for the old house," the renovated Warren property infused the surrounding neighborhood with its identity.[104] Buyers as well as sellers could point to the house, grounds, and old elm trees throughout the neighborhood to imprint subdivided properties with distinctive historical markers of place.[105] Residents of these new lots could resist critiques that their homes were cookie-cutter houses built by greedy capitalists by framing their real estate transactions as acts of evolutionary preservation. They too could secure the permanence of historic family estates in new residential forms.

Warren and like-minded men, of course, hoped to write their own histories with the management of ancestral properties. Many of their intimates complied. Observers celebrated John Pickering's preservation and transformation of his family estate. In 1846, eulogist Daniel Appleton White did so in the same breath, noting that on the old family tract of land "stands the ancient and picturesque mansion, the late summer residence of our deceased friend, who by his skilful [*sic*] arrangements converted the greater portion of the farm into a beautiful and flourishing village."[106] Mary Orne Pickering perpetuated the same narrative in her biography of her father. In 1874, she identified the Pickering family house by its municipal street address—No. 18 Broad Street—both when she stated the date of its construction and identified her own place of residence. She noted the property deed from 1642 had conveyed to her first North American ancestor "a part of the estate in Salem which descended in the Pickering family, and of which a large portion has been laid out in streets and sold in house-lots within the two centuries since elapsed." She claimed this development as an enduring part of her family's legacy, not an attenuation of their property, when she pointedly stated that the deed and the house were still "preserved in the family."[107]

Of course, every time that proprietors and commentators declared that these estates were retained by "the family," they validated current proprietors to the exclusion of others who might have claimed that role. John Pickering and John Collins Warren both inherited ancestral estates from bachelor uncles. Stephen Van Rensselaer IV was the first Van Rensselaer heir to inherit a divided estate after his half-brother received half of the manor. All men fashioned themselves as lineal heirs to suggest a proprietorship defined by unbroken biology. Yet when they defined generation by chain of title, they manufactured a patriarchal genealogy that denied mothers, siblings, and cousins proprietorship of a relative's property. Descendants of other genealogical lines made these omissions apparent when they publicized their personal connections to ancestral properties. In 1860, for instance, when newspapers from Hallowell, Maine, to San Francisco, California, reported the death of Jane Warren Paine on the auspicious Revolutionary date of April 19, they identified her birthplace as the Warren family homestead. Her father, Ebenezer Warren, brother to Joseph and John Warren, had lived in the old farmhouse during the War for Independence. It was "now known as the 'Warren House,' in Roxbury, Mass.," the papers reported.[108] John Collins

Warren had written these relatives out of the domestic history chiseled on the new façade. But as public commentators conflated the new house and the old, they perpetuated the memory of other Warren descendants with it.

Some dispossessed descendants used documentary view making to preserve their ancestral estates in mobile forms. Stephen Van Rensselaer IV's half-brother William commissioned Thomas Cole to paint views of the manor house and gardens. Cole stepped outside his typical artistic style to record views that captured a likeness of the property. William Van Rensselaer hoped that the paintings would provide his mother and sister with an enduring connection to the property after Stephen's inheritance necessitated their removal.[109] The Meriwether family in Albemarle County, Virginia, did the same a decade later with new photographic technology. Margaret Douglas Meriwether Nelson inherited the family estate, Clover Fields, on the death of her father in 1845. The family graveyard and house, built by Colonel Nicholas Meriwether III on his marriage to Margaret's namesake in 1760, stood on land patented from the British Crown in the 1730s.[110] Nelson and her brother used deed strictures to ensure that Margaret's children from a previous marriage would inherit the property. But they also preserved their ancestral seat for future generations with a daguerreotype of the old house, taken just before Margaret's husband, Francis Kinloch Nelson, demolished it in a campaign for rural improvement in 1848.[111]

Rebecca Brown preserved the old Warren house in a different form: a model made with wood and moss collected from it.[112] The architectural miniature offered her a way to maintain a material connection to the Warren estate when her brother had not recorded her name on the new house. In the mid-nineteenth century, historians referred to her house model almost as often as they did the new house in Roxbury—albeit with the names of her husband and father rather than herself. In 1852, when James Loring described the "elegant stone building" built by John Collins Warren, he noted that the old house still stood as well: "An exact model of it, made partially of the original materials, is retained in the family of Dr. Brown, who married a daughter of Dr. John Warren."[113] After Rebecca Warren's death in 1855, the model marked her own material legacy among her heirs. It attracted attention when her son, Buckminster Brown, loaned it to a display that raised funds for the preservation of the Old South Meetinghouse in 1876.[114] In Edwin Whitefield's book *Homes of Our Forefathers*, Rebecca Brown's legacy replaced her brother's: Whitefield depicted the Warren House by drawing a picture of the miniature model, not the stone house in Roxbury.[115]

It is hard to know if these women were satisfied with their movable replicas of their ancestral seats. Rebecca Brown may have envied the capital that her brother generated from the sale of his inheritance. Her husband's meager earnings from experimental medical work and his real estate losses—including his

development project on former Warren land—left Rebecca Brown trying to capitalize on her family's history with biographical writing. As she put it in 1828 when
defending her pecuniary motivations for writing, "I find that, unless I put my
shoulder to the wheel of Fortune, it makes no evolution in my favour."[116] By her
son's report in later years, the family remained in modest financial straits.[117] Other
women might have felt a sentimental loss when renovations or sales transformed
their family estates. Sarah Endicott expressed this in 1839 when she entreated
her mother to stop her stepfather from selling her childhood home. "I could not
bear to think I should never again have a paternal home where I with my children,
could pass every year at least a few most happy days, I hope now there will be
made some better arrangement," she pleaded.[118] While marriage afforded her stepfather the legal right to sell the property, she implied, she had moral claims to
the property by blood. His sale of the property would sunder the experiential
inheritance due to her children as well as herself.

Yet the architecture of rural improvement stirred up the politics of demolition. Its proponents professed that revivalist architecture preserved historic structures from the physical and moral decay that old buildings endured at the hands
of "the lower order of Society," as Stephen Gould put it.[119] Indiana residents, for
instance, remembered that the old blockhouses of Fort Wayne were torn down in
the 1840s and early 1850s because "the ruined, dilapidated buildings became the
rendezvous of undesirable citizens."[120] In 1854, Charles F. Briggs reported that
the Folger family home on Nantucket, once inhabited by Benjamin Franklin's
grandfather and mother, had fallen into "a very dilapidated condition." At his last
visit, "there were no evidences of the surrounding grounds having been cultivated, and a wretched family inhabited the ruin."[121] John Collins Warren himself
noted in 1849 that when he had visited the Green Dragon Tavern in Boston
years earlier, he found the Revolutionary landmark "inhabited by poor people,
the rooms cut up into small apartments, and in some of the poorest rooms were
seen the remains of gilded cornices, which had probably been set up by the Masonic fraternity for their celebrations."[122] The building was demolished five years
later. Rural improvers of ancestral estates joined urban improvers of public architecture in claiming that their work preserved evidence of the past by creating historic structures that did not invite uncivil behavior and, in turn, demolition.

Opponents of evolutionary preservation, however, cast the designs of rural
improvement as the destruction of historic architecture by the hand of private
interest. In suburbanizing districts, many looked to mechanisms of urban improvement to make the historic features of family estates permanent *and* public.
In 1846, some Boston newspapers opposed the demolition of the old Warren
house in this way. They admitted that the "venerable building . . . ha[d] been in a
decaying and dilapidated state for some years." But they took issue with its removal

because they suspected that its owner demolished it "probably with a view to the laying out the grounds for building lots" and expressed "regret that this old building, unsightly as it was in its appearance, has been removed." They wished instead "that Roxbury had purchased the building, repaired it, and laid out a portion of the grounds attached to it as a public walk or common."[123] When this desire to make the Warren birthplace a piece of public property did not come to fruition, residents of Roxbury laid claim to its public image as a marker of civic identity. In 1852, local donors to the Washington Monument inscribed their contribution from the "City of Roxbury, Mass.,—The Birth-place of General Joseph Warren."[124] Later that year, a contingent of Roxbury Whigs carried a banner "delineated in truthful colors, 'The Birth-place of Warren.'"[125] The elderly John Collins Warren avoided harsh public criticism and intrusions on his domestic privacy since he did not live at the site. But the tensions between the legal rights to shape an ancestral estate and public claims to its historic features would permeate national debates over economy and morality in the 1850s.

Public Claims to Private Estates

In September 1853, the estate of the late Henry Clay went up for sale near Lexington, Kentucky. Newspaper editors across the United States published notices of the impending auction of the famed house and grounds at Ashland—a sale directed by the will of the deceased proprietor.[126] During the statesman's lifetime, political biographies, campaign materials, sheet music, and the agricultural press had tied admiring images of the estate to Clay's identity as the "Sage of Ashland."[127] Popular print culture encouraged attention to the house and grounds as evidence of Clay's character, and many strangers made their way to Ashland hoping to see Clay "in private" (Figure 29).[128] As Horace Greeley wrote of the place, "Our business is not here with Tariffs, Bankes, Vetoes, and Presidential contests and aspirations. Our theme is the *man* Henry Clay,—what he was intrinsically, and in his daily dealings with, and deportment toward, his fellow-beings."[129] In the oft-repeated words of one Whig writer, "Ashland is one of the household words of the American people. Having been deeply lodged in their affections, so long as the memory of the great proprietor is cherished, it cannot fail to have a place in history."[130]

Yet newspaper reports feared that the estate's buyer would not maintain it in historic form. They seized on the language of sacred space, popularized by partisan writers before them, to encourage the preservation of Ashland in its current state. *New York Weekly Herald* editor James Gordon Bennett argued that such "homes of the great men of our history" should be maintained "inviolate from

Figure 29. Thomas Sinclair's lithograph of Henry Clay's home was one of many popular images of Ashland that circulated during the statesman's lifetime. This hand-colored print depicts a house set amid pleasure grounds, connoted by a foregrounded lawn and a couple strolling on the path that encircles it. Perhaps a writer for the *Cleveland Daily Herald* had this image in mind in 1855 when he wrote, "Those who have a lithograph of the home of Henry Clay, should carefully preserve it, for the original has been razed to the ground." "Ashland: The Home of Henry Clay" (Philadelphia: T. Sinclair's Lithography, 1852). Kentucky Historical Society, 2004.41.622.

destruction or innovation." Though his newspaper had endorsed James Polk over Clay in the 1844 presidential election, Bennett still hoped that Ashland would "pass into the hands of some man of soul and patriotism, who will respect its sanctity."[131] A writer for the *Ohio State Journal* agreed. "That the homes of our great men have but too frequently fallen into strange and impious hands, is to be regretted: and shows a lamentable indifference on the part of our country. Mount Vernon and Monticello scarcely present one feature now which recall the memories of Washington and Jefferson." If Ashland sold to the wrong person, "In a few years from now it will present a painful contrast to its present interesting beauty and loveliness—for all that would preserve the memory of its former guardian will be scarred and marked by a fashionable taste." But it was not too late to preserve the "rather antique architectural appearance" of the "old form" in which Clay had dwelt.[132] A new proprietor might heed popular calls to "let it be preserved."[133]

One week later, newspaper editors breathed a collective sigh of relief when they reported that James Brown Clay, a son of the statesman, had purchased the estate. The new proprietor paid just over $47,000 for the title to the two-hundred-acre core of his father's estate—and the right to position himself as the heir to his father's legacy.[134] As one acquaintance wrote to James's wife, Susan Jacob Clay, "I am delighted that Mr. Clay has become possessor of Ashland, connecting it with its great owner; I could not but wish it to belong to one who will venerate . . . it not only as the residence of his father, but likewise as a residence that will ever be contemplated [by every] American and foreigner with interest as recalling the memory of its Sage."[135] Clay professed his intention to do just that. In September, he completed the first step of his long-planned preservation campaign: he leveled the mansion to the ground.[136]

The public firestorm that ensued illuminates how a new definition of preservation emerged out of conversations about the social costs of economic privilege perpetuated by family wealth. In 1854, newspapers in all corners of the nation resounded the stark report: "Henry Clay is dead, and Ashland is a ruin."[137] As the Kansas-Nebraska Act broke down Henry Clay's Compromise of 1850, the house's demise seem to portend greater destruction. As one North Carolina newspaper editor put it, "We fear that the demolition of this mansion of Henry Clay is typical of the demolition of another structure: . . . the American Union."[138] Yet the political press engaged Ashland as more than a metaphor for Henry Clay's legacy. Observers assessed James Clay's proprietorship of Ashland as statements of the social and economic motives that guided his political actions at a time of broad-scale party realignment.[139] Clay had moved to Ashland to fashion himself his father's heir against rival claims of his brother, Thomas Hart Clay. Susan Jacob Clay, a favorite confidante of her father-in-law, had convinced her husband to purchase the estate because she, too, was eager to shape Ashland as a statement of Henry Clay's legacy and a source of her family's authority in public as well as private matters.[140]

James Clay used the architecture of rural improvement much in the same way that Van Rensselaer, Pickering, and Warren did in previous years: to preserve his family seat in "a style suitable to my own taste, and not wholly unworthy of my father."[141] The new proprietor built a new house in the same foundation trenches as the old one. He reconstructed its floor plan and massing as well, retaining the central Palladian window, staircase, and skylights. Inside, he restyled salvaged wood into paneling and shutters and appointed some rooms with his father's furnishings. In his view, this project perpetuated his father's legacy not only in continuities of form but also by carrying out the late proprietor's wishes. Though Henry Clay had built the core of the house in 1805 and enlarged it a few years later, faulty masonry threatened its structural integrity.[142] James Clay argued that the new house embodied his father's expressed desire for architectural improvement and permanence that the original structure could not provide. He pursued this vision of continuous improvement by hiring his father's chosen architect, British-trained Thomas Lewinski, to build a mansion house that would match the gardener's cottage and renovations that Henry Clay had commissioned from Lewinski in 1846.[143]

James Clay infused his renovations with the principles of rural improvement to pursue a campaign of evolutionary preservation. He ordered Lewinski to jettison the whitewash of his parents' generation for red brick walls and to restyle the entire house with Italianate details, arched windows, and, as one observer noted, a "roof of sheet iron painted red [that] has a flashing, new, appearance" (Plate 7).[144] Decorative cast-iron and heavy wood paneling showed the latest fashions for revival styles. Clay bridged British and American family heritage by designing a family crest in the Old English style, marked with "H C" in Gothicized text. He emblazoned it on a parlor cabinet, a personal seal, the arched entryway of the house, and Gothic chairs fashioned from ash wood from the demolished house.[145] All elements framed James Clay as a patriarchal presence for current residents.[146]

Sympathetic viewers saw this as a successful campaign to preserve the estate of Henry Clay. One set of travelers who reported a visit to the "mass of ruins" in 1854 described how Americans "love . . . to look upon the very house and rooms once occupied by the illustrious dead. But the home of Henry Clay, like his own noble form, could not stand the ravages of time. It was found to be beyond repair, and had to be taken down and built anew, with the same general features, but in fresher bloom and increased beauty." The so-called "hand of reform" brought simultaneous change and permanence.[147] Other responses conveyed a more casual willingness to accept the new house as the old, or perhaps an unconscious slippage. One owner of a printed view of the first house at Ashland colored its walls red in the image of the second structure (Plate 8).[148]

Yet detractors used the design of James Clay's campaign for permanence to draw him into the well-formulated politics of demolition. The *Cincinnati Gazette* issued a reprimand when it broke the news that the house had been "totally demolished" and reduced to "a pile of bricks and rubbish" in 1854. The writer was not consoled with the news that "a son of Henry Clay—is about to erect on the site of the old dwelling, a new edifice of its exact form and character. This will make some amends for the work of demolition he has completed, but it will hardly pardon it. The old house might have been repaired; it should not have been destroyed."[149] A year later, *Louisville Journal* editor George Prentice launched a sustained diatribe against James Clay by charging that he managed Ashland as a form of immoral commerce designed to profit from the sale of his patrimony.[150] Prentice had established himself as a Henry Clay disciple by publishing a biography of him two decades earlier; now he parlayed his Whig roots into support for the Know-Nothing, or American, Party, along with Thomas Hart Clay.[151] Prentice condemned James Clay in terms that resonated with charges made by William Duane and Edmund Quincy in previous decades. He accused Clay of "vandalism" and "barbarism" in "demolishing the sacred old dwelling of your father, and selling the lumber."[152] To Prentice, James Clay's desire to make a dollar on his father's house was apparent not only in the sale of raw architectural salvage but also in his manufacture of keepsakes marketed to his father's devotees. Residents of Lexington had reported that Clay was selling canes, boxes, and other souvenirs to individuals who wished to have a relic of Henry Clay's home. As a later critic put it, "Unless watched, he will have Clay's bones out of his grave."[153]

Prentice used his commentary on Ashland to disparage James Clay in familial and racialized terms calibrated to economic and social debates of the day. Clay's demolition of the Ashland mansion was uncivil, Prentice argued, because it treated his family's house no differently than a rude slave dwelling constructed for utilitarian needs. "It was his *property*; he *owned* it; he had a right to do what he pleased with it," Prentice scoffed. "He had by law as much control over it as over any of his negro-huts; and so, without a thought of the immortal father whose presence had consecrated every beam and rafter and plank and brick and shingle to the hearts of hundreds and thousands of American freemen, he *tore it down*." Clay, in other words, acted as an unfeeling man of law and market who managed his father's house as real estate rather than a family home. In turn, this "unfilial" act revealed that James Clay used his inherited privilege to exert control rather than benevolence toward members of his household and, in turn, to fellow citizens. "Are there not some memorials of the mighty and illustrious dead," Prentice asked, "which, although the legal title to them may be in private individuals, are in an important sense the property of the whole civilized world of mankind?"[154] The implications were clear to the white Americans that Prentice courted after Clay's recent political speech at Ashland: James Clay would use his political influence to aggrandize his own wealth at the expense of other citizens, whom he would not hesitate to relegate to the order of slaves.[155]

James Clay lambasted Prentice for making such serious charges against his character. He felt aggrieved enough to challenge Prentice to a duel. (It went unaccepted.)[156] But he also swung back blow for blow in the language of market morality developed by previous generations. His proprietorship satisfied the definition of filial piety, he averred, because it fulfilled his deathbed promise to his father than he would not let Ashland "pass into the hands of strangers." Clay secured the estate not by the privilege of inheritance but by his "own exertions" and personal expenditures.[157] "Leaving Missouri and sacrificing prospects of a brilliant fortune," he explained, "I became again a citizen of Kentucky, purposely to preserve Ashland in the family—from becoming a mule pen."[158] His personal restraint from maximum profit, in other words, ensured that his father's home would not become a gathering place for crass political partisanship of half-breed Whigs. It was Prentice, in Clay's view, who had broken "the sanctity of private life" by bringing family business—and particularly his aging mother—before the public eye.[159]

James Clay defended demolition as an act of good domestic economy. He conjured images of old houses as havens for the immoral poor when he claimed that building a new house was better "than to leave standing an old mansion, through which the water coursed, and whose walls were cracked to such an extent, as to render it positively unsafe, as a harbor for rats, and a resort for thieves and runaway negroes."[160] As for the sale of architectural salvage, Clay described it as a form of moral commerce. The refashioning of demolished features showed his thrift by repurposing "old lumber that was useless to me to a good and worthy use." Relic making was a form of "public charity," as he "employed a cabinetmaker, himself almost an object of charity . . . in these hard times," to make the souvenirs and planned to donate sales profits to disadvantaged citizens.[161] Since his return to Ashland, Clay had "been greatly annoyed by persons coming to my place and carrying away whatever they fancied, either from the old house, or plants and growing shrubs, without asking the permission of any one."[162] His relic business turned the tables on these guerrilla collectors, reproaching them not only for disrupting the estate's domestic privacy and beauty but also for depriving a charity of funds.

Sympathetic observers endorsed James Clay's explanation. In 1856, Clay had thrown his support behind the James Buchanan presidential ticket and succeeded in his own candidacy for the U.S. House of Representatives. In 1857, the fundraising campaign to build a public monument to Henry Clay in Lexington's rural cemetery drew more attention to Ashland. A wave of reports championed James Clay's renovations for enabling future generations of Americans to see Ashland for themselves. One report insisted, "The clamor about the devastation of Ashland by Mr. James B. Clay is in great part humbug. His house is the perfection of the idea of the architect who designed the old one."[163] It formed what he called an "exaggeration of the original" house—an enhancement of its character. The *Cultivator*, ever the champion of rural improvement, affirmed that the house, "worn and dilapidated by time, has been pulled down, and on its site stands an elegant brick mansion, built in excellent style by its present proprietor, James B. Clay, a son of Henry." The correspondent maintained that the newness of the house at Ashland did not diminish its historic value. "Like Mount Vernon, Monticello, and Marshfield, and some other distinguished places," he wrote, "it will for all future time remain one of those Meccas for Pilgrimage to those who love to look upon the homes of the great statesmen whose labors and influence have shed a halo of glory upon their country."[164] As another writer imagined at Daniel Webster's former estate at Marshfield, this citizenry would extend to "future pilgrims from Maine to Mexico, wandering, thoughtful, through the chambers and over the grounds," of family estates kept up by noble scions.[165]

A contemporaneous newspaper feature offered readers a tantalizing view of what they might see inside. On July 4, 1857, a front-page spread entitled "Ashland As It Was" greeted readers of the *Cincinnati Gazette* (Figure 30). Though the correspondent visited Lexington to report on the Clay monument in Lexington Cemetery, the visual hierarchy of the cover images spoke to Ashland's primacy. A large view of Henry Clay's house sat directly under the masthead and above smaller images of his gravesite and birthplace. "The identical house occupied by Henry Clay has been torn down since his death," the journalist explained, "and a new and more elegant edifice erected upon the same spot, and with but slight modifications of the same plan. The venerated edifice of the father had become insecure," he continued, "and his son James deemed that the associations to be kept permanent could be better attained by the visitor and pilgrim to this shrine observing that care had been taken to enclose the interesting memorials of the Patriot in an edifice which would defy the storm and the fast appearing ravages of decay."[166]

When Susan Clay admitted the writer to Ashland, he entered—in his mind—"Henry Clay's library." Though the dark paneled study certainly appeared different from the original one, its identical dimensions convinced him that he sat in Henry Clay's private quarters. "Here," the writer emphasized, "are old tables and sofas as they were used by the Ashland sage." He described sitting in Clay's chair at his desk, lifting the pen from his inkwell, "handl[ing] the paper folder, which Mrs. Clay said she could almost fancy retained the delicate touchings of his long, lithe fingers," and cradling the seal "used so much that his fingers had worn the plating."[167] The domestic arrangement of these objects enabled the writer to conceive that he took part in a doubled spatial experience with the deceased statesman. After so much attention to how the new façade and revitalized grounds preserved Henry Clay's spirit of improvement, this article suggested that James and Susan Clay preserved the private domain of Henry Clay for public access as well.

The couple certainly did not envision a regular stream of guests traipsing through their house. They remained deeply interested in shaping the public legacy of Henry Clay and abided some visitors. But as James Clay stated so clearly

Figure 30. This front-page spread of the *Cincinnati Gazette* depicts nodes in a memorial landscape dedicated to Henry Clay. Ashland reigned supreme in this popular imaginary of sites, even here where the writer reported on the new monument being built in Lexington Cemetery. The *Gazette* depicted a view of the demolished house copied from Sinclair's lithograph, yet the writer praised the new house that stood on site as "a new and more elegant edifice" that retained several features of the old one. "Ashland As It Was," *Cincinnati Gazette*, July 4, 1857, p. 1. Image number N385_V72_18570704.tif. Courtesy Ohio History Connection.

to George Prentice, he conceived of Ashland as private property. On the one hand, he insisted that he had made Ashland fully his own by purchasing it with his capital and renovating it to suit his family. He gave his father's ideas as much credence in the preservation of Ashland as he did in "the preservation of our glorious Union": "It is men of our age and time that must save the Union if it can be saved," James Clay wrote. "Most of the old men have been weighed in the ballance [*sic*]."[168] While he honored his father's contributions at home and in politics, he shaped both with a mind toward generational independence.

On the other hand, James Clay managed Ashland to preserve the privilege he *had* inherited. His purchase of Ashland included a favorable directive to hold two-thirds of the purchase money in hand during his mother's life and then collect annuities from a family trust to be created after her death. He also laid claim to the labor of people his father had enslaved—and in some cases freed. Henry Clay had willed enslaved people to his wife and sons and provided for the gradual manumission of children born to enslaved women after 1850. James B. Clay had announced that he would not farm Ashland with enslaved labor, but he and his wife had no compunction claiming his father's former slaves as inherited laborers, even if they earned wages.[169] In 1855, for instance, Susan Clay wrote to her sister that she had "a new photograph of Mammy Lotty" with two Clay children. "She deserves to be thus handed down to posterity for she has been far more useful in her generation than many who are above her in station and whiter of skin and her likeness deserves to be prized by my children."[170] Charlotte Dupuy had been a free woman since 1840, when Henry Clay had manumitted her a decade after she had sued for her freedom. Yet Susan Clay laid claim to Dupuy's memory as a heritable possession for a new generation of Clays, who continued to cite Dupuy's service as evidence of Clay family benevolence.[171] Likewise, newspapers characterized her husband, Aaron Dupuy, as a relic of Henry Clay's old family estates in Virginia and Kentucky rather than someone who likely felt drawn to his own family residing at Ashland.[172]

James and Susan Clay encouraged these material links between generations to establish James as patriarch of the Clay family for a new era. Like Van Rensselaer, Pickering, and Warren before him, Clay used the architecture of rural improvement to establish himself as a moral heir to the family legacy that he articulated. He did so, however, by using this evolutionary mode of preservation to erase the presence of slavery from his father's estate even as he maintained the institution in his own financial practices and partisan alliances.[173] In presenting the development of Ashland as one that resulted in his independent proprietorship of the estate with no enslaved laborers, James Clay sought to create a family property that modeled the development of American "improvement" as a process by which slavery simply died out of U.S. society and economy. It was, of course, an argument for the preservation of slavery in the present. Yet the national stream of commentary about Clay's demolition/preservation of Ashland points to the way that Clay stepped into a broader debate about the nature of capitalism in the United States. Many observers saw his proprietorship as an example of how the nation's most powerful citizens—white men of means—managed private property to the detriment of public welfare. In this respect, commentators placed James Clay in the company of the "scion of Washington" who inhabited Mount Vernon.[174] Their comparison points to the way that Clay shaped Ashland not only against partisan men who claimed his father's legacy but also under the spotlight of women who challenged patriarchal control of historic family estates.

Rethinking Mount Vernon
and Legacies of Preservation

Three months after the demolition of Ashland in 1853, an appeal "To the Ladies of the South" went out in the Charleston *Mercury*. Its author, describing herself as a daughter of Virginia and current resident of South Carolina, urged women to save the estate of George Washington from capitalist development. Her appeal used the language of financial sacrifice for the common good that had marked calls for architectural preservation since the 1780s: she called on readers to exercise the "unselfish love of country" in a nation where "love of money and speculation alone seems to survive." Mount Vernon sat on the rural banks of the Potomac River several miles south of Alexandria, but the writer summoned images of urban industrialism as the potential fate of the property. Can you imagine Mount Vernon "sold as a possession of speculative machinists," she asked readers? "Can you be still with closed hearts and purses," she asked, while the site becomes "the seat of manufacturers and manufactories; noise and smoke, and the 'busy hum of *men*' destroying all sanctity and repose" around Washington's grave? "Never," she cried, should the estate be "forgotten, and surrounded by blackening smoke and deafening machinery, where money, money, only money ever enters the thought, and gold, only gold, moves the heart or moves the arm!" The federal government, she argued, had fallen prey to the same lust for power and corruption that had infiltrated the industrial economy. Since Congress had refused to purchase the estate as a national shrine, it was up to southern women "to purchase and preserve Mount Vernon" from "Northern capital, and its devotion to money-making purposes." They would protect the estate from "the grasp of the speculator and the worldling!"[1]

It is hard to imagine a starker condemnation of "money power" than the one penned by Ann Pamela Cunningham. The self-styled "Southern matron" responded to newspaper reports that John A. Washington III, a grandnephew of George Washington, was preparing to sell the dwelling, grave, and grounds of his ancestral estate to a band of "speculators."[2] When she fleshed out her image of capitalist greed and environmental degradation, she issued her call for preservation in the contentious language of industry and slavery. Rather than driving a wedge between readers from different regions and partisan loyalties, however, Cunningham's appeal interested an array of U.S residents.[3] In the coming years, women and men who aligned with Whig, Know-Nothing, Democratic, and Republican causes all got on board with Cunningham's project. While some did express trepidation over certain language or political alliances, partners in the Mount Vernon cause did not disentangle their participation from their partisan stances. Instead, they invested their various political positions with the display of virtue demonstrated by the preservation of a historic estate apart from economic development. This environmental ethic of permanence remained a shared touchstone for U.S. residents even as their battles for the memory and legacy of the American Revolution tore them apart.[4]

The main conflicts engendered by the proposal to purchase Mount Vernon emerged from long-standing questions about how to define the contours of capitalist economies in the United States. The transaction was, after all, a real estate deal. Between 1853 and 1858, women and men involved in Cunningham's project debated associational constitutions, terms of incorporation, and means of raising and investing their funds. For a decade after that, leaders of the Mount Vernon Ladies' Association (MVLA) focused on negotiating a purchase contract with John A. Washington, fulfilling their payment schedule, and securing a clear title to the property after Washington's untimely death. Participants in and detractors of these activities shaped larger arguments about economy and society from which partisan divides extended. Ann Pamela Cunningham developed her proposal for associational stewardship of Washington's ancestral estate as newspapers across the nation debated the fate of Ashland at the hand of James B. Clay. Yet Cunningham's project weighed in on questions not only about the social effects of inherited family wealth but also about issues of corporate governance of public architecture addressed by Rufus Putnam and William Duane, the gendered authority of domestic economy contested by Sarah Hale and John Fanning Watson, and the character of commercial profits assessed by William Brown and Edmund Quincy.

Future generations would celebrate the MVLA as the birth of the preservation movement because of the widespread support it garnered to make George Washington's estate a house museum. Many characterize the organization's founders as visionaries of historic preservation who placed themselves outside the era's sectional politics to maintain a piece of the past for the benefit of "all" Americans—Union *and* Confederate for a time. This origin story accords with notions of a democratic republic where citizens set aside their differences to support a public good defined by a shared heritage. But it obscures the ways that the MVLA emerged from longstanding debates about economy and morality that turned on different ways of valuing architecture and land in a capitalist economy. A fresh look at the creation of the MVLA shows how its members engaged in highly contentious practices of corporatism, consumerism, and labor to define Mount Vernon and its meaning. It reveals how MVLA supporters consolidated a mode of preservation defined by rules of the market as well as idealized visions of the past.

Competing Proposals

John A. Washington had tried to sell Mount Vernon many times. Having moved to the estate as a boy, he had spent most of his life seeing the incursions of strangers on his family home, not least of all on the deathbed of his father in 1832. When Washington became the estate's proprietor for his widowed mother in 1841, desire for domestic privacy and low returns on agricultural products formed strong inducements to put Mount Vernon on the market. Five years later, he tried to sell the estate to the federal government for $100,000. His mother, Jane Washington, encouraged her son to rethink the asking price in light of the historic qualities of the estate that she long had struggled to share with visitors while keeping it a private family home. "As we approach the transaction," she wrote, "there is something so repugnant to me in parting with M V for Money, that I seem to recoil from it, as if it were almost sacrilegious. The Sum you mention . . . has ever seemed to me extortionate."[5] Jane Washington's hesitation stemmed from her inability to square the characterization of a sacred site with a market price. She would be more comfortable with the sale, she confessed, if Congress could pay what it wished.

John A. Washington refused to lower his asking price, and Congress refused to make the purchase. So Mount Vernon's proprietor turned to other efforts to monetize public interest in the estate. In doing so, he stepped into a debate about moral commerce. In 1850, Washington lifted his ban on steamboat landings at Mount Vernon. As he arranged a schedule with the steamboat captain, he also invested in the company and instructed enslaved workers to sell refreshments to tourists. So, too, did he invest in transportation developments to improve travel to Mount Vernon by land routes. It is easy to see how these investments in transportation infrastructure would have enticed buyers interested in commercial development of the site in 1853. When the impending sale reported by newspapers that year did not come to fruition, Washington turned to a different method of selling the estate: the commercial relic trade. The proprietor sold trees to a souvenir company that issued certificates of authenticity with their products.[6] Some customers certainly regarded their purchases as wise consumerism that showed their devotion to historical study and veneration of George Washington. Others characterized John Washington as a crass businessman looking to turn a profit on the destruction of a sacred site.

Ann Pamela Cunningham believed that women could offer Washington a more morally sound deal. When she sent her appeal to the press, she also made a private supplication to John's wife, Eleanor Selden Washington. Cunningham conveyed her understanding that Congress was considering the purchase of Mount Vernon to prevent the intended sale to real estate developers. She asked Washington to delay the sale and make the "aspirants" of the women's association the preferred buyers. "As a resident of an agricultural state, where combinations cannot be made rapidly," Cunningham entreated, "you must be aware that it requires time to circulate and arouse action on anything."[7] Perhaps Cunningham had heard of the difficulty that other historical associations had in raising money for similar causes and wanted Eleanor Washington to buy her some time. Washington's response, however, made clear that her opinion of the sale did not matter. She passed along her husband's response of polite dismissiveness: he appreciated "their ardent enthusiasm and untiring devotion and patriotism" but felt "constrained to decline the proposition you have so eloquently made, in behalf of the Ladies of the South."[8] Her husband, she relayed, would sell only to the state of Virginia or the U.S. Congress.

Yet Cunningham's public appeals quickly generated support. Despite her appeal to southern women, correspondents across the country answered her call. In Philadelphia, where Cunningham launched her campaign while seeking medical treatment, Elizabeth Whitney Milward offered immediate support. So, too, did her friend Martha Fondey, visiting from Albany. Milward framed their regional identities in terms of a racialized concept of genealogy promoted by popular history writers and espoused in Milward's nativist politics. She was from "Mayflower stock," as she described, and Fondey hailed from the "earliest families" of Albany—presumably Dutch colonizers and not Haudenosaunee peoples. "For one," wrote Milward, "I am rejoiced that a way seems to have been opened by my southern sisters to avert the stigma which would assuredly attach itself to this nation, if 'Mount Vernon' with the sacred ashes of our Washington were permitted to pass into the hands of speculating private individuals."[9] The politics of profit operated in an economy that spanned regional as well as generational divisions.

Women in the South responded quickly to Cunningham's call as well. In March 1854, Cunningham received a bank book from Richmond, Virginia, showing contributions that city residents had deposited at the Farmers' Bank for her cause.[10] William H. MacFarland oversaw the funds and was one of two men who joined thirty elite women in Virginia's capital to preserve Mount Vernon as a point of state pride. The other man was a local lawyer, John H. Gilmer, who drafted a constitution for the association in July 1854. "To preserve the Home and Grave of Washington from passing into Decay—to secure that hallowed spot from the grasp of selfish speculation—to possess, maintain and perpetuate it without mutilation, as the treasure of hearts that venerate his character and services, as the Father of our Country," the founding document affirmed, "is indeed an object worthy of the United and earnest efforts and Devotion of the patriotic Daughters of America!"[11] Julia Mayo Cabell assumed the office of president, while MacFarland served as treasurer and Gilmer became corresponding secretary. The latter sent a letter to Cunningham reporting the association's organization and then another to John A. Washington conveying their interest in purchasing Mount Vernon for the state of Virginia.[12]

The conflicting claims to authority that arose between this Virginia association and the broader network of participants who responded to Cunningham's call forced all parties to confront the challenges of securing collective property ownership in the United States. Women across the country began raising funds for the purchase of Mount Vernon. As Cunningham corresponded with them, she assured many that her project welcomed participation from every corner of the United States and that she would secure Mount Vernon as a national property. Yet her correspondence with John Gilmer quickly revealed that he worked at cross-purposes and refused to take direction from her. He had framed the constitution of the Virginia association to give it "a business aspect" that would "secure the confidence of the country" and encourage John A. Washington to answer "promptly and in a business way."[13] Gilmer fancied this advice part of his broader mission to help women navigate business and legal matters in which he presumed their sex to be ineffectual. After all, he viewed Julia Cabell as a source of "life and light" rather than leadership, and he invoked the dependency of "lady clients" in Richmond.[14] He also ignored Cunningham's pleas to acknowledge the contributions of women across the country.[15]

This contest for authority blew up in spectacular fashion when Gilmer finally told Cunningham that he could not approve her plan because it partnered with Americans who threatened the institution of slavery. "Its very discussion would open up the flood gates of sectional animosity," he wrote, "and tarnish the soil of Virginia—with the polluted breath of northern fanaticism. For one—as a Virginian—I could never consent to a joint tenancy in Mount Vernon—with the craven-spirited God offending hypocritical wretches of the North who are even now seeking to incite the slaves of the South to the overthrow of our domestic peace and safety. Let us keep away from the unholy alliance." He continued to publish appeals with similar invective in Cunningham's name—directly against her wishes.[16]

In 1855, Cunningham hoped to reclaim her public authority by publishing a letter that she had sent to Gilmer in the previous year. She followed the printed letter with an account of the formation of the Central Committee, a group of women who appointed Cunningham president and repudiated the influence of Gilmer. "An Appeal for Mount Vernon" solicited contributions from Maine to Texas and aimed to win back support from women driven away by the association's mixed messages and power struggles.[17] Cunningham's strategy worked. Gilmer resigned, and Virginia affiliates of the Central Committee worked to repair relationships with women on the Virginia state committee. With Gilmer gone, Cunningham turned to the task of designing a mechanism of ownership that would substantiate her desire for a property owned by a national citizenry and not a state or federal government.

Incorporation

The debacle with Gilmer convinced Cunningham that she needed to straighten out the "business aspect" of the association, as he had put it.[18] Previously, she had insisted that fundraisers strike while public outrage was hot; they could leave organizational details of the Mount Vernon purchase for later. "It is the 'full purse' which gains 'the cause'—not the merits!!!" she had explained.[19] Women would be more likely to encourage the Virginia legislature to purchase Mount Vernon if they showed up with money in hand, and they would be more likely to solicit donations when threats of capitalist development of the estate were fresh. But now Cunningham saw how the structure of the organization, not just the source of the funds, would shape the meaning of the preservation project. She turned to her partners for advice.

In Richmond, Anna Cora Ritchie demurred from giving Cunningham advice on constitutions after her tangle with Gilmer's committee. She wished to wash her hands of "business matters," by which she meant "discussing constitutions and deciding what is legal and what is not." She did, however, recommend several women "who can comprehend them."[20] But Ritchie proved indispensable by using her husband's associates as a Richmond newspaper editor to seek advice on getting the Central Committee's purchase approved by the Virginia legislature. Men with statehouse connections recommended what antiquaries had been proposing for two decades: to incorporate an association that would hold the property in perpetuity. James Murray Mason insisted that "it must not be presented to the State of Va but the Ladies must hold it themselves and appoint trustees to manage and protect it." State legislators would not want to own a property that might accrue debts and liabilities, he wrote, "and it will be much more beautiful for the Ladies to retain it and make it the Westminster of America." Lawyer H. C. Harrison relayed this advice with a template for a corporate charter, which asked the ladies to define specifically how they would use the land and whether they would charge admission fees. He also cautioned them not to get their application for incorporation "involved in any political party" because "if it is taken up by the American party it will be the death of it!!"[21] The women already had determined that the political weight of their preservation project extended from its stated partisan disinterestedness, and they would have to try again to ensure that men followed their lead.

Not everyone was on board with this plan. Anna Maria Mead, for instance, tried to convince Susan J. Adams of New Hampshire to support the cause of state ownership as a necessity. The politics of states' rights inflected Mead's claim that Virginia would not give up its land to the United States because it was a sovereign state. "Therefore the State of Virginia must by [sic] it, allowing the women of the Union to pay for it."[22] When word of her appeal got back to Ann Pamela Cunningham, Mead apologized that her appeal did not correspond with the association's approach but defended her explanation as the correct one "because, as a sovereign state, she alone can make the purchase or hold the Title—This is so—our delegates and wisest statesmen assure us there is no other . . . measure that will be listened to by the Legislature!"[23] A few weeks later, Governor Henry A. Wise seemed to think otherwise. H. C. Harrison asked him "whether he would give his sanction to this scheme, and he replyed [sic] very unhesitatingly no— that he was entirely opposed to it." Though Harrison pled the women's case for preservation, he reported that Wise "was not to be convinced by me, he said he would rather see Mount Vernon sunk into the bottom of the Potomac than to see it in the hands of a corporate company—and as to its being presented to the State by the Ladies, he should consider the state degraded by accepting such a gift—so much for Mr. Wise."[24] It remained unclear what his wife thought of the matter; she did not reply to the letter that inquired.

Wise's response revealed his conflation of corporations with business designs and his reluctance to see women as moral real estate agents. O. W. Langfitt believed that his fellow state legislators would have the opposite reaction. When he drafted the bill to incorporate the women's association, he emphasized the sex of the applicants: "I interpolated the word 'Lady' in the title of your association because I thought that in a public law it should appear plainly, who were entitled to the credit." He also reversed what Cunningham originally had desired for stewardship. The state of Virginia would serve as trustee of associational funds, earning the women a 6 percent return semiannually and making cash available for state-funded improvements—an arrangement similar to the one that managed the Newport synagogue trust. The Mount Vernon Lady Association Fund would have "the full power of improvement & custody but inasmuch as it contemplates perpetuity." If future generations did not abide this corporate mission, the state of Virginia had the right to step in to care for the estate. According to state law, a board of visitors would review operations periodically to ensure compliance with the terms of incorporation. Langfitt was optimistic that the bill would pass without opposition from Governor Wise since he did not have the power to veto a law passed by both legislative houses.[25] The closing of Langfitt's letter to Cunningham epitomized the difference of his approach from Gilmer's: Langfitt noted that the enclosed draft of the bill "is copied partly by wife, & partly by myself."[26]

Virginia state legislators expressed more opposition than Langfitt predicted. Cunningham also continued to ask if the Virginia governor and the president of the United States could serve as cotrustees of the corporation.[27] But after two months, the bill passed both houses and became, as Langfitt put it, "the law of the land."[28] It created an organizational structure that accorded with neither the recommendations of Harrison nor the wishes of Cunningham. It incorporated the "Mount Vernon Ladies Association of the Union" as the owner of the money collected by "ladies of the United States . . . to purchase and improve two hundred acres of Mount Vernon." However, it directed that their funds would be used to purchase land to be "converted into public property, and forever held by the state of Virginia, sacred to the memory of the 'Father of this Country.'"[29] It also placed the responsibility of negotiating the deed in the hands of the governor. Cunningham decidedly had not wanted Virginia alone to hold the deed to the property, even if it recorded an acknowledgment that the money came from a national organization. But it seemed too late to change the provisions now. The women were corporate trustees, and they had to file their constitution and bylaws with the governor, prompt him to secure a contract for a property he did not want, and raise $200,000.

Constitution and Contract

Incorporation filled women in Virginia with a renewed sense of purpose and authority. Anna Cora Ritchie reinvigorated fundraising efforts. Unlike most of her peers, she had worked for pay as a writer and an actress, and she desired to "labor" for the cause rather than organize it.[30] During statehouse debates over the bill, she had confessed, "I have planned out a deal of work for myself as soon as I hear that the bill is passed and I hope to stir up a great many now apathetic lookers on—who doubt that we can do anything and therefore will not 'lend a hand.'"[31] Her orientation toward work made her one of the most effective women in raising funds, smoothing over committee disagreements, writing editorials, and winning political allies. Secretary Susan Pellet took the opportunity to remind Julia Cabell of her subordinate place to the newly incorporated association. Officers were empowered by the state of Virginia to act with the authority of a national organization; Cabell operated only in the bounds of Virginia as a contributing member to the larger organization. She had no authority, Pellet reminded her, to correspond with John A. Washington about the sale of Mount Vernon.[32] Incorporation also solidified the support of renowned Massachusetts orator Edward Everett. He joined fundraising efforts only after asking if the association was chartered by Virginia or remained "a voluntary body without Corporate power."[33]

His question, however, pointed to an ongoing concern: Mount Vernon had a corporate buyer, but it did not yet have a seller. John A. Washington had nearly sunk the bill to incorporate the MVLA to the bottom of the Potomac, right where Governor Wise wanted it. The legislature had tabled the bill because one delegate had heard that Washington would not sell the estate to the association or anyone except the state of Virginia or the federal government. State representatives settled this uncertainty by giving the association five years to raise the money and close the deal. In that time, legislator Langfitt reasoned, Washington "may change his mind, and agree to accept $200,000—for the credit reputation and bones of his grandfather."[34] His commentary inverted the criticisms circulating against James B. Clay to frame the sale of Washington's ancestral estate and family tomb as a moral transaction.

The uncertainties of the business deal undercut the association's new authority. Julia Cabell appeared as a sheep in wolf's clothing when she asked Cunningham to clarify the status of the potential sale. It would prevent the whole operation running on rumors, she suggested, if Cunningham would just publish the letters between her and Washington.[35] Word about Washington's refusal to sell spread well beyond Virginia. Elizabeth Walton dashed off a letter from her husband's store in St. Louis when she saw the news. "I am almost heart broken having just read in our evenings paper, the news of Mr Washingtons refusal to sell 'Mount Vernon'! What is to be done? It cannot, nor will it be permitted to rest thus."[36] Two days later, Walton followed with a wish "that we may be spared the mortification of not holding Mount Vernon as our [sic]; the possession of which is so richly deserved, and that you most noble of women who has so nearly given your life to rescue it from desecrating hands."[37] Given Cunningham's repeated insistence that Virginia alone would not hold the title, most women likely shared Walton's belief that the association would possess the deed.

Many women believed that the lure of cash might convince Washington to sell, and they turned to the business of benevolence to raise the funds. Many used the appeals of self-denial that Sarah Hale had promulgated in support of the Bunker Hill Monument.[38] Calls to action in Delaware appealed to public schoolchildren to practice the self-denial of luxury: "You, all of you have sometimes money to buy a top, marbles, dolls or candy," the article intoned. "Now if you would be willing to deny yourselves the indulgence of those pleasures, and put that money aside, in a short time your School . . . will be enabled to raise how much?" Newspaper appeals in Alabama solicited donations for the MVLA as responsible consumerism as well.[39] Women also pursued fundraising as a form of competitive business. Every community was filled with benevolent causes, and the MVLA had to develop a pitch to convince potential volunteers and donors to support their cause over others. Julia Gardiner Tyler gave a glimpse of this difficulty when she explained her limited success in raising money for the MVLA. "We have [a] church in process of erection and that is also drawing upon the liberality of our County," she reported to Anne Cora Ritchie.[40] Elizabeth Milward noted that MVLA donation boxes in Independence Hall sat in competition with a collection for the Washington Monument.[41]

Many MVLA volunteers took the opportunity to develop their business acumen. Elizabeth Walton sought advice from Ann Pamela Cunningham. "I really do not know how to act," she wrote, "—if you cannot advise me, get your brother or dear mother to—I am so green—excuse the expression—about business that I fear I have already made many blunders."[42] The large number of donations that she reported from St. Louis families, however, indicate that she was a quick study. Other women found an outlet for a well-developed business sense. Mary Hamilton, for instance, opened a Manhattan office to stake a claim in New York's philanthropic market. Yet other women were wrapped up with the business of financial markets themselves. M. B. Green wished she "could bring about a patriotic feeling" with one of her female friends, she reported, but "she is too much engaged with improvements and Rail Road Stock."[43] Business-minded women were susceptible to the charge of Mammon worship as much as their male counterparts.

Some women infused MVLA fundraising efforts with an expertise in the protocols of corporate governance. In Tennessee, Mary Rutledge Fogg consistently referred to herself as an "agent"—a term that carried connotations of market investments that Cunningham hoped to avoid with her preferred term of "lady manager."[44] Fogg worked with men as well as women to collect funds, as she was determined to raise "as large a fund as Language can extort from the rich and the competent the incompetent and all."[45] Yet Fogg took great care to ascertain her duties and authority in the association's hierarchy before throwing herself into fundraising efforts. "Having on more than one occasion presented Petitions to the Legislature of Tennessee, and obtained Charters for various societies created at my request and of which I had the honor to be elected President," she explained to Cunningham, "I was too well aware of the duties and responsibilities involved by such department of those associations, to take a single step towards the accomplishment of the views of the Mount Vernon Association, without an accurate knowledge of the platform on which it was erected, and possessed an official right to perform the part which my heart so warmly dictated." Fogg wrote many paragraphs about the gravity she accorded the structures of chartered institutions and emphasized that she drew her authority from Cunningham "alone as President of a 'Chartered Institution'" to fulfill her "office of trust and responsibility" as head of the Tennessee campaign. Her professed commitment to procedure, fiduciary responsibility, and financial powers showed a remarkable depth of associational experience.[46]

Ann Pamela Cunningham seemed to devote the opposite amount of care to the organizational structure of the MVLA. In the summer of 1856, she focused her efforts on convincing John A. Washington to sell Mount Vernon to them. After begging him to ignore inflammatory and inaccurate reports in the press and deal directly with her, she moved Washington to meet with her and consider direct proposals from state leaders. It was a victory considering how much Washington hated Governor Wise.[47] A sympathetic politician from Georgia confirmed that Cunningham's best option was to let the Virginia officials try to arrange the sale, as Washington openly announced he "could not recognize the ladies association."[48] As Cunningham pressed Wise and Washington to negotiate a deed agreement, Edward Everett and O. W. Langfitt prodded Cunningham to submit the final paperwork needed to enact the incorporation of the association. The state could not charter the MVLA without a constitution and by-laws on file. Langfitt included suggestions for how she might structure a hierarchical institution that allowed for subordinate state chapters with county associations that reported to them.[49] This structure matched the extensive network already forming by the work of Cunningham and her allies. Yet donations and lecture fees continued to stream into bank accounts under the name of an association that remained unincorporated—and unprotected by the privileges extended to corporate bodies.

For two years, Cunningham pled her case to John A. Washington. Their exchanges and the ongoing appeals from the preservation of Mount Vernon were articulated in the now-familiar language of financial crisis—this time, a depression of market prices prompted by a panic in 1857.[50] All the while, Cunningham neglected to submit the constitution that would activate the association's corporate privileges and protect the funds given to its stewards. Yet she protected the donations in a different way—by preventing the association from incorporating under the existing law. A constitution for the association would put the Mount Vernon deal in the hands of the Virginia governor and make the historic estate state property. Cunningham's stalling paid off. On March 19, 1858, the Virginia legislature moved to incorporate the Mount Vernon Ladies' Association again. This time, amendments to the original bill gave the association the right "to purchase, hold and improve, two hundred acres of Mount Vernon, including the late mansion, as well as the tomb of George Washington, together with the garden, grounds and wharf, and landing . . . and to this end they may receive from the owner and proprietor of the said land, a deed in fee simple, and shall have and exercise full power over the use and management of the same." The state of Virginia would step into trusteeship if the association dissolved, and the General Assembly would have to approve a lease of the property. But the association would contract directly with John A. Washington for the purchase of the estate.[51] Two weeks later, Cunningham paid $18,000 cash out of associational coffers and agreed to an installment system for paying the remaining $182,000 plus interest. The final payment was due on February 22, 1862. Cunningham signed her name with monikers that marked her evolution as leader of the MVLA: "Ann Pamela Cunningham, A Southern Matron, Regent."[52]

MVLA leadership circulated a copy of the constitution and the contract together in the following weeks. It explained the structure of the association to women who might serve in the new position of vice regent: "The object of the Association is to secure perpetual guardianship for Mt Vernon, that it may be kept national property, sacred for all time, to the memory of the Father of our Country. Its constitution, designing to secure perpetuation for the Association, from generation to generation must necessarily be an instrument, drawn up principally for the purpose of providing such regulations as may seem best adapted to attain this end, and thus avoid what must occur in case of the future neglect of the property, viz—forfeiture to the state in which it lies, and its inevitable loss to the people of the Union." Individual vice regents were charged to collect funds by recording the name, amount, and residence of donors for the records of Mount Vernon and state archives. The MVLA wanted it to be "known forever, who purchased and consecrated, the Home and grave of Washington."[53]

The obligation to raise such an extraordinary sum kicked off a new era of fundraising. Many observers celebrated the federal structure of the organization: vice regents headed up fundraising in every state. Many noted how it drew support from the far reaches of the nation, sometimes even beyond. In 1859, California's committee included a large advisory council of men of Anglo American and Spanish American descent under vice regent Magalden G. Blanding. In Maine, contributions included donations from "American" residents of St. John's

Bay, New Brunswick, and a captain of the U.S. ship *Savannah* in port. The "priv-ilege of being a purchaser" also extended to immigrants.[54]

It was the corporate body of this association that enabled the MVLA to make the case that all donors became joint owners of Mount Vernon. As one associa-tion member pitched it to schoolchildren, "When in after life you visit Mount Ver-non, a place sacred to every American, and stand by the grave of Washington, and walk over the pleasant paths through the beautiful groves that surround, you will feel that by your self-denial you have aided in the purchase, and become one of the legal owners of so holy a spot."[55] This ownership status matched the per-petuity of the estate itself. In 1856, the original charter had ordered the state to record the names of all donors in two books, one to be "kept forever in the ar-chives of Virginia; and the other deposited in the least distructable [*sic*] part of any monument or other improvement which may hereafter be erected on said Mount Vernon Place."[56] Ann Pamela Cunningham conceived of this record of purchase as a marker of heritage, something that could be passed down "through all time to the childrens [*sic*] children" who can feel "the same pride that is now felt by the descendants of the signers of the declaration of our national Indepen-dence."[57] The corporate form enabled "a more direct participation of the People in the result" than did a purchase made by a stroke of governmental legislation.[58] But it also, as Edward Everett put it, placed Mount Vernon "under the protection and guardianship of a permanent institution co-extensive with the Republic."[59] It was a moment, however, when the Union did not seem so permanent.

Postbellum Permanence and Moral Economy

Edward Everett became one of the most influential voices in defining the char-acter of the Mount Vernon project of preservation. He had begun a lecture series to raise funds for the cause in 1856. In 1858, the editor of the *New York Ledger* had written to Everett, offering him $10,000 for the MVLA fund if the statesman would contribute a weekly article to the newspaper for a year. With a circulation of three hundred thousand subscribers at his disposal, Everett accepted the offer in the hope that his essays would reach a million individuals who would contrib-ute a small sum to the purchase and restoration of Washington's estate. Everett's popularity offered a business opportunity to *Ledger* publishers as well: they hoped to attract more family subscribers with weekly original content from the famed New England orator.[60]

At the end of 1858, in his third column for the series, Everett made the case for the preservation of Mount Vernon by speaking about the demolition of an-other historic building: Benjamin Franklin's childhood home. In 1837 and

1847, Edmund Quincy had said that shame would befall Bostonians if they allowed the building to be destroyed. But in 1858, Everett offered a different take: the building had to go. The narrow streets in Boston's old districts presented not just an inconvenience, he insisted, but also a danger to all who labored, shopped, and passed through the booming commercial district. With truck drivers forced to complete astounding maneuvers to deliver goods, someone was bound to get hurt.

Improvement arrived at the doorstep of the Franklin house on November 10, 1858. Or rather it removed the doorstep. City councillors had ordered Union Street to be widened by fifteen feet—the exact frontage of the Franklin house on Hanover Street where it met Union. Everett assured his readers that the merits of the street improvements outweighed the benefits of preserving the house in place. He had had several "confidential" meetings with city leaders and the property's owner, and ultimately they agreed that the house should be taken down.[61] "Little has been demolished that could be saved," he wrote, "and nothing that was worth saving."[62] In Everett's mind, it would have been a "deceptive operation" to remove the old house to new ground and use new materials to rebuild an ancient form whose appearance no one could document.[63]

Everett's column provided a timely update on a well-known historic structure.[64] But it also revealed a new view of preservation emerging in the Mount Vernon campaign: historic sites should be secured by the rules of modern economy and historical objectivity. "If the living Franklin, grown up to the height of his world-wide renown, had stood upon the spot," Everett surmised, "he must have stepped aside or been run down by the Charlestown Omnibus"; Franklin's alter ego, Poor Richard, would have done the same, for he "was not the man who would have allowed a sentimental feeling about a ruinous old house to prevent the widening of a great thoroughfare."[65] Everett did not disdain remnants of the past. But, in his mind, the character of historic properties needed to fulfill conditions of the past *and* of the present.

This is why Everett was raising money for Mount Vernon: John A. Washington had every right to set the asking price for Mount Vernon at $200,000. He had secured a purchase agreement for that price in previous years, and the costs of keeping up a farm and a tourist attraction added up fast. "Considered merely as a patrimonial farm, [Washington] surely has the right to take care of it or neglect it at his pleasure," he admitted. Everett agreed with popular veneration for Mount Vernon's "great national and patriotic associations," but he encouraged citizens who wanted to ensure the preservation of the site as sacred to stop condemning its proprietor and start contributing money. If the public desired to use the house and grounds as public space, they should be willing to invest in its purchase and legalize their access to it.[66]

The market ethics articulated in these arguments reveal how debates over historic architecture formed an integral part of debates over slavery and free labor in the late 1850s. Everett's departure from Edmund Quincy's pleas to preserve the Franklin house stemmed from a deeper difference between the two men. They did not value historic architecture in different ways; they disagreed over how much Americans should let the principles of strict political economy shape it—and the rest of life in the United States. Everett shared his views of the Franklin home with Robert C. Winthrop, president of the Massachusetts Historical Society, who had collected wood from the old house before facilitating its demolition. Both men expressed their devotion to a free market in a moderate politics of accommodation that stood in sharp contrast to Quincy's principles. Winthrop and Quincy had been close friends as young men but kept only a civil acquaintance after the latter began to support Garrisonian reforms. Everett professed a similar disdain for antislavery politics, and his argument for preserving the Union was an economic one.[67]

The MVLA fundraising campaign only served to embroil the fate of Mount Vernon in these contestations. Observers joined MVLA leaders in describing the estate as evidence of the moral constitution of its owner. Viewed as a family home, the historic estate seemed to reveal the commercial greed and poor domestic economy of its modern-day proprietor. For some, the poor physical condition of the house and grounds evinced John Washington's "want of ordinary thrift"—mismanagement of financial resources and labor marked by the decline of domestic virtue.[68] Antislavery advocates lambasted the presence of enslaved laborers (despite the fact that many descended from ancestors enslaved by George Washington).[69] In 1858, Horace Greeley echoed George Prentice's evocation of Ashland as a "negro-hut" when he criticized John A. Washington for human trafficking: "Here we have Mount Vernon transmogrified into a regular slave shamble, where human beings are sold out to the highest bidder—the proprietor living on their wages—until they are returned on his hands."[70] That same year, Elizabeth Cady Stanton expressed her views of moral economy in a refusal to serve as a vice regent of the MVLA: she believed that the cause of abolition better fulfilled the founding principles of the nation.[71]

These descriptions ratcheted up the politicization of the MVLA's management of the estate. The association proved itself a thrifty proprietor by paying off its debt ahead of schedule. During the Civil War, its resident caretakers declared Mount Vernon neutral ground—a political statement in itself. After the war, observers cast the estate as evidence of the moral superiority of free labor. John Trowbridge, for example, reported that individuals formerly hired out by John Washington were earning wages by keeping up George Washington's estate for the MVLA and the good of the nation.[72] Observers also cited the wages of the association's free white caretaker, Sarah Tracy, as evidence of the fair labor practices of Mount Vernon's new proprietors.[73]

The economic and moral conflicts that engendered the Civil War also changed the meaning of architectural permanence as well as the politics of labor. At Mount Vernon, caretakers maintained neutral ground during wartime as a means of self-preservation, both as an institution and as a property located on the border of two belligerent nations. MVLA stewards achieved this goal by defining their project of preservation as one devoted solely to restoring evidence of the past as it had looked in previous years. Residents of both the Confederacy and the Union could visit the grounds; soldiers were welcome only if they left their weapons elsewhere and obscured all markers of their national loyalties.[74] In effect, they had to conduct themselves as if they were part of the MVLA's efforts to restore the physical condition of the place to 1799, when the individuals living on both sides of the Mason-Dixon line were residents of the same nation. The war remained apparent to all who lived at and visited Mount Vernon. But the MVLA used its mission of restoring conditions of the past as the grounds for achieving unity—if not Union—grounded in a shared heritage rather than a common trajectory of historical development.

Across the broken nation, communities did the same thing. Residents of the United States and the Confederacy tried to keep historic architecture intact even as Americans destroyed properties high in financial and cultural value. Historical iconoclasm was a tactic of warfare.[75] But in 1863, the former house of John Hancock was threatened not by artillery, scavenging soldiers, or newly free African Americans but by real estate developers. After failed attempts to lobby the state to purchase the house, T. O. H. P. Burnham posted broadsides around the city, crying out to passersby in large letters and red ink: "BOSTONIANS! Save the Old John Hancock Mansion!" His call to action offered a visual crescendo that warned of impending damage (see Plate 9): "There is time yet, although the work of demolition has commenced." He acknowledged that the developers had made "an honest purchase" of the property and admitted his "full recognition of their rights in this respect" to do what they wished. But he wanted to "admonish them how dearly is purchased any good thing which costs the sacrifice of public associations as noble as those that cluster around the Hancock House." The developers might find their new houses poor investments, Burnham cautioned, when they faced a lifetime—indeed, an eternity—of complaints lodged against them by the public and "their remotest posterity" for destroying collectively cherished evidence of the past. In contrast, the property's owners could "earn a title to public gratitude by an act of simple self-denial."[76]

The developers enacted their original plans of demolition. Individuals who had been eager to keep the Hancock house standing documented the structure in a variety of ways. They took photographs of the house, creating some of the earliest domestic interior views with the new stereographic process.[77] They hired an architect to make measured drawings of the dwelling. They carried off innumerable furnishings and architectural fragments of the mansion. Entrepreneurs even sold carte-de-visite prints so that those not lucky enough to secure an artifact from the estate would at least have a photographic record of it.[78] One person who bought a photographic copy of a print of the house augmented his copy of a copy with material relics, pasting a piece of wallpaper from the house on the back and noting that its frame was made of wood from a tree in the yard of the house.[79] Yet Americans who partook in these documentary efforts roundly characterized them as evidence of the irretrievable loss of historic architecture.

Individuals who did manage to preserve historic structures during the Civil War devoted ever more painstaking attention to restoring these sites to professedly original condition. They claimed to attend solely to incontrovertible evidence of how sites looked in the past. In Salem, members of the Essex Institute trudged out to the yard of David Nichols in 1860 to investigate an old cowshed that risked disintegration with agrarian decline. The men had heard reports that its timbers were the remnants of the first church in Salem, built in 1634. In their institutional records, they reported a close study of written records, family accounts of their property, and a minute examination of the building's fabric. They concluded that it "be removed to some suitable place and fitted up internally and externally as nearly as possible to its original appearance, where it would be more accessible to the public."[80]

The Salem antiquaries reported the subsequent deconstruction and reconstruction of the building as a painstaking process of objective inquiry, classification, and spatial reasoning. In 1865, the committee "removed with care the outer covering of the building, the boards and the shingles; they marked and numbered every part of the frame; they noted the positions of the posts, braces, plates, rafters, ridge-pole, gallery-beam, tie-beam, mortices and cock-tenants: these were carefully examined and questioned as to their story of the past: the responses were prompt, and so satisfactory to those who could understand their language, that their origin and mission were placed beyond doubt."[81] In their view, walls could talk through structural analysis, and they sought "to erect them into their original positions and form, that they might repeat to coming generations the same story they had whispered to your representatives." In their written report, they stressed that they abstained from guesswork and ideological influence, and they sought to prove their objectivity in the transparency of their work. New architectural features, added to support the materials recovered from Nichols's field, were "colored brown, to distinguish them from the original materials." They hoped that Salem's oldest building would be thus "preserved to those who come after us, and handed down from generation to generation as a valued trust."[82] First secured as corporate property of the Essex Institute, the reconstructed building still stands on the grounds of its heir, the Peabody Essex Museum.

The MVLA undertook a less extreme project of reconstruction in the years after the Civil War. They began "to restore the mansion and the grounds from their present state of melancholy neglect and decay, as far as possible, to their original condition, and to make adequate provision for their permanent conservation and care."[83] Amid the beginning of this concerted restoration effort, Ann Pamela Cunningham worked to complete the one step remaining to secure Mount Vernon as property of the MVLA: executing and recording a final deed of sale. John A. Washington had died in the Confederate Army in 1861, after the MVLA had closed the contract but before he had signed the property title. The association had to sue his heirs to get them to sign the deed in their father's stead.[84] In 1868, Ann Pamela Cunningham faced a final hurdle in recording the deed: a new stamp tax.[85] She launched yet another appeal for the support of Mount Vernon—this time to the U.S. Secretary of the Treasury for a tax exemption. She painted a picture of a struggling estate: "The Association is poor," she explained, and "has to struggle to keep its pledges to the country to support Mt Vn as a public resort, to exact the secure stamp tax on the sum of 200,000 would be very onerous at a time when they have not even the means to repair the leaking roof of the Mt Vn mansion."[86] Tax authorities absolved the liability of the MVLA, and on May 13, 1869, fifteen years after she launched her effort to raise money for the purchase of Mount Vernon, Ann Pamela Cunningham recorded a deed to Mount Vernon.

Legacies

Cunningham remained at the helm of the MVLA for another five years before she retired. She died at her South Carolina home in 1875. After giving twenty years of her life to the MVLA, Cunningham bequeathed three more gifts to the organization: a group of photographs of a visit to Mount Vernon, the lamp that lit her first years of work for the estate, and "the gold pen with paper knife (presented to me by Dr. H. L. Hodge of Phila) with which the contract for Mt Vernon was signed."[87] The objects that she chose to keep for herself until death, and then to donate to the MVLA, speak to her desire to commemorate herself with the tools of her labor.

No object exemplifies the significance of debates over preservation at mid-century better than Ann Pamela Cunningham's pen (Plate 10). Cunningham viewed it as the instrument used to secure the purchase of Mount Vernon. The history of preservation laid out in this book helps us to understand the meaning that Cunningham attributed to the object. In signing the contract, she created a legal agreement that would make the land and buildings of Mount Vernon property of a corporate body composed solely of women. This was nothing new: it drew on a long history of female benevolence that had secured the right of women to hold property as corporate leaders, even where married women's property laws otherwise would have prevented it.[88] The Mount Vernon purchase agreement did assert a new statement of female independence, however. It was a stance not of radical women's equality but of women's complementary status to men. State legislatures had begun to debate the abolition of coverture in the late 1830s as a response to the volatile market swings of the preceding years. Many had decided to expand the rights of married women to hold their own assets as individual property to limit the damage that men's financial failures could wreak on household wealth. In 1858, the Mount Vernon purchase agreement extended this argument to the civic realm—especially in a state that had voted down the expansion of married women's property laws in the previous decade.

Cunningham substantiated this complementarity in a new way when she signed the purchase agreement for Mount Vernon. The contract secured a legal arrangement between two equal parties: a man of the market and a women's organization that promised to fulfill his financial demand.[89] This document confirmed a definition of preservation as a means of securing permanence that operated by the strictures of a free market. It framed an environmental ethic of complementarity that tried to draw sharper lines between public and private interests, as well as improvement and preservation, as separate but equal entities. Architectural permanence occurred, then, when market interests agreed. The MVLA offered a model that the ability to secure that agreement demanded a sacrifice from the people at large. When individuals decided to make substantial outlays of capital to achieve permanence, they earned a new title: philanthropist.[90]

Our willingness to accept this principle as a starting point for preservation obscures how it emerged from a sustained engagement with questions about how to shape corporate responsibility, commercial profit, and family life in capitalist society. It fixes our baseline view of preservation in a contract model of architectural permanence created to appease the demands of capital. Perhaps that is fitting for our own age of high capitalism. But maybe it is time to try something new. The longer history of preservation should inform our decision.

As we reckon with the white supremacy inscribed by the U.S. memorial landscape, the history of preservation demands that we recognize this book's subjects as cocreators of this landscape (Figure 31). Their ideas and actions shaped the historic landscape that we see in printed images, museum artifacts, preservation rhetoric, and environmental absences as well as extant structures.

Figure 31. A historical marker in Mound Cemetery, placed by the Washington County Historical Society in 1968, perpetuates the myth that the Marietta earthworks were built and abandoned by a mysterious prehistoric people who bore no relationship to eighteenth-century Indigenous residents of the Ohio Valley. It is one of many memorials in Marietta that continue to imprint the perspective of Rufus Putnam and his peers on the local environment. These narratives celebrate the founding of Marietta as an act of preservation by ignoring its use as a tool of Indigenous dispossession and erasure. Photograph by author, 2015.

Confronting the origins of these artifacts in the ethic of architectural preservation can bring to light the exclusions, transformations, and demolitions enacted to secure particular remnants of the past. It can help us recognize the shared costs incurred by this drive for permanence and consider how to account for these losses in the sites we preserve today and the histories we tell at and about them. More broadly, it reminds us that we construct a specific notion of "the public" when we decide who to empower to make these decisions.[91] The best solutions to competing claims to sites, structures, and memorials must address the complexity of the past as well as the present.

Materiality is a critical component of these conversations. Architects, artists, and digital engineers continually experiment with methods of preservation. They have introduced architectural materials such as structural glass to old sites, printed 3-D models to re-create historic landscapes, and used virtual reality to simulate visitation. Historians have cheered and critiqued the ways that these efforts communicate or obscure knowledge of the past and the work of history. They have taken the lead on experimental work in the built environment mainly through practices of placemaking that generate new means of spatial use and record memories of place.[92] Preservation today needs more conversations across the architect and humanist divide in pursuit of deeper practical engagement with histories of environmental materiality. This call does not aim to universalize the importance of material history or to fetishize notions about authenticity of place. Quite the opposite. It encourages historians to make visible the ways that people in different times and places have shaped material meaning to exert and to resist power, and then to call attention to the power of architectural preservation to do the same today.

Like it or not, this power is shaped by capitalism—even at sites that claim to preserve evidence of the past outside of market forces. In the United States, this has been true for over two hundred years. By studying the ways that previous generations defined preservation as an environmental ethic, we can better recognize debates over historic architecture today as economic ones, at once social and financial. Preservation still shapes the value of real estate, the principles of consumer ethics, and the worth of labor in our communities. Of late, architectural studies have encouraged the financial assessment of privately owned historic buildings to show how adaptive reuse can be a tool for creating sustainable communities, economic empowerment, and resistance to gentrification. Yet the preservation of "public" history sites run by municipalities, nonprofit corporations, and governmental agencies are measured in financial costs and benefits too. These sites are shaped by the presence or absence of philanthropic donors, real estate market values, caretaker trusts, prices of admission, and wages. When we demand that influence in shaping these sites requires a financial sacrifice, we risk perpetuating the social inequality that tracks growing economic inequality. We propagate remnants of this early ethic of preservation for a new age of capitalism when we define a stakeholder's sway in proportion to his financial contribution or encourage budding professionals to work for the love of doing history rather than a living wage. The stakes are too high not to invest in the development of historical perspectives needed to inform decisions about preservation today. They are, after all, statements of how we value people, not buildings.

Notes

Works frequently cited have been identified by the following abbreviations:

AAS American Antiquarian Society, Worcester, Massachusetts

HABS Historic American Buildings Survey, Prints and Photographs Online Catalog, Library of Congress, http://www.loc.gov/pictures/collection/hh/

HALS Historic American Landscapes Survey, Prints and Photographs Online Catalog, Library of Congress, http://www.loc.gov/pictures/collection/hh/

HCFP Henry Clay Family Papers Series II, Library of Congress, Washington, D.C.

HSP Historical Society of Pennsylvania, Philadelphia

MDOCA Manuscripts and Documents of the Ohio Company of Associates, Special Collections, Marietta College, Marietta, Ohio

MVLAER Mount Vernon Ladies Association Early Records, Fred W. Smith National Library for the Study of George Washington, Mount Vernon, Virginia

NIRC Narragansett Indian Records Collection, Rhode Island State Archives, Providence

RIHS Rhode Island Historical Society, Providence

RISA Rhode Island State Archives, Providence

RPP Rufus Putnam Papers, Special Collections, Marietta College, Marietta, Ohio

TSTFR Touro Synagogue Trust Fund Records (ID 06/06.01/1636-1836 C#27), Treasury Department Trust Fund Records, 1823–1891, Rhode Island State Archives, Providence

Preface

1. "Confident Philadelphia Officials Preemptively Raze Center City to Make Room for Amazon Headquarters," *Onion*, Nov. 16, 2017, https://www.theonion.com/confident-philadelphia-officials-preemptively-raze-cent-1820509855.

2. For current definitions of preservation, conservation, rehabilitation, reconstruction, and restoration, see William J. Murtagh, *Keeping Time: The History and Theory of Preservation in America*, 3rd ed. (Hoboken: John Wiley and Sons, 2006), 4–9.

3. On trees as historic markers, see Laura Turner Igoe, "'The limb in my Fathers arms': The Environmental and Material Creation of a Treaty Elm Relic," *Common-place: Journal of Early American Life* 17:1 (Fall 2016), http://common-place.org/book/the-limb-in-my-fathers-arms-the-environmental-and-material-creation-of-a-treaty-elm-relic/; Robert F. Trent, "The Charter Oak Artifacts," *Connecticut Historical Society Bulletin* 49:3 (Summer 1984), 125; Thomas J. Campanella, *Republic of Shade: New England and the American*

Elm (New Haven: Yale University Press, 2003). On settler colonial conservation of green spaces, see Richard H. Grove, *Green Imperialism: Colonial Expansion, Tropical Island Edens and the Origins of Environmentalism, 1600–1860* (Cambridge: Cambridge University Press, 1995); Elizabeth Milroy, *The Grid and the River: Philadelphia's Green Places, 1682–1876* (University Park: Pennsylvania State University Press, 2016); Richard William Judd, *The Untilled Garden: Natural History and the Spirit of Conservation in America, 1740–1840* (New York: Cambridge University Press, 2009); Michael Rawson, *Eden on the Charles: The Making of Boston* (Cambridge, MA: Harvard University Press, 2010); Adam Wesley Dean, *Agrarian Republic: Farming, Antislavery Politics, and Nature Parks in the Civil War Era* (Chapel Hill: University of North Carolina Press, 2015).

Introduction

1. "Ritual deposition" refers to burials of objects, flora, and fauna that melded sacred and secular meanings. Archaeologists believe that the monumental conical mound was likely built between 800 BCE and 100 CE and the other geometric earthworks were constructed between 100 CE and 500 CE as a ceremonial complex aligned with seasonal solar positions. Archaeological research indicates that people inhabited the surrounding area during the Middle Woodland and Mississippian eras but did not make physical interventions to the earthworks. William F. Roman, *Mysteries of the Hopewell: Astronomers, Geometers, and Magicians of the Eastern Woodlands* (Akron: University of Akron Press, 2000), 129–142; A. Martin Byers, *The Ohio Hopewell Episode: Paradigm Lost and Paradigm Regained* (Akron: University of Akron Press, 2004); Darlene Applegate and Robert C. Mainfort Jr., *Woodland Period Systematics in the Middle Ohio Valley* (Tuscaloosa: University of Alabama Press, 2005); William H. Pickard, "1990 Excavations at Capitolium Mound (33WNI3), Marietta, Washington County, Ohio: A Working Evaluation," in *A View from the Core: A Synthesis of Ohio Hopewell Archaeology*, ed. Paul J. Pacheco (Columbus: Ohio Archaeological Council, 1996), 274–285.

2. Archaeologists sometimes refer to the Adena and the Hopewell as separate cultural groups, but Indigenous knowledge and recent academic research eschew these divisions in favor of a narrative of continuous development. Members of many Indigenous nations in the United States and Canada descend from these groups. Lisa A. Mills, "Mitochondrial DNA Analysis of the Ohio Hopewell of the Hopewell Mound Group," PhD diss., Ohio State University, 2003; Elliott M. Abrams, "Hopewell Archaeology: A View from the Northern Woodlands," *Journal of Archaeological Research* 17:2 (June 2009), 169–204; Jarrod Burks and Robert A. Cook, "Beyond Squier and Davis: Rediscovering Ohio's Earthworks Using Geophysical Remote Sensing," *American Antiquity* 76:4 (Oct. 2011), 667–689; Geoffrey Sea, "Key Adena Earthworks and Preserve Saved in Ohio," Apr. 8, 2014, Indian Country Today Media Network, https://newsmaven.io/indiancountrytoday/archive/key-adena-earthworks-and-preserve-saved-in-ohio-PvAXN6og5Uy026cZrj-acg/; Eric Gary Anderson, "Earthworks and Contemporary Indigenous American Literature: Foundations and Futures," *Native South* 9 (2016), 1–26; Marti L. Chaatsmith, "Singing at a Center of the Indian World: The SAI and Ohio Earthworks," *American Indian Quarterly* 37:3 (Spring 2013), 181–198; Edward R. Henry, "Building Bundles, Building Memories: Processes of Remembering in Adena-Hopewell Societies of Eastern North America," *Journal of Archaeological Method and Theory* 24:1 (Mar. 2017), 188–228.

3. Residents of the early United States continued early modern debates about the relationship between principles of classical republicanism and classical liberalism. The debates extended from the belief that the material and moral states of men were linked. Albert O.

Hirschman, *The Passions and the Interests: Political Arguments for Capitalism Before Its Triumph*, rev. ed. (Princeton: Princeton University Press, 2013); Barbara Clark Smith, *The Freedoms We Lost: Consent and Resistance in Revolutionary America* (New York: New Press, 2010); Harry L. Watson, *Liberty and Power: The Politics of Jacksonian America* (New York: Hill and Wang, 1990), 42–64; Peter S. Onuf, *Statehood and Union: A History of the Northwest Ordinance* (Bloomington: Indiana University Press, 1987), 24; Brian Phillips Murphy, *Building the Empire State: Political Economy in the Early Republic* (Philadelphia: University of Pennsylvania Press, 2015), 10–13.

4. On cultural definitions of citizenship in the early United States, see Martin Brückner, *The Geographic Revolution in Early America: Maps, Literacy, and National Identity* (Chapel Hill: University of North Carolina Press, 2006); Dell Upton, *Another City: Urban Life and Urban Spaces in the New American Republic* (New Haven: Yale University Press, 2008); Thomas M. Allen, *A Republic in Time* (Chapel Hill: University of North Carolina Press, 2008); Mary Kelley, *Learning to Stand and Speak: Women, Education, and Public Life in America's Republic* (Chapel Hill: University of North Carolina Press, 2006); Carolyn Eastman, *A Nation of Speechifiers: Making an American Public After the Revolution* (Chicago: University of Chicago Press, 2009); Wendy Bellion, *Citizen Spectator: Art Illusion, and Visual Perception in Early National America* (Chapel Hill: University of North Carolina Press, 2011); Jennifer Van Horn, *The Power of Objects in Eighteenth-Century British America* (Chapel Hill: University of North Carolina Press, 2017).

5. The work of Pierre Nora inspired a boom in studies of historic places through the lens of collective memory. In English, see Pierre Nora, "Between Memory and History: Les Lieux de Mémoire," *Representations* 26 (Spring 1989), 7–24. For an excellent overview of memory studies as related to histories of place, see Christine M. DeLucia, *Memory Lands: King Philip's War and the Place of Violence in the Northeast* (New Haven: Yale University Press, 2018), 1–25. For studies of early America that examine architectural preservation as the creation of historical memory, see Susan M. Stabile, *Memory's Daughters: The Material Culture of Remembrance in Eighteenth-Century America* (Ithaca: Cornell University Press, 2004), 1–73; Charlene Mires, *Independence Hall in American Memory* (Philadelphia: University of Pennsylvania Press, 2002); Daniel Bluestone, *Buildings, Landscapes, and Memory: Case Studies in Historic Preservation* (New York: W. W. Norton, 2011); Gary B. Nash, *First City: Philadelphia and the Forging of Historical Memory* (Philadelphia: University of Pennsylvania Press, 2002); Lydia Mattice Brandt, *First in the Homes of His Countrymen: George Washington's Mount Vernon in the American Imagination* (Charlottesville: University of Virginia Press, 2011).

6. On preservation as nationalism, see Rosemary Sweet, *Antiquaries: The Discovery of the Past in Eighteenth-Century Britain* (London: Hambledon, 2006), 277–307; Miles Glendinning, *The Conservation Movement: A History of Architectural Preservation* (New York: Routledge, 2013), 65–115; Kevin D. Murphy, "The Historic Building in the Modernized City: The Cathedrals of Paris and Rouen in the Nineteenth Century," *Journal of Urban History* 37:2 (2011), 278–296.

7. Alfred F. Young, *The Shoemaker and the Tea Party* (Boston: Beacon, 1999); Thomas A. Chambers, *Memories of War: Visiting Battlegrounds and Bonefields in the Early American Republic* (Ithaca: Cornell University Press, 2012); Seth C. Bruggeman, *Here, George Washington Was Born: Memory, Material Culture, and the Public History of a National Monument* (Athens: University of Georgia Press, 2008); Sarah J. Purcell, *Sealed with Blood: War, Sacrifice, and Memory in Revolutionary America* (Philadelphia: University of Pennsylvania Press, 2002); Michael A. McDonnell, Clare Corbould, Frances M. Clarke, and W. Fitzhugh Brundage, eds., *Remembering the Revolution: Memory, History, and Nation Making from Independence to the Civil War* (Amherst: University of Massachusetts Press, 2013).

8. DeLucia, *Memory Lands*; Karen Halttunen, "Transnationalism and American Studies in Place," *Japanese Journal of American Studies* 18 (2007), 5–19; Halttunen, "Grounded Histories: Land and Landscape in Early America," *William and Mary Quarterly* 68:4 (Oct. 2011), 513–532.

9. "The Old Fort Demolished!" *Springfield Republican*, Aug. 3, 1831, p. 3.

10. On early republican taste in material culture, see Upton, *Another City*; Nora Pat Small, *Beauty and Convenience: Architecture and Order in the New Republic* (Knoxville: University of Tennessee Press, 2003); John Styles and Amanda Vickery, eds., *Gender, Taste, and Material Culture in Britain and North America, 1700–1830* (New Haven: Yale University Press, 2006); Maurie D. McInnis and Louis P. Nelson, eds., *Shaping the Body Politic: Art and Political Formation in Early America* (Charlottesville: University of Virginia Press, 2011); Catherine Kelly, *A Republic of Taste: Art, Politics, and Everyday Life in Early America* (Philadelphia: University of Pennsylvania Press, 2016); Van Horn, *Power of Objects*.

11. Historians have characterized architectural demolition in the early United States as evidence of an exceptional disdain of the past or a "historicidal" attitude. Mike Wallace, *Mickey Mouse History and Other Essays on American Memory* (Philadelphia: Temple University Press, 1996), quotation from ix, see also 4–5, 178–181. See also Thomas H. O'Connor, *The Athens of America: Boston 1825–1845* (Amherst: University of Massachusetts Press, 2006), xiii; Young, *Shoemaker and the Tea Party*, 143–154; Nash, *First City*, 2; Michael Kammen, *Mystic Chords of Memory: The Transformation of Tradition in American Culture* (New York: Knopf, 1991), 53; David Lowenthal, *The Past Is a Foreign Country* (Cambridge: Cambridge University Press, 1985), xviii. On buildings as metaphor, see Robert Blair St. George, *Conversing by Signs: Poetics of Implication in Colonial New England Culture* (Chapel Hill: University of North Carolina Press, 1998); Duncan Faherty, *Remodeling the Nation: The Architecture of American Identity, 1776–1858* (Hanover: University Press of New England, 2007).

12. I prefer the terms "material culture" and "environment" over "cultural landscape" because they invoke the agentive qualities of the physical world. On materiality, see George Kubler, *The Shape of Time: Remarks on the History of Things* (New Haven: Yale University Press, 1962; rev. ed., 2008); Robert Friedel, "Some Matters of Substance," in *History from Things: Essays on Material Culture*, ed. Steven Lubar and W. David Kingery (Washington, DC: Smithsonian Institution Press, 1993), 41–50; Bruno Latour, *Pandora's Hope: Essays on the Reality of Science Studies* (Cambridge, MA: Harvard University Press, 1999), 179–200; Henry Glassie, *Material Culture* (Bloomington: Indiana University Press, 1999); Daniel Miller, "Materiality: An Introduction," in *Materiality*, ed. Miller (Durham: Duke University Press, 2005); Van Horn, *Power of Objects*, esp. 8–26. Jennifer Van Horn employs a synthetic material cultural approach to the built environment in her discussion of burying grounds in *The Power of Objects* (156–213). Environmental studies of the early United States that attend to the particularities of architecture and material culture include Jennifer Anderson, *Mahogany: The Costs of Luxury in Early America* (Cambridge, MA: Harvard University Press, 2012); Philip Herrington, "The Exceptional Plantation: Slavery, Agricultural Reform, and the Creation of an American Landscape," PhD diss., University of Virginia, 2012; and Catherine McNeur, *Taming Manhattan: Environmental Battles in the Antebellum City* (Cambridge, MA: Harvard University Press, 2014). For recent historical studies that analyze vernacular architecture as part of a broader material world, see Bernard Herman, *Town House: Architecture and Material Life in the Early American City* (Chapel Hill: University of North Carolina Press, 2005); Maurie D. McInnis, *The Politics of Taste in Antebellum Charleston* (Chapel Hill: University of North Carolina Press, 2005); and Louis P. Nelson, *Architecture and Empire in Jamaica* (New Haven: Yale University Press, 2016). For studies that employ object-based studies

of material culture and historical consciousness, see Laurel Thatcher Ulrich, *The Age of Homespun: Objects and Stories in the Creation of an American Myth* (New York: Vintage, 2001); Teresa Barnett, *Sacred Relics: Pieces of the Past in Nineteenth-Century America* (Chicago: University of Chicago Press, 2013); Lindsay DiCuirci, *Colonial Revivals: The Nineteenth-Century Lives of Early American Books* (Philadelphia: University of Pennsylvania Press, 2018).

13. I see the discursive and material definitions of preservation as part of the broader process of producing space defined in Henri Lefebvre, *The Production of Space* (Oxford: Blackwell, 1991); Delores Hayden, *The Power of Place: Urban Landscapes as Public History* (Cambridge, MA: MIT Press, 1997); Edward W. Soja, *Thirdspace: Journeys to Los Angeles and Other Real-and-Imagined Places* (Cambridge: Blackwell, 1996); and Karin Ikas and Gerhard Wagner, eds., *Communicating in the Third Space* (New York: Routledge, 2009). On discursive definitions of the built environment, see Glassie, *Material Culture*; Bernard L. Herman, "On Being German in British America: Gravestones and the Inscription of Identity," *Winterthur Portfolio* 45:2/3 (Summer/Autumn 2011), 195–208; Amy Catania Kulper, "Representing the Discipline: The Operations of Architecture's Discursive Imagery," *Architecture and Culture* 1:1/2 (Nov. 2013), 42–66.

14. On conceptions of architectural permanence around the world before 1850, see Glendinning, *Conservation Movement*, 9–62; David Karmon, *The Ruin of the Eternal City: Antiquity and Preservation in Renaissance Rome* (New York: Oxford University Press, 2011); Fabio Rambelli, "Floating Signifiers: The Plural Significance of the Grand Shrine of Ise and the Incessant Re-signification of Shinto," *Japan Review* 27 (2014), 221–242; Jukka Jokilehto, *A History of Architectural Conservation* (Oxford: Butterworth Heinemann, 1999), 1–173.

15. Kevin Murphy, *Memory and Modernity: Viollet-le-Duc at Vézelay* (University Park: Pennsylvania State University Press, 2000); Martin Bressani, *Architecture and the Historical Imagination: Eugàne-Emmanuel Viollet-le-Duc, 1814–1879* (Farnham: Ashgate, 2014); Michael Wheeler and Nigel Whiteley, *The Lamp of Memory: Ruskin, Tradition, and Architecture* (Manchester: Manchester University Press, 1992).

16. Kariann Akemi Yokota, *Unbecoming British: How Revolutionary America Became a Postcolonial Nation* (Oxford: Oxford University Press, 2011); Van Horn, *Power of Objects*.

17. Whitney A. Martinko, "Progress Through Preservation: History on the American Landscape in an Age of Improvement," PhD diss., University of Virginia, 2012, 80–115; H. G. Jones, ed., *Historical Consciousness in the Early Republic: The Origins of State Historical Societies, Museums, and Collections, 1791–1861* (Chapel Hill: University of North Carolina Press, 1995); Alea Henle, "Preserving the Past, Making History: Historical Societies and Editors in the Early Republic," PhD diss., University of Connecticut, 2012; George Callcott, *History in the United States: Its Practice and Purpose* (Baltimore: Johns Hopkins University Press, 1970); Michael O'Brien, *Conjectures of Order: Intellectual Life and the American South, 1810–1860*, vol. 2 (Chapel Hill: University of North Carolina, 2004), 591–682.

18. Emma Hart, *Building Charleston: Town and Society in the Eighteenth-Century British Atlantic World* (Charlottesville: University of Virginia Press, 2009); Glendinning, *Conservation Movement*, 75–77; Carole Shammas, ed., *Investing in the Early Modern Built Environment: Europeans, Asians, Settlers, and Indigenous Societies* (Leiden: Brill, 2012), esp. 1–31; Drew R. McCoy, *The Elusive Republic: Political Economy in Jeffersonian America* (Chapel Hill: University of North Carolina Press, 1980), 13–47.

19. Upton, *Another City*; Small, *Beauty and Convenience*; D. W. Meinig, *The Shaping of America: A Geographical Perspective on 500 Years of History*, vols. 1–2 (New Haven: Yale University Press, 1986–1993); Claudio Saunt, *A New Order of Things: Property, Power, and the Transformation of the Creek Indians, 1733–1816* (Cambridge: Cambridge University Press, 1999); Alan Taylor, *Liberty Men and Great Proprietors: The Revolutionary Settlement on the*

Maine Frontier, 1760–1820 (Chapel Hill: University of North Carolina Press, 1990); Brendan McConville, *These Daring Disturbers of the Public Peace: The Struggle for Property and Power in Early New Jersey* (Ithaca: Cornell University Press, 1999); Honor Sachs, *Home Rule: Households, Manhood, and National Expansion on the Eighteenth-Century Kentucky Frontier* (New Haven: Yale University Press, 2015).

20. Here I engage and extend the theories of nationalism and the public sphere articulated in Jürgen Habermas, *The Structural Transformation of the Public Sphere* (Cambridge, MA: MIT Press, 1989); and Benedict Anderson, *Imagined Communities: Reflections on the Origin and Spread of Nationalism* (London: Verso, 1983).

21. Glendinning, *Conservation Movement*, 67–74; Kirk Savage, *Monument Wars: Washington, D.C., the National Mall, and the Transformation of the Memorial Landscape* (Berkeley: University of California Press, 2009).

22. I owe this formulation to Laura Edwards's discussion of local law in *The People and Their Peace: Legal Culture and the Transformation of Inequality in the Post-Revolutionary South* (Chapel Hill: University of North Carolina Press, 2009), 90–98, 105–107.

23. On construction of public space, see William J. Novak, *The People's Welfare: Law and Regulation in Nineteenth-Century America* (Chapel Hill: University of North Carolina Press, 1996), esp. 117; Jon C. Teaford, *The Municipal Revolution in America: Origins of Modern Urban Government, 1650–1825* (Chicago: University of Chicago Press, 1975); Morton J. Horwitz, *The Transformation of American Law, 1780–1860* (Cambridge, MA: Harvard University Press, 1977); Hendrik Hartog, *Public Property and Private Power: The Corporation of the City of New York in American Law, 1730–1870* (Chapel Hill: University of North Carolina Press, 1983); Elizabeth Blackmar, "Appropriating 'the Commons': The Tragedy of Public Rights Discourse," in *The Politics of Public Space*, eds. Setha Low and Neil Smith (New York: Routledge, 2006), 49–80; B. Murphy, *Building the Empire State*; Kevin Butterfield, *The Making of Tocqueville's America: Law and Association in the Early United States* (Chicago: University of Chicago Press, 2015); Carol Rose, *Property and Persuasion: Essays on the History, Theory, and Rhetoric of Ownership* (Boulder: Westview, 1994). On public structures built by national and state governments in early modern Britain and the United States, see Martha McNamara, *From Tavern to Courthouse: Architecture and Ritual in American Law, 1658–1860* (Baltimore: Johns Hopkins University Press, 2004); McInnis, *Politics of Taste*; Ryan Quintana, "Planners, Planters, and Slaves: Producing the State in Early National South Carolina," *Journal of Southern History* 81:1 (Feb. 2015), 79–116; Gautham Rao, *Custom Houses and the Making of the American State* (Chicago: Chicago University Press, 2015); and Jo Guldi, *Roads to Power: Britain Invents the Infrastructure State* (Cambridge, MA: Harvard University Press, 2012), 1–24.

24. Alison Stanley, "The Praying Indian Towns: Encounter and Conversation Through Imposed Urban Space," in *Building the British Atlantic World: Spaces, Places, and Material Culture, 1600–1850*, ed. Daniel Maudlin and Bernard L. Herman (Chapel Hill: University of North Carolina Press, 2016), 142–161; Saunt, *New Order of Things*, 70–73.

25. The specific programs for and results of these colonizing strategies differed in place and time. Steven Stoll, *Larding the Lean Earth: Soil and Society in Nineteenth-Century America* (New York: Hill and Wang, 2002), 44–46, 86–88; Stephanie Yuhl, *A Golden Haze of Memory: The Making of Historic Charleston* (Chapel Hill: University of North Carolina Press, 2005); William Glover, *Making Lahore Modern: Constructing and Imagining a Colonial City* (Minneapolis: University of Minnesota Press, 2008); Zeynep Çelik, *Empire, Architecture, and the City: French-Ottoman Encounters, 1830–1914* (Seattle: University of Washington Press, 2008); Michael Holleran, *Boston's "Changeful Times": Origins of Preservation and Planning in America* (Baltimore: Johns Hopkins University Press, 1998); Stephanie R. Ryberg, "Historic Preservation's Urban Renewal Roots: Preservation and Planning in Mid-

Century Philadelphia," *Journal of Urban History* 39:2 (2013), 193–213; Federico Caprotti, *Mussolini's Cities: Internal Colonialism in Italy, 1930–1939* (Youngstown: Cambria, 2007); Francesca Russello Ammon, *Bulldozer: Demolition and Clearance of the Postwar Landscape* (New Haven: Yale University Press, 2016); Anne Mitchell Whisnant, *Super-Scenic Motorway: A Blue Ridge Parkway History* (Chapel Hill: University of North Carolina Press, 2006); Mark David Spence, *Dispossessing the Wilderness: Indian Removal and the Making of the National Parks* (Oxford: Oxford University Press, 1999); Katrina M. Powell, *"Answer at Once": Letters of Mountain Families in Shenandoah National Park, 1934–1938* (Charlottesville: University of Virginia Press, 2009).

26. Susan Juster, *Sacred Violence in Early America* (Philadelphia: University of Pennsylvania Press, 2016), 218–223, 241.

27. On religious iconoclasm in colonial North America, see Juster, *Sacred Violence,* 192–241. On political iconoclasm in British North America, see St. George, *Conversing by Signs*; Brendan McConville, *The King's Three Faces: The Rise and Fall of Royal America* (Chapel Hill: University of North Carolina Press, 2007), 295–300, 306–311; and Wendy Bellion, *Iconoclasm in New York: Revolution to Reenactment* (University Park: Pennsylvania State University Press, 2019). For later studies of the political and cultural meaning of demolition in the United States, see Megan Kate Nelson, *Ruin Nation: Destruction and the American Civil War* (Athens: University of Georgia Press, 2013); and Ammon, *Bulldozer.*

28. Ruth Bogin, "Petitioning and the New Moral Economy of Post-Revolutionary America," *William and Mary Quarterly* 45:3 (July 1988), 391–425; Christopher Clark, *The Roots of Rural Capitalism: Western Massachusetts, 1780–1860* (Ithaca: Cornell University Press, 1992), 195–227; Stephen Innes, *Creating the Commonwealth: The Economic Culture of Puritan New England* (New York: W. W. Norton, 1995); Emma Hart, "From Field to Plate: The Colonial Livestock Trade and the Development of an American Economic Culture," *William and Mary Quarterly* 73:1 (Jan. 2016), 107–140; Michael Zakim and Gary J. Kornblinth, eds., *Capitalism Takes Command: The Social Transformation of Nineteenth-Century America* (Chicago: University of Chicago Press, 2012), 1–12; Joshua J. Yates and James Davison Hunter, eds., *Thrift and Thriving in America: Capitalism and Moral Order from the Puritans to the Present* (Oxford: Oxford University Press, 2011), 61–159.

29. On perfectionism and reform, see Daniel Walker Howe, *What Hath God Wrought: The Transformation of America, 1815–1848* (Oxford: Oxford University Press, 2007), 170–202, 285–327, 613–636; John L. Thomas, "Romantic Reform in America, 1815–1865," *American Quarterly* 17:4 (Winter 1965), 656–681. On environment and reform, see Upton, *Another City,* 113–278, esp. 245, 262; Jeffrey Sklansky, *The Soul's Economy: Market Society and Selfhood in American Thought, 1820–1920* (Chapel Hill: University of North Carolina Press, 2002), 33–72.

30. On market culture and religion, see Charles Sellers, *The Market Revolution: Jacksonian America, 1815–1846* (New York: Oxford University Press, 1991), 28–31, 202–236, 364–395; Howe, *What Hath God Wrought,* 164–202, 285–327, 613–657; Sklansky, *Soul's Economy,* 33–72; Zakim and Kornblinth, *Capitalism Takes Command*; Cathy Matson, ed., "Markets and Morality: Intersections of Economy, Ethics, and Religion in Early North America," special issue, *Early American Studies* 8:3 (Fall 2010), 475–683; and David Morgan, *Protestants and Pictures: Religion, Visual Culture, and the Age of American Mass Production* (New York: Oxford University Press, 1999).

31. Gretchen Buggeln is one of few scholars to make the point that the word *sacred* in the eighteenth and early nineteenth centuries meant special and set apart from the ordinary world and was not tied exclusively to religious meaning. Other studies of natural vistas, battlegrounds, and political language in the early United States link "sacred" subjects broadly

to religious meaning. Buggeln, "New England Orthodoxy," in *American Sanctuary: Understanding Sacred Spaces*, ed. Louis P. Nelson (Bloomington: Indiana University Press, 2006), 18, 31–34; John Sears, *Sacred Places: American Tourist Attractions in the Nineteenth Century* (New York: Oxford University Press, 1989), 5–7; Chambers, *Memories of War*; Watson, *Liberty and Power*, 46–48. On the sacralization of church buildings and cemeteries in the early United States, see Kevin M. Sweeney, "Meetinghouses, Town Houses, and Churches: Changing Perceptions of Sacred and Secular Space in Southern New England," *Winterthur Portfolio* 28:1 (Spring 1993), 59–93; Gretchen Buggeln, *Temples of Grace: The Material Transformation of Connecticut's Churches, 1790–1840* (Lebanon: University Press of New England, 2003); Louis Nelson, *The Beauty of Holiness: Anglicanism and Architecture in Colonial South Carolina* (Chapel Hill: University of North Carolina Press, 2008); and Upton, *Another City*, 203–205.

32. Jeffrey Sklansky makes a similar argument about Transcendental moral reformers. Sklansky, *Soul's Economy*, 4. See also Michael Sandel, *What Money Can't Buy: The Moral Limits of Markets* (New York: Farrar, Straus and Giroux, 2012).

33. On resistance to commodification of land by Euro-American agrarians, see Stephen Stoll, *Ramp Hollow: The Ordeal of Appalachia* (New York: Hill and Wang, 2017); and Daegan Miller, *This Radical Land: A Natural History of American Dissent* (Chicago: University of Chicago Press, 2018).

34. The history of architectural preservation in the early United States before 1860 is treated most comprehensively in the first chapter of Charles Hosmer, *Presence of the Past: The History of the Preservation Movement in the United States Before Williamsburg* (New York: Putnam, 1965). Most scholars point to the 1850s as the genesis of popular efforts to preserve historic sites from demolition as a counterweight to change and discord induced by industrialization, immigration, and slavery. Some histories of preservation locate its origins in the late nineteenth century. See, e.g., Steven Conn, "Rescuing the Homestead of the Nation: The Mount Vernon Ladies' Association and the Preservation of Mount Vernon," *Nineteenth-Century Studies* 11 (1997), 71–93; Patricia West, *Domesticating History: The Political Origins of America's House Museums* (Washington, DC: Smithsonian Institution Press, 1999), 1–37; Jean B. Lee, "Historical Memory, Sectional Strife, and the American Mecca: Mount Vernon, 1783–1853," *Virginia Magazine of History and Biography* (2001), 255–300; Brandt, *First in the Homes of His Countrymen*; William B. Rhoads, "The Colonial Revival and American Nationalism," *Journal of the Society of Architectural Historians* 35:4 (Dec. 1976), 239–254; Michael Holleran, "The Old South: The Meetinghouse and the American Preservation Movement," *Old-Time New England* 76 (Spring/Summer 1998), 49–77; James M. Lindgren, *Preserving the Old Dominion: Historic Preservation and Virginia Traditionalism* (Charlottesville: University of Virginia Press, 1993); and Sarah L. Giffen and Kevin D. Murphy, eds., *"A Noble and Dignified Stream": The Piscataqua Region in the Colonial Revival, 1860–1930* (York: Old York Historical Society, 1992).

35. Charles Dellheim is one of few scholars to see the ways that individuals used preservation to promote industrialization. Dellheim, *The Face of the Past: The Preservation of the Medieval Inheritance in Victorian England* (Cambridge: Cambridge University Press, 2004).

36. Samuel P. Hays, "From the History of the City to the History of the Urbanized Society," *Journal of Urban History* 19/4 (Aug. 1993), 3–25. On market development in the early United States, see Sellers, *Market Revolution*; John Lauritz Larson, *The Market Revolution in America: Liberty, Ambition, and the Eclipse of the Common Good* (Cambridge: Cambridge University Press, 2009); Sven Beckert and Seth Rockman, eds., *Slavery's Capitalism: A New History of American Economic Development* (Philadelphia: University of Pennsylvania Press, 2016); David Jaffee, *A New Nation of Goods: The Material Culture of Early America* (Philadelphia: University of Pennsylvania Press, 2010).

37. Scholars of the "new capitalism" have emphasized that capitalism developed according to human decisions in particular times and places, not along a natural, inevitable, or monolithic course. For studies that encourage cultural approaches to capitalism, see Sklansky, *Soul's Economy*; Jane Kamensky, *The Exchange Artist: A Tale of High-Flying Speculation and America's First Banking Collapse* (New York: Viking, 2008); Rosanne Currarino, "Toward a History of Cultural Economy," *Journal of the Civil War Era* 2:4 (Dec. 2012), 564–585; Jeffrey Sklansky, "The Elusive Sovereign: New Intellectual and Social Histories of Capitalism," *Modern Intellectual History* 9:1 (2012), 233–248; Jessica M. Lepler, *The Many Panics of 1837: People, Politics, and the Creation of a Transatlantic Financial Crisis* (Cambridge: Cambridge University Press, 2013); Brian Luskey and Wendy Woloson, eds., *Capitalism by Gaslight: Illuminating the Economy of Nineteenth-Century America* (Philadelphia: University of Pennsylvania Press, 2015); Ellen Hartigan-O'Connor, "Gender's Value in the History of Capitalism," *Journal of the Early Republic* 36:4 (Winter 2016), 613–635; Joanna Cohen, *Luxurious Citizens: The Politics of Consumption in Nineteenth-Century America* (Philadelphia: University of Pennsylvania Press, 2017). For studies of the early American built environment and capitalism, see Elizabeth Blackmar, *Manhattan for Rent, 1785–1850* (Ithaca: Cornell University Press, 1989); Donna Rilling, *Making Houses, Crafting Capitalism: Builders in Philadelphia, 1790–1850* (Philadelphia: University of Pennsylvania Press, 2000); A. K. Sandoval-Strausz, *Hotel: An American History* (New Haven: Yale University Press, 2008); Upton, *Another City*; and Ryan K. Smith, *Robert Morris's Folly: The Architectural and Financial Failures of an American Founder* (New Haven: Yale University Press, 2014). On the history of moral commerce and benevolence, see Kathleen D. McCarthy, *American Creed: Philanthropy and the Rise of Civil Society* (Chicago: University of Chicago Press, 2003); Lori D. Ginzberg, *Women and the Work of Benevolence: Morality, Politics, and Class in the Nineteenth-Century United States* (New Haven: Yale University Press, 1990); Lawrence J. Friedman and Mark D. McGarvie, eds., *Charity, Philanthropy, and Civility in American History* (Cambridge: Cambridge University Press, 2003); Rob Reich, Chiara Cordelli, and Lucy Bernholz, eds., *Philanthropy in Democratic Societies: Histories, Institutions, Values* (Chicago: University of Chicago Press, 2016); Julie L. Holcomb, *Moral Commerce* (Ithaca: Cornell University Press, 2016); and Bronwen Everill, *Not Made By Slaves: Ethical Capitalism in the Age of Abolition* (Cambridge, MA: Harvard University Press, forthcoming).

38. Jay Kinsbruner, *The Colonial Spanish-American City: Urban Life in the Age of Atlantic Capitalism* (Austin: University of Texas Press, 2005); Upton, *Another City*; Stoll, *Ramp Hollow*; William Cronon, *Nature's Metropolis* (New York: W. W. Norton, 1992); David Harvey, *Paris, Capital of Modernity* (New York: Routledge, 2005); Catherine McNeur, "Parks, People, and Property Values: The Changing Role of Green Spaces in Antebellum Manhattan," *Journal of Planning History* 16:2 (2017), 98–111.

39. Scholars who agree include Blackmar, "Appropriating 'the Commons,'" 49–80; B. Murphy, *Building the Empire State*; and Milroy, *Grid and the River*. For overviews of preservation and real estate markets in the late nineteenth and twentieth centuries, see Wallace, *Mickey Mouse History*, 185–246; and Andrew Hurley, *Beyond Preservation* (Philadelphia: Temple University Press, 2010), 3–30.

Chapter 1

1. For an account of the first steps of building Marietta, see Kim M. Gruenwald, *River of Enterprise: The Commercial Origins of Regional Identity in the Ohio Valley, 1790–1850* (Bloomington: Indiana University Press, 2002), 27–29.

2. Sachs, *Home Rule*, 27–40; Stoll, *Ramp Hollow*, 9, 90–106.

3. Archer Butler Hulbert, ed., *The Records of the Original Proceedings of the Ohio Company* (Marietta: Marietta Historical Commission, 1917), vol. 2, Jan. 5, 1791, 68; Eric Hinderaker, *Elusive Empires: Constructing Colonialism in the Ohio Valley, 1673–1800* (Cambridge: Cambridge University Press, 1997), 226–244; Gregory Evans Dowd, *A Spirited Resistance: The North American Indian Struggle for Unity, 1745–1815* (Baltimore: Johns Hopkins University Press 1992), esp. 90–122. For more on the bloodshed at Big Bottom on January 2, 1791, and its significance for U.S. Indian policy, see Patrick Griffin, "Reconsidering the Ideological Origins of Indian Removal: The Case of the Big Bottom 'Massacre,'" in *The Center of a Great Empire: The Ohio Country in the Early Republic*, ed. Andrew R. L. Cayton and Stuart D. Hobbs (Athens: Ohio University Press, 2005), 11–35.

4. Hulbert, *Records*, vol. 2, Jan. 5, 1791, 68–73 ("general war" from 68); Feb. 21, 1791, 77; Mar. 7, 1791, 79–81.

5. By the end of the year, migrants to the Scioto Company tract would expose the fraudulent dealings of its organizers that left them with no land holdings. Timothy J. Shannon, "The Ohio Company and the Meaning of Opportunity in the American West, 1786–1795," *New England Quarterly* 64:3 (Sept. 1991), 404–405.

6. Hulbert, *Records*, vol. 1, Feb. 21, 1791, 77.

7. Hulbert, *Records*, vol. 1, Mar. 7, 1791, 79–81.

8. Both men also had a hand in Ohio Valley land speculation. Adam Costanzo, *George Washington's Washington: Visions for the National Capital in the Early American Republic* (Athens: University of Georgia Press, 2018); Bob Arnebeck, *Through a Fiery Trial: Building Washington, 1790–1800* (Lanham: Madison Books, 1991), 1–82; Michael Blaakman, "Speculation Nation: Land and Mania in the Revolutionary American Republic, 1776–1803," PhD diss., Yale University, 2016.

9. Bethel Saler, *The Settlers' Empire: Colonialism and State Formation in America's Old Northwest* (Philadelphia: University of Pennsylvania Press, 2014), 1–2.

10. Many U.S. residents believed that Indigenous Americans attacked U.S. migrants under incitement of British forces, and they wanted to claim the Ohio country to remove the lingering influence of British colonial power and to prevent incursions from Spanish colonists along the Mississippi. See, e.g., Josiah Harmar to William S. Johnson, Nov. 26, 1785, William S. Johnson Papers, reel 1, frames 150–152, Library of Congress. For a more comprehensive history of the Ohio Valley, see Andrew Cayton, *The Frontier Republic: Ideology and Politics in the Ohio Country* (Kent: Kent State University Press, 1986); Douglas Hurt, *The Ohio Frontier: Crucible of the Old Northwest, 1720–1830* (Bloomington: Indiana University Press, 1998); Richard White, *The Middle Ground: Indians, Empires, and Republics in the Great Lakes Region, 1650–1815* (Cambridge: Cambridge University Press, 1991); Lawrence Hatter, *Citizens of Convenience: The Imperial Origins of American Nationhood on the U.S.-Canadian Border* (Charlottesville: University of Virginia Press, 2016); and Rob Harper, *Unsettling the West: Violence and State Building in the Ohio Valley* (Philadelphia: University of Pennsylvania Press, 2017). A map done by Dudley Woodbridge shows how Ohio Company associates tried to follow the stipulations of the Land Ordinance of 1785. However, exceptions for continued federal administration of natural resources and specified township sections proved nearly impossible to enforce. Woodbridge, "Appropriated Lotts," 1793, series 4, oversize drawer 4, MDOCA; Onuf, *Statehood and Union*; Malcolm Rohrbaugh, *The Land Office Business: The Settlement and Administration of American Public Lands* (Oxford: Oxford University Press, 1968), 7–11; John Opie, *The Law of the Land: Two Hundred Years of American Farmland Policy* (Lincoln: University of Nebraska Press, 1987), 12.

11. Winthrop Sargent, diary, July 27, 1786 (microfilm: reel 1), Winthrop Sargent Papers, Massachusetts Historical Society, Boston (hereafter Sargent Papers).

12. Many Indigenous Americans today view earthworks as spiritually significant sites and vessels of collective memory. Scholars continue to debate how Indigenous architects conceived of and used earthworks throughout the Ohio Valley. Jay Miller, *Ancestral Mounds: Vitality and Volatility of Native America* (Lincoln: University of Nebraska Press, 2015); Lindsay Jones and Richard D. Shiels, eds., *The Newark Earthworks: Enduring Monuments, Contested Meanings* (Charlottesville: University of Virginia Press, 2016).

13. Winthrop Sargent, "Plan of the Ruins of an Antient Town or Fortified Camp near the Confluence of the Ohio and Muskingum Rivers," D. Blommart copy, 1787, AAS. Winthrop Sargent recorded first seeing the earthworks on July 24, 1786, after arriving at Fort Harmar. In the same journal entry, he noted a plan of the earthworks in the making. Sargent drew a plan at some point before March 1787, when he sent one to the American Academy of Arts and Sciences. This is likely the same plan that D. Blommart copied "by permission" in 1787. Despite broad similarities, Sargent's plan seems to be distinct from Jonathan Heart's plan engraved in the *Columbian Magazine* in May 1787. Blommart's copy of Sargent's plan is also distinct from the sketch that Samuel Holden Parsons made for Ezra Stiles on May 3, 1786. Winthrop Sargent, diary, July 24, 1786 (microfilm: reel 1), Sargent Papers; Jonathan Heart, "Account of some Remains of ancient Works, on the Muskingum, with a Plan of these Works," *Columbian Magazine* 1:9 (May 1787), 424–427; Terry A. Barnhart, *American Antiquities: Revisiting the Origins of American Archaeology* (Lincoln: University of Nebraska Press, 2015), 94–109; Thomas H. Smith, *The Mapping of Ohio* (Kent: Kent State University Press, 1977), 35–37.

14. James Winthrop to Winthrop Sargent, Feb. 26, 1788 (microfilm: reel 2), Sargent Papers; American Philosophical Society, *List of the Members of the American Philosophical Society* (Philadelphia: private printing, 1890), 17–18.

15. Susan Scott Parrish, *American Curiosity: Cultures of Natural History in the Colonial British Atlantic World* (Chapel Hill: University of North Carolina Press, 2006); Kathleen S. Murphy, "Translating the Vernacular: Indigenous and African Knowledge in the Eighteenth-Century British Atlantic," *Atlantic Studies* 8:1 (2011), 29–48; Cameron B. Strang, *Frontiers of Science: Imperialism and Natural Knowledge in the Gulf South Borderlands, 1500–1850* (Chapel Hill: University of North Carolina Press, 2018).

16. Sweet, *Antiquaries*, 119–187.

17. James Winthrop to Winthrop Sargent, Feb. 26, 1788 (microfilm: reel 2), Sargent Papers. See also Hugh Williamson to Thomas Worthington, Apr. 23, 1804, box 2, folder 7 (microfilm 96, series 15, roll 3), Thomas Worthington Papers, Ohio History Connection, Columbus (hereafter Ohio History Connection).

18. Manasseh Cutler to Rufus Putnam, Nov. 18, 1788, in *Life, Journals and Correspondence of Rev. Manasseh Cutler, LL.D.*, ed. William Parker Cutler and Julia Perkins Cutler (Cincinnati: Robert Clarke and Co., 1888), vol. 1, 436.

19. Yokota, *Unbecoming British*, esp. 153–191; Onuf, *Statehood and Union*, 24–36.

20. Saler, *Settler's Empire*, 1–3.

21. Heart, "Account of Some Remains of Ancient Works," 424–427; Whitney A. Martinko, "'So Majestic a Monument of Antiquity': Landscape, Knowledge, and Authority in the Early National West," *Buildings and Landscapes* 16:1 (Spring 2009), 29–61.

22. Manasseh Cutler to Winthrop Sargent, Mar. 24, 1786, in Cutler and Cutler, *Life, Journals and Correspondence*, vol. 1, 187–189.

23. Saler, *Settlers' Empire*, 42–49.

24. Cayton, *Frontier Republic*, 11; Rohrbaugh, *Land Office Business*, 15–16.

25. Kathryn E. Sampeck, "From Ancient Altepetl to Modern Municipios: Surveying as Power in Colonial Guatemala," *International Journal of Historical Archaeology* 18:1 (Mar. 2014), 175–203; Neil Safier, *Measuring the New World: Enlightenment Science and South*

America (Chicago: University of Chicago Press, 2008); R. Hunter and A. Sluyter, "How Incipient Colonies Create Territory: The Textual Surveys of New Spain, 1520s–1620s," *Journal of Historical Geography* 37 (2011), 288–299.

26. Cutler's manuscript notes on the survey of Quadraniou and on the examination of its trees, with a note in Putnam's handwriting, are located in box 3, folder 10, RPP. Reports of this certification circulated in U.S. newspapers. See, e.g., "Extract of a letter from a gentlemen at Marietta, to his friend in Middletown, Connecticut, dated September 8," *New-York Morning Post*, Oct. 16, 1788, p. 2; "Middletown, October 13," *Connecticut Courant*, Oct. 20, 1788, p. 3; "Middletown, October 12," (Philadelphia) *Independent Gazetteer*, Oct. 20, 1788, p. 2; "Massachusetts, dated 8th September, 1788," *Pennsylvania Gazette*, Oct. 22, 1788, p. 2; "Middletown, Oct. 13," *Providence Gazette and Country Journal*, Nov. 1, 1788, p. 3; "Extract of a Letter from a gentleman at Marietta to his friend in Massachusetts, dated 8th September, 1788," (Windsor) *Vermont Journal*, Nov. 17, 1788, p. 2.

27. Stanley, "Praying Indian Towns," 142–161; Saunt, *New Order of Things*, 70–79.

28. Though people around the world offered many theories about the origins of the earthworks' architects, most Ohio Company members agreed with the proposition that the moundbuilders were indigenous to the Ohio Valley and either had migrated to Central and South America or had died and dispersed before European colonization. For more on these debates and the production of knowledge and regional identity, see Martinko, "So Majestic a Monument of Antiquity." For more on the moundbuilder myth, see Robert Silverberg, *Mound Builders of Ancient America: The Archaeology of a Myth* (Athens: Ohio University Press, 1968); Roger Kennedy, *Hidden Cities: The Discovery and Loss of Ancient North American Civilization* (New York: Free Press, 1994); Angela Miller, "'The Soil of an Unknown America': New World Lost Empires and the Debate over Cultural Origins," *American Art* 8:3/4 (Summer–Autumn 1994), 9–27; Gordon Sayre, "The Mound Builders and the Imagination of American Antiquity in Jefferson, Bartram, and Chateaubriand," *Early American Literature* 33:3 (1998), 225–249; and Barnhart, *American Antiquities*.

29. Frazer McGlinchey has observed that Ohio Company associates framed the earthworks as evidence of the lower civilization status of their Indigenous contemporaries. However, he overlooks the town-building activities of the Ohio Company and writes that they had no intention of preserving the mounds. McGlinchey, "'A Superior Civilization': Appropriation, Negotiation, and Interaction in the Northwest Territory, 1787–1795," in *The Boundaries Between Us: Natives and Newcomers Along the Frontiers of the Old Northwest Territory, 1750–1850*, ed. Daniel Barr (Kent: Kent State University Press, 2006), 123.

30. Indigenous populations continued to use earthworks in other Ohio regions as sites of burial and spiritual meaning into the seventeenth and eighteenth centuries. Rob Mann argues that Euro-Americans ignored this evidence to create the "moundbuilder myth," which separated Indigenous peoples into prehistoric and historic populations to assert colonial power over the land. Mann, "Intruding on the Past: The Reuse of Ancient Earthen Mounds by Native Americans," *Southeastern Archaeology* 24:1 (Summer 2005), 1–10.

31. Hulbert, *Records*, Aug. 30, 1787, vol. 1, 15–16; and Nov. 21, 1787, vol. 1, 20–21; Manasseh Cutler to Ebenezer Hazard, Sept. 18, 1787, in Cutler and Cutler, *Life, Journals and Correspondence*, vol. 1, 330.

32. Upton, *Another City*, 1–3, 113–144.

33. Euro-Americans broadly saw the grid as a tool of Enlightenment study, order, and classification of environment, society, and political economy in the late eighteenth century. For more on systematic thinking and orthogonal planning, see Upton, *Another City*, 123–137.

34. In 1788, for instance, Rufus Putnam described the complex as "the Town or principle works," amending the sentence to include "City" but then crossing it out to let his original

phrasing stand. Rufus Putnam to Isaiah Thomas [wrapper says to Thomas May in Putnam's handwriting], May 17, 1788, series 2, box 1, folder 1, MDOCA.

35. On Roman classicism and U.S. identity, see Eran Shalev, *Rome Reborn on Western Shores: Historical Imagination and the Creation of the American Republic* (Charlottesville: University of Virginia Press, 2009), 2; Caroline Winterer, *The Mirror of Antiquity: American Women and the Classical Traditions, 1750–1900* (Ithaca: Cornell University Press, 2007); John C. Shields, *American Aeneus: Classical Origins of the American Self* (Knoxville: University of Tennessee Press, 2001), esp. 259, 268–277; and Purcell, *Sealed with Blood*, esp. 1–10, 49–91. On European views of Roman ruins in the late eighteenth century, see Rosemary Sweet, "The Changing View of Rome in the Long Eighteenth Century," *Journal for Eighteenth-Century Studies* 33:2 (2010), 154.

36. Company members debated variations on the town name Castrapolis in acknowledgment of the ancient fortifications and the creation of the new city by military men. Some derided the mixing of Roman and Greek linguistic conventions; others pleaded modesty in not wanting to honor themselves as founders. Ohio Company leaders eventually decided to honor the queen of France. Josephine E. Phillips, "The Naming of Marietta," *Ohio Archaeological and Historical Quarterly* 55:2 (Apr.–June 1946), 106–137.

37. Famiano Nardini's *Roma Antica* (1688) was widely reprinted and contained a rough map of the seven hills of ancient Rome. Dominique Magnan's *La ville de Rome* included street maps of Rome's various districts; the footprints of earthworks in Marietta appear very similar to ancient features indicated on these maps. See http://gallica.bnf.fr /ark:/12148/bpt6k208643z/f34.item.zoom. Visually, the urban plan was a frame for monumental antiquities. British imprints did not contain street maps of modern Rome until J. Salmon's *An Historical Description of Ancient and Modern Rome* in 1800. For more on eighteenth-century views of Rome, see Sweet, "Changing View of Rome." Rosemary Sweet, *Cities and the Grand Tour: The British in Italy, 1690–1820* (West Nyack: Cambridge University Press, 2012).

38. Hulbert, *Records*, vol. 1, 51; Rufus Putnam, emendations to "Plan of the City" by Edward Ruggles, oversize file, series 4, drawer 3, item 4, MDOCA. The Ohio Company at first considered dedicating, or even deeding, this square to the queen of France in gratitude for French support for the American Revolution. This plan presumably died away when the French Revolution toppled the monarchy. The last mention in the Ohio Company records of honoring Marie Antoinette with the dedication of the square came on May 16, 1789. In the manuscript minutes for the March 7, 1791, meeting, the directors omitted the name of the square when setting out directions for its preservation. Hulbert, *Records*, vol. 1, July 2, 1788, 51; and May 16, 1789, 108; Records of the Origin and the Proceedings of the Ohio Company, Mar. 7, 1791, manuscript, 148, MDOCA.

39. David Karmon, *The Ruin of the Eternal City: Antiquity and Preservation in Renaissance Rome* (New York: Oxford University Press, 2011), esp. 6–13, 34–45.

40. Stoll, *Ramp Hollow*.

41. U.S. armed forces regularly deployed environmental destruction to gain control of contested territories inhabited by Indigenous peoples and Euro-American agrarians. The Continental Army had used environmental destruction to wage war against the Haudenosaunee in western New York—a tactic that earned George Washington the moniker of "Town Destroyer." U.S. troops and settlers used similar tactics to destroy the buildings, crops, and orchards of Ohio country residents in the 1780s and 1790s. Hinderaker, *Elusive Empires*, 226, 238–242; Max M. Mintz, *Seeds of Empire: The American Revolutionary Conquest of the Iroquois* (New York: New York University Press, 1999), 86–155; Harper, *Unsettling the West*; Rufus Putnam letter to [Fisher Ames?], Jan. 6, 1791, box 1, folder 10, RPP.

42. Nine of the eleven attendees at the first organizational meeting of the company were members of the Society of the Cincinnati. Shannon, "Ohio Company and Meaning of Opportunity," 396.

43. Saler, *Settlers' Empire*, 5.

44. On taste and political power, see Kelly, *Republic of Taste*, 4–9; Van Horn, *Power of Objects*, 9–11; and Sweet, *Antiquaries*, 155.

45. On urban planning as a statement of taste, see Richard L. Bushman, *The Refinement of America: Persons, Houses, Cities* (New York: Vintage, 1993), 139–160.

46. Manasseh Cutler to Winthrop Sargent, Apr. 20, 1786, in Cutler and Cutler, *Life, Journals and Correspondence*, vol. 1, 189–191.

47. Company directors consistently referred to their planned settlement as a *city*. They said so in their foundational document, noting that they would set aside a tract of land for a *city* at the confluence of the Ohio and Muskingum Rivers. Hulbert, *Records*, vol. 1, Aug. 30, 1787, 15. Rufus Putnam referred to the spot as "the Plot of ground laid out for building the Citty" in a letter to newspaper printer Isaiah Thomas, written with instructions to publish. Putnam to Thomas, May 17, 1788, series 2, box 1, folder 1, MDOCA.

48. Hart, *Building Charleston*, 159–168; Milroy, *Grid and the River*, 11–49; Upton, *Another City*, 1–15.

49. Richard C. Wade still provides the best overview of the importance of urban commercial and cultural development to the U.S. project of settling western territories and states. Richard C. Wade, *The Urban Frontier: The Rise of Western Cities, 1790–1830* (1959; repr. Urbana: University of Illinois Press, 1996). See also John Reps, *Town Planning in Frontier America* (Princeton: Princeton University Press, 1969), 261–303.

50. Steven Bullock, *Revolutionary Brotherhood: Freemasonry and the Transformation of the American Social Order, 1730–1840* (Chapel Hill: University of North Carolina, 1998); Sweet, *Antiquaries*, 131–132.

51. Many Ohio Company leaders were members of the Masonic American Union Lodge, founded in 1776 in Roxbury, Massachusetts, and reconstituted in Newburgh, New York, in 1779 as a traveling military lodge. Marietta freemasons ultimately decided that Jonathan Heart had inherited the appointment of provincial grand master over all of North America and had the authority to re-create a lodge in federal territory. On February 7, 1791, Jonathan Heart, Daniel Story, and Return J. Meigs Jr. sent letters from the Marietta lodge to the Grand Lodges of New York, Pennsylvania, and Massachusetts, asking for acceptance in a "Brethren of Confederated States," as a "Masonic Body corporate within the Federal Territory, and duly invested with every power necessary to constitute, rule and govern the same, agreeable to the Constitutions and ancient customs of the Royal Craft throughout the world." Charles S. Plumb, *The History of American Union Lodge No. 1, Free and Accepted Masons of Ohio* (Marietta, 1934), 1–34, 87–102, quotations from 99–102.

52. Rufus Putnam, draft letter to "Dear Sir," c. late 1788–89, box 3, folder 10, RPP. It is unclear which specific lodge Putnam described. Most Masons met in taverns during the eighteenth century, not in grand lodges. But it is uncertain where Boston freemasons were meeting at the time other than the Green Dragon Tavern, purchased by the St. John Order in 1764. At this moment, Masons were starting to become more insular and private, meeting more in lodges that they defined as private space rather than in public taverns. By 1816, the Columbian Lodge met at the Grand Lodge of Massachusetts. Bullock, *Revolutionary Brotherhood*, 241–242, 259.

53. Edward Ruggles, "Plan of the City Marietta," 1789, AAS. Jonathan Heart had called the largest mound a pyramid but also had noted that it was circular. See Heart, "Account of some Remains of ancient Works," 424–427.

54. Rufus Putnam, emendations to "Plan of the City" by Edward Ruggles, oversize file, series 4, drawer 3, item 4, MDOCA. Thomas H. Smith does not include these maps in his history of mapping Ohio earthworks. Smith, *Mapping of Ohio*, 32–55. For a more extensive bibliography of U.S. maps of the Northwest Territory, see J. C. Wheat and C. F. Brun, *Maps and Charts Published in America Before 1800*, rev. 2nd ed. (New Haven: Yale University Press, 1978), 144–149.

55. Plumb, *History of American Union Lodge No. 1*; Hulbert, *Records*, Dec. 3, 1788, vol. 1, 89; vol. 1, Mar. 7, 1791, 79–81; and vol. 2, Jan. 21, 1796, 209.

56. John D. Hamilton, *Material Culture of the American Freemasons* (Hanover: University Press of New England, 1994), 16.

57. Putnam to Thomas, May 17, 1788, series 2, box 1, folder 1, MDOCA.

58. Johann Neem, *Creating a Nation of Joiners: Democracy and Civil Society in Early National Massachusetts* (Cambridge, MA: Harvard University Press, 2008), 30–32.

59. Savage, *Monument Wars*, 25–32.

60. On baroque urban planning in the early United States, see Upton, *Another City*, 118–119.

61. Robert Clarke, *Record of the Distribution and Sale of Lots in the Town of Losantiville (now Cincinnati) 1789*, 1802, Rare Books, University of Cincinnati, https://www.libraries .uc.edu/content/dam/libraries/arb/images/urban-studies/maps/cincinnati-1802-plan.jpg.

62. Upton, *Another City*, 120–121.

63. Hulbert, *Records*, vol. 2, Jan. 21, 1796, 209. For more on Indigenous construction of monumentality, see Gregory D. Wilson, "Community, Identity, and Social Memory at Moundsville," *American Antiquity* 75:1 (Jan. 2010), 3–18; and Richard L. Burger and Robert M. Rosenswig, eds., *Early New World Monumentality* (Gainesville: University Press of Florida, 2012), 3–52, 78–110.

64. Hulbert, *Records*, Mar. 7, 1791, vol. 2, 80.

65. Winthrop to Sargent, Feb. 26, 1788 (microfilm: reel 2), Sargent Papers.

66. Putnam to Cutler, May 16, 1788, in Cutler and Cutler, *Life, Journals and Correspondence*, vol. 1, 377.

67. John May, journal, May 27, 1788, *The Western Journals of John May, Ohio Company Agent and Business Adventurer* (Cincinnati: Historical and Philosophical Society of Ohio, 1961), 48.

68. Bushman, *Refinement of America*, 165–169.

69. Hulbert, *Records*, Dec. 3, 1788, vol. 1, 89. See also July 29, 1790, vol. 2, 51; Feb. 21, 1791, vol. 2, 77; Mar. 7, 1791, vol. 2, 79–81; and Jan. 21, 1796, vol. 2, 208–210.

70. Hulbert, *Records*, Mar. 7, 1791, vol. 2, 79–81.

71. Bushman, *Refinement of America*, 383–390.

72. Rufus Putnam draft letter to "Dear Sir," undated (c. 1788–89), box 3, folder 10, RPP. For a map of the mall around 1780, see Rawson, *Eden on the Charles*, 66.

73. James Bowdoin served as governor of Massachusetts from 1785 to 1787 and is best remembered for his opposition to Shays' Rebellion during his governorship, when he called out the militia to western Massachusetts to break up the men who gathered to protest state taxes. He was also the first president of the American Academy of Arts and Sciences, and Winthrop Sargent had sent him a description and plan of the Muskingum earthworks on March 27, 1787. Bowdoin and his wife, Elizabeth, held a total of nine shares in the Ohio Company. They tried to sell their shares in 1789, but they were not able to find a buyer at the price they desired. Neem, *Creating a Nation of Joiners*, 39; Smith, *Mapping of Ohio*, 38; James and Elizabeth Bowdoin to John May, Apr. 21, 1789, in Western Reserve Historical Society, "Side Lights on the Ohio Company of Associates from the John May Papers," ed. Elbert Jay Benton (Cleveland, 1917), 145.

74. Rufus Putnam draft letter to "Dear Sir," undated (c. 1788–89), box 3, folder 10, RPP.

75. John May, journal, Apr. 30, 1789, *Western Journals of John May*, 88. See also Blackmar, *Manhattan for Rent*, 79–80; Bushman, *Refinement of America*, 353–357.

76. In 1768, Christian Remick composed a view of the Common with the mall in the foreground. He situated his viewer's perspective above pedestrians on the mall, looking across the Common toward John Hancock's prominent house. Remick, "A Prospective View of part of the Commons," watercolor, c. 1768, Collections of the Concord Museum, Concord, MA.

77. Minerva Nye to Mrs. Stone, Sept. 19, 1788, box 2, folder 1, Tupper family papers typed, Ohio History Connection.

78. John May, journal, May 23, 1788, *Western Journals of John May*, 44.

79. Here I draw on historical geographer D. W. Meinig's model of empire and Bethel Saler's discussion of the role of place in state formation in the Northwest Territory. Meinig, *The Shaping of America: A Geographical Perspective on 500 Years of History*, vol. 1 (New Haven: Yale University Press, 1988), 370; Saler, *Settlers' Empire*, 5.

80. Minutes of the July 2 meeting, including the naming of the earthworks and the squares, were published widely. See, e.g., "Salem, September 30," *Salem Mercury*, Sept. 30, 1788, p. 3; "Meeting at Marietta," *Massachusetts Centinel*, Oct. 1, 1788, 19; "Salem, September 30," (Salem) *Independent Chronicle*, Oct. 2, 1788, p. 3; "At a Meeting of the Directors and agents of the Ohio Company," *Massachusetts Gazette*, Oct. 3, 1788, p. 1; "Portsmouth, October 4," (Portsmouth) *New-Hampshire Spy*, Oct. 4, 1788, p. 287; "At a Meeting of the Directors and Agents of the Ohio Company," *Providence Gazette and Country Journal*, Oct. 4, 1788, p. 2; "Boston, October 1; Meeting at Marietta," (Philadelphia) *Federal Gazette*, Oct. 9, 1788, p. 3. Newspapers in Northampton, Massachusetts; New York, New York; Worcester, Massachusetts; New London, Connecticut; New Haven, Connecticut; and Elizabethtown, New Jersey, printed similar notices. Isaac Pitman of Newport, Rhode Island, likely included these minutes for sale along with the Independence Day speeches of James Varnum and Arthur St. Clair. Advertisement, Sept. 25, 1788, *Newport Herald*, p. 3.

81. Joseph Gilman to Nicholas Gilman, May 11, 1789, in Emily Noyes, *A Family History in Letters and Documents, 1667–1837*, vol. 1 (private printing, 1919), 160–161.

82. Shannon, "Ohio Company and Meaning of Opportunity," 393–413; Gruenwald, *River of Enterprise*, 10–18.

83. Opie, *Law of the Land*, 15–17.

84. See, e.g., Rufus Putnam, journal of his service to the Ohio Company, box 4, RPP; Winthrop Sargent expenses, series 1, box 5, MDOCA; Records of Origins and Proceedings of the Ohio Company, series 1, box 1, 269–270, MDOCA.

85. Dudley Woodbridge Jr. to James Backus, Feb. 15, 1799, Backus Woodbridge Papers, Ohio History Connection; quoted in Gruenwald, *River of Enterprise*, 47.

86. Onuf, *Statehood and Union*, 24–36. See also B. Murphy, *Building the Empire State*.

87. Henry Knox to Samuel Holden Parsons, Mar. 29, 1785, Henry Knox Papers, Gilder-Lehrman Collection online, http://www.gilderlehrman.org/collections/7ec7e2e6-29db-41c7-8a58-022056334106. See also Shannon, "Ohio Company and Meaning of Opportunity," 398–399.

88. Samuel Holden Parsons to William S. Johnson, Nov. 26, 1785, reel 1, frames 150–152, William S. Johnson Papers, Manuscripts Division, Library of Congress. Emphasis in original. See also Joseph Gilman to Nicholas Gilman, May 11, 1789, in Noyes, *Family History*, vol. 1, 160; and Rufus Putnam to Fisher Ames, Jan. 9, 1790, Mss. Misc. Boxes P, folder 4, Rufus Putnam Papers, AAS.

89. Indigenous Americans and white agrarians—so-called squatters—defined public lands as commons accessible to all citizens. Lisa Brooks, "Two Paths to Peace: Competing

Vision of Native Space in the Old Northwest," in *The Boundaries Between Us: Natives and Newcomers Along the Frontiers of the Old Northwest Territory, 1750–1850*, ed. Daniel P. Barr (Kent: Kent State University Press, 2006), 87–117; Stoll, *Ramp Hollow*; John R. Van Atta, *Securing the West: Politics, Public Lands, and the Fate of the Old Republic, 1785–1850* (Baltimore: Johns Hopkins University Press, 2014), 41–42, 45–46.

90. Putnam to Thomas, May 17, 1788, series 2, box 1, folder 1, MDOCA.

91. Putnam to Thomas, May 17, 1788, series 2, box 1, folder 1, MDOCA.

92. John Opie argues that the federal system of land division and farmland policy ultimately benefited speculative private enterprise. The federal government repeatedly bolstered this principle with farmland policy in subsequent decades. Opie, *Law of the Land*, xi.

93. Cutler to Hazard, Sept. 18, 1787, in Cutler and Cutler, *Life, Journals and Correspondence*, vol. 1, 330.

94. Martinko, "So Majestic a Monument of Antiquity," 29–61.

95. "Extract of a letter from Pittsburgh November 18," (Philadelphia) *National Gazette*, Dec. 5, 1791, p. 43. Reprinted throughout the Mid-Atlantic region and New England. See also Manasseh Cutler to "Dear Sir," Oct. 21, 1790 (microfilm: reel 3), Manasseh Cutler Collection, Northwestern University (microfilm: Ohio University).

96. Reps, *Town Planning in Frontier America*, 261–303; Wade, *Urban Frontier*, 27-29.

97. Reps, *Town Planning in Frontier America*, 288–289.

98. On the geographical distribution of shareholders, see Shannon, "Ohio Company and Meaning of Opportunity," 408–413.

99. Manasseh Cutler, diary, July 27, 1787, in Cutler and Cutler, *Life, Journals and Correspondence*, vol. 1, 305.

100. Manasseh Cutler, diary, Oct. 27, 1787, in Cutler and Cutler, *Life, Journals and Correspondence*, vol. 1, 326.

101. These 148 shareholders had defaulted by nonpayment by May 1789. William Duer, Andrew Craigie, and Royal Flint were appointed trustees of this group of Ohio Company shares. Shaw Livermore, *Early American Land Companies: Their Influence on Corporate Development* (New York: Oxford University Press, 1939), 141.

102. Shannon, "Ohio Company and Meaning of Opportunity," 403–405.

103. Editors of their printed records, however, state that no record of that application exists. Hulbert, *Records*, Mar. 6, 1788, vol. 1, 41–42.

104. Manasseh Cutler to Agents of the Ohio Company, Nov. 19, 1788, in Western Reserve Historical Society, "Side Lights," ed. Benton, 130.

105. For instance, Rufus Putnam tried unsuccessfully to approve a company clause stating that Ohio Company directors could be held liable only for decisions for which they had personally voted to approve. Company record-keepers still recorded the names of dissenting voters. B. Murphy, *Building the Empire State*, ix–x; Livermore, *Early American Land Companies*, 141–142; Neem, *Creating a Nation of Joiners*, 4.

106. Gruenwald, *River of Enterprise*, 27.

107. Hulbert, *Records*, Dec. 3, 1788, vol. 1, 89.

108. Hulbert, *Records*, Dec. 3, 1788, vol. 1, 89.

109. Hulbert, *Records*, Mar. 7, 1791, vol. 2, 79–81.

110. It was not unusual to have public green spaces with different sections devoted to recreation and productive space. Boston Common, for instance, included a burying ground and tree-lined walks as well as open space for pasturage. Rawson, *Eden on the Charles*, 28–35, 66.

111. Rufus Putnam, Manasseh Cutler, and Robert Oliver, Petition of the Directors of the Ohio Company to Congress, Mar. 2, 1792, p. 3, series 1, box 4, folder 3, MDOCA. They argued that Congress should give clear title to the Ohio Company at a lower than agreed on

price so that the company could execute deeds and maintain security and defense of the tract.

112. Manasseh Cutler to Rufus Putnam, Nov. 24, 1791 (microfilm: reel 3), Manasseh Cutler Collection, Northwestern University (microfilm: Ohio University).

113. On Ohio migration after 1795, see Saler, *Settlers' Empire*, 56–60.

114. Thaddeus Mason Harris, *A Journal of a Tour into the Territory Northwest of the Alleghany Mountains, Made in the Spring of the Year 1803* (Boston, 1805), 53. For citations of Harris's account, see Caleb Atwater, "Description of the Antiquities Discovered in the State of Ohio and Other Western States," in *Archaeologia Americana, Transactions and Collections of the American Antiquarian Society* 1 (Cambridge, MA, 1820), 134–140; and John Delafield Jr., "A Brief Topographical Description of the County of Washington, in the State of Ohio" (New York: J. M. Elliott 1834), AAS.

115. H. M. Brackenridge to Thomas Jefferson, July 25, 1813, Jefferson Papers, Founders Online, http://founders.archives.gov/documents/Jefferson/03-06-02-0269.

116. H. M. Brackenridge, *Views of Louisiana; Together with a Journal of a Voyage Up the Missouri River, in 1811* (Pittsburgh, 1814), 121.

117. Brackenridge, *Views of Louisiana*, 186. Architects of this site built its earthworks at least five hundred years after the last major phase of construction of the Muskingum earthworks. For an overview of the site's history, see Timothy R. Pauketat, *Cahokia: Ancient America's Great City on the Mississippi* (New York: Viking, 2009).

118. Deed Book A, Aug. 4, 1810, 27, Pickaway County, Ohio, Recorder's Office. The first printed images and descriptions of these earthworks appeared in the *Royal American Magazine* in 1775. Smith, *Mapping of Ohio*, 34–35.

119. Journal of the Court of Common Pleas, July 27, 1810, vol. 1-2-3, 14, Court of Common Pleas, Pickaway County, Ohio.

120. Deed Book A, 28, 67, Recorder's Office, Pickaway County, Ohio.

121. Caleb Atwater to Isaiah Thomas, Mar. 3, 1820, box 1, folder 2, Caleb Atwater Papers, AAS.

122. "To the Editors of the Farmer," (Bridgeport, CT) *Republican Farmer*, Aug. 28, 1816; "Of the Aborigines of the Western Country," *Port-folio* 2:1 (July 1816), 1–8. Excerpts of this article that mentioned Circleville were reprinted widely in U.S. newspapers in the summer of 1816—from Washington, D.C., to New York City, to Columbia, South Carolina, to Winchester, Kentucky.

123. "Topographical: Circleville, Ohio," *Daily National Intelligencer*, June 16, 1816, p. 2. Reprinted in Philadelphia's *Weekly Aurora*, June 25, 1816, p. 162; and "Topographical: Circleville, Ohio," (Charlestown, VA) *Farmer's Repository*, June 26, 1816, p. 1.

124. "Essex Register: Salem—Wednesday, June 26, 1816," *Essex Register*, June 26, 1816, p. 2.

125. Leatitia Ware, Aug. 21, 1816, "Memorandum kept on a visit to the Meetings of Friends in the State of Ohio some parts of Pennsylvania & Virginia Perform'd by Leatitia Ware accompanied by Martha Rose & Halliday Jackson," 56–59, Halliday Jackson Manuscripts, Swarthmore Friends Historical Library, Swarthmore, PA.

Chapter 2

1. Council Records, Town of Marietta, vol. 1, Mar. 22, 1810, 139; Mar. 29, 1811, 154; Apr. 15, 1811, 159–161, Special Collections, Marietta College, Marietta, Ohio. The original survey and committee report made in April 1811 are not included in the town council rec-

ords held in Special Collections at Marietta College. An account of that report comes from vol. 1, Jan. 3, 1817, 265–268 ("be improved as a burying ground" from 265).

2. Blanche Linden, *Silent Cities on a Hill: Picturesque Landscapes of Memory and Boston's Mount Auburn Cemetery* (Amherst: University of Massachusetts Press, 2007), 86–93, 120–124; Upton, *Another City*, 203–241.

3. Council Records, Town of Marietta, vol. 1, Special Collections, Marietta College. See, e.g., May 7, 1803, 43; Apr. 19, 1805, 65; May 28, 1805, 81; Mar. 30, 1808, 114; Apr. 17, 1809, 124.

4. John Carter, *Views of Ancient Buildings in England*, 6 vols. (London, 1793).

5. Rosemary Sweet, *The Writing of Urban Histories in Eighteen-Century England* (Oxford: Oxford University Press, 1997). On chorography, or place-writing, in early U.S. town histories, see Halttunen, "Grounded Histories," 513–532.

6. Allison built his theories on John Locke's conception of sensationalism, which held that views of particular landscapes shaped the minds and imaginations of individuals. In this view, writers drew on the specific aspects of a place's environment and history to encourage readers to translate sensationalism into national feeling. Angela Miller, *The Eye of Empire: Landscape Representation and American Cultural Politics, 1825–1875* (Ithaca: Cornell University Press, 1993), 9–11; Buggeln, *Temples of Grace*, 129–131; Robert Streeter, "Association Psychology and Literary Nationalism in the North American Review, 1815–1825," *American Literature* 17:3 (Nov. 1945), 253–254.

7. Deborah Norris Logan, diary, Aug. 17, 1825, vol. 8, 98, Deborah Norris Logan Diaries, 1815–1839, HSP (hereafter Logan Diaries).

8. On ruins and picturesque appreciation of landscape in the early United States, see Nick Yablon, *Untimely Ruins: An Archaeology of American Urban Modernity, 1819–1919* (Chicago: University of Chicago Press, 2009), 1–45; Chambers, *Memories of War*; W. Maynard Barksdale, "'Best, Lowliest Style!' The Nineteenth-Century Rediscovery of American Colonial Architecture," *Journal of the Society of Architectural Historians* 59:3 (Sept. 2000), 338–357.

9. Joseph Lathrop, "God's mercies recollected in the midst of his Temple: A Sermon preached in the Old Church of the First Society in West Springfield, on June 20th, 1802, the Sabbath which closed the assembling in that Church, and preceded the Dedication of the New Church" (Springfield: Ashley and Brewer, 1802), 7.

10. Lathrop, "God's mercies," 13.

11. Lathrop, "God's mercies," 8.

12. This wave of new construction made neoclassical features a popular marker of new public buildings. See Novak, *People's Welfare*; Upton, *Another City*; Buggeln, *Temples of Grace*; McNamara, *From Tavern to Courthouse*.

13. Teaford, *Municipal Revolution in America*, 64, 129 n.1.

14. Town residents sometimes challenged this model by submitting petitions and new municipal charter drafts asking city councils to attend to public safety and spaces other than markets. Teaford, *Municipal Revolution in America*, 1–34; Jessica Choppin Roney, *Governed by a Spirit of Opposition: The Origins of American Political Practice in Colonial Philadelphia* (Baltimore: Johns Hopkins University Press, 2014), 38–58; Milroy, *Grid and the River*, 30–31.

15. "Sketch of the Origin and Present State of Philadelphia," *Literary Magazine, and American Register* 2:9 (June 1804), 162.

16. Jon C. Teaford has characterized this as the "municipal revolution." Teaford, *Municipal Revolution in America*, 36–47.

17. Petition to incorporate Marietta, Addressed to Governor, Legislative Council, House of Representatives in the General Assembly of the Northwest Territory, Nov. 6, 1800 [dated by legislature clerk], unpublished material, State Archives Series 2895, Ohio History Connection.

18. Teaford, *Municipal Revolution in America*, 67–78.

19. Petition to incorporate Marietta, Addressed to Governor, Legislative Council, House of Representatives in the General Assembly of the Northwest Territory, Nov. 6, 1800 [dated by legislature clerk], unpublished material, State Archives Series 2895, Ohio History Connection; Northwest Territory, General Assembly, House of Representatives, *Journal of the House of Representatives of the Territory of the United States, North-West of the River Ohio: At the Second Session of the First General Assembly, A.D. 1800, and of the Independence of the United States of America the Twenty-fifth* (Chillicothe: Winship & Willis, 1800), 23, 35, 58. Ohio Company members had agitated for incorporation as a means of municipal governance as early as 1790, when Thomas Wallcut complained that Marietta had no public means of providing for indigent residents. When Ohio Company leaders stopped the association's management of the town in 1796, they set out intermediate modes of trusteeship and governance in anticipation of future municipal incorporation. As a business entity, however, the Ohio Company never officially settled its final accounts because of lasting controversy over the payment of company debts with forged loan certificates in 1792. The Supreme Court finally dismissed remaining claims on these certificates in 1870. At that time, Nahum Ward was the sole proprietor of all traceable shares; he never recorded a formal dissolution of the company. Thomas Wallcut, *Journal of Thomas Wallcut*, Feb. 2, 1790, ed. George Dexter (Cambridge: Cambridge University Press, 1879), 12; Hulbert, *Records*, vol. 2, Jan. 21, 1796, 208–210; Livermore, *Early American Land Companies*, 146.

20. Putnam, Cutler, and Sargent supported the passage of the congressional acts creating the ministerial sections even though they came to challenge their application in Marietta. Ministerial lands existed only in lands sold in the Ohio Company purchase and the Symmes purchase. William E. Peters, *Ohio Lands and Their Subdivision*, 2nd ed. (Athens: Private printing, 1918), 358–366; Ohio Constitutional Modernization Commission, "Report and Recommendation Ohio Constitution Article VI Section 1 Funds for Religious and Educational Purposes" (2015), 3, http://www.ocmc.ohio.gov/ocmc/uploads/Uploaded%20Files/OCMC%20-%20R&R%20Art.VI%20Sec.1%20(Funds%20for%20Religious%20and%20Educational%20Purposes)%20-%20ES%20(2016.01.20).pdf.

21. By 1796, Ohio Company directors relented and plotted an extension of the Marietta town plat, where they deeded new lots to company investors originally assigned lots within the ministerial section. Though equal in size, the new lots offered none of the advantages of lots in the center of town. Beginning in 1800, Washington County trustees of the ministerial section divided the rental income proportionally among houses of worship according to their number of members. Rental of these lands continued until 1818, when the federal government agreed to survey remaining "public lots," beyond the ones set aside for the support of education, for sale as public land in federal territories. Putnam quotation from Rufus Putnam to William Gridley, Feb. 8, 1801, series II, box 1, folder 6, MDOCA. On Fairhaven and lot conflicts, see Rufus Putnam to Manasseh Cutler, Feb. 19, 1796 (microfilm: reel 3), Manasseh Cutler Collection, Northwestern University (microfilm: Ohio University); Benjamin Tallmadge to Rufus Putnam, Jan. 3, 1806, series 2, box 1, folder 6, MDOCA; and Rufus Putnam to William C. Park, July 8, 1808, series II, box 1, folder 6, MDOCA. On ministerial lands in Marietta, see Ministerial Trustees Minutes, box 1, Washington County Ministerial Lands Trustees' Records, 1800–1915, State Archives Series 514, Ohio History Connection; and *A Compilation of Laws, Treaties, Resolutions, and Ordinances, of the General and State Governments, which Relate to the Lands in the State of Ohio* (Columbus: George Nashee, 1825), 24–25.

22. Levi Barber and Joseph Holden issued the request from the town council. Ministerial Trustees Minutes, May 7, 1811, box 1, folder 2, Washington County Ministerial Lands Trustees' Records, 1800–1915, State Archives Series 514, Ohio History Connection. See also Council Records, Town of Marietta, vol. 1, Apr. 15, 1811, 160, Special Collections, Marietta College.

23. The copy of the protest into the town council minutes on April 15, 1811, indicates that three town council members—William Woodbridge, Jeremiah Dare, and William Skinner—originally composed it on November 6, 1810. These men were not original shareholders of the Ohio Company. William Woodbridge arrived in Marietta from Norwich, Connecticut. Jeremiah Dare, a native of New Jersey, had moved to Marietta from Baltimore around 1805. William Skinner hailed from central Pennsylvania. For a list of town officers in Marietta, see *Ordinances of the City of Marietta: In Force April 1, 1893* (Marietta: City Council, 1893), 186–188. Council Records, Town of Marietta, vol 1., Apr. 15, 1811, 164–169, Special Collections, Marietta College.

24. Council Records, Town of Marietta, vol. 1, Apr. 15, 1811, 165, Special Collections, Marietta College.

25. Council Records, Town of Marietta, vol. 1, Apr. 15, 1811, 166, Special Collections, Marietta College.

26. Council Records, Town of Marietta, vol. 1, Apr. 15, 1811, 168, Special Collections, Marietta College.

27. Citizens of Boston wrote preservation mandates into their new city charter in 1822. They barred the sale of Faneuil Hall, the former site of town meetings made obsolescent by the new mayor and town council, and Boston Common, a green space undergoing "improvements" to regulate its use. Rawson, *Eden on the Charles*, 42–43.

28. C. D. to Enos Bronson, "For the United States' Gazette," (Philadelphia) *United States Gazette for the Country*, Mar. 10, 1813, daily edition, p. 2, AAS.

29. Mires, *Independence Hall*, 1–30; Benjamin L. Carp, *Rebels Rising: Cities and the American Revolution* (Oxford: Oxford University Press, 2007), 172–211.

30. Philadelphia Select Council Minutes, Apr. 2, 1811, CNL 18 (Mar. 28, 1811–Mar. 24, 1814), 82–85, Philadelphia City Archives; A. B. to Enos Bronson, "For the United States' Gazette," (Philadelphia) *United States Gazette for the Country*, Mar. 9, 1813, daily edition, p. 2. Reprinted in the semiweekly edition, Mar. 13, 1813, p. 1. William Duane reiterated these legal arguments and defended them in his *Aurora for the Country* in 1816.

31. For a history of municipal governance, urban planning, and public health, see Simon Finger, *The Contagious City: The Politics of Public Health in Early Philadelphia* (Ithaca: Cornell University Press, 2012); and Milroy, *Grid and the River*.

32. Philadelphia Select Council Minutes, Mar. 11, 1813, CNL 18 (Mar. 28, 1811–Mar. 24, 1814), 133–134, Philadelphia City Archives.

33. Philadelphia Select Council Minutes, Mar. 11, 1813, CNL 18 (Mar. 28, 1811–Mar. 24, 1814), 133, Philadelphia City Archives.

34. Commissioners for the Erection of the Public Buildings, *Reply of the Commissioners for the Erection of the Public Buildings, to the Request of Hon. Samuel G. King, Mayor of Philadelphia, for a Statement of Their Operations During the Year 1883, and for Such Other Information As Will Be of Interest to the City of Philadelphia: To Which Is Added Communications From the Commissioners to Councils, and Opinion of William Rawle, to the Common Council of the City of Philadelphia, May 28, 1799, As to the Right of the City to the Centre (Penn) Square, and to Erect a Building for Public Purposes Upon the Intersection of Broad and High (Market) Streets* (Philadelphia, 1884), 33–37; Milroy, *Grid and the River*, 156–157, 168–169.

35. [William Duane], "Stupefaction," (Philadelphia) *Aurora for the Country*, Feb. 28, 1816, daily, p. 1, AAS.

36. Not all citizens had access to these spaces: the square had been enclosed at various times, and the statehouse admitted those who had business there. For more on the statehouse yard, see Milroy, *Grid and the River*, 39–43.

37. [William Duane], "The Brazen Age of Pennsylvania," (Philadelphia) *Aurora for the Country*, Feb. 10, 1816, daily, p. 1, AAS.

38. Council Records, Town of Marietta, vol. 2, Mar. 25, 1820, 80, Special Collections, Marietta College. The town council first recorded inquiries to Willard on Nov. 1, 1819, vol. 2, 73.

39. Council Records, Town of Marietta, vol. 1, Apr. 17, 1820, 315, Special Collections, Marietta College.

40. Disagreements between Willard and the city continued for years and ended in an arbitrated settlement. Martin R. Andrews, *History of Marietta and Washington County, Ohio and Representative Citizens* (Chicago: Biographical Publishing Company, 1902), 21.

41. Daniel Kurt Ackerman, "Embracing the Sacred in the Secular: Synagogue Architecture, Community, and God in Willemstad, Curaçao, and Newport, Rhode Island," in *New England and the Caribbean*, ed. Peter Benes (Historic Deerfield, 2012), 138–139; Susan R. Slade, "Touro Synagogue, Congregation Jeshuat Israel," HABS RI-278 (1972).

42. "Communication," (Newport) *Rhode-Island Republican*, May 29, 1822, p. 2. On Jeshuat Israel as a marker of religious toleration, see Mordecai Manuel Noah, "Discourse, delivered at the consecration of the synagogue of K. K. Shearith Israel, in the city of New-York, on . . . the 17th of April, 1818" (New York: Van Winkle, 1818), AAS.

43. Will of Abraham Touro, TSTFR, 2.

44. Touro may have sought to quell contemporary fears that charitable trusts consolidated the wealth of religious congregations to the detriment of public welfare. On private charitable trusts in the early United States, see Jonathan Levy, "Altruism and the Origins of Nonprofit Philanthropy," in *Philanthropy in Democratic Societies: Histories, Institutions, Values*, ed. Rob Reich, Chiara Cordelli, and Lucy Bernholz (Chicago: University of Chicago Press, 2016), 26–27. On debates over church property, see Sarah Barringer Gordon, "The First Disestablishment: Limits on Church Power and Property Before the Civil War," *University of Pennsylvania Law Review* (Jan. 2014), 307–372; Kellen Funk, "Church Corporations and Conflict of Laws in Antebellum America," *Journal of Law and Religion* 32:2 (2017), 263–284; and Lawrence M. Friedman, *Dead Hands: A Social History of Wills, Trusts, and Inheritance Law* (Stanford: Stanford Law Books, 2009), 149–154.

45. Will of Abraham Touro, TSTFR, 2. On streets as public space, see Novak, *People's Welfare*, 120–133.

46. Stephen Gould to Titus Wells, Nov. 22, 1822, Stephen Gould Letter Book, Newport Historical Society, Newport, Rhode Island (hereafter Gould Letter Book). Executors questioned whether Touro intended to set up his bequest as a fund to be used directly to support his wishes or as a trust whose interest only should be spent. They also debated whether Touro intended for the synagogue funds to be made available to a new congregation for any use, in an effort to attract new Jewish residents, or solely for the town to keep the property in good repair in case a future congregation resumed worship. See Stephen Gould to Titus Welles, Jan. 1823; Apr. 19, 1823; and July 1823, Gould Letter Book.

47. Rhode Island General Assembly, "An Act to Secure and Appropriate the Touro Jewish Synagogue Fund," June session 1823, TSTFR, 5.

48. Novak, *People's Welfare*, 106; Hartog, *Public Property and Private Power*, 98; B. Murphy, *Building the Empire State*; Andrew M. Schocket, *Founding Corporate Power in Early National Philadelphia* (DeKalb: Northern Illinois University Press, 2007).

49. Horwitz, *Transformation of American Law*, 112; Pauline Maier, "The Revolutionary Origins of the American Corporation," *William and Mary Quarterly* 50:1 (Jan. 1993), 65; Mark D. McGarvie, "The *Dartmouth College* Case and Legal Design of Civil Society," in *Charity, Philanthropy, and Civility in American History*, ed. Lawrence J. Friedman and Mark D. McGarvie (Cambridge: Cambridge University Press, 2003), 91–105.

50. Novak, *People's Welfare*, 107; Teaford, *Municipal Revolution in America*, 89–90.

51. McGarvie, "*Dartmouth College* Case," 91–105; Neem, *Creating a Nation of Joiners*, 70.

52. McGarvie, "*Dartmouth College* Case," 101–102.

53. Henry Wheaton, *Reports of Cases Argued and Adjudged in the Supreme Court of the United States. February Term, 1819*, vol. 4 (New York: R. Donaldson, 1819), 637.

54. Horwitz, *Transformation of American Law*, 112; Maier, "Revolutionary Origins of the American Corporation," 65.

55. Novak, *People's Welfare*, 107–108; Jonathan Levy, "From Fiscal Triangle to Passing Through: Rise of the Nonprofit Corporation," in *Corporations and American Democracy*, ed. Naomi R. Lamoreaux and William J. Novak (Cambridge, MA: Harvard University Press, 2017), 213–244.

56. McGarvie, "*Dartmouth College* Case," 103.

57. See, e.g., Buggeln, *Temples of Grace*; McInnis, *Politics of Taste in Antebellum Charleston*; McNamara, *From Tavern to Courthouse*.

58. Hartog, *Public Property and Private Power*, 159, 182.

59. Hartog, *Public Property and Private Power*, 133, 146–147; Gordon, "First Disestablishment," 307–372; Schocket, *Founding Corporate Power*, 7–10, 30, 50.

60. Text of the Senate bill printed in "State House Yard," *United States Gazette*, Feb. 17, 1813, semiweekly, p. 3. Philadelphia Council described this as to be "sold in the manner therein specified to the highest and best bidders." Philadelphia Select Council Minutes, CNL 18 (Mar. 28, 1811–Mar. 24, 1814), Mar. 10, 1813, Philadelphia City Archives.

61. Text of the Senate bill printed in "State House Yard," *United States Gazette*, Feb. 17, 1813, semiweekly, p. 3. Philadelphia men debated this price for several years. By 1816, men such as John Reed still felt that the asking price was too high but supported paying it to avoid losing the opportunity to purchase. John Reed to Nicholas Biddle, Feb. 21, 1816, Biddle Papers (microfilm: reel 2), Van Pelt Library, University of Pennsylvania.

62. William Rawle and Peter S. DuPonceau, "Opinion of W. Rawle and Peter S. Duponceau on the title to the State-House yard, in the city of Philadelphia" [Philadelphia: 1816], 4. The question of whether a public entity could sell public squares to build public coffers continued to grow. William Novak discusses a number of mid-nineteenth-century legal cases about this issue in *People's Welfare*, 146–148.

63. [Duane], "Stupefaction." Emphasis in original.

64. Nathanial Ingersoll Bowditch, *A History of the Massachusetts General Hospital* (Boston: John Wilson and Son, 1851), 3–10.

65. Charles Shaw, *A Topographical and Historical Description of Boston, from the First Settlement of the Town to the Present Period; with Some Account of Its Environs* (Boston: Oliver Spear, 1817), 290.

66. Caleb Snow, *History of Boston* (Boston, 1825), 245.

67. Austin was a full member of the First Church until he revoked his membership around the time of the Old Brick's demolition. Arthur B. Ellis, *History of the First Church in Boston, 1630–1880* (Boston: Hall and Whiting, 1881), 241–242.

68. Peter S. Field, *Ralph Waldo Emerson: The Making of a Democratic Intellectual* (Lanham: Rowman & Littlefield, 2002), 16–23.

69. Sweeney, "Meetinghouses, Town Houses, and Churches," 59–93; Amanda Porterfield, *Corporate Spirit: Religion and the Rise of the Modern Corporation* (Oxford: Oxford University Press, 2018), 72–76.

70. "Communications," (Boston) *Independent Chronicle*, July 25, 1808, p. 3.

71. Edward Buck, *Massachusetts Ecclesiastical Law* (Boston: Gould and Lincoln, 1866), 19–20.

72. When members sought incorporation by the state in 1828, they argued that they had exercised corporate powers for over half a century and should be granted incorporation because they had been operating as one. Massachusetts did not disestablish state religion

until 1833. Leo W. Collins, *This Is Our Church: The First Church in Boston, 1630–2005* (Boston: Society of the First Church in Boston, 2005), 140–144.

73. "Communications," (Boston) *Independent Chronicle*, July 25, 1808, p. 3. See also "Old Brick's Soliloquy," *Boston Democrat*, Aug. 3, 1808, p. 3.

74. *New-England Palladium*, July 22, 1808, p. 2. The site, Cornhill Square, was developing into the heart of Boston's commercial district that would stretch along Washington Street. For details on the era's building projects, see Kamensky, *Exchange Artist*, 73–80.

75. [Duane], "Brazen Age of Pennsylvania." Emphasis in original.

76. [Duane], "Stupefaction." Emphasis in original.

77. "Communications," (Boston) *Independent Chronicle*, July 25, 1808, p. 3.

78. "Poetry. From the Boston Chronicle. The Old Brick Bell's Farewell to the Churches in Boston," (Stonington, CT) *America's Friend*, Sept. 7, 1808, p. 4; advertisement, (Boston) *Columbian Centinel*, June 25, 1808, p. 3.

79. Sweet, *Antiquaries*, 292–293, 306–307.

80. Timothy Touch [John Carter] to Mr. Urban, Sept. 8, 1806, *Gentleman's Magazine*, 76:2 (1806), 817–818. Rosemary Sweet identifies John Carter as the author of these articles. Sweet, *Antiquaries*, 294–295.

81. Letter to Mr. Urban, July 15, 1807, *Gentleman's Magazine*, 77:2 (1807), 710–711.

82. Horwitz, *Transformation of American Law*, 54.

83. As John Corrigan notes, in 1771, the worth of Benjamin Austin's property placed him in the top 12 percent of Boston's property owners. Corrigan, *The Hidden Balance: Religion and the Social Theories of Charles Chauncy and Jonathan Mayhew* (Cambridge: Cambridge University Press, 1987), 122.

84. Phyllis Cole, *Mary Moody Emerson and the Origins of Transcendentalism: A Family History* (New York: Oxford, 1998), 127.

85. Austin offered commentary on criminal law, municipal management, and constitutional law to weigh individual rights and the common good. See, e.g., Benjamin Austin, "Speech of the Hon. Benjamin Austin, Jun. Esq. at Faneuil-Hall, on Thursday last, previous to the question, whether the town would accept the report of the committee, as amended; with respect to the police of the town" (Boston, 1792); Benjamin Austin, "Constitutional Republicanism, in Opposition to Fallacious Federalism" (Boston: Adams and Rhoads, 1803); Benjamin Austin, "Memorial to the Legislature of Massachusetts" (Boston, 1808).

86. Kamensky, *Exchange Artist*, 115–164; Thorp Lanier Wolford, "Democratic-Republican Reaction in Massachusetts to the Embargo of 1807," *New England Quarterly* 15:1 (1942), 35–61.

87. For a full discussion of Republican politics in early national Pennsylvania, see Andrew Shankman, *Crucible of American Democracy: The Struggle to Fuse Egalitarianism and Capitalism in Jeffersonian Pennsylvania* (Lawrence: University of Kansas Press, 2004).

88. [Duane], "Brazen Age of Pennsylvania." Emphasis in original.

89. [Duane], "Brazen Age of Pennsylvania." Emphasis in original.

90. "Extraction of a Letter," (Philadelphia) *Aurora for the Country*, Mar. 1, 1816, daily, p. 1, AAS.

91. Jane Kamensky describes this attitude of "romantic capitalism," which she attributes to Richard D. Brown. Kamensky, *Exchange Artist*, 55.

92. Carol Rose makes the argument that creating physical impassability was one of the only feasible strategies for private citizens to resist the usurpation of private property for public access, particularly roads, in the nineteenth century. I apply this principle to disputes over different claims to public use of spaces. Carol Rose, "The Comedy of the Commons: Custom, Commerce, and Inherently Public Property," *University of Chicago Law Review* 53 (1986), 711–81. See also Novak, *People's Welfare*, 123–124.

93. Before this time, most Americans buried their dead anonymously, marked graves with impermanent markers, or expected that graves would be disturbed by future burials. Only elite Euro-Americans erected substantial stone memorials to deceased individuals. Frederick Dalcho, *An Historical Account of the Protestant Episcopal Church, in South-Carolina* (Charleston: E. Thayer, 1820), 252; Upton, *Another City*, 203–241; Linden, *Silent Cities on a Hill*, 92–93, 120–124.

94. As part of a broader vision of urban planning in the late 1790s, James Hillhouse sought to remove burials from the multiuse New Haven town green and place them in a ten-acre cemetery where architecture and corporate ownership secured the permanence of graves. Josiah Meigs, a lawyer and mathematics professor at Yale University, set out the cemetery plan after incorporation in 1797. He likely communicated the details of the project to his brother Return Jonathan Meigs, an Ohio Company surveyor and Marietta resident until 1801. Albert E. Van Dusen, *The Public Records of the State of Connecticut*, vol. 9 (Hartford: Connecticut State Library, 1953), 120–121; "Report of the Committee, Appointed to Inquire into the Condition of the New Haven Burying Ground, and to Propose a Plan for Its Improvement" (New Haven: B. L. Hamlin, 1839); Linden, *Silent Cities on a Hill*, 86–89; Upton, *Another City*, 217–222.

95. Milroy, *The Grid and the River*, 167.

96. "The Monument Mound," (Marietta) *American Friend*, Dec. 27, 1816, p. 3. The poem echoes Byron's *Childe Harold*, first published in 1812.

97. As one jurist put it in an 1821 lawsuit in Maine, not only were graves themselves sacred, but they also worked "to attach a character of sacredness to the grounds dedicated and inclosed as cemeteries of the dead." Simon Greenleaf, *Reports of Cases Argued and Determined in the Supreme Judicial Court of the State of Maine*, vol. 1 (Portland: Dresser, McLellan, 1876), 227.

98. Marietta Town Council Minutes, Oct. 4, 1813, vol. 1, 215; Apr. 23, 1814, vol. 1, 222. On sexton duties and burial regulations, see Sept. 19, 1816, vol. 1, 259; Jan. 3, 1817, vol. 1, 265–268; May 21, 1817, vol. 1, 279–280; June 2, 1817, vol. 2, 47; July 7, 1817, vol. 2, 48; Nov. 1, 1819, vol. 2, 72–73; Jan. 14, 1822, vol. 2, 105. All in Special Collections, Marietta College.

99. Marietta Town Council Records, Jan. 3, 1817, vol. 1, 267, Special Collections, Marietta College.

100. Atwater, *Archaeologica Americana*, 165.

101. Atwater, *Archaeologica Americana*, 134–135.

102. Marietta Town Council Minutes, Mar. 12, 1822, vol. 1, 348; Mar. 27, 1822, vol. 1, 349, Special Collections, Marietta College.

103. Hendrik Hartog, "Pigs and Positivism," *Wisconsin Law Review* 4 (1985), 899–935; Novak, *People's Welfare*; Hartog, *Public Property and Private Power*, esp. 10, 71–221; Blackmar, *Manhattan for Rent*, 77–95; McNeur, *Taming Manhattan*; Dell Upton, "Inventing the Metropolis: Civilization and Urbanity in Antebellum New York," in *Art and the Empire City*, ed. Catherine Hoover Voorsanger and John K. Howat (New Haven: Yale University Press, 2000), 5–9.

104. Horwitz, *Transformation of American Law*, 30–45; Novak, *People's Welfare*, 105–111.

105. Hartog, *Public Property and Private Power*, 73–79.

106. Their arguments aligned with the reasoning of one Maine judge, who wrote in an 1821 decision that the maintenance of burial markers was a matter of "public feelings" as well as the sensibilities of relatives of the deceased. Hartog, *Public Property and Private Power*, 74, 79; Greenleaf, *Reports of Cases Argued and Determined in the Supreme Judicial Court of the State of Maine*, vol. 1, 227. For more on histories of cemetery law, see Alfred L. Brophy,

"Grave Matters: The Ancient Rights of the Grave Yard," *BYU Law Review* 6 (2006), 1469–1516. On private property and charter rights, see Novak, *People's Welfare*, 108–109.

107. *Mayor of New York v. Slack*, 3 Wheeler's Criminal Cases 237, 245–247, quoted in Hartog, *Public Property and Private Power*, 76.

108. Hartog, *Public Property and Private Power*, 142; Hartog, "Pigs and Positivism," 913.

109. Gould expressed an antiquarian interest in Newport's Jewish community years before Abraham Touro's death. See "The Gould Family and the Jews of Newport," *Publications of the American Jewish Historical Society* 27 (Baltimore: Lord Baltimore Press, 1920), 424–426.

110. The terms of the Touro bequest and the Shearith Israel trusteeship have created highly contentious legal disputes over ownership of historic Jeshuat Israel congregational property, such as the silver *rimonim* made by renowned colonial silversmith Myer Myers. See, e.g., Barry Bridges, "Touro Outcome in Hands of Federal Judge," *Newport This Week*, Sept. 24, 2015, http://www.newportthisweek.com/news/2015-09-24/Front_Page/Touro _Outcome_in_Hands_of_Federal_Judge.html.

111. Stephen Gould to Moses Lopez, Jan. 1823, Gould Letter Book. Gould had first tried to charter the Newport Historical and Antiquarian Society in 1820. He served as cabinet keeper of the RIHS from 1822 to 1829 and again from 1835 to 1837. He died the following year. Stephen Gould et al., Petition to the General Assembly, Oct. 28, 1820, folder 1820 #61-86 October Session, Petitions Failed/Withdrawn, Archives of the General Assembly, RISA; Minute book, June 1822, vol. 1, 3, Records of RIHS; *Proceedings of the Rhode Island Historical Society* (Providence, 1872), 18.

112. Rebecca Touro, petition to the Rhode Island House of Representatives, Touro Family Papers, American Jewish Historical Society, New York City. The petition, signed by Rebecca Touro but penned by a different hand, is undated, but a note on the wrapper indicates that it was received by the state legislature on January 11, 1825. In the *Publications of the American Jewish Historical Society*, vol. 27 (1920), see Moses Lopez to Stephen Gould, Dec. 15, 1822 (postscript of Dec. 12, 1822, letter); Dec. 10, 1823, 427; Jan. 20, 1825, 430; Jan. 28, 1825, 433–434. On women's petitions to state legislatures in the early United States, see Cynthia Kierner, *Beyond the Household: Women's Place in the Early South, 1700–1835* (New York: Cornell University Press, 1988), 97–104.

113. B. B. Howland (Council Clerk), Newport Town Council records, vol. 1819–1836, Apr. 17, 1826, 170, Newport Historical Society, Newport, Rhode Island.

114. Benjamin Howland, marked House of Representatives received May 2, 1826, folder May 1826, Petitions Failed/Withdrawn, Archives of the General Assembly, RISA.

115. Moses Lopez to Stephen Gould, Sept. 29, 1826, *Publications of the American Jewish Historical Society* 27 (1920), 437.

116. Gould also had the cemetery deed re-recorded on June 7, 1827, to ensure that future generations could find a record of clear title in municipal records. "The Gould Family and the Jews of Newport," *Publications of the American Jewish Historical Society* 27 (1920), 423.

117. The carpenter seems to have created a design from William Kent's *Designs of Inigo Jones* (London, 1727) and Batty Langley's *The City and Country Builder's and Workman's Treasury of Design* (London, 1740). Slade, "Touro Synagogue," 9. Esther I. Schwartz first made the case that the ark extant in the Newport synagogue today was "a radical alteration made in the early nineteenth-century program of preservation." She points to the difference between the sketch of the ark made by Ezra Stiles in 1763 and the ark in place in an 1872 photograph of the synagogue interior. Schwartz, "Touro Synagogue Restored, 1827–29," *Journal of the Society of Architectural Historians* 17:2 (Summer 1958), 23–26.

118. "Town Meeting," *Rhode-Island Republican*, Sept. 15, 1825, p. 2.

119. *Two Hundred Years of American Synagogue Architecture* (Waltham: American Jewish Historical Society, 1976), 10.

120. Rhode Island General Assembly, "An Act to Secure and Appropriate the Touro Jewish Synagogue Fund," June session 1823, TSTFR, 5–7; B. Hazard, May 10, 1828, vol. 8, no. 79, Committee Reports (1818–1830), Archives of the General Assembly, RISA; Benjamin Howland, Jan. 7 and 13, 1829, vol. 8, no. 86, Committee Reports (1818–1830), Archives of the General Assembly, RISA.

121. B. Hazard, May 10, 1828, vol. 8, no. 79, Committee Reports (1818–1830), Archives of the General Assembly, RISA. A full financial accounting of the project is included in this report.

122. Moses Lopez to Stephen Gould, Sept. 7, 1827, *Publications of the American Jewish Historical Society* 27 (1920), 440.

123. General Assembly, "An Act to Secure and Appropriate the Touro Jewish Synagogue Fund," June session 1823, TSTFR, 5–7; B. Hazard, May 10, 1828, folder 1828 vol. 8, no. 79, Committee Reports (1818–1830), Archives of the General Assembly, RISA.

124. Stephen Gould noted the steady depreciation of Newport real estate in the early 1820s. Stephen Gould to Benjamin Dix, Aug. 28, 1824, Gould Letter Book.

125. Howland filled his office with local "antiquities" and served as cabinet keeper for the RIHS from 1829 to 1835 and again in 1838. *Proceedings of the Rhode Island Historical Society* (Providence, 1872), 18. After his death forty years later, he was remembered as a long-serving clerk for the bank, the city, and several historical institutions, as well as a leader in the First Baptist Church of Newport. "Town Meeting," *Rhode-Island Republican*, Sept. 15, 1825, p. 2; "Obituary: Benjamin B. Howland," *New York Herald*, Oct. 22, 1877, p. 10; *Proceedings of the Rhode Island Historical Society, 1877–1888*, (Providence, 1888), 112–115.

126. Benjamin B. Howland, bankruptcy petition, Dec. 20, 1815, inventory 39, vol. 44, Petitions to the General Assembly, Petitions Received (01/01.13/C#0165), RISA.

127. Stephen Gould to Benjamin Dix, Oct. 7, 1824, Gould Letter Book.

128. Stephen Gould to Titus Welles, July 1823, Gould Letter Book. In 1823, the General Assembly invested the trust funds in 3 percent stock of the United States at a loan office in Providence. General Assembly, "An Act to Secure and Appropriate the Touro Jewish Synagogue Fund," June session 1823, 5–7, TSTFR.

129. In 1828, Harvard College sued the trust fund manager of John McLean's bequest to the college in 1823. Trust manager Francis Amory, they argued, invested the funds in stocks whose risk went against McLean's wishes for the funds to be invested in "safe and productive stock." In 1830, the Supreme Court ruled in favor of Amory, arguing that all investment involved risk and a wise investor had to consider risk but not avoid it entirely. Octavius Pickering, *Reports of Cases Argued and Determined in the Supreme Judicial Court of Massachusetts*, vol. 9 (Boston: Hilliard, Gray, Little, and Wilkins, 1831), 446–465, quotation from 461; Friedman, *Dead Hands*, 114–115.

130. Mires, *Independence Hall*, 67.

131. *Register of Pennsylvania*, Mar. 8, 1828, 153.

132. *Register of Pennsylvania*, Mar. 8, 1828, 153.

133. *Register of Pennsylvania*, Apr. 23, 1831, 265; and Nov. 5, 1831, 292. For a fuller account of this reconstruction, see Mires, *Independence Hall*, 73–79. Architectural renovations in the mid-twentieth century showed just how far Haviland departed from evidence of the room's eighteenth-century appearance. Penelope Hartshorne Batcheler, "Independence Hall: Its Appearance Restored," in *Building Early America: Contributions Toward the History of a Great Industry*, ed. Charles E. Peterson (Radnor: Chilton, 1976), 298–318.

134. C. E. Gadsden, Daniel Cobia, and William Mason Smith, "Circular of the Congregation of St. Philip's Church," Feb. 18, 1835, South Carolina Historical Society; "Circular of the Congregation of St. Philip's Church," *Charleston Courier*, Mar. 4, 1835, p. 2.

135. "Calamitous Fire," *Charleston Mercury*, Feb. 16, 1835, p. 2; "Awful Conflagration," *Charleston Courier*, Feb. 16, 1835, p. 2; Maurie D. McInnis, "Conflating Past and Present in

the Reconstruction of Charleston's St. Philip's Church," *Perspectives in Vernacular Architecture* 9 (2003), 41.

136. William H. Pease and Jane H. Pease, *The Web of Progress: Private Values and Public Styles in Boston and Charleston, 1828–1843* (New York: Oxford University Press, 1985), 8.

137. Daniel Cobia, "The House of God in Ashes: A Sermon, preached in St. Michael's Church, Charleston, before the Congregation of St. Philip's, on Friday, Feb. 20, 1835; a day set apart for religious reflection, humiliation and prayer, in consequence of the Destruction of their Church by Fire" (Charleston: A. E. Miller, 1835).

138. "Calamitous Fire," p. 2.

139. "Awful Conflagration," p. 2. Emphasis in original.

140. Gadsden, Cobia, and Smith, "Circular of the Congregation of St. Philip's Church."

141. "York Minster," *Monthly Supplement of the Penny Magazine of the Society for the Diffusion of Useful Knowledge* 53 (Jan. 1833), 36.

142. A Citizen, "To the City Council of Charleston," *Charleston Mercury*, Apr. 21, 1835, p. 2.

143. David McCord, ed., *Statutes at Large of South Carolina*, vol. 7 (Columbia: A. S. Johnston, 1840), 136. After the Revolution, the interests of Charleston residents and those represented by the state legislature diverged. The placement of the new state capital inland in Columbia tracked the westward trajectory of upland cotton production and population. By the second quarter of the nineteenth century, fewer members of the state assembly had seasonal homes in Charleston or direct stakes in the development of the urban plan. Pease and Pease, *Web of Progress*, 10.

144. Here I revise the argument of Maurie McInnis in "Conflating Past and Present," 42–45. The issue of weighing the interests of particular landholding citizens against the broader welfare of a populace were familiar to the general assembly and the city council. In the early 1830s, both governmental bodies had heard opposing arguments of citizens about environmental changes demanded by a new railroad built by a corporation for shareholders' profit and also ostensibly for the good of the city and state economy. Pease and Pease, *Web of Progress*, 60–62, 104–106.

145. Journal of the Board of Commissioners for Opening and Widening of Streets, Lanes and Alleys, June 6, 1835, 63, Charleston Public Library Special Collections. The city paid the church $2,500 for the land claimed for the city street and the designation of the ground under the portico as a public right-of-way. McInnis, "Conflating Past and Present," 42.

146. The state of South Carolina incorporated St. Philip's Episcopal Church in 1785. McCord, *Statutes at Large of South Carolina*, vol. 8, 130–132.

147. State Commissioners Records, June 6, 1835, 65–66, Charleston Public Library Special Collections; printed in the *Charleston Courier*, June 12, 1835, p. 2 (with different punctuation).

148. A Member of St. Philip's Congregation, "St. Philip's Church," *Charleston Courier*, Aug. 13, 1835, p. 2. This member showed knowledge of the chain of authority that governed conflicts over the space as well. He dared the city council, if not satisfied by this compromise, to find fifty men to petition the state legislature to compel the church to move the new footprint.

149. Cornerstone text quoted in McInnis, "Conflating Past and Present," 48.

150. McInnis, "Conflating Past and Present," 46–48.

151. "St. Philip's Church," *Charleston Courier*, May 13, 1836, p. 2.

152. McInnis, "Conflating Past and Present," 48–50.

153. Milroy, *The Grid and the River*, 156–157, 168–169.

154. Joseph A. Conforti, *Imagining New England: Explorations of Regional Identity from the Pilgrims to the Mid-Twentieth Century* (Chapel Hill: University of North Carolina Press, 2001), 124–144.

Chapter 3

1. John Rubens Smith, del., James Kidder, eng., "Historical Sketches, No. III," *Polyanthos*, July 1813, 169. For more on James Kidder's career as an imagemaker, see Whitney Martinko, "'A Natural Representation of Market-Street, in Philadelphia': An Attribution, a Story, and Some Thoughts on Future Study," *Common-place: The Journal of Early American Life* 16:3 (Summer 2016), http://common-place.org/book/a-natural-representation-of-market-street-in-philadelphia-an-attribution-a-story-and-some-thoughts-on-future-study/.

2. On the production of commercial goods, including print, in the early nineteenth century, see Jaffee, *A New Nation of Goods*; Lawrence A. Peskin, *Manufacturing Revolution: The Intellectual Origins of Early American Industry* (Baltimore: Johns Hopkins University Press, 2004), 133–161; and Rosalind Remer, *Printers and Men of Capital: Philadelphia Book Publishers in the New Republic* (Philadelphia: University of Pennsylvania Press, 2000). On consumerism in the second quarter of the nineteenth century, see Cohen, *Luxurious Citizens*; Upton, *Another City*, 149; and Joanna Cohen, "Promoting Pleasure as Political Economy: The Transformation of American Advertising, 1800–1850," *Winterthur Portfolio* 48:2/3 (Summer/Autumn 2014), 163–190. For earlier histories of consumerism in the British Atlantic world, see Claire Walsh, "Shops, Shopping, and the Art of Decision Making in Eighteenth-Century England," in Styles and Vickery, *Gender, Taste, and Material Culture*, 151–177; and John Brewer and Roy Porter, eds., *Consumption and the World of Goods: Consumption and Society in the Seventeenth and Eighteenth Centuries* (London: Routledge, 1993).

3. On respectability and commercial capitalism in Great Britain, see Joel Mokyr, *The Enlightened Economy: An Economic History of Britain 1700–1850* (New Haven: Yale University Press, 2009), 383–388; and Cohen, *Luxurious Citizens*, 1–13.

4. Sweet, *Antiquaries*, 301; James Ackerman, *Origins, Imitation, Conventions: Representation in the Visual Arts* (Cambridge, MA: MIT Press, 2002), 98–99. For examples of measured drawings of buildings, see, e.g., Charles-Louis Clerisseau, *Antiquitiés de la France* (Paris, 1778); James Stuart and Nicholas Revett, *The Antiquities of Athens* 4 vols. (1762–1818) (New York: Princeton Architectural Press, 2008); John Britton, *The Architectural Antiquities of Great Britain, represented and illustrated in a series of views, elevations, plans, sections, and details, of various Ancient English Edifices*, five vols. (London: vol. 1, 1807; vol. 2, 1809; vol. 3, 1812; vol. 4, 1814; vol. 5, 1826); Augustus Charles Pugin, *Pugin and Le Neux's Specimens of the Architectural Antiquities of Normandy* (London: J. Britton, 1827); John Sell Cottman, *Architectural Antiquities of Normandy* (London: J. and A. Arch, 1822); George Ledwell Taylor, *The Architectural Antiquities of Rome* (London: G. L. Taylor, 1821–22); William Dickinson, *Antiquities Historical, Architectural, Chorographical, and Itinerary, in Nottinghamshire and the adjacent counties* (Newark: Holt and Hage, 1801–1819); and James Norris Brewer and James Sargent Storer, *History and Antiquities of the Cathedral Churches of Great Britain* (London: Rivingtons, 1814–1819). U.S. view makers did not publish the expensive folios of measured drawings that some European antiquaries produced. But elite Euro-Americans could access these volumes in the private libraries of wealthy gentlemen and lending libraries such as the Library Company of Philadelphia.

5. John Carter, "Present State of York [1806]," *Gentleman's Magazine* 76:2 (1806), 1027. See also Dale Townshend, "Architecture and the Romance of Gothic Remains: John Carter

and *The Gentleman's Magazine, 1797–1817*," in *The Gothic and the Everyday: Living Gothic*, ed. Lorna Piatti-Farnell and Maria Beville (Houndmills: Palgrave Macmillan, 2014), 173–194; and Bernard Nurse and Mordaunt Crook, "John Carter, FSA (1748–1817): 'The Ingenious, and Very Accurate Draughtsman,'" *Antiquaries Journal* 91 (Sept. 2011), 211–252. On rejection of picturesque conventions by British antiquaries, see Sweet, *Antiquaries*, 307.

6. Elizabeth M. Covart, "'Dam'd Paving Yankees' and Dutch New Yorkers': The Post-Revolution New England Migration and the Creation of American Identity in the Upper Hudson River Valley, 1783–1820," *Hudson River Valley Review* 291 (Autumn 2012), 2–25.

7. Covart, "Dam'd Paving Yankees and Dutch New Yorkers," 17.

8. The congregation paid Putnam and Hooker $25,000 to build the new church, completed in 1799. Joel Munsell, *The Annals of Albany*, vol. 3 (Albany: Joel Munsell, 1852), 189. Hooker also served in municipal positions and built private homes for a number of Albany's prominent residents beginning in 1797. For more on Hooker, see Diana S. Waite, ed., *Architects in Albany* (Albany: Mount Ida Press, 2009), 1–4; and Mary Raddan Tomlan, ed., *A Neat Plain Modern Style: Philip Hooker and His Contemporaries, 1796–1836* (Amherst: University of Massachusetts Press, 1993).

9. Tammis K. Groft and Mary Alice Mackay, eds., *Albany Institute of History and Art: 200 Years of Collecting* (New York: Hudson Hills, 1998), 362–363.

10. Whether commissioned by the vestry or donated by a congregant, these views show the artist's attention to the distinctive features of the façade and side elevation. For more on the congregation's changing engagement with German and Anglo-American culture, see Nelson, *Beauty of Holiness*, 353–360.

11. Ann Bermingham, "System, Order, and Abstraction: The Politics of English Landscape Drawing Around 1795," in W. J. T. Mitchell, ed., *Landscape and Power*, 2nd ed. (Chicago: University of Chicago Press, 2002), 88–93; Bellion, *Citizen Spectator*, 171–229.

12. I discuss the print in the collections of the Albany Institute that was donated by George W. Carpenter in 1840 (1840.1.1). Evert A. Duyckinck donated a copy of this first print to the New-York Historical Society in 1849 (Print Room, Geographic File: PR 020—New York State Views—Medium Prints—Albany). The Yale University Art Gallery owns another copy (1946.9.9). *Proceedings of the NYHS for the Year 1849* (New York: Press of the Historical Society, 1849/1861), 91.

13. Snyder engraved a number of architectural views during a career that spanned New York City, Albany, and Boston. David McNeely Stauffer, *American Engravers upon Copper and Steel*, vol. 1 (New York: Burt Franklin, 1907), 256; Groft and Mackay, *Albany Institute of History and Art*, 321 (cat. 105, note 4).

14. Given the fine nature of Snyder's engraving in the first plate, the high quality of the lines in the print struck from this second version of the plate suggests that Snyder did not touch up his first round of work. It seems likely that at least some of these prints would have been printed on Albany presses since Snyder worked there for a time. With Hooker's original drawing not located, it is unclear whether he included the street view in his image. I write about the hand-colored copy in the collections of the AAS. Philip Hooker, del., Henry Snyder, eng., John Low, printer, "A View of the Late Protestant Dutch Church in the City of Albany," 1806. Copies of this print (not colored) are in the collections of the Miriam and Ira D. Wallach Division of Art, Prints and Photographs: Print Collection, New York Public Library, and the Print Room of the New-York Historical Society (Geographic File: PR 020—New York State Views—Medium Prints—Albany).

15. On the masthead of his journal, Spofford announced his authorship of geographic texts as well as his membership in the New-York Historical Society, American Antiquarian Society, Society for the Promotion of Useful Arts, and Berkshire Agricultural Society. John

Scoles, eng., "A View of the Late Protestant Dutch Church in the City of Albany," *American Magazine* 3:1 (Aug. 1815), 97, and frontispiece verso 97.

16. It is also possible that Henry W. Snyder drew the printwork pattern, as he returned to Albany in 1813. Groft and Mackay, *Albany Institute of History and Art*, 321 (cat. 105, note 4).

17. Unidentified marker, pier glass, c. 1806–1815, collections of the Albany Institute (1919.4.10), in Groft and Mackay, *Albany Institute of History and Art*, 220–221.

18. Annatie and Maria Gourlay, the likely embroiderers of the piece, were born in 1799 and 1801, respectively. Their parents married in the New Dutch Church in 1799. Unidentified artist, Gourlay Print-Work Memorial, c. 1814, collections of the Albany Institute (1952.4.15), in Groft and Mackay, *Albany Institute of History and Art*, 274–275.

19. Andrew Stevenson was one of the lead producers of Staffordshire transferware for the U.S. market between 1809 and 1829. He produced views of a number of U.S. buildings from prints. Sam Laidacker, *Anglo-American China*, vol. 2 (Bristol: private printing, 1951), 72.

20. For more on portraits as images meant to preserve their subjects, see Margaretta Lovell, *Art in a Season of Revolution: Painters, Artisans, and Patrons in Early America* (Philadelphia: University of Pennsylvania Press, 2005), 27.

21. Lee Clark Mitchell, *Witnesses to a Vanishing America* (Princeton: Princeton University Press, 1981), 117–121. McKenney and his partner James Hall reproduced these paintings with lithographs in *History of the Indian Tribes of North America*. Though they met with financial ruin when they could not recover their costs with sales, their publication ultimately preserved the paintings: approximately seventy of a hundred portraits went up in flames at the Smithsonian Institution in 1865.

22. George Catlin, *Letters and Notes on the Manner, Customs, and Condition of the North American Indians*, vol. 1 (London, 1841), 2–3.

23. Jennifer L. Roberts, *Transporting Visions: The Movement of Images in Early America* (Berkeley: University of California Press, 2014), 69–115, esp. 108–109; John Hausdoerffer, *Catlin's Lament: Indians, Manifest Destiny, and the Ethics of Nature* (Lawrence: University Press of Kansas, 2009), 76–77.

24. Soon after the invention of photography in 1839, American antiquaries turned to daguerreotypy to fix a "true copy" of a building on a silver plate. For more on the use of photography to preserve the built environment, see Whitney A. Martinko, "'Worthy of Being Thus Preserved': American Daguerreotype Views and the Preservation of History," in *Documenting History, Charting Progress, Exploring the World: Nineteenth-Century Photographs of Architecture*, ed. Micheline Nilsen (Farnham: Ashgate, 2013), 37–58.

25. Cohen, *Luxurious Citizens*, 94–111.

26. Holcomb, *Moral Commerce*; Everill, *Not Made by Slaves*; "Journeymen Cabinet Makers Wareroom," *Philadelphia Inquirer*, Mar. 8, 1834, p. 4.

27. R. Laurence Moore, *Selling God: Religion in the Marketplace of Culture* (New York: Oxford University Press, 1994), 1–117; Ginzberg, *Women and the Work of Benevolence*, 36–66, esp. 46–47.

28. Roberts, *Transporting Visions*, 112–115; Gregory Nobles, *John James Audubon: The Nature of the American Woodsman* (Philadelphia: University of Pennsylvania Press, 2017), 5–6, 91–119.

29. Catlin, *Letters and Notes*, 261.

30. Hausdoerffer, *Catlin's Lament*, 52–54, 68.

31. Preservational views might be considered part of a broader visual culture, including fine art, that critiqued the speculative, capitalist land economy of the 1820s and 1830s. See, e.g., Ross Barrett, "Bursting the Bubble: John Quidor's Money Diggers and Land Speculation," *American Art* 30:1 (Spring 2016), 28–51.

32. "Antiquities of New-York: German Church in Frankfort-Street," *New-York Mirror* 9:21 (Nov. 26, 1831), 161.

33. The original edition was entitled *The Picture of New-York, and Stranger's Guide Through the Commercial Emporium of the United States: Containing, also, a Description of the Environs, with Several Pleasant Tours and Summer Excursions Around the Neighbouring Country; with Plan of the City, and Numerous Views of Public Buildings* (New York: A. T. Goodrich, 1818).

34. Goodrich, *Picture of New-York*, iii–iv; A. T. Goodrich, *The Picture of New-York, or the Stranger's Guide to the Commercial Metropolis of the United States* (New York: A. T. Goodrich, 1825), iii–v.

35. A. T. Goodrich, *The Picture of New-York, and Stranger's Guide to the Commercial Metropolis of the United States* (New York: A. T. Goodrich, 1828), iii–iv.

36. On local history writing in the early United States, see David J. Russo, *Keepers of Our Past: Local History Writing in the United States, 1820s–1930s* (Westport: Greenwood, 1988), 1–76; Halttunen, "Grounded Histories."

37. Shaw, *Topographical and Historical Description of Boston*, 3–6.

38. Snow, *History of Boston*, iii–iv. When Bowen purchased the copyright to Shaw's work, he caused a rift with John Foster Jr., with whom he had first contracted for a history of Boston. Foster then tried to garner subscriptions for his own town history. Bowen paid Snow three hundred dollars for his work on the history published in 1825 and fifty dollars for the 1828 edition. John Foster Jr., "To the Public," *Nantucket Inquirer*, July 12, 1824, p. 4; contracts between Abel Bowen and Caleb Snow, box 4, Caleb Hopkins Snow Papers, Massachusetts Historical Society (hereafter Snow Papers).

39. Abel Bowen, *Bowen's Picture of Boston, or the Citizen's and Stranger's Guide to the Metropolis of Massachusetts, and Its Environs* (Boston: Abel Bowen, 1829), 3; Caleb Snow, *A Geography of Boston, County of Suffolk, and the Adjacent Towns with Historical Notes* (Boston: Carter and Hendee, 1830), iii–iv.

40. Shaw, *Topographical and Historical Description of Boston*, 198; William Henry Whitmore, "Abel Bowen," *Bostonian Society Publications* 1 (Boston, 1886), 34.

41. Two seventeenth-century buildings, known as Julien's Restorator and the Triangular Warehouse, were demolished in 1824. Snow, *History of Boston*, 107, 244.

42. Snow, *History of Boston*, 107.

43. Snow, *History of Boston*, 107.

44. Snow, *History of Boston*, 206–207.

45. Snow, *History of Boston*, verso 378.

46. Snow, *History of Boston*, 247.

47. By 1826, for instance, tavern keepers in Plymouth reported that they profited from their proximity to the supposed landing site of the Pilgrims, which drew boarders who traveled to see the landmark. "The Plymouth Rock," (Providence) *Rhode-Island American*, Jan. 6, 1826, p. 1. On historic tourism, see John Seelye, *Memory's Nation: The Place of Plymouth Rock* (Chapel Hill: University of North Carolina Press, 1998); Chambers, *Memories of War*, 1–16; Dona Brown, *Inventing New England: Regional Tourism in the Nineteenth Century* (Washington, DC: Smithsonian Institution Press, 1995); Richard Gassan, *The Birth of American Tourism: New York, the Hudson Valley, and American Culture, 1790–1830* (Amherst: University of Massachusetts Press, 2008); Sears, *Sacred Places*; Barbara G. Carson, "Early American Tourists and the Commercialization of Leisure," in *Of Consuming Interests: The Style of Life in the Eighteenth Century*, ed. Cary Carson, Ronald Hoffman, Peter J. Albert (Charlottesville: University of Virginia Press, 1994), 373–405.

48. Upton, *Another City*; David Henkin, *City Reading: Written Words and Public Spaces in Antebellum New York* (New York: Columbia University Press, 1998).

49. Luskey and Woloson, *Capitalism by Gaslight*.

50. Ann Smart Martin, "Commercial Space as Consumption Arena: Retail Stores in Early Virginia," in *People, Power, Places*, ed. Sally McMurry and Annmarie Adams (Knoxville: University of Tennessee Press, 2000), 201–218; Ellen Hartigan-O'Connor, *The Ties That Buy: Women and Commerce in Revolutionary America* (Philadelphia: University of Pennsylvania Press, 2009), 129–160.

51. Daniel Pomroy and John K. Simpson, upholsterers, were listed at 1 Ann Street in *The Boston Directory* (Boston: John Frost and Charles Stimson Jr., 1820), 169.

52. John K. Simpson trade card (c. 1820–1829), AAS.

53. Simpson was not previously acquainted with Bowen, as he addressed the letter to "Mr. Bowen publisher of the History of Boston." J. K. Simpson to Abel Bowen, n.d. [1824], folder 3, Snow Papers.

54. Bowen included a near duplicate of the Kidder and Hoogland view in his 1829 *Picture of Boston*, as did Caleb Snow in his 1830 geography of Boston. Bowen, *Bowen's Picture of Boston*, 225; Snow, *Geography of Boston*, 43.

55. Washington Society, *An Historical View of the Public Celebrations of the Washington Society, and Those of the Young Republicans* (Boston: True and Greene, 1823), 30; George Washington Warren, *The History of the Bunker Hill Monument Association During the First Century of the United States of America* (Boston: James R. Osgood, 1877), 418.

56. Simpson's name appeared as resident business proprietor of the building in "Editorial Correspondence," *Crystal Fount and Rechabite Recorder* 4:15 (June 21, 1845), 233.

57. (Boston) *Columbian Centinel*, Mar. 16, 1825, p. 2.

58. Abel Bowen, *Picture of Boston* (Boston: Abel Bowen, 1838), 238.

59. Payton Stewart is listed as dealing in clothes at 27 Union Street in an 1839 Boston directory. In 1841, he had removed to 50 Endicott Street. In the mid-1840s, he or a son boarded in the home of prominent African American tailor and activist John P. Coburn. Payton (or Patton) Stewart Sr. or Jr. established a gymnasium in 1849 and became a prominent physical trainer of elite white Bostonians by the mid-1850s. John Collins Warren, a physician and leading antiquary, was one of the most vocal supporters of Stewart's gymnasium. *Stimpson's Boston Directory* (Boston: Charles Stimpson Jr., 1839), 430; *Stimpson's Boston Directory* (Boston: Charles Stimpson Jr., 1841), 487; Kathryn Grover and Janine V. Da Silva, "Historic Resource Study—Boston African American National Historic Site," unpublished paper, Dec. 31, 2002, 118; William C. Nell, *The Colored Patriots of the American Revolution* (Boston: Robert F. Wallcut, 1855), 112; Louis Moore, "Fit for Citizenship: Black Sparring Masters, Gymnasium Owners, and the White Body, 1825–1886," *Journal of African American History* 96:4 (Fall 2011), 448–473.

60. Edmund Quincy, journal, Aug. 8, 1838, 75, Quincy Family Papers, Massachusetts Historical Society (hereafter Quincy Family Papers); D.Y. [Edmund Quincy], "From Our Boston Correspondent, No. XII," *Anti-Slavery Standard*, Jan. 21, 1847, p. 135.

61. For more on the secondhand clothing economy of the era, see Robert J. Gamble, "The Promiscuous Economy: Cultural and Commercial Geographies of Secondhand in the Antebellum City," in Luskey and Woloson, *Capitalism by Gaslight*, 31–52.

62. Peter DuPonceau, John Read, and John Jay Smith all were political and social leaders devoted to shaping the modern municipal government and landscape. Roberts Vaux, William Meredith, Richard Peters Jr., Thomas Biddle, Joseph Watson, Zachariah Poulson, Joseph Parker Norris, and Thomas I. Wharton also attended. John Fanning Watson, an eccentric bank clerk from nearby Germantown, had ingratiated himself with these men as a devoted antiquary who performed the fastidious research that led them to the tavern.

63. "Proceedings of a Meeting," *Poulson's American Daily Advertiser*, Nov. 27, 1824, p. 2, Library Company of Philadelphia.

64. The commission brought relics into the tavern for the celebration, including furniture purported to be William Penn's and chairs made from the "Old Kensington Elm," or the Treaty Tree, which blew down in a storm in 1810. Logan, diary, Nov. 18, 1824, vol. 7, 144, Logan Diaries.

65. Deborah Norris Logan recorded these impressions after reading newspaper accounts of the dinner and speaking with attendees. Logan, diary, Nov. 18, 1824, vol. 7, 144, Logan Diaries.

66. "Penn's House," (Newark, NJ) *Emporium*, Nov. 26, 1825, p. 3.

67. Logan, diary, Jan. 31, 1825, vol. 7, 209, Logan Diaries.

68. John Fanning Watson to Roberts Vaux, Nov. 6, 1824, box 2, folder 17, Roberts Vaux Papers, HSP.

69. A. K. Sandoval-Strausz, *Hotel: An American History* (New Haven: Yale University Press, 2007), 48, 187.

70. On the boom of hotel building in this era, see Sandoval-Strausz, *Hotel*, 45–74.

71. A. K. Sandoval-Strausz argues that hotels, designed to fit the needs of a self-consciously republican and commercial society, comprised distinctive types of gathering places, for local residents as well as travelers, that helped to shape early U.S. civil society. Sandoval-Strausz, *Hotel*, 45, 232.

72. Logan, diary, Jan. 31, 1825, vol. 7, 209, Logan Diaries.

73. Receipt from Daniel Rubicam and Mary Rutter, Oct. 24, 1825, and Nov. 12, 1825; receipt from John Kelley, Oct. 25, 1825, Records of the Society for the Commemoration of the Landing of William Penn, HSP. The 1825 Philadelphia city directory listed Rubicam as an innkeeper at the Washington Hotel and the proprietor of a liquor and wine store. Thomas Wilson, *The Philadelphia Directory and Strangers' Guide for 1825* (Philadelphia, 1825), 120; William Woys Weaver, *Thirty-Five Receipts from "The Larder Invaded"* (Philadelphia: Library Company of Philadelphia and Historical Society of Pennsylvania, 1986), 35.

74. "William Penn Tavern, Beef Steak, Terrapin, and Oyster House, head of Laetitia Court," *Poulson's Daily Advertiser*, Dec. 8, 1826, p. 3; also Dec. 9 and 11, p. 4. Emphasis in original. Attendees of the third annual Penn Society dinner at Masonic Hall, which had grown to include the mayor of Philadelphia, foreign dignitaries, and guests from South Carolina and Alabama, had heard about these renovations as well: "The ancient residence of William Penn, in Laetitia Court, now occupied as a Tavern, by John Doyle, had recently been repaired, and the addition of a large room, for public purposes, has been made." "Commemoration of the Landing of William Penn," *Poulson's Daily Advertiser*, Oct. 28, 1826, p. 2.

75. "Penn House," *Poulson's Daily Advertiser*, June 8, 1827, p. 3; June 9 and 10, 1827, p. 4. "To Be Sold," *Poulson's Daily Advertiser*, June 6, 1827, p. 3.

76. Landauer Collection, PR 031, Series II—Large—2NW, Case 7, Drawer 16—Men's Clothing, New-York Historical Society.

77. Landauer Collection, PR 031, Series II—Large—2NW, Case 7, Drawer 16—Men's Clothing, New-York Historical Society.

78. On linking ready-made clothing to U.S. democracy, see Michael Zakim, *Ready-Made Democracy: A History of Men's Dress in the American Republic, 1760–1860* (Chicago: University of Chicago Press, 2003).

79. Cohen, "Promoting Pleasure as Political Economy," 173; Hartigan-O'Connor, *Ties That Buy*, 129–160; Upton, *Another City*, 149–157.

80. "Views of Public Buildings: The Engraving," *New-York Mirror* 7:37 (Mar. 20, 1830), 289. On Morris and his contribution to print culture, see Trudie A. Grace and David B. Dearinger, *George Pope Morris: Defining American Culture* (Cold Spring: Putnam County Historical Society and Foundry School Museum, 2009). For a history of the *Mirror*, see Frank Luther Mott, *A History of American Magazines, 1741–1850* (New York: D. Appleton, 1930), 320–330.

81. "Dutch Architecture: The Old House in Broad-Street," *New-York Mirror* 8:1 (July 10, 1830), 1.

82. "Dutch Architecture."

83. Davis had produced architectural drawings for many years, both as images of extant buildings and as illustrations of architectural designs. He worked in a variety of media and had studied technical printing and drafting as well as the fine arts. In the late 1820s, he made a number of drawings for the *Mirror*'s public buildings series and began to earn public praise as a skilled draftsman. He was only beginning the architectural career that would garner him praise for his work in the Gothic Revival style. Mason learned the trade of woodcut engraving in England and worked his way up to leadership in the London Mechanics' Institution in the 1820s. He had been in the United States for less than a year when he undertook commissions for the *Mirror* in 1830. That year, he was named an associate of the National Academy of the Arts of Design; two years later, he was named a professor of woodcut engraving. Amelia Peck, ed., *Alexander Jackson Davis: American Architect, 1803–1892* (New York: Rizzoli, 1992). Richard J. Koke, *American Landscape and Genre Paintings in the New-York Historical Society: A Catalog of the Collection, Including Historical, Narrative, and Marine Art* (New York: New-York Historical Society, 1982), vol. 1, 249; Benson J. Lossing, *History of New York City*, vol. 1 (New York: Perine Engraving and Publishing, 1884), 246–247.

84. "Antiquities of New-York: Old Dutch House in New-Street," *New-York Mirror* 10:31 (Feb. 2, 1833), 241.

85. Bowen published this newsletter between 1825 and 1827, during the interstitial years of his two editions of Snow's *History of Boston*.

86. *Mirror* editors commissioned their views from the most highly praised wood engravers in New York City at the time, Abraham J. Mason and Alexander Anderson. Anderson was well-known as being an early and skilled practitioner of this method, and his name would have invested the images with his reputation as the best engraver in a method that enabled widespread distribution. Although the images were small and printed from woodblocks, *Mirror* editors achieved a remarkable, widely noted quality of in-text image because of it. Printing from woodblocks was cheaper than copperplate engraving and better for wide distribution. It was printed on the same paper as type and could be used 900,000 times without serious damage to the block. Copperplate prints, however, needed special paper and time-consuming upkeep because they began to show wear after a few thousand impressions. "Engraving on Wood," *New-York Mirror*, Sept. 27, 1834; Jane R. Pomeroy, *Alexander Anderson: Wood Engraver and Illustrator*, vol. 2 (New Castle: Oak Knoll, 2005), 1089 (catalog entry 969). For a detailed biography and astonishing catalogue of Anderson's work, see Pomeroy, *Alexander Anderson*, 3 vols. For a description of the end-grain boxwood technique that Anderson used, see Pomeroy, *Alexander Anderson*, vol. 1, lxxv–lxxvi.

87. *New-York Mirror* engravings done from extant buildings appear in William Dunlap, *A History of New York, for Schools* (New York, 1837), vol. 1, 22, 167, 180, 194; vol. 2, 131, 170. These volumes were reprinted in 1838 and 1844. For more, see Pomeroy, *Alexander Anderson*, vol. 3, 1882–1883 (catalog entry 1771).

88. The same thing, they wrote, had happened to the old French church that they had profiled. "Antiquities of New-York: German Church in Frankfort-Street," *New-York Mirror* 9:21 (Nov. 26, 1831), 161.

89. "Dutch Architecture," *New-York Mirror* 8:26 (Jan. 1, 1831), 201.

90. "Dutch Architecture," *New-York Mirror* 8:37 (Mar. 19, 1831), 289.

91. Samuel Woodworth cofounded the *Mirror* with George Pope Morris in 1823. Though he withdrew his support less than a year later, Morris remained friends with him and continued to publish his prose and favorable reviews of his work in the *Mirror*. For more, see Kendall B. Taft, "Samuel Woodworth," PhD diss., University of Chicago, 1936, 82.

92. Samuel Woodworth, "New-York Antiquities: History of the Old Stuyvesant Mansion," *New-York Mirror* 10:26 (Dec. 31, 1831), 201.

93. Here he used the term "money diggers" and referred to Irving's stories about men who dug up Dutch cemeteries looking for buried treasure. John Quidor painted a historical scene of this activity in 1832; it is now in the Brooklyn Museum. For more, see Barrett, "Bursting the Bubble."

94. A. J. Davis, sepia watercolor on paper, 9 1/8 × 12 1/16 inches, New-York Historical Society 1912.33, in Koke, *American Landscape and Genre Paintings*, vol. 1, 256.

95. Davis drew a partial floor plan on the back of this image. A. J. Davis, sepia watercolor on paper, 6 1/2 × 9 inches, New-York Historical Society 1912.32, in Koke, *American Landscape and Genre Paintings*, vol. 1, 255.

96. Woodworth recommended a route from Manhattan's center that led travelers to approach the house from this side. Woodworth, "New-York Antiquities."

97. The author of a brief biography, published in 1869, remembered happening upon Breton in 1824 as he sat sketching the Stritzel House on Church Street in Philadelphia soon before the old structure was taken down. Martin Snyder claims that Watson and Breton did not meet until the spring of 1828. However, Watson was advertising some of Breton's pictures for sale as early as the summer of 1826. The Historical Society of Pennsylvania, the Downs Collection and museum collections at Winterthur, the Library Company of Philadelphia, the Athenaeum of Philadelphia, and the collections of the Philadelphia History Museum all hold Breton views. Martin L. Snyder, "William L. Breton, Nineteenth-Century Artist," *Pennsylvania Magazine of History and Biography* 85:2 (April 1961)," 178–209; John Baum? to John Fanning Watson, 11 June? 1826, box 2, John Fanning Watson Collection, HSP; "Brereton [*sic*], (18 July 1827), See Notice of Drawings of Ancient Buildings," Accessions Book, vol. 1, 4, Institutional Records of the Historical Society of Pennsylvania, with the Balch Institute for Ethnic Studies, 1824–2005, HSP (hereafter Records of HSP); John Fanning Watson, "List of Old houses—to be drawn by W. L. Breton," HSP; John Fanning Watson to Gen. Thomas Cadwalader, Jan. 16, 1830, box 66, folder 5, Cadwalader Papers, HSP; *Philadelphia in 1830–1; or a brief account of the various institutions and public objects in this metropolis* (Philadelphia: E. Carey and A. Hart, 1830), 221–222; Nash, *First City*, 208.

98. Breton sold views of historic sites to Samuel Atkinson's *Casket*, Godey's *Lady's Book*, publishers of various books, and lithographic firms who published individual prints for sale. Snyder, "William L. Breton," 201.

99. William L. Breton, "N. E. View of the Old Court House in Market St, Philada.," Print Department, Library Company of Philadelphia.

100. William L. Breton, "S. W. View of the Old Court House in Market St. Philada. at the time of its being taken down (7th April 1837)," Print Department, Library Company of Philadelphia.

101. John F. Watson, *Annals of Philadelphia, Being a collection of Memoirs, Anecdotes, and Incidents of the City and Its Inhabitants from the Days of the Pilgrim Founders* (Philadelphia: Carey and Hart, 1830), 295–299; *Philadelphia in 1830–1*, 219–220.

Chapter 4

1. Wolbert rented the ground level of the Old Hall for $350 per year. Auction duties for 1829 indicate that he ran a small, less prosperous business than most Philadelphia auctioneers. Records of the Carpenters' Society, Minutes of Managing Committee, 1823–1838, July 9, 1828, July 23, 1828 (reel 6, item 5G), American Philosophical Society; Records of the Carpenters' Society, Minutes 1826–1857, Jan. 19, 1857, p. 337 (reel 3, item 4c), American

Philosophical Society; "Auction Commissions" and "Auction Duties," *Register of Pennsylvania* 3:12, Mar. 21, 1829, p. 177.

2. [Charles G. DeWitt], "The Days of Old," *Richmond Enquirer*, Feb. 2, 1830, p. 4. This article identified the author of the letter as the editor of the *Ulster Sentinel*, though subsequent publishers identified the author as a Virginian.

3. [DeWitt], "Days of Old"; [Charles G. DeWitt], "Patrick Henry," *Trumpet and Universalist Magazine* 2:46 (May 15, 1830), 184; John F. Watson, *Annals of Philadelphia and Pennsylvania in the Olden Time*, vol. 1 (Philadelphia: King and Baird, 1850), 419.

4. Erskine Mason, "A Rebuke to the Worldly Ambition of the Present Age: A Sermon, Preached in the Bleecker-Street Church, N.Y. July 10, 1836" (New York: West & Trow, 1836), quoted in Lepler, *Many Panics of 1837*, 70. See also Old-Fashioned Man, "The Pressure and Its Causes" (Boston, 1837), 16–20.

5. Cohen, *Luxurious Citizens*, 90–91, 95–99, 102–106.

6. Thomas P. Hunt's *The Book of Wealth; In Which It Is Proved from the Bible, That It Is the Duty of Every Man, to Become Rich* (New York: Ezra Collier, 1836) exemplifies the gospel of wealth articulated in this era. Amanda Porterfield, John Corrigan, and Darren E. Grem, "Introduction," *The Business Turn in American Religious History* (New York: Oxford University Press, 2017), 7. See also "How to Get Rich," *Manual of Self-Education* 1:1 (Aug. 1842), 66–67.

7. [DeWitt], "Days of Old."

8. The phenomenon that I label a doubled spatial experience parallels an aural experience that Leigh Eric Schmidt explains: when early Americans read texts aloud, they simultaneously heard their own voices and the one of the author of the written text. Schmidt, *Hearing Things: Religion, Illusion, and the American Enlightenment* (Cambridge, MA: Harvard University Press, 2000), 35.

9. The antiquated features of the dining room's interior made it a "hallowed place" and a "sanctuary," in his mind. "Proceedings of a Meeting," *Poulson's American Daily Advertiser*, Nov. 27, 1824, p. 2, Library Company of Philadelphia.

10. Stephen Gould to John Howland, Oct. 13, 1835, box 1, Henry Bull Papers, RIHS (hereafter Bull Papers).

11. For more on perceptual capabilities, see Oliver Sacks, "The Mind's Eye: What the Blind See," in *Empire of the Senses: The Sensual Cultural Reader*, ed. David Howe (New York: Berg, 2005), 25–42.

12. Leading Romantic intellectuals in Europe only had begun to differentiate the words "imagination" as a tool of serious research and "fancy" as a playful activity of the mind, an intellectual distinction that had existed since the time of Augustine. J. M. Cocking, *Imagination: A Study in the History of Ideas* (London: Routledge, 1991), xiii.

13. For more on the relationship between imagination and reason, see Cocking, *Imagination*, vii–xvi, 268–274.

14. [DeWitt], "Days of Old."

15. For more on Wirt's biography, see Christopher Looby, *Voicing America: Language, Literary Form, and the Origins of the United States* (Chicago: University of Chicago Press, 1996), 266–278; and Scott Casper, *Constructing American Lives: Biography and Culture in Nineteenth-Century America* (Chapel Hill: University of North Carolina Press, 1999), 19–66.

16. John F. Watson, *Annals of Philadelphia* (Philadelphia: E. L. Carey and A. Hart, 1830), 151.

17. Schmidt, *Hearing Things*, 164–168; Bellion, *Citizen Spectator*, 231–234, 239, 244–245.

18. William Wirt, *Life of Patrick Henry* (Philadelphia: J. Webster, 1817), 107, see also 60, 250, 296, 413.

19. Wirt, *Life of Patrick Henry*, 296.

20. Looby, *Voicing America*, 275–276.

21. [DeWitt], "Days of Old."

22. Phillippe-Auguste de Sainte-Foix, *The Palace of Silence: A Philosophic Tale* (London, 1775), 188; William Gilpin, *Observations, Relative Chiefly to Picturesque Beauty*, vol. 2 (London, 1786), 247; George Crabbe, "The Borough" (Philadelphia: Bradford and Inskeep, 1810), 259; James Lawson, *Tales and Sketches* (New York: T. Snowden, 1830), 13–14; X. X., "For the Mercury," *New Bedford Mercury*, Mar. 30, 1838, p. 4; "Scenes in Matamoras," *Boston Daily Atlas* 15:29 (Aug. 3, 1846), p. 2 (republished from *New Orleans Tropic*).

23. Schmidt, *Hearing Things*, 26–27; Bellion, *Citizen Spectator*, 231–234, 239, 244–245.

24. Y.D. [Edmund Quincy], "Old Houses," *American Monthly Magazine*, Oct. 1837, 347; see also Edmund Quincy, "Old Houses in Boston," manuscript, Quincy Family Papers; and Edmund Quincy, journal, June 29, 1837, 14, Quincy Family Papers.

25. Some writers continued to focus on the secretive, sensational aspect of past activities that had occurred within old walls. A writer for the *New-York Mirror* described the architectural features of one of the last remaining Dutch colonial buildings in Manhattan this way in 1830: "'Could its old walls tell tales,' there is no knowing what heart-thrilling secrets of 'love and murder' might be collected by a good stenographer." "Dutch Architecture: The Old House in Broad-Street," *New-York Mirror* 8:1 (July 10, 1830), 1. See also Samuel L. Knapp, *Tales of the Garden of Kosciuszko* (New York: West and Trow, 1834), 9; A Southern Gentleman, "Sketches of a Visit to Europe," *Southern Rose* 5:22 (June 24, 1837), 172; "Priestly Corruption," *Zion's Herald* 6:47 (Nov. 25, 1835), 186. For more on the link between these characterizations and Gothic fiction, see Kate Ellis, *The Contested Castle: Gothic Novels and the Subversion of Domestic Ideology* (Champaign: University of Illinois Press, 1989); Fred Botting, *Gothic* (London: Routledge, 2005); and Anne Williams, *Art of Darkness: A Poetics of the Gothic* (Chicago: University of Chicago Press, 2005).

26. Bellion, *Citizen Spectator*, 306–315; Schmidt, *Hearing Things*, 153–163; Robert Vincent Sparks, "Abolition in Silver Slippers: A Biography of Edmund Quincy," PhD diss., Boston College, 1978, 192–193.

27. Louis Nelson, "Building Confessions: Architecture and Meaning in Nineteenth-Century Places of Worship," in *Sacred Spaces: Building and Remembering Sites of Worship in the Nineteenth Century*, ed. Virginia Chieffo Raguin, Mary Ann Powers, and Georgia Brady Barnhill (Worcester: College of the Holy Cross, 2002), 12.

28. Joseph Story, "Address at the Consecration of Mount Auburn" (Boston: Joseph T. and Edwin Buckingham, 1831), 7, 18–19.

29. Sears, *Sacred Places*, 5–7.

30. David Kling, *Field of Divine Wonders: The New Divinity and Village Revivals in Northwest Connecticut, 1792–1822* (State College: Pennsylvania State University Press, 1993).

31. [DeWitt], "Days of Old."

32. S., "Journal of a Traveller to Louisville" (Baltimore) *American Farmer* 50:7 (Mar. 3, 1826), 399. See also Ware, "Memorandum," 58; Atwater, *Archaeologica Americana*, 143–144.

33. Edmund Flagg, *The Far West*, vol. 1 (New York: Harper and Brothers, 1838), 127–128.

34. Basil Hall, *Travels in North America, In the Years 1827 and 1828* (Edinburgh: Cadell and Co., 1829), vol. 2, 375–376. See also Michel J. Chevalier, *Society, Manners, and Politics in the United States*, trans. T. G. Bradford (Boston: Weeks, Jordan, 1839), 298–304.

35. "House Lots in Charlestown," *Columbian Centinel*, Apr. 10, 1822, p. 3.

36. "At Auction," *Boston Daily Advertiser*, Apr. 12, 1822, p. 3.

37. "Bunker Hill," *Independent Chronicle and Boston Patriot*, Apr. 17, 1822, p. 2. Reprinted as "Bunker Hill," Charleston, S.C., *City Gazette and Commercial Daily Advertiser*, May 1, 1822, p. 2.

38. Snow, *History of Boston*, 112.

39. Logan, diary, vol. 3, May 23, May 28, June, Sept. (?) 1818, 108–110, 114, 156, Logan Diaries. Susan Stabile analyzes Logan's memory making of her family home in *Memory's Daughters*, 1–8.

40. Larson, *Market Revolution in America*, 39–45.

41. Logan, diary, Sept. 8, 1829, vol. 12, 268, Logan Diaries.

42. Stephen Mihm, *A Nation of Counterfeiters: Capitalists, Con Men, and the Making of the United States* (Cambridge, MA: Harvard University Press, 2009), 103–107; on the founding of the Second Bank of the United States, see Scott Reynolds Nelson, *A Nation of Deadbeats: An Uncommon History of America's Financial Disasters* (New York: Alfred A. Knopf, 2012), 62–66.

43. George Strickland, "United States Bank," engraved by William E. Tucker, frontispiece, *Souvenir* (Philadelphia, 1827), AAS. See also Charles Burton, "United States Bank, Philadelphia," engraved by Fenner, Sears, and Co., 1831, Marian S. Carson Collection, Library of Congress.

44. Cephas Childs, "The Bank of the United States," in *Views in Philadelphia and Its Vicinity; Engraved from Original Drawings* (Philadelphia: C. G. Childs, 1827), n.p.

45. Frances Trollope, *Domestic Manners of the Americans* (New York, 1832), 266; Lepler, *Many Panics of 1837*, 14–15.

46. Logan, diary, Sept. 8, 1829, vol. 12, 268, Logan Diaries.

47. Karen Halttunen, *Confidence Men and Painted Women: A Study of Middle-Class Culture in America 1830–1870* (New Haven: Yale University Press, 1986); Roberts, *Transporting Visions*, 117–160; Mihm, *Nation of Counterfeiters*.

48. Records of the Carpenters' Society, Minutes, 1826–1857, Mar. 12 1827, 14 (reel 3, item 4c), American Philosophical Society.

49. [DeWitt], "Days of Old."

50. See, e.g., "Mammon," *Philadelphia Album and Ladies Literary Gazette* 3:20 (Oct. 15, 1828), 159 (reprinted in [Boston] *American Traveller*, Jan. 6, 1829, p. 4); "Hindrances to Prosperity in Christian Churches; The Fifth Circular Letter of the Several Ministers and Messengers of the Churches, Composing the South Devon and Cornwall Baptist Association, Assembled at Helston, May 13th and 14th, 1829" (Plymouth, 1829), 4; Robert Southey, *Sir Thomas More: Or, Colloquies on the Progress and Prospects of Society*, vol. 1 (London, 1829), 173; [Sarah Hale], "The Worth of Money," *Ladies Magazine and Literary Gazette* 3:2 (Feb. 1830), 49; John Harris, *Mammon; or, Covetousness the Sin of the Christian Church* (Boston: Gould, Kendall, & Lincoln, 1836); Stewart Davenport, *Friends of the Unrighteous Mammon: Northern Christians and Market Capitalism, 1815–1860* (Chicago: University of Chicago Press, 2008); Mark A. Noll, "Protestant Reasoning About Money and the Economy, 1790–1860," in *God and Mammon: Protestants, Money, and the Market, 1790–1860*, ed. Mark Noll (New York: Oxford University Press, 2002), 265–294; Kenneth Startup, "'A Mere Calculation of Profits and Loss': The Southern Clergy and the Economic Culture of the Antebellum North," in Noll, *God and Mammon*, 217–235.

51. See, e.g., [Seth Luther?], "A Confederacy Against the Constitution and the Rights of the People; with an Historical View of the Component Parts of the Diabolical Transaction" ([1833?]), Print Department, Library Company of Philadelphia.

52. Mihm, *Nation of Counterfeiters*, 143–152.

53. As Seth Rockman put it, "The chains of credit between large investment houses, state-chartered banks, and entrepreneurial borrowers rendered property ownership into a social fiction, one whose flimsiness was all too often revealed whenever the chain broke." Rockman, "What Makes the History of Capitalism Newsworthy?" *Journal of the Early Republic* 34:3 (Fall 2014), 452.

54. Old-Fashioned Man, "The Pressure and Its Causes," 26.

55. "The Old Fort Demolished!" *Springfield Republican*, Aug. 3, 1831, p. 3, col. 3–4, Boston Public Library. For more on the Pyncheon house, see Bushman, *Refinement of America*, 103.

56. Robin Pearson, "The Impact of Fire and Fire Insurance on Eighteenth-Century English Town Buildings and the Populations," in Shammas, *Investing in the Early Modern Built Environment*, 74–76; Blackmar, *Manhattan for Rent*, 161, 167, 183–192; Ted Cavanagh, "Balloon Houses: The Original Aspects of Conventional Wood-Frame Construction Re-Examined," *Journal of Architectural Education* 51:1 (Sept. 1997), 5–15; Rilling, *Making Houses, Crafting Capitalism*.

57. Scholars and archivists have characterized this piece as an essay because of the first-person narration, yet it is better classified as a type of historical fiction. Quincy arrived at his signature by taking the initials of his name spelled backward: Ycniuq Dnumde. He signed some of his letters D. Y: Dnumde Ycniuq. Both sets of backward initials emphasize the importance of looking backward. But the former signature seems to connote his assumption of an elderly persona while the latter signals his own perspective on historic structures in contemporary society. Sparks, "Abolition in Silver Slippers"; Geoffrey D. Smith, "The Reluctant Democrat and the Amiable Whig: Nathaniel Hawthorne, Edmund Quincy and the Politics of History," *Nathaniel Hawthorne Review* 18:2 (1992), 9–14.

58. Y.D. [Quincy], "Old Houses," 337, 347, 348.

59. Y.D. [Quincy], "Old Houses," 344, 346, 345–346.

60. Old-Fashioned Man, "The Pressure and Its Causes," 30, see also 64.

61. Y.D. [Quincy], "Old Houses," 338, 346.

62. On criticism, and continued support, of business corporations in the late 1820s and 1830s, see Horwitz, *Transformation of American Law*, 109–139, esp. 136–137; Robert E. Wright, "The Rise of the Corporation Nation," in Zakim and Kornblinth, *Capitalism Takes Command*, 149, 160–161; John Majewski, "Toward a Social History of the Corporation: Shareholding in Pennsylvania, 1800–1840," in *The Economy of Early America: Historical Perspectives and New Directions*, ed. Cathy Matson (University Park: Pennsylvania State University Press, 2006), 294–316.

63. For more, see Lepler, *Many Panics of 1837*, 8–15.

64. Hartog, *Public Property and Private Power*, 76–79; Larson, *Market Revolution in America*, 25; Novak, *People's Welfare*, 107. For a full history of this legal decision in social context, see Stanley I. Kutler, *Privilege and Creative Destruction: The Charles River Bridge Case* (Philadelphia: J. B. Lippincott, 1971). On how this ruling prompted commentators to revisit issues of public welfare and private profit addressed in the 1819 Dartmouth case, see A Citizen of Boston [David Henshaw], "Remarks upon the Rights and Powers of Corporations, and of the Rights, Power, and Duties of the Legislature Toward Them" (Boston: Beals and Greene, 1837); and Horwitz, *Transformation of American Law*, 136–137.

65. Old-Fashioned Man, "The Pressure and Its Causes," 11–12.

66. The desire for "expensive living" had "swept over the whole country, like an epidemic." Old-Fashioned Man, "The Pressure and Its Causes," 13 (in text), 15, 29. Emphasis in original.

67. Old-Fashioned Man, "The Pressure and Its Causes," 14.

68. Old-Fashioned Man, "The Pressure and Its Causes," 29.

69. [Edmund Quincy], "Reminiscences of a Walker Round Boston," *United States Magazine and Democratic Review*, Sept. 1838, 86. I have identified Quincy as the author of this piece from his journal, in which he noted, "At Pemberton's office saw the Demo Mag. for Sept. wh. contained my 'Walks round Boston.'" Quincy, journal, Oct. 16, 1838, 87, Quincy Family Papers.

70. Thomas L. Haskell, "Capitalism and the Origins of the Humanitarian Sensibility," 2 parts, *American Historical Review* 90:2 (Apr. 1985), 339–361; and 90:3 (June 1985), 547–566.

71. For more on fast property, see Michael Zakim and Gary J. Kornblinth, "An American Revolutionary Tradition," in Zakim and Kornblinth, *Capitalism Takes Command*, 3.

72. Sean Wilentz, *The Rise of American Democracy: Jefferson to Lincoln* (New York: W. W. Norton, 2005), 309–329.

73. Of course, many Americans would not have considered these changes radical. Workingmen advocated for shorter work days, land redistribution, and the end of imprisonment for debt. African Americans and female laborers also advocated for civil rights. Daniel Walker Howe gives an overview of many of these movements in the 1820s and 1830s in *What Hath God Wrought*, 539–557.

74. The Jacksonian vision of expanded democracy empowered white men at the expense of African Americans, Indigenous Americans, and women. For more on the limits of Jacksonian democracy, see Watson, *Liberty and Power*, 12–14; and David Roediger, *The Wages of Whiteness: Race and the Making of the American Working Class*, rev. ed. (New York: Verso, 1999), 65–94.

75. For an overview of mainline Jacksonian politics, see Watson, *Liberty and Power*.

76. On Martin Van Buren and Thomas Ritchie's efforts to consolidate a national political party, see Howe, *What Hath God Wrought*, 279–280.

77. DeWitt's critiques extended to the schoolmaster upstairs, where John Willetts rented rooms for his private school. Records of the Carpenters' Society, Minutes of Managing Committee, 1823–1838, Aug. 11, 1824 (reel 6, item 5G), n.p., American Philosophical Society.

78. Edgar A. Poe, "The Fall of the House of Usher," *Burton's Gentleman's Magazine* (Sept. 1839), 145–146. My interpretation of these Gothic tropes, both in fictional and nonfictional prose, supports the argument of Sian Silyn Roberts that American writers adapted Gothic tropes to address particular conditions and concerns of politics, economy, and society in the United States. It also agrees with her conjecture that these appropriations bolstered rather than challenged rational, observational thought frequently characterized as stemming from the Enlightenment. Roberts, *Gothic Subjects: The Transformation of Individualism in American Fiction, 1790–1861* (Philadelphia: University of Pennsylvania Press, 2014). On American Gothic as a form of social critique leveraged on conceptions of the American past, see Teresa A. Goddu, *Gothic America: Narrative, History, and Nation* (New York: Columbia University Press, 1997).

79. Nathaniel Hawthorne, "Edward Randolph's Portrait," *Twice-Told Tales*, vol. 2 (Boston: Ticknor, Reed, and Fields, 1851), 41.

80. Emphasis added.

81. These stories were first published in the *United States Magazine and Democratic Review* issues of May 1838 (129–140), July 1838 (360–369), Dec. 1838 (321–332), and Jan. 1839 (51–59). Hawthorne's stories were republished together in the second volume of *Twice-Told Tales* in 1842 and 1851–1853. C. E. Frazer Clark Jr., *Nathaniel Hawthorne: A Descriptive Bibliography* (Pittsburgh: University of Pittsburgh Press, 1978), 417–418; Michael T. Gilmore, *American Romanticism and the Marketplace* (Chicago: University of Chicago Press, 1985), 62; William Charvat, *Literary Publishing in America, 1790–1850* (Philadelphia: University of Pennsylvania Press, 1959), 9.

82. Yonatan Eyal, *The Young America Movement and the Transformation of the Democratic Party, 1828–1861* (Cambridge: Cambridge University Press, 2007), 65–92.

83. Thomas Waite kept the tavern from 1835 until approximately 1849. He appears in the *Directory of Boston for 1849* (Boston: George Adams, 1849) at the "Old Province House" at the rear of 165 Washington Street (p. 281) but not in the *Directory of Boston for 1850* (Boston:

George Adams, 1850), compiled by Adams in May and June of that year, or in Boston rolls of the 1850 U.S. census.

84. Nathaniel Hawthorne, "Howe's Masquerade," *Twice-Told Tales*, vol. 2 (Boston: Ticknor, Reed, and Fields, 1851), 5.

85. Hawthorne, "Howe's Masquerade," 6–8.

86. Hawthorne, "Howe's Masquerade," 24.

87. Nathaniel Hawthorne, "Lady Eleanore's Mantle," *Twice-Told Tales*, vol. 2 (Boston: Ticknor, Reed, and Fields, 1851), 42–43.

88. For more on Duyckinck (1816–1878) and Young American politics and literature, see Eyal, *Young America Movement*, 3–5; and Edward Widmer, *Young America: The Flowering of Democracy in New York City* (Oxford: Oxford University Press, 1999).

89. Felix Merry [Evert Duyckinck], "The City and the Country," *American Monthly Magazine*, May 1838, 414. Reprinted in *New Yorker* 10:8 (May 12, 1838), 114.

90. Merry [Duyckinck], "The City and the Country," 415–416.

91. The similarity of Hawthorne's and Quincy's subjects and narrative structures is remarkable, and they certainly were aware of one another's writing. See, e.g., Y. D., "Old Houses," 344; and Hawthorne, "Howe's Masquerade," 9.

92. On historical memory and abolitionism, see Seelye, *Memory's Nation*, 216–222; Margot Minardi, *Making Slavery History: Abolitionism and the Politics of Memory in Massachusetts* (Oxford: Oxford University Press, 2010).

93. Quincy drew on his father's real estate holdings, as well as the family wealth of his mother, Susan Morton Quincy of New York, and his wife, Lucilla Pinckney Parker of Boston. Sparks, "Abolition in Silver Slippers," 46–47, 66–68.

94. Quincy published a series of thirty-eight columns for the *Anti-Slavery Standard* that regularly commented on historic sites in Boston. The first appeared July 2, 1846 (p. 19) and the final appeared Oct. 12, 1848 (p. 79).

95. D.Y. [Quincy], "From Our Boston Correspondent, No. XII."

96. "An Old Settler," *Salem Observer*, June 15, 1839, p. 2 (microfilm: Phillips Library of the Peabody Essex Museum, Rowley, MA [hereafter Phillips Library]). Editors of the *Salem Register* excerpted this article to report the building's demolition as a loss of one of the last buildings to provide "a strong and visible tie with the ages that are past." They excised all praise of the commercial development of the city. "Ancient Building," *Salem Register*, June 17, 1839, p. 2 (microfilm: Phillips Library).

97. "The State House," (Philadelphia) *Public Ledger*, Nov. 16, 1836, p. 4; "Our State House," (Philadelphia) *Public Ledger*, Dec. 13, 1836, p. 2.

98. The *Philadelphia Inquirer* reported that "the pressure in the Money Market" had "palsied the hands of our capitalists and enterprising mechanics." "City Improvements," *Philadelphia Inquirer*, May 13, 1837, p. 2.

99. Lepler, *Many Panics of 1837*, 119.

100. "Antiquities," (Philadelphia) *Public Ledger*, Apr. 12, 1837, p. 2. Philadelphia newspapers carried news of the building's demolition alongside reports of urban improvements and commercial developments. Some notices remarked on the building's age and the fact that Whitefield had preached from its balcony. See., e.g., "Clear the Way for Improvements," *Public Ledger*, Apr. 8, 1837, p. 2; "City Improvements," *Pennsylvanian*, Apr. 13, 1837, p. 2; "The Old Court House," (Newark) *Centinel of Freedom*, Apr. 18, 1837, p. 3.

101. "The Improvement of Our City," (Philadelphia) *Public Ledger*, Mar. 1, 1837, p. 2.

102. "Antiquities," (Philadelphia) *Public Ledger*, Apr. 12, 1837, p. 2.

103. "Antiquities."

104. Robert Seager II, *And Tyler Too: A Biography of John and Julia Gardiner Tyler* (New York: McGraw-Hill, 1963), 114–115, 128–129.

105. John Tyler, "An Oration Delivered by John Tyler, At York Town, October 19th, 1837," *Southern Literary Messenger* 3:12 (Dec. 1837), 747.

106. Tyler, "Oration," 748–749.

107. John M. Galt et al. to John Tyler, Oct. 21, 1837, in *Southern Literary Messenger* 3:12 (Dec. 1837), 747.

108. Tyler, "Oration," 751.

109. Y. D. [Edmund Quincy], "Old Houses," *Southern Literary Messenger* 5:12 (Dec. 1839), 793–798.

110. Abel Upshur, "Domestic Slavery," *Southern Literary Messenger*, Oct. 1839, 677–687, quotes from 682.

111. "Bunker Hill," *Independent Chronicle and Boston Patriot*, May 1, 1822, p. 2. See also "Bunker Hill," *Independent Chronicle and Boston Patriot*, May 4, 1822, p. 1.

112. They paid $23,232.42 for the purchase of ten lots. G. Rodger Evans, Charles W. Snell, and Stull Associates, *Historic Structure Report, Bunker Hill Monument, 1818–1916*, vol. 1 (Denver: National Park Service, U.S. Department of the Interior, 1982), 23–33; Charles W. Snell, ed., *Documents Relating to the Organization and Purpose of the Bunker Hill Monument Association and to the Construction of the Bunker Hill Monument, 1823–1846*, vol. 2 (Denver: National Park Service, U.S. Department of the Interior, 1982), 3–6, 16–26.

113. Henry A. S. Dearborn, "Address to Gentlemen of Massachusetts," Feb. 1829, in Snell, *Documents Relating to the Organization and Purpose of the Bunker Hill Monument Association*, 96.

114. [George E. Ellis], *Sketches of Bunker Hill Battle and Monument: With Illustrative Documents*, 2nd ed. (Charlestown: C. P. Emmons, 1843), 156; Linden, *Silent Cities on a Hill*, 109–113.

115. "Monument Land," *Boston Courier*, Apr. 7, 1836, p. 4.

116. "Bunker Hill Monument," *Hampshire Gazette*, Sept. 12, 1838, p. 3.

117. Warren recorded in his journal that he met with the association and made "some remarks with a view of preventing the building on the Battle ground." John Collins Warren, journal, vol. 73, Sept. 8, 1838, John Collins Warren Papers, Massachusetts Historical Society (hereafter Warren Papers).

118. "Bunker Hill Monument," (New Orleans) *Daily Picayune*, Sept. 19, 1838, p. 2.

119. Evans, Snell, and Stull Associates, *Historic Structure Report*, vol. 1, 76–77.

120. "Bunker Hill Resolutions," *New York Evening Post*, July 8, 1837, p. 2; "Alexander H. Everett," *New York Evening Post*, Aug. 8, 1837, p. 2; "The Bunker Hill Convention," (Philadelphia) *National Gazette*, Sept. 15, 1840, p. 4.

121. Old-Fashioned Man, "The Pressure and Its Causes," 26.

122. Snell, *Documents Relating to the Organization and Purpose of the Bunker Hill Monument Association*, 19, 76.

123. Snell, *Documents Relating to the Organization and Purpose of the Bunker Hill Monument Association*, 84.

124. Benson J. Lossing, *The Pictorial Field-book of the Revolution*, vol. 2 (New York: Harper Brothers, 1852), 264.

125. Records of the Carpenters' Society, Minutes 1826–1857, Jan. 21, 1856, 327; Apr. 21, 1856, 328–329; Jan. 19, 1857, 337; April 20, 1857, 342; July 20, 1857, 345 (reel 3, item 4c), American Philosophical Society.

Chapter 5

1. Y.D. [Quincy], "Old Houses," 337, 336, 347.

2. Quincy, journal, Aug. 8, 1838, 75, Quincy Family Papers.

3. On the politics of voluntary associations, see Roney, *Governed by a Spirit of Opposition*; Albrecht Koschnik, *"Let a Common Interest Bind Us Together": Associations, Partisanship, and Culture in Philadelphia, 1776–1840* (Charlottesville: University of Virginia Press, 2007); Neem, *Creating a Nation of Joiners*.

4. On conceptions of the connections between family and state governance, see Gordon J. Schochet, *Patriarchalism in Political Thought: The Authoritarian Family and Political Speculation and Attitudes, Especially in Seventeenth-Century England* (Oxford: Oxford University Press, 1975); Jeanne Boydston, *Home and Work: Housework, Wages, and the Ideology of Labor in the Early Republic* (New York: Oxford University Press, 1990), 27–34; Kathleen M. Brown, *Good Wives, Nasty Wenches, and Anxious Patriarchs: Gender, Race, and Power in Colonial Virginia* (Chapel Hill: University of North Carolina Press, 1996); and Sachs, *Home Rule*.

5. For more on the link between selfhood and domestic space, see Gillian Brown, *Domestic Individualism: Imagining Self in Nineteenth-Century America* (Berkeley: University of California Press, 1990); Mary Ryan, *Cradle of the Middle Class: The Family in Oneida County, New York, 1790–1865* (Cambridge: Cambridge University Press, 1981), 146–155; Nancy F. Cott, *The Bonds of Womanhood: "Women's Sphere" in New England, 1780–1835*, 2nd ed. (New Haven: Yale University Press, 1997), 63–100; and Catherine Kelly, *In the New England Fashion: Reshaping Women's Lives in the Nineteenth Century* (Ithaca: Cornell University Press, 1999), 188–192.

6. Caroline Kirkland, "Washington," in *Homes of American Statesmen; With Anecdotal, Personal, and Descriptive Sketches*, ed. George P. Putnam (New York: G. P. Putnam, 1854), 3–4.

7. See, e.g., Watson, *Annals of Philadelphia*, 151; Brandt, *First in the Homes of His Countrymen*, 33–34.

8. Oliver Goldsmith, *The Life of Richard Nash, Esq.* (London, 1762), quoted in Michael McKeon, *The Secret History of Domesticity: Public, Private, and the Division of Knowledge* (Baltimore: Johns Hopkins University Press, 2005), 339.

9. Benjamin Latrobe, Aug. 3, 1796, *The Virginia Journals of Benjamin Henry Latrobe, 1795–1798*, ed. Edward Carter (New Haven: Yale University Press, 1977), vol. 1, 181. For more on William Berkeley's construction of this house in the 1670s (his second on site), see David A. Brown, "Domestic Masonry Architecture in 17th-Century Virginia," *Northeast Historical Archaeology* 27:1 (1998), 96–97.

10. Latrobe, Aug. 3, 1796, *Virginia Journals*, vol. 1, 181–183.

11. William Bentley, Feb. 8, 1796, *The Diary of William Bentley, D.D., Pastor of the East Church, Salem, Massachusetts*, vol. 2 (Gloucester: Peter Smith, 1962), 172.

12. "Antiquities," *Boston Courier*, May 16, 1833, p. 2. For more on the Clarke-Frankland House, see Edward B. Allen, *Early American Wall Paintings, 1710–1850* (New Haven: Yale University Press, 1926), 3–7.

13. "Selected Summary," (Boston) *American Traveller*, Apr. 2, 1833, p. 2 (microfilm: Boston Public Library); Abbott Lowell Cummings, "The Foster-Hutchinson House," *Old-Time New England* 54 (1964), 59–76; Abbott Lowell Cummings, "The Beginnings of Provincial Renaissance Architecture in Boston (1690–1725): Current Observations and Suggestions for Further Study," *Journal of the Society of Architectural Historians* 43 (Mar. 1983), 43–53; Peter Hoffer, *Sensory Worlds in Early America* (Baltimore: Johns Hopkins University Press, 2003), 205–214.

14. "Antiquities," *Boston Courier*. See also Lydia Maria Francis, *The Rebels, of Boston Before the Revolution* (Boston: Cummings, Hilliard, 1825), 8; James Fenimore Cooper, *Lionel Lincoln; or the Leaguer of Boston* (London: John Miller, 1825), 69–71; Logan, diary, Feb. 15, 1825, vol. 7, 218, Logan Diaries; Eliza Leslie, *Cards of Boston: Comprizing a Variety of Facts and Descriptions Relative to that City, in Past and Present Times* (Boston: Munroe and Fennels, 1831), Game Collection, AAS.

15. Bushman, *Refinement of America*, 100–138; Kevin Sweeney, "Mansion People: Kinship, Class, and Architecture in Western Massachusetts in the Eighteenth Century," *Winterthur Portfolio* 19:4 (Winter 1984), 231–255; Barbara Mooney, *Prodigy Houses of Virginia: Architecture and the Native Elite* (Charlottesville: University of Virginia Press, 2008); Dell Upton, "Black and White Landscapes in Eighteenth-Century Virginia," *Places* 2:2 (1984), 59–72. On the domestic architectural use of Anglo-American classicism by Indigenous leaders, see Saunt, *New Order of Things*, 71–72; Tiya Miles, *The House on Diamond Hill: A Cherokee Plantation Story* (Chapel Hill: University of North Carolina Press, 2010), 71–74, 164–170.

16. Guests had been scrawling on the walls at least since David Garrick's Shakespeare Jubilee in 1769. Julian North, *The Domestication of Genius: Biography and the Romantic Poet* (Oxford: Oxford University Press, 2010), 11–30; McKeon, *Secret History of Domesticity*, 337–342; Aaron Santesso, "The Birth of the Birthplace: Bread Street and Literary Tourism Before Stratford," *ELH* 71:2 (Summer 2004), 377–403; Glendinning, *Conservation Movement*, 112–115; Dan Hinchen, "The Bostonian and the Bard," *The Beehive: Official Blog of the Massachusetts Historical Society*, Dec. 23, 2016, http://www.masshist.org/blog/1441.

17. François Furstenberg, *In the Name of the Father: Washington's Legacy, Slavery, and the Making of the Nation* (New York: Penguin, 2006); Barbara J. Mitnick, "Parallel Visions: The Literary and Visual Image of George Washington," in *George Washington: American Symbol*, ed. Barbara J. Mitnick and William S. Ayres (New York: Hudson Hills, 1999), 63–65.

18. Charles H. Ruggles to Sarah C. Ruggles, Apr. 28, 1822, quoted in Jean B. Lee, "Jane C. Washington, Family, and Nation at Mount Vernon, 1830-1855," in *Women Shaping the South: Creating and Confronting Change*, ed. Angela Boswell and Judith N. McArthur (Columbia: University of Missouri Press, 2006), 37.

19. Lee, "Jane C. Washington," 30–31.

20. Upton, *Another City*; Herman, *Town House*; Small, *Beauty and Convenience*; Jack Larkin, *Where We Lived: Discovering the Places We Once Called Home: The American Home from 1775–1840* (Newtown: Taunton, 2006); Bushman, *Refinement of America*, 238–279; Clifton Ellis and Rebecca Ginsburg, eds., *Cabin, Quarter, Plantation: Architecture and Landscapes of North American Slavery* (New Haven: Yale University Press, 2010); McInnis, *Politics of Taste in Antebellum Charleston*, 160–239.

21. Quincy, journal, June 29, 1837, 14–15, Quincy Family Papers. See also Robert Johnston, journal, Apr. 23 to June 16, 1835, folder 2, box 51, Powel Family Papers, HSP.

22. Latrobe, *Virginia Journals*, vol. 1, Aug. 3, 1796, 182; Aug. 3, 1797, 247; Benjamin Henry Latrobe sketchbooks, Museum Department, Maryland Historical Society (1960.108.1.2.33).

23. Bentley, *Diary*, vol. 2, Feb. 8, 1796, 172; Feb. 5, 1796, 172.

24. The Bostonian Society does contain an associational relic from the Hutchinson house: a splinter of wood reportedly collected from it (object X0079).

25. "Antiquities," *Boston Courier.*

26. Many of these buyers, or scavengers, later donated these objects to historical societies. *Proceedings of the Massachusetts Historical Society* 17 (Nov. 1879) (Boston: Massachusetts Historical Society, 1880), 234; Nancy Carlisle, *Cherished Possessions: A New England Legacy* (Boston: SPNEA, 2003), 112–115; Allen, *Early American Wall Paintings,* 3–7; chair from Clarke-Frankland house, Bostonian Society, object 1957.0002.

27. (Boston) *Columbian Centinel,* May 29, 1833, quoted in Cummings, "Foster-Hutchinson House," p. 73; "Antiquity," *Salem Observer,* June 1, 1833, p. 2; Minutes of Recording Secretary, May 30, 1833, vol. 4, Records of the Massachusetts Historical Society, 77.

28. "The Hutchinson House," *American Magazine of Useful and Entertaining Knowledge* 1 (Feb. 1836), 237.

29. Faherty, *Remodeling the Nation*, 18–20, 32; Milette Shamir, *Inexpressible Privacy: The Interior Life of Antebellum American Literature* (Philadelphia: University of Pennsylvania Press, 2006).

30. Bowen, *Bowen's Picture of Boston*, 225.

31. Christopher Columbus Baldwin, diary, Oct. 25, 1831, *A Place in My Chronicle: A New Edition of the Diary of Christopher Columbus Baldwin, 1829–1835*, ed. Caroline Sloat and Jack Larkin (Worcester: American Antiquarian Society, 2010), 104.

32. Ellen Randolph Coolidge to Martha Jefferson Randolph, Aug. 7, 1831, box 3, Correspondence of Ellen Wayles Randolph Coolidge, Small Special Collections, University of Virginia (hereafter Coolidge Correspondence). Bracketed parts are missing in manuscript letter.

33. Cornelia Jefferson Randolph to Ellen Wayles Randolph Coolidge, July 6, 1828, box 2, Coolidge Correspondence.

34. Martha Jefferson Randolph to Ellen Wayles Randolph Coolidge, Aug. 15, 1831, box 3, Coolidge Correspondence.

35. John H. B. Latrobe, quoted in John Edward Semmes, *John H. B. Latrobe and His Times, 1803–1891* (Baltimore: Norman, Remington, 1917), 248.

36. For a complete overview of the historical studies of Elihu Hoyt and his fellow local historians, see Michael Batinski, *Pastkeepers in a Small Place: Five Centuries in Deerfield, Massachusetts* (Amherst: University of Massachusetts Press, 2004), 81–119.

37. Baldwin, diary, Sept. 16, 1833, *A Place in My Chronicle*, 140.

38. Elihu Hoyt had 280 copies of his pamphlet, "A Brief Sketch of the First Settlement of Deerfield, Mass.," in his home upon his death that year. Donald R. Friary, "A Family Enterprise: Collecting Deerfield's Past," in *New England Collectors and Collections*, ed. Peter Benes (Boston: Boston University Press, 2006), 53–68.

39. "Biographical Mania," *New-York Mirror*, May 15, 1830, 359, Library Company of Philadelphia. See also Casper, *Constructing American Lives*, 38–42, 202–211.

40. The growing number and geographical distribution of printing presses created a reading public that expanded well beyond the economic and cultural bounds of the urban middle classes. Howe, *What Hath God Wrought*, 627–628; James N. Green, "The Rise of Book Publishing," in *An Extensive Republic: Print, Culture, and Society in a New Nation, 1790–1840*, ed. Robert A. Gross and Mary Kelley (Chapel Hill: University of North Carolina Press, 2010), 75–127.

41. Jared Sparks, *Works of Benjamin Franklin*, vol. 1 (Boston: Hilliard, Gray, 1840), 8.

42. Briggs was born on Nantucket in 1804. Charles Briggs, "Franklin," in Putnam, *Homes of American Statesmen*, 68.

43. Washington Irving, "New York State Documents, Washington's Head Quarters at Newburgh," *Richmond County Mirror* 3:13 (Apr. 27, 1839), 107.

44. Mary P. Ryan, *The Empire of the Mother: American Writing About Domesticity, 1830–1860* (New York: Haworth, 1982), 19–43; Boydston, *Home and Work*, 99; Blackmar, *Manhattan for Rent*, 109–138; Michael Grossberg, *Governing the Hearth: Law and the Family in Nineteenth-Century America* (Chapel Hill: University of North Carolina Press, 1985), 6–8. U.S. homes were not, in fact, separate from the market in material composition or practice. Historians of gender have shown this to great effect when challenging the boundaries of the cult of domesticity. See, e.g., Linda K. Kerber, "Separate Sphere, Female Worlds, Woman's Place: The Rhetoric of Women's History," *Journal of American History* 75:1 (June 1988), 9–39; Boydston, *Home and Work*, xiv–xv.

45. Uriah Levy to David Coddington, Dec. 1, 1842, quoted in Mark Leepson, *Saving Monticello: The Levy Family's Epic Quest to Rescue the House That Jefferson Built* (New York: Free Press, 2001), 60.

46. (Portland, ME) *Eastern Argus*, Oct. 18, 1833, p. 2, reprinted from the *Richmond Compiler*.

47. *Baltimore Patriot*, Apr. 10, 1834, p. 2.

48. *Richmond Enquirer*, Apr. 15, 1834, p. 4.

49. See Leepson, *Saving Monticello*, 72–74.

50. Lee, "Jane C. Washington," 44–46.

51. Jane Washington to G. C. Washington, May 25, 1840, quoted in Lee, "Jane C. Washington," 38–39.

52. Jane Washington to John A. Washington, Feb. 18 and Dec. 13, 1846, quoted in Lee, "Jane C. Washington," 42; Lee, "Jane C. Washington," 40–45.

53. After building the house in 1759, John Vassall Jr. abandoned the property when he refused to join the Revolutionary cause in 1774. George Washington made the house his headquarters when he assumed control of the Continental Army in 1775. Longfellow became acquainted with the house's history in the 1830s, while boarding with the widow of the famed land speculator Andrew Craigie, who had purchased the property after the Revolution. Fanny Appleton Longfellow to Nathan Appleton, [Sept. 1843], in Fanny Appleton Longfellow, *Mrs. Longfellow: Selected Letters and Journals*, ed. Edward Wagenknecht (New York: Longmans, Green, 1956), 93.

54. Fanny Appleton Longfellow to Thomas G. Appleton, Aug. 30, 1843, in F. Longfellow, *Mrs. Longfellow*, 92–93; John Trumbull to Jared Sparks, June 12, 1843, box 140, folder 70, Henry Wadsworth Longfellow Dana Papers, Longfellow National Historic Site, Cambridge, Massachusetts.

55. Fanny Appleton Longfellow and Henry Wadsworth Longfellow, "The Craigie House," Henry Wadsworth Longfellow Papers, Houghton Library, Harvard University.

56. Henry Wadsworth Longfellow, journal, Apr. 9, 1844, quoted in Catherine Evans, *Cultural Landscape Report for Longfellow National Historic Site* (Boston: National Park Service, 1993), 33.

57. Fanny Appleton Longfellow to Nathan Appleton, [Sept. 1843], in F. Longfellow, *Mrs. Longfellow*, 93.

58. Fanny Appleton Longfellow to Nathan Appleton, July 20, 1843, in F. Longfellow, *Mrs. Longfellow*, 88; Fanny Appleton Longfellow to Harriot Sumner Appleton, Apr. 28, 1844, in F. Longfellow, *Mrs. Longfellow*, 110; Evans, *Cultural Landscape Report*, 42.

59. Washington Irving, *Life of George Washington* (New York: Putnam, 1857), 221.

60. Henry Wadsworth Longfellow to John Jay Smith, June 18, 1844, in an extra-illustrated edition of John Jay Smith, *Recollections of John Jay Smith* (Philadelphia: J. B. Lippincott, 1892), vol. 2., Library Company of Philadelphia. Emphasis in original.

61. Jared Sparks to John Trumbull, June 9, 1843, and John Trumbull to Jared Sparks, June 12, 1843, box 140, folder 70, Henry Wadsworth Longfellow Dana Papers, Longfellow National Historic Site, Cambridge, Massachusetts.

62. McCarthy, *American Creed*, 1–120.

63. Cornelia Randolph to Ellen Coolidge, June 29, 1831, box 3, Coolidge Correspondence.

64. Lee, "Jane C. Washington," 40–45.

65. Butterfield, *Making of Tocqueville's America*.

66. On John Fanning Watson's broader antiquarian pursuits, see Seth Cotlar, "Seeing Like an Antiquarian: Popular Nostalgia and the Rise of Modern Historical Subjectivity in the 1820s," in *Experiencing Empire: People, Power, and Revolution in Early America*, ed. Patrick Griffin (Charlottesville: University of Virginia Press, 2017), 212–231.

67. Roberts Vaux to John Fanning Watson, Nov. 2, 1824, and Deborah Logan to John Fanning Watson, Feb. 2, 1825, box 2, John Fanning Watson Collection; Watson, *Annals of Philadelphia*, 145–149.

68. Watson, *Annals of Philadelphia*, 147.

69. Watson, *Annals of Philadelphia*, 147.

70. Logan, diary, vol. 13, Nov. 2, 1830, 116, Logan Diaries.

71. John Fanning Watson to John Jay Smith, Feb. 22, 1834, in extra-illustrated edition of Smith, *Recollections*, vol. 3, Library Company of Philadelphia; *Desilver's Philadelphia Directory and Stranger's Guide for 1835 & 36* (Philadelphia: Robert Desilver, 1835), 88;

David C. Hammack, ed., *Making the Nonprofit Sector in the United States: A Reader* (Bloomington: Indiana University Press, 1998), 117; Levy, "Altruism and the Origins of Nonprofit Philanthropy," 23–29.

72. John Fanning Watson to John Jay Smith, Feb. 22, 1834, in Smith, *Recollections*, vol. 3, Library Company of Philadelphia.

73. Minute Book, July 7, 1835, vol. 1, 174, Records of RIHS.

74. Stephen Gould to John Howland, Oct. 13, 1835, box 1, Bull Papers; *Newport Mercury*, June 1, 1833, p. 3.

75. Correspondence and Reports, July 20, 1835, vol. 2, 6, Records of RIHS; Records of the Trustees, July 7, 1835, 79, Records of RIHS; Robert Johnston, journal, July 10, 11, and 15, 1835, folder 2, box 51, Powel Family Papers, HSP (hereafter Powel Papers).

76. Correspondence and Reports, July 20, 1835, vol. 2, 6, Records of RIHS.

77. Irving, "New York State Documents, Washington's Head Quarters at Newburgh," 107.

78. *Documents of the Assembly of the State of New-York, Sixty-Second Session*, vol. 6 (Albany: E. Croswell, 1839), 1–5; *Laws of the State of New-York, Passed at the Sixty-Second Session of the Legislature* (Albany: E. Croswell, 1839), 155.

79. A. J. Schenkman, *Washington's Headquarters in Newburgh: Home to a Revolution* (Charleston: History Press, 2009), 95.

80. Gulian C. Verplanck, "American Antiquities: View of Washington's Headquarters," *New-York Mirror*, Dec. 27, 1834, p. 201.

81. *Documents of the Assembly of the State of New-York, Sixty-Second Session*, vol. 6 (Albany: E Croswell, 1839), 1–5, quote from 4.

82. Watson, *Annals of Philadelphia*, 147.

83. John Fanning Watson to John Jay Smith, Feb. 22, 1834, in Smith, *Recollections*, vol. 3, Library Company of Philadelphia.

84. John Fanning Watson to John Jay Smith, Feb. 22, 1834, in Smith, *Recollections*, vol. 3, Library Company of Philadelphia.

85. Johnston, journal, July 11, 1835, folder 2, box 51, Powel Family Papers.

86. Harwood produced lithograph views of the house and donated prints to the Rhode Island Historical Society and the Historical Society of Pennsylvania. Robert Johnston, diary, July 4, 1835, folder 2, box 51, Powel Family Papers; Minute Book, vol. 1, 297, Records of RIHS; Accessions Book, Sept. 9, 1850, vol. 1, 55, Records of HSP.

87. Generations of the Brown family lived at Whitehall until the 1880s. The National Society of the Colonial Dames of America secured the property for restoration as a house museum in 1897. Whitehall Museum House website, http://www.whitehallmuseumhouse.org /history-of-the-whitehall-property/.

88. Correspondence and Reports, July 31, 1835, vol. 2, 89, Records of RIHS.

89. Jeremiah Day to Thomas H. Webb, Aug. 7, 1835, Correspondence and Reports, vol. 2, 90, Records of RIHS.

90. Colleen McDannell, *The Christian Home in Victorian America, 1840–1900* (Bloomington: Indiana University Press, 1986).

91. This revises the notion that house museums, or civic housekeeping more broadly, originated when women extended their domestic authority into the public realm. See, e.g., West, *Domesticating History*.

92. Antiquary, "The 'Old House' in Deerfield," Nov. 16, 1847, *Greenfield Gazette*, reprinted in *The New England Historical and Genealogical Register*, Jan. 1848 (Boston: Samuel G. Drake, 1848), 110–111. Emphasis in original.

93. Epaphras Hoyt, Stephen West Williams, M.D., Reverend Samuel Willard, Colonel John Wilson, and Pliny Arms, "To All Who Feel an Interest in the Antiquities of New-England," broadside, 1847, collections of Memorial Hall Museum, http://americancenturies

.mass.edu/collection/itempage.jsp?itemid=5725&img=0&level=advanced&transcription=1. The formation of the committee was announced by a communication from secretary John Wilson on Nov. 29, 1847, printed in the *Greenfield Gazette,* reprinted in *The New England Historical and Genealogical Register,* Jan. 1848 (Boston: Samuel G. Drake, 1848), 111.

94. Hoyt et al., "To All Who Feel an Interest in the Antiquities of New-England."

95. Antiquary, "'Old House' in Deerfield." See also David W. Hoyt, *A Genealogical History of John Hoyt of Salisbury, and David Hoyt of Deerfield* (Boston: C. Benjamin Richardson, 1857), 124–127.

96. The Hoyts kept architectural relics of the old house, and Catherine Wells Hoyt donated them to U.S. centennial and local history exhibitions in the 1870s and 1880s. Batinski, *Pastkeepers in a Small Place,* 86; Harley J. McKee, "John Sheldon 'Old Indian House,'" HABS MASS-649 (1959). For a history and photographs of buildings on the site, see Susan McGowan and Amelia F. Miller, *Family and Landscape: Deerfield Homelots from 1671* (Deerfield: Pocumtuck Valley Memorial Association, 1996), 26–28. For an overview of changes in the material life of the Hoyt family and region, see J. Ritchie Garrison, *Landscape and Material Life in Franklin County, Massachusetts, 1770–1860* (Knoxville: University of Tennessee Press, 1991).

97. Cohen, *Luxurious Citizens,* 130–138; Bushman, *Refinement of America,* 256–279; Jaffee, *New Nation of Goods;* Wendy A. Woloson, *Refined Tastes: Sugar, Confectionary, and Consumers in Nineteenth-Century America* (Baltimore: Johns Hopkins University Press, 2002).

98. Cohen, *Luxurious Citizens,* 108–111, 132; Boydston, *Home and Work,* 24–28.

99. Martha Coffin Wright to [Lucretia Mott], [Dec.] 18, [1841], Martha Coffin Wright Correspondence, 1825–1841, Garrison Papers, Smith College, quoted in Boydston, *Home and Work,* 117.

100. Stabile, *Memory's Daughters;* Hannah Mather Crocker, *Reminiscences and Traditions of Boston,* ed. Eileen Hunt Botting and Sarah L. Houser (Boston: NEHGS, 2011); Alea Henle, "The Widow's Mite: Hannah Mather Crocker and the Mather Libraries," *Information and Culture: A Journal of History* 48:3 (2013), 323–343; Ulrich, *Age of Homespun.*

101. Logan, diary, Sept. 3, 1827, vol. 7, 1, Logan Diaries; Kathleen Brown, *Foul Bodies: Cleanliness in Early America* (New Haven: Yale University Press, 2009), 284, 291, 326.

102. Logan, diary, Jan. 16, 1823, vol. 6, 9; May 13, 1824, vol. 6, 192; Jan. 15, 1827, vol. 10, 158–159; May 26, 1830, vol. 13, 28–29, Logan Diaries. Emphasis in original.

103. Logan, diary, June 8, 1832, vol. 14, 52 (typescript: Winterthur), Logan Diaries.

104. Francis, *Rebels,* 8; L. M. Francis to Mary and Catherine Byles, May 6, 1826, Mary and Catherine Byles letterbook (1825–1827), Series A, Almon Family Fonds (microfilm: Nova Scotia Archives, Halifax, Nova Scotia).

105. Lydia Maria Child, *The American Frugal Housewife,* 16th ed. (Boston: Carter, Hendee, 1835), 3–6. Emphasis in original.

106. Child expressed her expansive commitment to these economic principles in her support for Garrisonian antislavery and for Indigenous American resistance to forced migration. Carolyn L. Karcher, *The First Woman in the Republic: A Cultural Biography of Lydia Maria Child* (Durham: Duke University Press, 1998), 86–213.

107. Karcher, *First Woman in the Republic,* 128–129.

108. Leslie, *Cards of Boston;* Whitney Martinko, "Byles Versus Boston: Historic Houses, Urban Development, and the Public Good in an Improving City," *Massachusetts Historical Review* 18 (2016), 119–151.

109. Catherine Beecher, *A Treatise on Domestic Economy, for the Use of Young Ladies at School* (New York: Harper and Brothers, 1845), 181, 185; Boydston, *Home and Work,* 142–143, 171–176.

110. Diana Strazdes, "Catherine Beecher and the American Woman's Puritan Home," *New England Quarterly* 82:3 (Sept. 2009), 452–489; Boydston, *Home and Work,* 109–112.

111. Ginzberg, *Women and the Work of Benevolence*, 11–66; Kathleen D. McCarthy, "Spreading the Gospel of Self-Denial: Thrift and Association in Antebellum America," in *Thrift and Thriving in America: Capitalism and Moral Order from the Puritans to the Present*, ed. Joshua J. Yates and James Davison Hunter (Oxford: Oxford University Press, 2011), 160–182; Cynthia A. Kierner, *Beyond the Household: Women's Place in the Early South, 1700–1835* (Ithaca: Cornell University Press, 1998), 180–211.

112. [Sarah Hale], "The Worth of Money," *Ladies Magazine and Literary Gazette* 3:2 (Feb. 1830), 49.

113. [Hale], "The Worth of Money," 49.

114. [Sarah Hale], "The Bunker Hill Monument," *Ladies' Magazine and Literary Gazette* 3:3 (Mar. 1830), 135. Emphasis in original.

115. Eleven Boston women signed this appeal and invited women all over New England to form societies devoted to the same cause. "To the Women of New England," *Ladies' Magazine and Literary Gazette* 3:4 (Apr. 1830), 171.

116. [Hale], "Bunker Hill Monument," 135.

117. [Hale], "Bunker Hill Monument," *Ladies' Magazine and Literary Gazette* 6:6 (June 1833), 280.

118. Abigail Carroll, "Of Kettles and Cranes: Colonial Revival Kitchens and the Performance of National Identity," *Winterthur Portfolio* 43:4 (2009), 335–364; Frances M. Clarke, "Old-Fashioned Tea Parties: Revolutionary Memory in Civil War Sanitary Fairs," in *Remembering the Revolution*, ed. McDonnell, Corbould, Clarke, and Brundage, 294–312; Ulrich, *Age of Homespun*.

119. Ellen Randolph Coolidge to Virginia Trist, Apr. 15, 1834, box 3, Coolidge Correspondence.

120. "First Brick House Built in Philadelphia," *The Building Age*, July 1, 1913, 355; "Letitia Street House," HABS PA-184 (1938).

121. Minutes, May 4, 1846, vol. 3, 25, Records of HSP.

122. Minutes, Nov. 10 and Dec. 8, 1851, vol. 3, 276, 279, Records of HSP.

123. Chapter 181, New York State Legislature (Senate and Assembly), Apr. 15, 1839. *Laws of the State of New-York, Passed at the Sixty-Second Session of the Legislature* (Albany: E. Croswell, 1839), 155.

124. Richard Caldwell, *A True History of the Acquisition of Washington's Headquarters at Newburgh by the State of New York* (Middletown: Stivers, Slauson & Boyd, 1887).

125. George P. Putnam, ed., *Homes of American Authors; Comprising Anecdotal, Personal, and Descriptive Sketches* (New York: G. P. Putnam, 1853), 126; Putnam, *Homes of American Statesmen*, n.p. [iii].

126. Articles about notable Americans often included facsimiles of signatures, portraits, and views of houses. Edward W. Johnston, "Madison," in Putnam, *Homes of American Statesmen*, 181–182.

Chapter 6

1. [Rebecca Warren Brown], *Stories about General Warren* (Boston: James Loring, 1835), 12–14. This versatile apple variety is more commonly known as the Roxbury russet today. It was cultivated by North American colonizers a century before Joseph Warren died from a fall in his apple orchard on October 23, 1755. *Boston Evening-Post*, Oct. 27, 1755, pp. 1–2.

2. Edward Warren, *The Life of John Collins Warren, M.D.*, 2 vols. (Boston: Noyes, Holmes, 1874), vol. 1, 9, and vol. 2, 25.

3. On the financial calculations of nineteenth-century slaveholders, see Caitlin Rosenthal, *Accounting for Slavery: Masters and Management* (Cambridge, MA: Harvard University Press, 2018); and Beckert and Rockman, *Slavery's Capitalism*, 105–178.

4. Elizabeth Blackmar, "Inheriting Property and Debt: From Family Security to Corporate Accumulation," in Zakim and Kornblinth, *Capitalism Takes Command*, 93–117.

5. Louisa Catherine Johnson Adams to John Quincy Adams, July 20, 1822," *Founders Online,* National Archives, last modified June 13, 2018, http://founders.archives.gov /documents/Adams/99-03-02-4090. See also Louisa Catherine Johnson Adams to John Quincy Adams, 6 August 1822," *Founders Online,* National Archives, last modified June 13, 2018, http://founders.archives.gov/documents/Adams/99-03-02-4118.

6. James A. Jacobs, "Addendum to the Woodlands," HABS PA-1125 (2002), 14–16.

7. On the "market revolution" of the 1810s to 1840s, see Sellers, *Market Revolution*.

8. Most scholars state that Commuck moved to New York in 1825, but Commuck dated his move to 1822 or 1823. Petition of Thomas Commuck, July 7, 1840, NIRC.

9. The Narragansett Indian Records Collection contains a number of petitions, legislative acts, and reports that convey these conditions. Petition by the Narragansett Indian tribe, Oct. 1823, NIRC. See also Ruth Wallis Herndon and Ella Wilcox Sekatau, "The Right to a Name: The Narragansett People and Rhode Island Officials in the Revolutionary Era," *Ethnohistory* 44:3 (Summer 1997), 433–462; Narragansett Indian Tribe, "Perseverance," http:// narragansettindiannation.org/history/perseverance/; Jean O'Brien, *Firsting and Lasting: Writing Indians out of Existence in New England* (Minneapolis: University of Minnesota Press, 2010); and Daniel Mandell, *Tribe, Race, History: Native Americans in Southern New England, 1780–1880* (Baltimore: Johns Hopkins University Press, 2010), 1–103. Today, the Brothertown Indian Nation identifies its six "parent tribes" as the Mohegan, Montaukett, Narragansett, Niantic, Pequot, and Tunxis. Brothertown Indian Nation, "Tribal Alliance," http://brothertownindians.org/heritage/tribal-alliance.

10. On genealogy as a process of claiming property in Anglo-America, see Karin Wulf, "Bible, King, and Common Law: Genealogical Legacies and Family History Practices in British America," *Early American Studies* 10:3 (Fall 2012), 467–502; Francesca Morgan, "Lineage as Capital: Genealogy in Antebellum New England," *New England Quarterly* 83:2 (June 2010), 250–282; and Toby L. Ditz, *Property and Kinship: Inheritance in Early Connecticut, 1750–1820* (Princeton: Princeton University Press, 1986), esp. 46–60.

11. Petition of Thomas Commuck, July 7, 1840, NIRC. See also Thomas Commuck to Elisha Potter, July 11, 1844, in *Dawnland Voices: An Anthology of Indigenous Writing from New England*, ed. Siobhan Senier (Lincoln: University of Nebraska Press, 2014), 501.

12. Thomas Commuck to Wilkins Updike, July 14, 1837, in Senier, *Dawnland Voices*, 501.

13. O'Brien, *Firsting and Lasting*.

14. Commuck's grandmother was a Narragansett woman in Rhode Island who turned twenty years old before the founding of the Brothertown nation. Moreover, Brothertown members spoke a number of Indigenous languages. Thomas Commuck to Lyman C. Draper, Aug. 22, 1855, printed as "Sketch of the Brothertown Indians," *Report and Collections of the State Historical Society of Wisconsin, for the Years 1857 and 1858*, ed. Lyman C. Draper, vol. 4 (Madison: James Ross, 1859), 297. On Brothertown origins, see David J. Silverman, *Red Brethren: The Brothertown and Stockbridge Indians and the Problem of Race in Early America* (Ithaca: Cornell University Press, 2010), 89–106.

15. Methodist hymnist Thomas Hastings composed the harmonies. Thomas Commuck, *Indian Melodies* (New York: G. Lane and C. B. Tippett, 1845), iv.

16. Thomas Commuck, R. Abner, Charles Anthony, and Alonzo D. Dick to C. C. Sholes, May 16, 1839, printed in "Brothertown Indians," (Madison) *Wisconsin Enquirer,* June 15,

1839, p. 3. On Indigenous American conceptions of civilization in this era, see Christina Snyder, "The Rise and Fall and Rise of Civilizations: Indian Intellectual Culture During the Removal Era," *Journal of American History* 104:2 (Sept. 2017), 386–409.

17. Commuck to Draper, Aug. 22, 1855, in Draper, *Report and Collections of the State Historical Society of Wisconsin*, 291.

18. Several petitioners followed suit in the 1840s after the state of Rhode Island authorized another confiscation and sale of Narragansett land to settle debts. Along with several Brothertown migrants, Narragansett Daniel Moody appealed for permission to sell his family land in the trust to fund the building of "a permanent residence" in Voluntown, Connecticut. He was included in the list of people authorized to sell lands and reinvest in Wisconsin, though he had asked to buy land in Connecticut. All petitioners seem to have received permission to sell except Matilda Congdon, who wanted to use money from the sale to repair her home rather than build a new one elsewhere. Resolution appointing E. R. Potter Commissioner of Indian Claims, Mar. 30, 1842; Daniel Moody to General Assembly, Oct. 1843; Nancy Stanton General Assembly, Oct. 1843; Moses Stanton to General Assembly, Oct. 1843; Matilda Congdon to General Assembly, Oct. 1843; Moses Stanton to General Assembly, May 1844, all NIRC; and *Acts and Resolves passed by the General Assembly of the State of Rhode Island and Providence Plantations* (Providence, 1843), May 1843, 10–11; June 1843, 77–78; Oct. 1843, 75–76.

19. Commuck recounted his history of these land disputes, treaties, and purchases in Commuck to Draper, Aug. 22, 1855, in Draper, *Report and Collections of the State Historical Society of Wisconsin*, 291–298. In 2009, the U.S. government cited the lack of communal land holdings, along with acceptance of U.S. citizenship in 1839, as a reason for denying federal recognition of Brothertown Indian Nation tribal sovereignty. https://www.bia.gov/sites/bia.gov/files/assets/as-ia/ofa/petition/067_brothe_WI/067_pf.pdf. On Brothertown land dealing in the real estate market, see Brad D. E. Jarvis, *The Brothertown Nation of Indians: Land Ownership and Nationalism in Early America, 1740–1840* (Lincoln: University of Nebraska Press, 2010).

20. Thomas Skidmore articulated the fullest argument against private property and inheritance in his *The Rights of Man to Property!* (New York, 1829). On Skidmore, see Sean Wilentz, *Chants Democratic: New York City and the Rise of the American Working Class, 1788–1850* (New York: Oxford University Press, 1984), 172–216. On inheritance and agrarian reform, see Charles W. McCurdy, *The Anti-Rent Era in New York Law and Politics, 1839–1865* (Chapel Hill: University of North Carolina Press, 2001), 87–88, 172–173.

21. Renters could sell their leases, but they would owe a quarter of the purchase price or an extra year's rent to the landlord. McCurdy, *Anti-Rent Era*, 1.

22. McCurdy, *Anti-Rent Era*, 10–12.

23. McCurdy, *Anti-Rent Era*, 10–15, 314.

24. McCurdy, *Anti-Rent Era*, 10–15, 314; Reeve Huston, *Land and Freedom: Rural Society, Popular Protest, and Party Politics in Antebellum New York* (New York: Oxford University Press, 2000), 77–87.

25. Historical investigations into proprietary titles occurred on other families' lands as well. McCurdy, *Anti-Rent Era*, 97–100, 163, 201, 214, 252–254, 301.

26. *Young America*, Feb. 8, 1845, quoted in Huston, *Land and Freedom*, 111.

27. Huston, *Land and Freedom*, 107–124.

28. Veto, "The Convention," *New York Evening Post*, Sept. 23, 1845, quoted in McCurdy, *Anti-Rent Era*, 211. See also McCurdy, *Anti-Rent Era*, 22–29, 205–233.

29. Ambrose Jordan, as recorded in Sherman Croswell and Richard Sutton, eds., *Debates and Proceedings in the New York State Convention, for the Revision of the Constitution* (Albany: Argus, 1846), 514–515.

30. Daniel S. Dickinson, "Address Delivered at the Fair of the Queens County Agricultural Society, October 17, 1843," quoted in McCurdy, *Anti-Rent Era*, 38.

31. McCurdy, *Anti-Rent Era*, 119, 200.

32. McCurdy, *Anti-Rent Era*, 172–173.

33. Huston, *Land and Freedom*, 181–186.

34. Quoted in McCurdy, *Anti-Rent Era*, 4. McCurdy, *Anti-Rent Era*, 5–7.

35. William Cullen Bryant, *New York Evening Post*, Dec. 18 and 23, 1844, quoted in McCurdy, *Anti-Rent Era*, 167.

36. Marc Levitt and Lilach Dekel's film, *Stories in Stone*, documents Narragansett stone masons talking about their construction methods and the meanings that they attribute to their structures. See also the photographs appended to the National Register of Historic Places Inventory for the "Former reservation of the Narragansett Tribe of Indians," Washington County, Rhode Island (1973), http://www.preservation.ri.gov/pdfs_zips_downloads/national_pdfs/charlestown/char_historic-village-of-the-narragansetts.pdf. For a broader view of historical placemaking and survivance in Narragansett country, see DeLucia, *Memory Lands*, 164–200.

37. Rae Gould, Eric Johnson, and Betsy Friedberg, National Register of Historic Places Registration Form for the "Hassanamisco Reservation," Worcester County, Massachusetts (2011), https://www.nps.gov/nr/feature/indian/2011/Hassanamisco.pdf.

38. Roderic H. Blackburn and Ruth Piwonka, *Remembrance of Patria: Dutch Arts and Culture in Colonial America, 1609–1776* (Albany: Albany Institute of History and Art, 1988), 62, 71–73.

39. Upjohn worked on the Van Rensselaer manor house from 1840 to 1844. Everard M. Upjohn, *Richard Upjohn: Architect and Churchman* (New York: Columbia University Press, 1939), 68, 93, 137, 207.

40. Stoll, *Larding the Lean Earth*, 20–24, 89–91.

41. Andrew Jackson Downing, *A Treatise on the Theory and Practice of Landscape Gardening Adapted to North America* (New York: Wiley and Putnam, 1841), 300–301; Downing, *Cottage Residences; or, A Series of Designs for Rural Cottages and Cottage-Villas, and their Gardens and Grounds—Adapted to North America.* (New York: Wiley and Putnam, 1842), 16; Dell Upton, "Pattern Books and Professionalism: Aspects of the Transformation of Domestic Architecture in America, 1800–1860," *Winterthur Portfolio* 19:2/3 (Summer–Autumn 1984), 118–119.

42. Downing, *Treatise*, viii. All citations from the first edition (1841) unless otherwise noted.

43. Downing, *Cottage Residences*, i, 34; Downing, *Treatise*, 67; Adam Sweeting, *Reading Houses and Building Books: Andrew Jackson Downing and the Architecture of Popular Antebellum Literature, 1835–1855* (Hanover: University Press of New England, 1996), 17–18.

44. James Pemberton Morris, "Address Delivered before the Agricultural Society of Bucks County" (Philadelphia: Clark and Raser, 1823), 12, quoted in Stoll, *Larding the Lean Earth*, 86. Andrew Jackson Downing quoted Alexis de Tocqueville's *Democracy in America* when discussing the particular qualities of U.S. citizens. Downing, *Treatise*, iii, viii–ix; David Schuyler, *Apostle of Taste: Andrew Jackson Downing, 1815–1852* (Baltimore: Johns Hopkins University Press, 1996), 54–55; Stoll, *Larding the Lean Earth*, esp. 19–25, 84–91, 199–202.

45. Downing, *Treatise*, 1st ed., (1841), 24.

46. Downing, *Treatise*, 2nd ed., (1844), 356.

47. Downing, *Treatise*, 4th ed., (1849), 50.

48. On the genealogical mode of viewing land, see Tim Ingold, *The Perception of the Environment: Essays in Livelihood, Dwelling, and Skill* (London: Routledge, 2000), 132–151.

49. Downing defined Americans as descendants of "English stock," for instance. Downing, *Treatise*, ii.

50. Timothy Pickering, "The Family of the Pickerings of Massachusetts," box 10, Pickering Family Papers (MSS 400), Phillips Library (hereafter Pickering Papers); Richard C. Armstrong,

The House That John Built: Ten Generations of the Pickering Family of Salem (Salem: Private Press, 2010), 117. For more on Pickering's antiquarian pursuits, see Mary Orne Pickering, *Life of John Pickering* (Boston: private printing, 1887), 334, 409, 424, 449, 453.

51. Dendrochronology and written evidence suggest that John Pickering II (a housewright like his father) built the house in 1664 and made additions in 1681 and 1682. "Pickering House," Massachusetts Cultural Resource Information System, inventory SAL.1044, http://mhc-macris.net.

52. Timothy Pickering, "The Family of the Pickerings of Massachusetts," box 10, Pickering Papers; "Pickering House," Massachusetts Cultural Resource Information System, inventory SAL.1044, http://mhc-macris.net.

53. Armstrong, *House That John Built*, 79, 99.

54. Armstrong, *House That John Built*, 135, 502, 519.

55. St. Peter's Episcopal (1833) and First Unitarian Church (1836) in Salem featured quatrefoil windows. Bryant F. Tolles, *Architecture in Salem: An Illustrated Guide* (Hanover: University Press of New England, 2004), 113–114; Henry-Russell Hitchcock, *Architecture: Nineteenth and Twentieth Centuries* (New Haven: Yale University Press, 1977), 155–156.

56. Downing's book was available in Salem before May of that year. Downing, *Treatise*, 62–63, 302–304, 328; "New Work on Gardening," *Salem Register*, May 13, 1841, p. 4.

57. "Pickering House," Massachusetts Cultural Resource Information System, inventory SAL.1044, http://mhc-macris.net; Elisa Tamarkin, *Anglophilia: Deference, Devotion, and Early America* (Chicago: University of Chicago Press, 2008), 69–71.

58. "Salem Improvements," *Salem Gazette*, June 29, 1841, p. 2.

59. Downing, *Treatise*, 331. See also Downing, *Cottage Residences*, 33.

60. Joseph B. Felt, *Annals of Salem*, 2nd ed., vol. 1 (Salem: W. and S. B. Ives, 1845), 411.

61. Felt, *Annals of Salem*, 2nd ed., vol. 1, 412–413.

62. Linden, *Silent City on a Hill*, 29–79, 293–294; Upton, *Another City*, 203–205.

63. Americans drew on eighteenth-century ideals of English picturesque gardens and Père Lachaise cemetery in Paris. David Schuyler, *The New Urban Landscape: The Redefinition of City Form in Nineteenth-Century America* (Baltimore: Johns Hopkins University Press, 1986), 37–58; Linden, *Silent City on a Hill*, 29–79, 293–294; Downing, *Treatise*, 308–311.

64. Charter, By-Laws and Regulations of the Woodlands Cemetery Company (1845 ed.), quoted in Aaron V. Wunsch, "Woodlands Cemetery," HALS PA-5, 128. See also Milroy, *Grid and the River*, 127–132; "An Act to Incorporate the Rose Family Burying Ground," *Laws of the General Assembly of the Commonwealth of Pennsylvania* (Harrisburg: Theo. Fenn, 1853), 726–729; Aaron V. Wunsch, "Addendum to Laurel Hill Cemetery," HABS PA 51–PHILA 100 (1999).

65. Henry Dearborn, "Mount Auburn Cemetery," *North American Review* 33 (Oct. 1831), 397–398.

66. "Monticello and the University of Virginia," *Salem Gazette*, Nov. 26, 1841, p. 2.

67. "Salem Improvements," *Salem Gazette*, June 29, 1841, p. 2; Tamara Plakins Thornton, *Cultivating Gentlemen: The Meaning of Country Life Among the Boston Elite* (New Haven: Yale University Press, 1989), 43–45, 60, 128–129; Felt, *Annals of Salem*, 2nd ed., vol. 1, 411; John W. Proctor, "Memoir of Colonel Pickering," *Cultivator* 8:3 (Mar. 1851), 100–102; Armstrong, *House That John Built*, 121.

68. Daniel Appleton White, "Eulogy of John Pickering, LL.D." (Cambridge: Metcalf and Company, 1847), 6.

69. John Collins Warren, diary, July 11, 1846 (vol. 82), Mar. 24 and 25, 1847 (vol. 83), Warren Papers. A transcription of the tablets appeared in "Gen. Warren House," *Gleason's Pictorial Drawing Room Companion*, June 28, 1851, 132.

70. This was the second time that Warren exhumed and reinterred the body of his uncle Joseph Warren. His son Jonathan Mason Warren took three photographs of the skull to preserve its appearance for posterity. Though John Collins Warren's name also appears on a gravestone in the Forest Hills family plot, he willed his body to Massachusetts General Hospital for study. Linden, *Silent City on a Hill*, 122–123, 294, 312; Warren, diary, Sept. 18, 1849, vol. 86, Warren Papers; Anthony M. Sammarco, "Dr. John Collins Warren," Forest Hills Educational Trust http://foresthillstrust.blogspot.com/2010/03/dr-john-collins-warren.html, accessed Aug. 5, 2012; Howard Payson Arnold, *Memoir of Dr. Jonathan Mason Warren, M.D.* (Boston: Boston University Press, 1886), 245.

71. The house appears most similar to Design IV in Downing's *Cottage Residences* (verso 88) based on the author's inspection of the extant house's footprint and ground-level floor plan in May 2014. Warren also purchased D. J. Browne's *The Trees of America* at the same time. Warren, diary, Aug. 19, Aug. 29, 1846, vol. 82, Warren Papers.

72. Bureau of the Census, U.S. Federal Census, 1850, Roxbury, Norfolk County, Massachusetts, p. 141; "Plan of Part of the Warren Estate in Roxbury" (Boston: Meisel Brothers Lithography, n.d. (1858?)), box 1 oversize, Warren Papers.

73. Warren, diary, Sept. 18, 1849, vol. 86, Warren Papers.

74. Andrew J. Downing, "The Multiplication of Horticultural Societies," *Horticulturist and Journal of Rural Art and Rural Taste* 2:1 (July 1847), 11.

75. Warren, diary, Sept. 18, 1849, vol. 86; Jan. 27, 1851, and Feb. 12, 1851, vol. 89, Warren Papers; John Collins Warren, *Genealogy of Warren* (Boston: Printed by John Wilson and Son, 1854), 42–45.

76. Alfred Thompson Bricher, "Warren House Roxbury," water color and graphite on paper, 1858, Boston Museum of Fine Arts (61.262).

77. On homecoming festivals, see Sarah L. Giffen and Kevin D. Murphy, eds., '*A Noble and Dignified Stream': The Piscataqua Region in the Colonial Revival, 1860–1930* (York: Old York Historical Society, 1992), 21–23; Ulrich, *Age of Homespun*, 11–40.

78. "The Old House at Home," *Cleveland Herald*, May 30, 1844, p. 3. The title of this article refers to the song by Thomas Haynes Bayly that became popular in Europe and America in the second quarter of the nineteenth century.

79. Henry Clay to John Cleves Short, June 16, 1851, in *Papers of Henry Clay*, ed. Melba Porter Hay and Carol Reardon, vol. 10 (Lexington: University of Kentucky Press, 1991), 898.

80. Putnam, *Homes of American Authors*, 140.

81. "The Oldest Town," *Salem Observer*, June 22, 1839, p. 2; Henry Miller, *Account of the Tour of the California Missions and Towns* (Santa Barbara: Bellerophon, 1856; 1987), 3, 5, 9, 13, 19, 33, 35, 37, 42, 55, 59; George R. Fairbanks, *The History and Antiquities of the City of St. Augustine, Florida, Founded A. D. 1565: Comprising some of the most interesting portions of the Early History of Florida* (New York: Charles B. Norton, 1858), 9–10.

82. R. K. Sewall, *Sketches of St. Augustine: With a View of its History and Advantages as a Resort for Invalids* (New York: George P. Putnam, 1848), 11–12, 17.

83. William Prescott argued that the Castilians descended from Visigoths and thus inherited the Roman disposition for liberty. In his view, the absolutism of the Catholic Church weakened Spanish society and empire and resulted in degenerate, racially mixed populations of their former colonies. David Levin, *History as Romantic Art: Bancroft, Prescott, Motley, and Parkman* (New York: AMS, 1967), 75–78, 93–96; Iván Jaksic, *The Hispanic World and American Intellectual Life* (New York: Palgrave Macmillan, 2007), 125–160.

84. McCurdy, *Anti-Rent Era*, 15–16.

85. McCurdy, *Anti-Rent Era*, 29.

86. Downing, *Treatise*, 4th ed. (1849), 50.

87. McCurdy, *Anti-Rent Era*, 308–309.

88. Armstrong, *House That John Built*, 100–106, 141. Salem gained five thousand residents in the 1840s. In 1850, it had over twenty thousand residents and ranked thirty-fourth in size of U.S. cities. Campbell Gibson, "Population of the 100 Largest Cities and Other Urban Places in the United States: 1790 to 1990," U.S. Bureau of the Census, www.census.gov/population /www/documentation/twps0027/twps0027.html.

89. Felt, *Annals of Salem*, vol. 1, 412–413.

90. John R. Stilgoe, *Borderland: Origins of the American Suburb, 1820–1939* (New Haven: Yale University Press, 1988), 69–77.

91. See, e.g., "The Old Brewery, and the New Mission House at Five Points" (New York: Stringer and Townsend, 1854), 45.

92. Warren, *Life of John Collins Warren*, vol. 1, 9.

93. Thornton, *Cultivating Gentlemen*, 141–145, 164, 167–168.

94. Lucius Manlius Sargent to Henry Wheatland, Mar. 29, 1845, box 1, Henry Wheatland Papers, Phillips Library.

95. The burden of this standard fell heavily on people of color and recent immigrants with few resources, particularly Irish workers. Brown, *Foul Bodies*, 284, 291, 326.

96. Cotting was a real estate agent for a firm called the Fifty Associates. Amos Cotting to John Collins Warren, Aug. 4, 1845, box 11, Warren Papers; Bureau of the Census, U.S. Federal Census, 1850, Brookline, Norfolk County, MA, p. 76; Nathan Crosby, *Annual Obituary Notices of Eminent Persons Who Have Died in the United States for 1857* (Boston: Phillips, Sampson, 1858), 103.

97. Construction proceeded steadily throughout 1846, and Warren saw the finished product for the first time in March 1847. Warren, diary, May 14, 1846; Sept. 18 and Sept. 23, 1846, vol. 82; Mar. 24, 1847, vol. 83, Warren Papers.

98. Warren, diary, Aug. 19, Aug. 29, 1846, vol. 82, Warren Papers.

99. Bureau of the Census, U.S. Federal Census, 1850, Roxbury, Norfolk County, Massachusetts, p. 141; George Adams, *The Roxbury Directory* (Roxbury: Bicknell, 1852), 37; "Plan of Part of the Warren Estate in Roxbury," Warren Papers; Sampson Davenport, *The Roxbury Directory* (Roxbury: John Backup, 1866), 34.

100. "Moreland Street Historic District," Suffolk County, Mass., National Register of Historic Places Nomination Form (1983), item 8, page 2.

101. Roxbury doubled in population in the 1840s. In 1850, Roxbury was the thirty-sixth largest city in the United States, with a population of more than 18,000 people. Henry Binford, *First Suburbs: Residential Communities on the Boston Periphery, 1815–1860* (Chicago: University of Chicago Press, 1985), 11–12, 134.

102. Warren, diary, May 11, 1847, vol. 83, Warren Papers; William B. Kingsbury of Board of Alderman, City of Roxbury, to [Warren?], May 10, 1847, box 11, Warren Papers; "Plan of Part of the Warren Estate in Roxbury," Warren Papers.

103. "Suburban Residences," *Ballou's Pictorial Drawing-Room Companion* 8:24 (June 16, 1855), 376.

104. "Suburban Residences."

105. "Plan of Part of the Warren Estate in Roxbury," Warren Papers.

106. White, "Eulogy of John Pickering, LL.D.," 6.

107. Mary Orne Pickering, *Life of John Pickering* (Cambridge: Cambridge University Press, 1887), vi.

108. "Mrs. Jane T. Paine," *Maine Farmer*, May 24, 1860, p. 2; "A Revolutionary 'Relict' Gone," (San Francisco) *Daily Evening Bulletin*, June 5, 1860, p. 1.

109. Blackburn and Piwonka, *Remembrance of Patria*, 77.

110. Sarah M. Dreller, Fiona L. Robertson, and Martha L. Teall, "Meriwether House (Cloverfields)," unpublished manuscript, 1997, Small Special Collections, University of Virginia.

111. Francis Kinloch Nelson, journal, vol. 2, 72, Small Special Collections, University of Virginia. Meriwether family descendants still own the daguerreotype. For more on daguerreotypes as a mode of preservation, see Martinko, "Worthy of Being Thus Preserved," 37–58.

112. It is possible that the house was made from the relics that John Collins Warren collected when he visited the old house for the last time. Warren, diary, May 21, 1846, vol. 82, Warren Papers.

113. James Spear Loring, *The Hundred Boston Orators Appointed by the Municipal Authorities and Other Public Bodies, from 1770 to 1852* (Boston: John P. Jewett, 1852), 47. See also Richard Frothingham, *Life and Times of Joseph Warren* (Boston: Little, Brown, 1865), 7.

114. Warren House miniature model and curatorial files (object #62, old #168), collections of the Old South Meetinghouse, Boston; *Catalog of the Loan Collection of Revolutionary Relics*, 5th ed. (Boston: George H. Ellis, 1876), 12.

115. Edwin Whitefield, *Homes of Our Forefathers, in Boston, Old England and Boston, New England* (Boston: Damrell and Upham, 1889), 52.

116. [Rebecca Warren Brown], "Preface," in *Tales of the Emerald Isle; or, Legends of Ireland* (New York: W. Borradaile, 1828), n.p.

117. Joseph Palmer, *Necrology of Alumni of Harvard College, 1851–52 to 1862–63* (Boston: John Wilson and Son, 1864), 9–10.

118. Charles Moses Endicott to Mrs. Jonathan Ingersoll, Dec. 2, 1839, box 1, Endicott Family Papers, Phillips Library.

119. Stephen Gould to John Howland, Oct. 13, 1835, box 1, Bull Papers.

120. Bert Joseph Griswold, *The Pictorial History of Fort Wayne, Indiana* (Chicago: Robert O. Law, 1917), 143.

121. Charles F. Briggs, "Franklin," in Putnam, *Homes of American Statesmen*, 68.

122. Warren, *Life of John Collins Warren*, 219.

123. *Boston Journal*, Sat. Evening, May 23, 1846, p. 2; (Boston) *Daily Atlas*, May 25, 1846, p. 2.

124. "Affairs in and about the City," (Boston) *Daily Atlas*, Aug. 20, 1852, p. 2; Judith M. Jacob, "The Washington Monument: A Technical History and Catalog of the Commemorative Stones" ([Lowell, MA]: National Park Service, U.S. Department of the Interior, 2005), 80.

125. "Glorious Whig Gathering in Old Norfolk," (Boston) *Daily Atlas*, Oct. 7, 1852, p. 2.

126. "Ashland for Sale," (Concord) *New Hampshire Statesman*, Sept. 3, 1853, p. 2; David S. Heidler and Jeanne T. Heidler, *Henry Clay: The Essential American* (New York: Random House, 2011), 484.

127. As one writer to the *Daily Cincinnati Gazette* put it in 1854, "Ashland has often been described by abler pens than ours, and its name has gone forth to the ends of the earth." "Henry Clay's Home and Grave," *Daily Cincinnati Gazette*, Sept. 26, 1854, p. 3.

128. G. E. D., "Ashland," *Daily Cincinnati Gazette*, Oct. 2, 1854, p. 1.

129. Horace Greeley, "Clay," in Putnam, *Homes of American Statesmen*, 378.

130. Calvin Colton, *The Life and Times of Henry Clay*, vol. 1 (New York: A. S. Barnes, 1846), 42. These sentences appeared in multiple editions throughout the 1840s and 1850s and in posthumous memorials to Clay. See, e.g., "Monument to Henry Clay," *Gleason's Pictorial Drawing-Room Companion* 4:2 (Jan. 8, 1853), 32.

131. James L. Crouthemel, *Bennett's New York Herald and the Rise of the Popular Press* (Syracuse: Syracuse University Press, 1989); Henkin, *City Reading*, 105–135.

132. "The Home of Henry Clay," (Columbus) *Ohio State Journal*, Sept. 20, 1853, p. 2.

133. "The Residence of Henry Clay at Public Auction," (New York City) *Weekly Herald*, Sept. 10, 1853, p. 293.

134. Executors auctioned off Ashland on September 20, 1853. "Ashland," *Daily* (Columbus) *Ohio Statesman*, Sept. 24, 1853, p. 2; "Ashland," *Daily Cleveland Herald*, Sept. 27, 1853, p. 2; "Sale of Ashland," *Trenton State Gazette*, Sept. 27, 1853, p. 2; "Ashland," *Daily* (Raleigh) *Register*, Oct. 1, 1853, p. 3; "Sale of Ashland," *Fayetteville Observer*, Oct. 3, 1853, p. 2; "Ashland," (Milwaukee) *Daily Sentinel*, Oct. 3, 1853, p. 2; "Ashland," *Daily Alabama Journal*, Oct. 5, 1853, p. 2; "Ashland," (Hannibal) *Missouri Courier*, Oct. 6, 1853, p. 2; "Ashland," *Pittsfield Massachusetts Sun*, Oct. 6, 1853, p. 3; "The Ashland Estate," *Liberator*, Oct. 7, 1853, p. 159; "Ashland," (Philadelphia) *North American and United States Gazette*, Oct. 14, 1853, p. 1; "The homestead of the late Henry Clay," (Salt Lake City) *Deseret News*, Dec. 1, 1853, p. 3.

135. Clay had moved to Ashland and planned to purchase the estate in coming months. Judge [Brederode?] to Mrs. Susan Clay, Mar. 8, 1853, box 42, HCFP.

136. As his brother-in-law put it seven months earlier, the "old house . . . too will soon be remembered among the things that were." Thomas Jacob to Susan Clay, Feb. 9, 1854, box 42, HCFP.

137. "Henry Clay's Home and Grave," *Daily Cincinnati Gazette*, Sept. 26, 1854, p. 3. Reprinted in *Daily Cleveland Herald*, Sept. 27, 1854, p. 2; *Baltimore Sun*, Sept. 29, 1854, p. 1; *Daily* (Chillicothe) *Scioto Gazette*, Oct. 2, 1854, p. 2; (Washington, DC) *Daily Globe*, Oct. 3, 1854, p. 3; *New York Times*, Oct. 3, 1854, p. 8; (Washington, DC) *Sentinel*, Oct. 4, 1854, p. 2; *New Hampshire Statesman*, Oct. 7, 1854, p. 3; (Auburn, NY) *Cayuga Chief*, Oct. 10, 1854, p. 1; (Worcester, MA) *National Aegis*, Oct. 11, 1854, p. 4; *Norwich Courier*, Oct. 11, 1854, p. 2; *Wisconsin Patriot*, Oct. 21, 1854, p. 2; *Rutland County Herald*, Nov. 3, 1854, p. 1; *Easton Star*, Nov. 14, 1854, p. 1. See also "Ashland Dismantled," *Trenton State Gazette*, Oct. 2, 1854, p. 2.

138. "Ashland," *Weekly Raleigh Register*, Oct. 11, 1854, p. 2. During Henry Clay's lifetime, many observers saw the estate as a working model of the political economy that he promoted. Daniel Walker Howe, *The Political Culture of the American Whigs* (Chicago: University of Chicago Press, 1979), 130.

139. On shifting party alliances in the 1850s, see Michael F. Holt, *The Rise and Fall of the American Whig Party* (Oxford: Oxford University Press, 1999), 765–985.

140. James B. Clay to Charles B. Calvert and Philip Fendall, Jan. 3, 1853, box 42, HCFP; Susan Clay to Thomas Jacob, June 16, 1853, box 42, HCFP.

141. James B. Clay to George Prentice, July 14, 1855, in "To the Public," ed. James B. Clay ([Lexington?]: private printing, 1855), 4, box 43, HCFP. James B. Clay printed this pamphlet to defend himself against George Prentice's charges. He included excerpts of both men's letters printed in the *Louisville Journal*.

142. For more on the construction of the Ashland estate before 1853, see Michael Fazio and Patrick Snadon, *The Domestic Architecture of Benjamin Henry Latrobe* (Baltimore: Johns Hopkins University Press, 2006), 579, 655–666.

143. Lewinski also designed houses for Henry Clay's sons, including James B. Clay, in the mid-1840s. Clay Lancaster, "Major Thomas Lewinski: Émigré Architect in Kentucky," *Journal of the Society of Architectural Historians* 11:4 (Dec. 1952), 13–20.

144. "Ashland As It Was," *Cincinnati Gazette*, July 4, 1857, p. 1.

145. "Ashland As It Was;" and Eric Brooks, *Ashland: The Henry Clay Estate* (Charleston: Arcadia, 2007), 36–37. For more on furnishings for the new house, see Robert Spiotta, "Remembering Father: James Brown Clay, Merchants, Material, and a New Ashland," MA thesis, Cooper-Hewitt Museum/Parsons School of Design, New York City, 1990, 36–84.

146. McInnis, *Politics of Taste in Antebellum Charleston*, 195–239.

147. "A Visit to Ashland," *Times Picayune*, Nov. 5, 1854, p. 2. See also "A Vulgarism," *New York Times*, July 23, 1855, p. 4.

148. This print is colored with the green shutters of the old house but the red brick of the new house. Written descriptions and depictions of the old house described white-washed walls. John Sartain, "Ashland" (Philadelphia, 1853), item 1985.6, Kentucky Historical Society.

149. "Henry Clay's Home and Grave," *Daily Cincinnati Gazette*, Sept. 26, 1854, p. 3. See also "Ashland," *Weekly Raleigh Register*, Oct. 11, 1854, p. 2.

150. Newspaper editors across the country carried reports of the dispute: "James B. Clay and 'Ashland,'" *Baltimore Sun*, July 21, 1855, p. 1; "Henry Clay's Family Mansion—Letter from His Son," *New York Times*, July 21, 1855, p. 6; "The Demolition of Ashland—Reply of the *Louisville Journal* to Mr. Clay," *New York Times*, July 24, 1855, p. 5; "James B. Clay," *New-Hampshire Patriot*, July 25, 1855, p. 2; "Henry Clay's Family Mansion—Letter from His Son," *Daily* (Savannah) *Morning News*, July 25, 1855, p. 1; "Mr. James B. Clay," *Weekly Raleigh Register*, July 25, 1855, p. 3; "Sacrilege," *Cleveland Daily Herald*, July 26, 1855, p. 2; "Mr. James B. Clay," *Chicago Times*, July 26, 1855, p. 2; "Henry Clay's Residence at Ashland," *New York Observer and Chronicle*, July 26, 1855 (33:30), p. 238; "James B. Clay and George D. Prentice—Interesting Correspondence" and "Mr. Clay Belligerent," *New York Times,* Aug. 2, 1855, p. 2; "James B. Clay and George D. Prentice," *Baltimore Sun,* Aug. 2, 1855, p. 1; "James B. Clay and George D. Prentice," *Boston Daily Advertiser*, Aug. 3, 1855, p. 1; "Kentucky Chivalry!" *Daily Cleveland Herald*, Aug. 1, 1855, p. 1; "Challenge Refused," (Savannah) *Daily Morning News*, Aug. 6, 1855, p. 2.

151. George D. Prentice wrote *The Biography of Henry Clay* (Hartford: Hanmer and Phelps, 1831), which went through multiple editions that year. Michael F. Holt describes the circumstances of the split between Kentucky Whigs who sympathized with Know-Nothing principles, such as Prentice and Thomas Hart Clay, and men who rejected them for old Whig principles, such as James B. Clay. See Holt, *Rise and Fall*, 936–937.

152. George Prentice to James B. Clay, July 21, 1855, in "To the Public," 7, box 43, HCFP.

153. "James B. Clay," *Daily Cleveland Herald*, July 24, 1856, p. 2; "James B. Clay," *Ohio State Journal*, July 30, 1856, p. 3. See also "Slaveholding Stumpers in Ohio," *Daily Cleveland Herald*, Sept. 5, 1856, p. 2.

154. "Mr. Jas. B. Clay's Letter," *Louisville Evening Bulletin*, July 18, 1855, p. 1. Emphasis in original.

155. On Clay's speech at Ashland, see "Son of Henry Clay on the Stump," *New York Daily Tribune*, July 19, 1855, p. 6; "A Voice from Ashland," *Semi-Weekly* (Jackson) *Mississippian*, July 27, 1855, p. 2.

156. "The Clay Whigs—James B. Clay, Son of Henry Clay," *Daily Ohio Statesman*, Aug. 5, 1856, p. 2; "Speech of Mr. James B. Clay," *Macon Weekly Telegraph*, Aug. 12, 1856, p. 2; "James B. Clay," *Ohio State Journal*, Sept. 17, 1856, p. 1; "Among the Political Schemes," *Ohio State Journal*, Oct. 22, 1856, p. 2.

157. "Speech of James B. Clay," *Baltimore Sun*, Aug. 23, 1856, p. 2.

158. "Letter from Henry Clay's Widow—Her Defence of Her Son," *New York Times*, Sept. 26, 1856, p. 2.

159. "James B. Clay and George D. Prentice," *Baltimore Sun*, Aug. 2, 1855, p. 1.

160. James B. Clay, letter to the public, July 24, 1855, in "To the Public," 1, box 43, HCFP.

161. James B. Clay to George Prentice, July 14, 1855, in "To the Public," 4, box 43, HCFP.

162. James B. Clay to George Prentice, July 14, 1855, in "To the Public," 5, box 43, HCFP.

163. "Laying of the Corner-Stone of the Clay Monument," *Baltimore Sun*, July 8, 1857, p. 1; "A Pilgrimage to Ashland," *Pittsfield* (Massachusetts) *Sun*, July 23, 1857, p. 1; "A Pilgrimage to Ashland," (Philadelphia) *Press*, Oct. 8, 1857, p. 1.

164. "A Day or Two in Fayette," *Cultivator* 5:1 (Jan. 1857), 11.

165. Putnam, *Homes of American Authors*, 337.

166. "Ashland As It Was."

167. "Ashland As It Was."

168. James B. Clay to Charles Anderson, Nov. 5, 1855, box 43, HCFP.

169. James B. Clay bought and sold enslaved people as a means of financial speculation. Henry Clay, Last Will and Testament, July 10, 1851, in Hay and Readon, *Papers of Henry Clay*, vol. 10, 900–904; "Mr. Clay's Family, etc.," *Pittsfield* (Massachusetts) *Sun*, July 29, 1852, p. 1; "Ashland for Sale," (Concord) *New Hampshire Statesman*, Sept. 3, 1853, p. 2; "The Lexington Observer," (Chillicothe) *Daily Scioto Gazette*, Sept. 3, 1853, p. 2; Lindsey Apple, *The Family Legacy of Henry Clay: In the Shadow of a Kentucky Patriarch* (Lexington: University of Kentucky Press, 2011), 101.

170. Susan Clay to Lucy Jacob, Oct. 29 1855, box 43, HCFP.

171. Heidler and Heidler, *Henry Clay*, 217–218; Apple, *Family Legacy of Henry Clay*, 142.

172. "Laying on the Corner Stone of the Clay Monument at Lexington," (Raleigh) *Biblical Reporter*, Aug. 20, 1857, p. 3; "Summary of News," *Philadelphia Inquirer*, Feb. 24, 1866, p. 2.

173. On the erasure of slavery with agricultural reform, see Philip Mills Herrington, "Agricultural and Architectural Reform in the Antebellum South: Fruitland at Augusta, Georgia," *Journal of Southern History* 78:4 (Nov. 2012), 855–866.

174. "Mr. Jas. B. Clay's Letter," *Louisville Evening Bulletin*, July 18, 1855, p. 1.

Epilogue

1. [Ann Pamela Cunningham], "To the Ladies of the South," (Charleston) *Mercury*, Dec. 2, 1853.

2. See, e.g., "Mount Vernon," (Middletown, CT) *Constitution*, July 6, 1853, p. 2; "Sale of Mount Vernon," *New York Weekly Herald*, Aug. 13, 1853, p. 261; "Mount Vernon," (New Orleans) *Daily Picayune*, Aug. 17, 1853, p. 2.

3. On the Mount Vernon Ladies' Association as mediators of sectional tensions and party politics, see West, *Domesticating History*, 1–37; Elizabeth R. Varon, *We Mean to Be Counted: White Women and Politics in Antebellum Virginia* (Chapel Hill: University of North Carolina Press, 1998), 124–136; Steven Conn, "Rescuing the Homestead of the Nation: The Mount Vernon Ladies' Association and the Preservation of Mount Vernon," *Nineteenth-Century Studies* 11 (1997), 71–94; Matthew Mason, "'The Sacred Ashes of the First of Men': Edward Everett, The Mount Vernon Ladies Association of the Union, and Late Antebellum Unionism," in McDonnell, Corbould, Clarke, and Brundage, *Remembering the Revolution*, 265–279.

4. On memory of the American Revolution and sectional politics, see Michael Morrison, *Slavery and the American West: The Eclipse of Manifest Destiny and the Coming of the Civil War* (Chapel Hill: University of North Carolina Press, 1997), 252–279; and Sarah J. Purcell, "Martyred Blood and Avenging Spirits: Revolutionary Martyrs and Heroes as Inspiration for the U.S. Civil War," in McDonnell, Corbould, Clarke, and Brundage, *Remembering the Revolution*, 280–293.

5. Jane C. Washington to John A. Washington, Dec. 13, 1846, quoted in Lee, "Jane C. Washington," 44.

6. Scott E. Casper, *Sarah Johnson's Mount Vernon: The Forgotten History of an American Shrine* (New York: Hill and Wang, 2008), 64–67; Jean B. Lee, "Historical Memory, Sectional Strife, and the American Mecca: Mount Vernon, 1783–1853," *Virginia Magazine of History and Biography* 109:3 (2001), 287, 291–292; "John Augustine Washington, III," George Washington Digital Encyclopedia, https://www.mountvernon.org/library/digitalhistory/digital-encyclopedia/article/john-augustine-washington-iii/#2.

7. Ann Pamela Cunningham to Mrs. John A. Washington, Dec. 19, 1853, box 14, MVLAER.

8. Mrs. John A. Washington to Ann Pamela Cunningham, Jan. 10, 1854, box 14, MVLAER.

9. Milward referred to a notice in the Philadelphia *Evening Bulletin* of April 29, 1854. Elizabeth Whitney Milward to Ann Pamela Cunningham, June 14, 1854, box 14, MVLAER. See also Elizabeth Whitney Milward to Ann Pamela Cunningham, Aug. 8 1854, box 14, MV-LAER; Elizabeth Whitney Milward to Ann Pamela Cunningham, Dec. 23, 1855, box 15, MV-LAER; Elizabeth Whitney Milward to Ann Pamela Cunningham, Jan. 14, 1857, box 17, MVLAER.

10. William H. MacFarland to Ann Pamela Cunningham, Mar. 4, 1854, box 14, MVLAER.

11. Constitution of the Virginia State Committee of the MVLA, July 1854, box 3, MVLAER.

12. Minutes of Richmond meeting, July 12, 1854, box 4, MVLAER; Report of Council meeting from Journal of Mrs. Susan Pellet, 1854, box 5, MVLAER.

13. John H. Gilmer to Ann Pamela Cunningham, July 22, 1854, box 14, MVLAER; see also John H. Gilmer to Ann Pamela Cunningham, Aug. 4, 1854, box 14, MVLAER.

14. John H. Gilmer to Ann Pamela Cunningham, July 21, 1854, box 14, MVLAER.

15. Ann Pamela Cunningham to John H. Gilmer, Dec. 19, 1854, box 14, MVLAER; Ann Pamela Cunningham to John H. Gilmer, Jan. 13, 1855, box 14, MVLAER; Ann Pamela Cunningham to John H. Gilmer, Jan. 25, 1855, box 14, MVLAER; Ann Pamela Cunningham to John H. Gilmer, Jan. 29, 1855, box 14, MVLAER.

16. John H. Gilmer to Ann Pamela Cunningham, June 21, 1854, box 14, MVLAER.

17. See, e.g., "An Appeal from Mount Vernon," (Brattleboro) *Vermont Phoenix*, July 28, 1855, p. 1.

18. John H. Gilmer to Ann Pamela Cunningham, July 22, 1854, box 14, MVLAER.

19. Ann Pamela Cunningham to John H. Gilmer, Jan. 13, 1855, box 14, MVLAER.

20. Anna Cora Ritchie to Ann Pamela Cunningham, June 18, 1855, box 14, MVLAER.

21. H. C. Harrison to Ann Pamela Cunningham, Sept. 1, 1855, box 15, MVLAER.

22. Anna Maria Mead to Susan J. Adams, Nov. 6, 1855, box 15, MVLAER.

23. Anna Maria Mead to Ann Pamela Cunningham, Nov. 22, 1855, box 15, MVLAER.

24. H.C. Harrison to Ann Pamela Cunningham, Dec. 11, 1855, box 15, MVLAER.

25. O. W. Langfitt to Ann Pamela Cunningham, Feb. 5, 1856, box 15, MVLAER.

26. O. W. Langfitt to Ann Pamela Cunningham, Dec. 31, 1855, box 15, MVLAER; see also O. W. Langfitt to Ann Pamela Cunningham, Jan. 9, 1856, box 15, MVLAER.

27. O. W. Langfitt to Ann Pamela Cunningham, Jan. 9, 1856, box 15, MVLAER; Anna Cora Ritchie to Ann Pamela Cunningham, Feb. 19, 1856, box 15, MVLAER; O.W. Langfitt to Ann Pamela Cunningham, Feb. 20, 1856, box 15, MVLAER.

28. O. W. Langfitt to Ann Pamela Cunningham, Mar. 17, 1856, box 15, MVLAER.

29. Bill No. 147, Virginia state legislature, Jan. 18, 1856, box 3, MVLAER.

30. Anna Cora Ritchie to Ann Pamela Cunningham, June 28, 1855, box 14, MVLAER.

31. Anna Cora Ritchie to Ann Pamela Cunningham, Feb. 19, 1856, box 15, MVLAER.

32. Susan L. Pellet to Julia Cabell, Mar. 29, 1856, box 15, MVLAER.

33. Edward Everett to John R. Thompson, Feb. 26, 1856, box 15, MVLAER.

34. O. W. Langfitt to Ann Pamela Cunningham, Feb. 20, 1856, box 15, MVLAER.

35. Julia Cabell to Ann Pamela Cunningham, Apr. 18, 1856, box 16, MVLAER.

36. [Elizabeth] Walton to [Ann Pamela Cunningham], Apr. 8, 1856, box 16, MVLAER; see also Samuel B. Ruggles to Miss Ann Pamela Cunningham, Apr. 1856, box 16, MVLAER.

37. [Elizabeth] Walton to [Ann Pamela Cunningham], Apr. 10, 1856, box 16, MVLAER.

38. Cunningham herself recognized a model in Hale. Hale renewed her attempts to raise contributions for the completion of the lingering Bunker Hill Monument construction project in 1840. Her organization of women's fairs raised the bulk of funds needed to finish the

memorial in 1843. John H. Gilmer to Ann Pamela Cunningham, Aug. 4, 1854, box 14, MVLAER; Sarah Hale to Ann Pamela Cunningham, Jan. 16, 1857, box 17, MVLAER; [Sarah Hale], "Editor's Table," *Godey's Ladies Book* 21 (Nov. 1840), 237; Sarah J. Purcell, "Commemoration, Public Art, and the Changing Meaning of the Bunker Hill Monument," *Public Historian* 25:2 (Spring 2003), 66.

39. Delaware Appeals and Alabama Appeals, box 6, MVLAER.

40. Julia Gardiner Tyler to Anna Cora Ritchie, Feb. 11, 1856, Papers of Anna Cora Ogden Mowatt Ritchie, Small Special Collections, University of Virginia.

41. Elizabeth Whitney Milward to Ann Pamela Cunningham, Apr. 9, 1856, box 16, MVLAER.

42. Elizabeth M. Walton to Ann Pamela Cunningham, June 12, 1857, box 18, MVLAER.

43. M. B. Green to Ann Pamela Cunningham, May 6, 1856, box 16, MVLAER.

44. Form letter, MVLA, n.d., box 1, MVLAER.

45. Mary Rutledge Fogg to Ann Pamela Cunningham, Aug. 21, 1856, box 16, MVLAER.

46. Mary Rutledge Fogg to Ann Pamela Cunningham, July 30, 1856, box 16, MVLAER.

47. Ann Pamela Cunningham to John A. Washington, May 6, 1856, box 16, MVLAER; [Edward Everett] to [Ann Pamela Cunningham], May 7, 1856, box 16, MVLAER.; Edward Everett to Miss Ann Pamela Cunningham, July 18, 1856, box 16, MVLAER; John A. Washington to Ann Pamela Cunningham, Aug. 4/22, 1856, box 16, MVLAER.

48. Robert Toombs to Ann Pamela Cunningham, Aug. 11, 1856, box 16, MVLAER.

49. Edward Everett to [Ann Pamela Cunningham], May 24, 1856, box 16, MVLAER; O. W. Langfitt to Ann Pamela Cunningham, June 4, 1856, box 16, MVLAER.

50. James L. Huston, *The Panic of 1857 and the Coming of the Civil War* (Baton Rouge: Louisiana State University Press, 1987).

51. Act of Incorporation, Mar. 19, 1858, box 3, MVLAER.

52. Agreement between John A. Washington and Ann Pamela Cunningham, Apr. 6, 1858, box 1, MVLAER.

53. Form letter, n.d., box 1, MVLAER.

54. California Appeals, box 6, MVLAER; Contributions received from Maine, n.d., box 11, MVLAER; Form letter, n.d., box 1, MVLAER.

55. "An Appeal in behalf of Mount Vernon to the Children of the Public and Private Schools in the City of Wilmington," Delaware Appeals, box 6, MVLAER.

56. Copy of bill, O. W. Langfitt to Ann Pamela Cunningham, Dec. 31, 1855, box 15, MVLAER.

57. Ann Pamela Cunningham, note on membership, n.d., box 1, MVLAER.

58. Edward Everett, *The Mount Vernon Papers* (New York: Appleton, 1860) 9, [491].

59. Everett, *Mount Vernon Papers*, 3.

60. The essays were collected and published as *The Mount Vernon Papers* in 1860. Everett, *Mount Vernon Papers*, 9. On the political dimensions of Everett's engagement with historical commemoration and the MVLA, see Matthew Mason, *Apostle of Union: A Political Biography of Edward Everett* (Chapel Hill: University of North Carolina, 2016), 213–242.

61. Everett, *Mount Vernon Papers*, 23–28.

62. Everett wrote that original pieces of wood, a partial window, an interior door, and other small elements had been removed for safekeeping. E. L. Stone had saved the sign of the blue ball that had hung above the door to Franklin's birthplace. In May 2012, the author found herself standing under the oft-described sign in the exhibition "Benjamin Franklin: In Search of a Better World," Lawrence F. O'Brien Gallery, National Archives, Washington, D.C. The sign is owned by the Bostonian Society (catalog number 1909.0028). Everett, *Mount Vernon Papers*, 22, 31.

63. Everett, *Mount Vernon Papers*, 29–31.

64. Newspapers as far away as Hawaii advertised the Franklin essay. The *Honolulu Friend* encouraged Hawaiian newspapers to republish Everett's essays because their newspa-

pers were not subject to the U.S. copyright that the *Ledger* had secured for Everett's essays. "The Mount Vernon Papers," *Boston Daily Advertiser*, Jan. 7, 1859, p. 2; "The Mount Vernon Papers," *Honolulu Friend*, March 5, 1859, p. 20.

65. Everett, *Mount Vernon Papers*, 31.

66. Everett, *Mount Vernon Papers*, 5–8.

67. *Proceedings of the Massachusetts Historical Society*, vol. 10 (Boston: Massachusetts Historical Society, 1869), 470; Sparks, "Abolition in Silver Slippers," 111–112; Mason, *Apostle of Union*, 90–122, 211–242.

68. Thomas P. Rossiter, "Mount Vernon, Past and Present: What Shall Be Its Destiny?" *Crayon* 5:9 (Sept. 1858), 243.

69. Maurie McInnis, "The Most Famous Plantation of All: The Politics of Painting Mount Vernon," in *Landscape of Slavery: The Plantation in American Art*, ed. Angela Mack (Columbia: University of South Carolina Press, 2008), 101; Casper, *Sarah Johnson's Mount Vernon*, 66–67, 77; Eric Foner, *Free Soil, Free Labor, Free Men: The Ideology of the Republican Party Before the Civil War* (Oxford: Oxford University Press, 2005), 41–72.

70. Quoted from the *New York Tribune* in Casper, *Sarah Johnson's Mount Vernon*, 72–73.

71. Mason, *Apostle of Union*, 222.

72. Casper, *Sarah Johnson's Mount Vernon*, 103–106.

73. Tracy earned an annual salary of four hundred dollars, paid in monthly installments. Agreement between Sarah C. Tracy and Ann Pamela Cunningham, box 1, MVLAER.

74. Casper, *Sarah Johnson's Mount Vernon*, 79–106.

75. Nelson, *Ruin Nation*; Leon F. Litwack, *Been in the Storm So Long: The Aftermath of Slavery* (New York: Vintage, 1980); Jennifer Van Horn, "'The Dark Iconoclast': African-Americans' Artistic Resistance in the Civil War South," *Art Bulletin* 99:4 (Dec. 2017), 133–167.

76. T. O. H. P. Burnham, "Bostonians!" broadside (Boston, 1863), Historic New England, Boston.

77. J. P. Soule, stereographs of the Hancock House, c. 1863, Special Photos—Hancock House Collection, Historic New England, Boston.

78. Lorna Condon and Richard Nylander, "A Classic in the Annals of Vandalism," *Historic New England* 6 (Summer 2005), 3–8; Rebecca Bertrand, "Myth and Memory: The Legacy of the John Hancock House," MA thesis, University of Delaware, 2010.

79. The frame had been removed. Hancock house, Cartes de visite Collection, AAS.

80. "Report of the Committee, on the Authenticity of the Tradition of the First Church, Built in 1634," *Historical Collections of the Essex Institute* 2:3 (June 1860), 145.

81. Francis Peabody, George D. Phippen, A. C. Goodell, Ira J. Patch, and C. W. Upham, "Report of the Committee of the Essex Institute on the First Church of the Pilgrims: Rendered June 19 1865," Phillips Library.

82. Peabody et al., "Report of the Committee of the Essex Institute," Phillips Library.

83. Everett, *Mount Vernon Papers*, 3.

84. Opinion on John A. Washington's will, c. 1868, box 5, MVLAER; Ladies of the MVLA versus the heirs of John A. Washington, Nov. 6, 1868, box 2, MVLAER; Bill for title suit, Nov. 7, 1868, box 2, MVLAER.

85. Validation of Mount Vernon deed to W. Arthur Taylor, n.d., box 1, MVLAER; Deed of bargain and sale by W. Arthur Taylor, May 13, 1869, box 2, MVLAER.

86. Ann Pamela Cunningham to Secretary of Treasury, 1868, box 2, MVLAER.

87. Copy of the Will of Ann Pamela Cunningham, Apr. 13, 1871, box 5, MVLAER; Codicil to Will of Ann Pamela Cunningham, Mar. 31, 1875, box 5, MVLAER.

88. These rights were defined in individual acts of incorporation granted by state legislatures. Ginzberg, *Women and the Work of Benevolence*, 48–53.

89. Amy Dru Stanley, *From Bondage to Contract: Wage Labor, Marriage, and the Market in the Age of Slave Emancipation* (Cambridge: Cambridge University Press, 1998).

90. For more on preservation and progressivism in the late nineteenth century, see Lindgren, *Preserving the Old Dominion*; James M. Lindgren, *Preserving Historic New England: Preservation, Progressivism, and the Remaking of Memory* (New York: Oxford University Press, 1995); and Holleran, *Boston's "Changeful Times."*

91. On preservation and public history as a means of inclusion, see Stephanie Meeks with Kevin C. Murphy, *The Past and Future City: How Historic Preservation Is Reviving America's Communities* (Washington, DC: Island Press, 2016); Franklin D. Vagnone and Deborah E. Ryan, *Anarchist's Guide to Historic House Museums* (New York: Routledge, 2016); Blog Forum, "When Does Preservation Become Social Justice," National Trust for Historic Preservation (July 2017), https://forum.savingplaces.org/blogs/forum-online/2017/07/26/blog-series-when-does-preservation-become-social-justice. On the promise of environmental histories to inform contemporary social movements, see Max Page and Randall Mason, "Rethinking the Roots of the Historic Preservation Movement," in *Giving Preservation a History: Histories of Historic Preservation in the United States*, ed. Max Page and Randall Mason (New York: Routledge, 2004), 3; William Cronon, "The Uses of Environmental History," *Environmental History Review* 17:3 (Autumn 1993), 1–22.

92. "'Plan or Be Planned For': Temple Contemporary's *Funeral for a Home* and the Politics of Engagement," *Public Historian* 37:2 (May 2015), 14–26; Lisa Stone, "Playing House/Museum," *Public Historian* 37:2 (May 2015), 27–41; Ryan and Vagnone, *Anarchist's Guide to House Museums*; Andrew Hurley, "Chasing the Frontiers of Digital Technology: Public History Meets the Digital Divide," *Public Historian* 38:1 (Jan. 2016), 69–88; Cathy Stanton, ed., *Public History in a Changing Climate*, National Council on Public History e-book (Mar. 2014), http://ncph.org/wp-content/uploads/2014/03/PHCC-2014.pdf.

Index

Acknowledgments

When I think about the intellectual roots of this book, I owe my first set of thanks to my college and graduate school mentors. At Harvard College, Joyce Chaplin, Lizabeth Cohen, Cathy Corman, Laurel Ulrich, Rick Bell, and Margot Minardi all taught me what it means to be a historian. They instilled in me an interest in material culture, the built environment, and the craft of writing that infuses this book. At the University of Virginia, Peter Onuf was the first person to believe in a set of inquiries that eventually became this book. He is a legendary mentor for a reason, and I am indebted to him for giving me the space to pursue intensive archival research while always pushing me to see the big picture. Max Edelson, Sophie Rosenfeld, Liz Varon, and Olivier Zunz also played formative roles in my intellectual and professional approaches to history. Dell Upton and Sheila Crane at the School of Architecture were equally formative to my thinking about urbanism, and I am indebted to Maurie McInnis and Louis Nelson for welcoming me into their early American art and architectural workshop and to Louis for introducing me to the joys of architectural fieldwork.

This book would not have come into being without two fellowships that provided support at a crucial moment. I sketched out the chapter outline of this book at the Lapidus Scholars' Workshop at the Omohundro Institute of Early American History and Culture. Martha Howard, Josh Piker, Brett Rushforth, Fredrika J. Teute, Karin Wulf, and Nadine Zimmerli all played a role in the structure of this book, as did fellow workshop participants Zara Anishanslin, Céline Carayon, Glenda Goodman, Rana Hogarth, and Christine Walker. A few weeks later, I moved to Worcester, Massachusetts, to start writing this book with the support of a Hench Postdoctoral Fellowship at the American Antiquarian Society. I am deeply grateful to every member of the AAS staff for their work during my year in residence, and I am particularly thankful to Gigi Barnhill, Lauren Hewes, the late "Doctor Ed" Koury, Cheryl McRell, and Nan Wolverton for their support. Fellow fellows Colleen Boggs, Seth Cotlar, Christine DeLucia, Elizabeth Eager, Amy Hughes, Cole Jones, Cynthia Kierner, Dwight McBride, Don James McLaughlin, Christen Mucher, Hunter Price, and Clay Zuba deserve special thanks for their camaraderie, counsel, and friendship. Most of all, this book would not have been possible without the critical feedback, encouragement, support, and humor of Paul Erickson. I cannot imagine how many books single out Paul's influence for thanks, but I am happy to add this book to the list.

In Philadelphia, this book was shaped by the intellectual community fostered by the McNeil Center of Early American Studies. I am deeply grateful to the center for a Summer Faculty Fellowship that gave me the time and space to finish writing the manuscript. I am also thankful for the support of my colleagues in the Department of History at Villanova University and for the various university funds that have supported the development of this book, including the Albert C. Lepage Research Fund, the History Department Summer Research Fund, and the University Summer Grant program. This book also has benefitted from the generosity of research fellowships sponsored by the Jay and Deborah Last Fund at the American Antiquarian Society, the Massachusetts Historical Society, the National Museum of American History, the New England Regional Consortium, the Phillips Library at the Peabody Essex Museum, and Winterthur Museum, Garden and Library.

It is impossible to thank by name all of the archivists, history professionals, conference panelists, and commentators that have helped me access and analyze sources and have sharpened my thinking and writing over the years. I am particularly grateful to the curators who have taken time to give me tours of historic properties, looked for difficult-to-find objects and images, and shared research files. Elizabeth Blackmar, Al Brophy, Tamara Thornton, Dell Upton and two anonymous reviewers all made this book better by providing me with critical and encouraging feedback on the manuscript at important moments. I am also grateful for the editorial counsel of Robert Lockhart, Dan Richter, Lily Palladino, and Pat Wieland at Penn Press. Two graduate research assistants at Villanova, Madison Bastress and Lori Wysong, deserve especial thanks for help with manuscript preparation.

This book is dedicated, in part, to my friends who have been an unceasing form of support and cheer during the past several years. I am thankful for the continuing friendship of David Flaherty, Philip Herrington, Randi Lewis Flaherty, Nic Wood, Rachel Shelden, and especially Lawrence Hatter and Martin Öhman from our days at the University of Virginia. Kate Gaudet, Matt Karp, and Nenette Luarca-Shoaf have remained steadfast friends since our first days at the McNeil Center. Craig Agule, Alice Bailey, Alicia Maggard, Matt McFarland, Emily Sandberg, and Sarah Schuetze offered encouragement and advice at crucial moments. In Philadelphia, Sara Altman, Zara Anishanslin, Mitch Fraas, Glenda Goodman, Julio Peña, Jess Roney, Adam Scales, Andy Shankman, and Cristina

Soriano have provided steady streams of friendship, and Jessica Baumert, Ben Boyd, Monica Fonorow, Joe DeVitis, Jamal Elias, Jennifer Harford Vargas, Starr Herr-Cardillo, Manuel Lopez, Mir Masud-Elias, and Katie Price have made our neighborhood home.

Above all, my greatest thanks go to my parents, Michael and Dana Martinko. Their love and support are the bedrock of this book. I only wish that my father had lived to see me complete it. Thanks, Mom and Dad, for everything.